Y0-BVO-938

Policy Analysis:

Perspectives, Concepts, and Methods

PUBLIC POLICY STUDIES: A MULTI-VOLUME TREATISE, VOLUME 6

Editor: Stuart Nagel, *Department of Political Science, University of Illinois*

PUBLIC POLICY STUDIES
A Multi-Volume Treatise

General Editor: Stuart Nagel, Department of Political
Science, University of Illinois

Policy Analysis:

Perspectives, Concepts, and Methods

Edited by **WILLIAM N. DUNN**
Graduate School of Public and
International Affairs
University of Pittsburgh

JAI PRESS INC.

Greenwich, Connecticut   *London, England*

Library of Congress Cataloging-in-Publication Data
Main entry under title:

Policy analysis.

  (Public policy studies ; v. 6)
  Bibliography: p.
  Includes indexes.
  1. Policy sciences—Addresses, essays, lectures.
2. Policy sciences—Moral and ethical aspects—Addresses,
essays, lectures. I. Dunn, William N. II. Series:
Public policy studies (Greenwich, Conn.) ; v. 6.
H97.P638 1986   361.6′1   85–23152
ISBN 0–89232–371–X

CONTENTS

PART III.   METHODS

ACKNOWLEDGMENTS

The editor gratefully acknowledges the assistance of Lina D'Amico, who typed portions of the manuscript, and Andrea Hegedus, who prepared the index. The publication of this volume also permits me to acknowledge my personal and professional gratitude to John H. Funari and Leon L. Haley, deans of the Graduate School of Public and International Affairs in the period 1973–1985. Their support and encouragement, over the years, not only helped complete this particular project, but also contributed to local and national projects undertaken by other colleagues who have been responsible for the meandering institutionalization of public policy and management (some call it administration) as a serious subject of interdisciplinary research and teaching. Deans Funari and Haley understood that policy analysis and other promising interdisciplinary ventures are shaped not only by the force of ideas, but also by those key institutions—programs, departments, schools, universities, professional associations—which are major sources of intellectual progress and retrogression. As reflective practitioners Funari and Haley not only knew the difference; they had the courage to try to make a difference.

INTRODUCTION

As an applied social science discipline policy analysis employs multiple methods of inquiry to produce and transform policy-relevant information that may be used to diagnose or alleviate some practical problem. The production and transformation of policy-relevant information is guided in part by aims which are descriptive, since policy analysts seek to uncover the causes and consequences of policy interventions of different kinds (Cook and Campbell, 1979). These descriptive aims are perhaps exemplified by the title of a standard text: *Policy Analysis: What Governments Do, Why They Do It, and What Difference It Makes* (Dye, 1976). Yet policy-relevant information is not confined to causal inferences. Policy analysts are also guided by normative aims which involve the production and transformation of information about right action. MacRae's characterization of policy analysis as an applied science punctuates this normative intent:

> It is perhaps obvious that applied science aims at goals or values and that when we ask what should be done we are asking a *valuative* question. But we often conceal from ourselves the valuative status of our dependent variables...we must realize that the use of these variables can lead toward theoretical structures other than those of basic science (MacRae, 1976:281).

The aims of policy analysis therefore embrace but go beyond the production of information about "facts"; as an applied discipline policy analysis seeks also to transform such factual information into statements about "values" and their realization through reflective public action. Accordingly, policy analysis provides answers to several important classes of questions (Dunn, 1981) whose intent is designative (What are the effects of the policy?), evaluative (Of what value are these effects?), and advocative (What should be done?). Policy analysis, to the degree that it supplies answers to these questions, borrows from those disciplines (political science, public administration, sociology, psychology, anthropology, economics) whose chief purpose is to describe and explain constraints and opportunities surrounding policy action (e.g., Dye, 1983; Quade, 1982; Stokey and Zeckhauser, 1978). Yet policy analysis also draws, thus far less generously, from political philosophy, jurisprudence, and ethics, disciplines whose primary subject matter is values and their relation to moral action (see, e.g., Beauchamp, 1975; Callahan and Jennings, 1982; Dunn, 1983).

This broad multidisciplinary charter, since it expands conventionally accepted boundaries of the social, behavioral, and management sciences, imposes on policy analysis a burden of new and unfamiliar methodological responsibilities. For this and other reasons discussed by contributors to this volume, policy analysts have been reluctant, unwilling, or unprepared to address a number of important issues surrounding the theoretical and practical status of this applied discipline.

Part I of this volume presents alternative perspectives of policy analysis. These perspectives, originating in intellectual history, general systems theory, critical social theory, philosophy, anthropology, and psychotherapy, make explicit numerous unresolved theoretical and practical issues facing policy analysis as an applied science. Adopting a historical perspective of the growth of the discipline, David Garson questions whether policy analysis, despite its origins in the global interdisciplinary contributions of Merriam and Lasswell, has not succumbed to overly narrow and self-sealing concepts, models, and methodologies. In an attempt to reextend the domain of policy analysis by reflecting on its intellectual origins, Garson affirms that current debates between now encrusted empirico-analytic and neo-pluralist traditions obscure the potential breadth and relevance of an applied discipline whose descriptive and normative aims are interdependent and intregral.

Employing a similar global perspective, Robert Backoff and Barry Mitnick reappraise the strengths and limitations of general systems theory as a unifying framework for the policy and management sciences. In this reappraisal they effectively resolve a number of issues surrounding the definition of "system" and the role of holistic thinking in social problem solving. Joining this debate about the proper boundaries of policy analysis, Fred Dallmayr shows how the quality of normative discourse may be improved by employing perspectives of critical social theory set forth by Jurgen Habermas and others. Alex Michalos, also concerned with boundary questions, argues from a philosophical perspective that there are good theoretical and practical reasons to avoid any appeals to a fact-value distinction in the assessment of technology or in any other area of policy analysis. Erve Chambers, bringing an anthropological perspective to bear on issues surrounding facts and values, argues that the processes and products of policy analysis must be situated securely within the sensibilities of the society in which they are developed. Part I is concluded by Baruch Fischhoff, who employs perspectives of psychotherapy to create an analogy in terms of which the promises and limitations of policy analysis may be assessed. Policy analysis, like psychotherapy, is confronted by crises surrounding its transformation from an art to a clinical science.

In Part II contributors develop and apply concepts whose function is to extend the boundaries of policy analysis beyond their current limits. Duncan MacRae, who elaborates the concept of democratic information systems, specifies possibilities for measuring general end-values, including equity and the common good, and including these as policy indicators that inform public debate. Guy Adams, appealing to Vico's idea of the *sensus communis*, offers a framework which illuminates the poverty of valuative discourse on public policy and the possibilities for its enrichment. Defining and elaborating the value of caring, William Leiss argues for a conservation ethic based on practical morality and public policy for a viable sense of well-being. Herbert Reid, extending the concept of ideology critique to issues of Appalachian social policy, argues that a static image of the region obscures the region's particular form of "modernization." Frederick Reamer, observing that policy analysts often face conflicts between ideological, empirical, and ethical statements, applies Louis Gewirth's Principle of Generic Consistency to show how policy claims may be justified on nonarbitrary, logical grounds. Finally, Stuart Nagel provides an inventory of basic concepts of public policy analysis, an inventory that may enlarge the boundaries of this relatively new, useful, and important field of applied multidisciplinary inquiry.

In Part III contributors critique, develop, or apply methods designed to address many of the issues raised in the first two parts of the volume. Michael Carley, reviewing several methods for attaching social values to quantitative data in policy analysis, argues that issues of distributional equity are best addressed without recourse to single, highly quantified weighting schemes which may obscure the value judgments which lie beneath aggregative indexes. Stephen Linder, addressing the same issue, argues for the systematic and explicit inclusion of "soft" values and moral claims in attempts to evaluate public policies and programs. In contrast to Carley and Linder, who concentrate on the need for innovations in quantitative methods of policy analysis and evaluation, George Graham draws from traditions of rhetoric and ethical discourse to establish a methodological basis for policy analysis and evaluation. Frank Fischer extends this search for a normative methodology by employing an informal logic of practical reasoning to specify a system of rules for mediating and integrating empirical and normative claims. Kevin Kearns, also appealing to an informal logic of practical argumentation, shows how a particular method of policy analysis and evaluation (the analytic hierarchy process of Thomas Saaty) may be strengthened by incorporating an explicit value-critical perspective that systematically surfaces assumptions underlying contending policy arguments. Finally, the concluding chapter develops and applies a cognitive methodology for investigating the cumulative movement and reinterpretation of policy through "systems of interpretation," a term coined by Hugh Heclo and others. In this concluding chapter William Dunn, Anthony Cahill, Mary Dukes, and Ari Ginsberg illustrate the potential of what they call the policy grid for investigating changes in the systems of interpretation by which individual and collective meanings are attached to observable events.

Contributions to this volume, individually and in their overall configuration, represent a kind of basic treatise on the prospects and problems of policy analysis. The central theme of the volume, represented by perspectives, concepts, and methods put forth in the three parts, is that of a reflective striving to extend the boundaries of policy analysis as an applied discipline, to recover the nexus between facts and values, and to reunite disciplines whose specialized trajectories have concealed prospects for the growth of knowledge. "Everywhere the unit sooner or later searches to comprehend its role by discovering a map of the whole" (Lasswell, 1968:41).

William N. Dunn

REFERENCES

Beauchamp, T. L. (1975) Ethics and Public Policy. Englewood Cliffs, NJ: Prentice-Hall.
Callahan, D. and B. Jennings (1982) Ethics, the Social Sciences, and Policy Analysis. New York: Plenum Press.
Cook, T. D. and D. T. Campbell (1979) Quasi-Experimentation. Boston: Houghton Mifflin.
Dunn, W. N. (1981) Public Policy Analysis. Englewood Cliffs, NJ: Prentice-Hall.
————(1983) "Values, ethics, and standards in policy analysis." In S. Nagel (ed.), Encyclopedia of Policy Studies. New York: Marcel Dekker.
Dye, T. R. (1976) Policy Analysis: What Governments Do, Why They Do It, and What Difference It Makes. University, AL: University of Alabama Press.

————(1983) Understanding Public Policy, 4th ed. Englewood Cliffs, NJ: Prentice-Hall.
Lasswell, H. D. (1963) The Future of Political Science. Chicago: Atherton.
MacRae, D. (1976) The Social Function of Social Science. New Haven, CT: Yale University Press.
Quade, E. S. (1982) Analysis for Public Decisions, 2nd ed. New York: Elsevier.
Stokey, E. and R. Zeckhauser (1978) A Primer for Policy Analysis. New York: W. W. Norton.

PART I

PERSPECTIVES

FROM POLICY SCIENCE TO POLICY ANALYSIS:

A QUARTER CENTURY OF PROGRESS

G. David Garson

ABSTRACT

This essay on the intellectual history of policy analysis traces the field from Merriam's concept of "intelligent planning" and Lasswell's vision of "policy sciences" to the present. Lasswell's vision is seen as a relevant if unrealized one in general dimensions. It is argued that the tie of policy analysis to traditional issues in political science is unbreakable and, because of this, attempts to develop an interdisciplinary policy science premised on the supposed unifying force of a common methodological core have led to fragmentation, not theoretical integration. The emergence of the synoptic/empirico-rational tradition and anti-synoptic/neo-pluralistic traditions in policy analysis in the 1950s and 1960s are discussed and strengths and weaknesses noted. Divisions over the question of values and normative theory are highlighted. A concluding section discusses alternative views on the proper scope of policy analysis as an emerging discipline, contrasting the "handmaiden" and "ivory tower" alternatives. A six-dimension outline of a map for policy analysis as a field is presented and the continued utility

Policy Analysis: Perspectives, Concepts, and Methods, pages 3–22.
ISBN: 0–89232–371–X

of Lasswellian concerns emphasized in contrast to the stalemated debate between synoptic and anti-synoptic viewpoints in American policy analysis.

INTRODUCTION

It has been over a quarter-century since Daniel Lerner and Harold Lasswell's *The Policy Sciences* (1951) was issued. In a discipline notoriously neglectful of its heritage it is perhaps now overdue to look back over the intervening years. While it is not necessarily true that those who are ignorant of past mistakes are condemned to repeat them, nonetheless such a retrospective can be instructive. Like the old professor who returns to teach the introductory course, such an enterprise gives us a challenging opportunity to review the origins of our field and the premises of our thought.

It is the thesis of this essay that Lasswell's vision of the policy sciences remains a relevant if unrealized one in its general dimensions. It is argued that the tie of policy analysis to traditional issues in political science is unbreakable, more so perhaps than Lasswell himself realized. Because of this, attempts to develop interdisciplinary policy sciences premised on the supposed unifying force of a common methodological core have led to fragmentation, not the integration of a new applied discipline. While the majority of policy analysts today welcome the resulting eclecticism, there is an equal yearning for placing the emerging discipline on a more satisfying theoretical basis.

A review of the current theoretical debate exposes conflict between systems and politics, quantitative methods and case analyses, planners and incrementers, analysts and muddlers. Institutionally, this debate has been stereotyped as the number-crunching "Harvard" school versus the politicking "Berkeley" school (Nelson, 1979). In this debate between empirico-analytic models and neo-pluralism the vision of policy sciences has become lost. The debate threatens to plunge policy analysis into the stagnant waters of issues disputed fruitlessly in political science in the 1950s and 1960s. How has policy analysis come to this state of affairs and what is to be done about it? It is these questions which are addressed in the present chapter.

The sections which follow treat three topics. First, the seminal contributions of Harold Lasswell and his Chicago mentor, Charles Merriam, are discussed for the light they throw on the early hopes for policy sciences. Second, the synoptic and anti-synoptic traditions which dominated the ensuing two decades are analyzed to explain the development of empirico-analytic and neo-pluralist models in policy analysis. Finally, the chapter concludes with a historical perspective on issues pertaining to the values and scope of modern policy analysis as an emerging discipline.

LASSWELL AND MERRIAM

Harold D. Lasswell has rightly been called "the modern-day founder of policy science" (Scott and Shore, 1979:46). A professor of political science at the University of Chicago (1922–1938), Lasswell went on to wartime research and consulting in Washington (1938–1947) and finished his active years on the faculty of the Yale Law School (1947–1973). One of the truly great American social scientists, Lasswell's influence was pervasive. Among his students are numbered such names as V. O. Key, David Truman, Herbert Simon, Gabriel Almond, and Edward Shils. Yet of him a biographer wrote:

> It should be noted that Lasswell has been out of step intellectually with many of the disciplinary accomplishments of the postwar decade . . . Only toward the end of his career has Lasswell's lifelong stress on the study of controversial major problems, his belief that contextual factors must not be neglected, and his appreciation of the dialectical difficulties of doing significant political research begun to evoke professional agreement (Marvick, 1977:7–8).

Ironically it was the very sweep of his vision of policy sciences that at once excited the development of this new field and at the same time led to stereotyping of his ideas as utopian.

Writing in *The Policy Sciences* (1951) Lasswell had expressed his dismay at the undermining of the unity of intellectual life in the postwar period. The "centrifugal forces" of specialization in science, philosophy, and the social sciences were perhaps inevitable. The result was the rupture of the harmony of science and practice. A policy orientation, Lasswell believed, would cut across the fragmented specializations and establish a new, unifying social science (Lerner and Lasswell, 1951:3–4).

The policy sciences were to be a break with the past. They were *not*, for example, applied social science of the type which proliferated in wartime Washington. Nor was Lasswell talking about activism for social scientists as he had a decade earlier in *Democracy Through Public Opinion* (1941). Instead, in Lasswell's vision, policy science was to revolve around a general theory of choice (Lerner and Lasswell, 1951:4). Topical issues of the moment were explicitly *not* the central concern of policy sciences (Lerner and Lasswell, 1951:8–10).

This vision of theoretically-oriented policy sciences was quite in contrast to the handmaiden-of-government tradition of policy analysis which was to become dominant in the decade ahead. Though practical men of affairs were to be an integral part of the policy sciences (Lerner and Lasswell, 1951:13), and though Lasswell lauded the Harvard Littauer School's seminars for graduates and practitioners, fundamentally Lasswell saw policy sciences as something far different from applied social science. Policy sciences would be concerned with the "fundamental problems of man in society" (Lerner and Lasswell, 1951:8). It would be global in perspective, emphasize the historical context of policy, and emphasize the study of change—diffusion, invention, revolution (Lerner and Lasswell, 1951:11–12). It was exemplified by Gunnar Myrdal's epic study of civil rights policy in *An American Dilemma* (1944).

In later years Lasswell continued to urge upon political scientists the opportunity which policy sciences afforded for the reconstitution of their discipline. In *The Future of Political Science* (1963) Lasswell gained American Political Science Association auspices to propound his most systematic thesis on this subject. In this work he urged a political science centered on the theory of choice in policy decision-making.

"It seems to me," he wrote, "that as political science faces the future it is in a remarkable position to take an important initiative in the creative integration of thought and organization at the higher as well as the lower levels of knowledge and policy. The prospect of realizing a working harmony among diverse approaches has provided political scientists with an opportunity which they have only partially utilized, to achieve a coherent conception of a problem-solving discipline oriented to the larger issues of the life of man in society" (Lasswell, 1963:38–9). In these prescient remarks Lasswell was calling on his colleagues to address their discipline to a more relevant set of policy and social issues. The relative failure to do so led to a variety of splits in political science later in the 1960s and early 1970s (Garson, 1978:chs. 4–5).

Part of the failure of political science to act on Lasswell's vision of policy sciences must be laid to Lasswell himself. Though any serious reading of his work reveals the depth of his humanistic concerns, it must be said that his enthusiasm for behavioral methods often dominated perceptions of what he was advocating. All too often the medium of research did become the message. *The Future of Political Science*, for example, was noted within the *American Political Science Review* (Zawodny, 1964:121–2) and elsewhere for an emphasis on quantitative methodology in the service of policy decision-making. The visionary message about policy science was there, but lost. The public impression was one of advocacy of advanced research centers, utilization of vast data surveys, micromodelling, and laboratory experimentation (Lasswell, 1963:chs. 3–10).

In Lasswell's vision of policy sciences one finds the juxtaposition of behaviorism and humanism:

> If, as political scientists, we were omniscient, we would have at our disposal descriptive and analytic tools enabling us to do the following: make a rapid survey of the predispositions found everywhere in the world, 'predict' (retrospectively) the conditioning factors accounting for the direction and intensity of these predispositions; predict the way in which these predispositions would express themselves under the impact of any conceivable constellation of future conditioning factors; predict the probable occurrence of future constellations; outline the strategies by which the probability of future factor constellations can be modified (at stated cost in terms of values); and connect past and prospective sequences of events with specifications of goal (in our case, the goal of realizing the dignity of man—and other advanced forms of life—on the widest scale).

This is a breathtakingly optimistic vision of the possibilities of behavioral methods to serve humanistic ends.

Later, in *A Preview of Policy Science* (1971), Lasswell defined the policy scientist as one who was "concerned with mastering the skills appropriate to enlightened decision in the context of public and civic order" (Lasswell, 1971:13). In this definition "skills" became emphasized in the field of policy analysis. "Context"—historical, cross-cultural, multi-method— represented a deep commitment in Lasswell's concept of policy science, but one which was obscured by sweeping projections of empirical skills. "Civic order," an even deeper philosophical concern, became lost altogether as the postwar decades transformed policy sciences in the service of democracy into policy analysis in the service of government. That transformation embodied a profound shift in premises.

Lasswell in the Context of Merriam

The ambiguity between the behavioral and humanistic bases of Lasswell's vision of policy sciences was a more extreme version of the same tension in the thought of Lasswell's mentor, Charles E. Merriam. Merriam was perhaps the foremost social scientist of the depression and war years. Intimately connected to the early years of the American Political Science Association, the founding of the Chicago Bureau of Municipal Research, and the establishment of the Social Science Research Council, Merriam symbolized a generation of social scientists interested in public policy: Louis Wirth, Harold Odum, Robert Park, John Commons, William Ogburn, and J. Allen Smith, to name a few. Merriam was a primary force in the Commission on the Social Studies (1932–5), the Commission on Administrative Management (1935–7), and the National Resources Planning Board (NRPB) (1933–43).

It is this last, the NRPB, that illustrated the early vision of policy science. In *Systematic Politics* (1945) Merriam described the NRPB as "an advisory planning agency, dealing with the highest and best use of national resources, both natural and human" (Merriam, 1945:157). It was part of a general interest in policy planning in the 1930s (see Garson, 1973). Merriam saw the NRPB as the basis for a national planning board which would advise the president on the coordination of various policies among the branches of government, establishing "long-term national policy in the larger sense of the term" (Merriam, 1945:158).

The NRPB, which Merriam headed, was relatively inconsequential in practice. Nonetheless it symbolized the vision of policy sciences. Merriam conceived planning as interdisciplinary science—not just economic analysis, agricultural planning, or other specialized perspectives. "It will be possible," he wrote, "to make full use of science and democracy in planning for the expansion of national production, for justice, for the fair distribution of national gains, for far higher standards of living, for liberty, for the recognition of the dignity of man, and for his right to participate fully in the civilization he has helped to create" (Merriam, 1945:337). In this statement we see the dual emphasis on scientific method and humanistic ends that was to characterize Lasswell.

Merriam, in fact, did more than any other social scientist of his day to encourage methodological sophistication. At Chicago, where he was department head, bright young protegés were brought in and encouraged to become involved in the new techniques that had been developed in other disciplines such as psychology and economics; Lasswell was one of these. Chicago became one of the few places in America where quantitative approaches to political science began to dominate. "It is possible to locate without difficulty," Lasswell later wrote, "the principle time and place in American political science at which the 'newer aspects' of the subject gained momentum. The creative center was the University of Chicago and the time was the 1920s and early 1930s. The leading figure was Charles E. Merriam, who encouraged a new emphasis at the university and through the American Political Science Association" (Lasswell, 1963:37). Later, in leading in the organization of the Social Science Research Council, Merriam spread the new gospel on a national basis.

Merriam was an organizer, adept at arranging private funding as well as public. In this he held up the desirability of bringing science to the service of democracy and bringing academics out of the library and into the world of affairs. He wrote:

> Intelligent planning involves systematic attention to the growth of the gains of civilization, the mode and range of their distribution, the principles of justice and freedom. In their practical application... this involves a guaranty by the government, as one of the underwriters, of security in employment, minimum standards of health, education, and the 'social securities,' and equal access to the development of creative possibilities in the human personality (Merriam, 1945:334).

This was a vision of social science as the enabling tool for national planning under the banner of positive government in a liberal and humanistic sense.

What is important today is to realize that this was an exciting vision, in many ways providing the motive force not only behind Merriam's work but also behind Lasswell's concept of policy sciences after the war. Merriam clearly understood that some would think scientific skills would come to *be* policy science. This was wrong, he stated. "Much more will be known about social and political science in the future than now, beyond question, but . . . there will always be the margin of alternatives— a margin where human values and choices will be important and conclusive . . . the maintenance of community morale is facilitated by community participation in community affairs" (Merriam, 1945:329). The emphasis on human values and on participating fully in the civilization he has helped to create was primary; skills were secondary. The motive behind policy science was not empirical methodology for science's sake but rather science for democracy's sake.

Merriam saw few problems in the marriage of science and democracy. Logically one might think his emphasis on value choices and civic participation would lead away from the empirico-analytic approach and toward the neo-pluralist tradition. Instead Merriam minimized the forces which would push in this direction. Notably, he optimistically believed in two possibilities minimizing political conflict and maximizing the potential for scientific analysis. First, he believed that men of affairs and scientists could easily work together on great issues of the day, much as they did on the NRPB he headed. Second, he believed that the value systems of business, religion, and government could be merged in a new enlightened consensus on the values of positive government in the service of democracy and the dignity of man (Merriam, 1945–340). With consensual values—plausible in the context of wartime unity—and direct participation in planning processes—another wartime mobilization theme—the joining of scientific analysis to democratic humanism seemed a reasonable and even inevitable development. Lasswell's vision of the policy sciences was a natural child of this optimistic wedding of scientific analysis and humanistic planning.

THE SYNOPTIC AND ANTI-SYNOPTIC TRADITIONS

This duality in the concept of policy sciences became pronounced in the 1950s and 1960s. Borrowing from Charles Lindblom we may label the two sets of premises "synoptic" and "anti-synoptic." Synopsis, meaning overview of the whole, was epitomized by systems analysis (e.g., by Easton, 1953), whereas anti-synoptic scholars emphasized the limits—in fact, impossibility—of comprehensive rational cognition of entire systems of action (e.g., Simon, 1952:1134–5). These two viewpoints provide the basis for some of the most striking contrasts in contemporary approaches to policy analysis. In particular, they underlie the divisions between the empirico-analytic and neo-pluralist orientations toward policy analysis.

While individual scholars often held complex and even self-contradictory views, two clusters of premises could be identified in the 1950s and 1960s. The pure synoptic cluster was marked by identification with systems analysis as a metatheory, statistical empiricism as methodology, and optimization of values as a decision criterion. The pure anti-synoptic cluster was marked by identification with pluralism as a metatheory, contextual and case analysis as methodology, and social rationality (integration of interests) as a decision criterion. Although the anti-synoptic view quickly became dominant in political science generally, the synoptic tradition proved far more viable in the fields of public administration and public policy.

Though not dominant in political science, the synoptic tradition was supported by powerful forces. First, it rode on the crest of the behavioral revolution in the political and social sciences, with its interdisciplinary emphasis, focus on quantitative precision, and goal of systematic empirical theory (see Ranney, ed., 1962). Second, it retained some of the mantle of legitimacy of the vision of service to national planning conferred on it by Lasswell, Merriam, and others. In contrast, the social ferment of the 1960s led to intense criticism of the pluralist alternative. Scholars like Lowi (1967) were highly influential in attacking pluralism (and, indirectly, the whole anti-synoptic tradition) as a vast default on leadership and accountability in the public sector.

Then, too, the synoptic tradition became more complex and sophisticated as the 1960s wore on. Advocates of national planning, such as Amitai Etzioni (1968), developed mixed models of rational decision-making. These avoided the unrealistic assumptions of pure comprehensive-rational approaches while still upholding planning and vigorously condemning incrementalism and other pluralist policy models.

The success of the economists with empirical methodology was a further strength of the synoptic tradition. The culmination of this was the adoption of Program Planning and Budgeting (PPBS) during the Kennedy-Johnson years, years which saw a dramatic increase in the number of economists in federal policy-making roles (Amacher, Tollison and Willett, eds., 1976:37). Though PPBS itself was later dismantled, the legacy of cost-benefit methodology and program evaluation came to be largely equated with policy analysis in many governmental circles.

While anti-synoptic critics continued to flail away at the straw man of the impossible pure rational decision model, more thoughtful commentators were concluding that the synoptic model was an acceptable ideal type. Like all ideal types it was meant to be treated as a standard which actual practice would be measured against but would not be expected to attain. Alice Rivlin, later to head the Congressional Budget Office, acknowledged the critics but basically upheld the rational approach in her highly influential *Systematic Thinking for Social Action* (1971), for example. Lasswell's (1971:46–60) own work said much the same.

A recent review of public policy education by Fry and Tompkins (1978:306) concluded, "The combination of apparent agreement on rational-comprehensive approaches to resource allocation coupled with an apparent lack of agreement on what else might constitute appropriate training in public policy raises questions regarding education in public policy." Fry and Tompkins note the strong representation of computer scientists, mathematicians, operations researchers, statisticians, and economists in existing public policy programs and go on to urge a redirection of policy studies.

There is, however, a strong reason for the prominent role of quantitative approaches and systems in public analysis. Caplan's (1976:231) study of knowledge use by federal executives found that utilization was highest by users oriented toward scientific methods. Noting this, Scott and Shore (1979:72) in their study of sociology and policy analysis ask, "What would a policy-making process have to be like in order for things that sociologists know and do to make a contribution to it?" They answer themselves, "We see that, as constituted, sociology could best contribute to what might be termed a scientifically-based system of planning." Scott and Shore argued that where the anti-synoptic approaches raised theoretical issues appealing to academics it was only in the synoptic approaches that social scientists had something to contribute which governmental users wanted to buy, as Caplan's study showed.

Given the heritage of planning, the driving force of behavioralism, the success of the economists, and the record of marketing research to governmental users, Fry and Tompkins's findings—the strong representation of empirico-analytic orientations in American public policy programs—is hardly surprising.

The Neo-Pluralist Reaction to the Synoptic Tradition

As every force has its counter-force, the synoptic tradition has its anti-synoptic counterpart, an alternative viewpoint supported by equally strong forces. Never a united intellectual movement, the anti-synoptic tradition shares little consensus except on the matter of the impossibility of rational-comprehensive methods due to intractable limitations on required

information and due to the critical intrusion of value questions throughout the policy-making process.

As the synoptic approaches draw on the scientific element in Lasswell's
policy sciences, the anti-synoptic draw on the humanistic. An example
is found in the writings of Dwight Waldo, the highly respected editor
of *Public Administration Review* for many years. In his essay, "Development
of Theory of Democratic Administration" (Waldo, 1952:97) he criticized
efficiency as an allegedly value-free standard in administrative analysis.
Rather, Waldo wanted to put the question of values at center stage. "The
history we experience," he wrote, "is the result of the ideals we pursue"
(Waldo, 1952:99). The pursuit of value-free scientific assessments of
policies was thus cast as a misguided attempt to side-step the more fundamental issues of societal values. Waldo's view was echoed repeatedly
in later attacks on the empirico-analytic approach for the trivialization
of social science.

An even more telling attack was launched the following year by two
of the leading American social scientists of the postwar period, Robert
A. Dahl and Charles E. Lindblom. In *Politics, Economics, and Welfare*
(1953) these authors argued that systems of rational calculation and
control were inherently inefficient if not unworkable. This sweeping
argument was applied not only to central planning and socialism but to
welfare state versions of public policy as well. All decision-making, including policy choice, was seen as reducible to four types: hierarchy,
polyarchy, bargaining, and markets. All systems were seen as requiring
a combination of all four types of decision-making since each type had
strengths and weaknesses. (Nonetheless, the weaknesses of hierarchy and
the strengths of bargaining and market pricing were emphasized.) Dahl
and Lindblom's argument was later buttressed by influential empirical
studies of public policy decision-making (Dahl, 1961) as well as more
refined theoretical formulations (Dahl, 1956; Braybrooke and Lindblom,
1963; Lindblom, 1965). These studies seemed to prove that while decision-makers may be taught synoptic methods in school, they actually
practice incrementalism, partisan mutual adjustment, and plain 'mud-
dling through.'

It should be noted that incrementalism was merely a policy-oriented
variant of pluralist theory. As articulated by Robert Dahl, pluralism
became the dominant explanatory framework for American political
process in political science. Since political science was more oriented
toward causal description and policy analysis toward prescription, and
since pluralism/incrementalism was more accurate as description than it
was reflective of prescriptive preferences, pluralism fared considerably
better in political science than incrementalism did in public administration and public policy.

Incrementalism in the narrow sense is rather uncontroversial. Budgets for a given year are best predicted in nearly all cases by extrapolation from the immediately previous years. In fact, each year's budget does increment the line items in the past year's. Incrementalism in the broad sense, however, suggested Lindblom's "partisan mutual adjustment." Mutuality in bargaining relationships was, though, an inadequate theoretical formulation of policy-making even for descriptive purposes. The work of Herbert A. Simon and James G. March provided a better and more influential—but still anti-synoptic—theoretical framework.

Where the Dahl-Lindblom conceptualization tended to merge hierarchy and planning, Simon's work presented a vision of hierarchical control without rational-comprehensive decision-making. This reasonable view clearly held top management to be in control of organizations and policies, not through planning but through less obtrusive controls (e.g., influence over the value structure of organizational culture). Decision-making was by a limited search process which accepted satisfactory (not necessarily optimal) alternatives ("satisficing"). Heavy reliance was placed on standard operating rules and action repertories, as well as socialization of organization members to organizational patterns. This was an anti-synoptic view of decision-making, but one far more complex than that of simple incrementalism. Its critique of central-rational planning approaches went beyond Dahl and Lindblom's decentralized-rational bargaining approach. In a more profound attack on the synoptic tradition, March and Simon were arguing for the importance of non-rational factors in understanding organizations and, by extension, policy decision-making. Though intensely involved in application of behavioral methods (March, 1955; Simon, 1957), March and Simon's modelling was in the service of academic theory, not governmental planning for the goals of democracy as Merriam envisioned.

In addition to development of anti-synoptic models of policy process, another important aspect of the reaction against the synoptic tradition elaborated on Dahl and Lindblom's enthusiasm for market pricing as a policy decision mechanism. Public choice theory came to prominence in the 1970s as a movement advocating reliance on market-like decision processes in public policy arenas. Partly this message came from economists directly importing their analyses into areas formerly trod only by political scientists (Niskanen, 1971). It also came, however, from political scientists seeing in public choice theory the way out of a perceived intellectual crisis in American public administration (Ostrom, 1973). These authors provided a more acceptable formulation of the marketing approach, a territory formerly held only by extreme conservatives such as Friedman (1962).

Finally, various empirical studies of policy-making showed an apparent inferiority of hierarchical decision-making and planning compared to approaches incorporating greater group conflict. A prominent early example was Aaron Wildavsky's *Dixon-Yates: A Study in Power* (1962). These studies, together with the compelling exercises in descriptive theory by Dahl, Lindblom, March, Simon and others, provided support convincing many students of public policy that the powerful synoptic tradition was leading policy analysis down the wrong road. To this was added the separate line of criticism represented by Waldo, that simple empiricism simply failed to address the most important questions, which were ones of value.

VALUES IN THE DEVELOPMENT OF POLICY ANALYSIS

In the early 1950s Lasswell had envisioned policy sciences, based on common methodological skills, as an emerging interdisciplinary movement simultaneously serving democratic values, academic theory-building, and governmental needs. Academics and practitioners would be, he believed, easily integrated in mutual endeavors serving the needs of both groups. Although the 1950s did see the rise of interdisciplinary research (e.g., urban studies, area studies), a historical review by Irving Louis Horowitz and James E. Katz (1975) showed that these hopes for mutually beneficial joint research were largely unfulfilled.

At the academic level the traditional departments proved a source of powerful resistance to the emerging interdisciplinary movement. More important, Horowitz and Katz's survey found that by the 1960s policy analysis had become characterized by what they termed the "handmaiden approach" (Horowitz and Katz, 1975:156–7). By this they meant theory-less research to federal specifications more akin to industrial extension work than academic research. Some, like David Truman (1968), had urged a more balanced approach to government-university collaboration, including interchange of staff, joint seminars, and conferences. Horowitz and Katz concluded by noting that, while little had come of suggestions like Truman's, and while applied social science continued to be contracted widely by governmental agencies, increasingly policy analysts who wished to write on national policies continued to do so outside governmental auspices.

In spite of some tendencies toward reversion to the "ivory tower" model of policy research, the "handmaiden approach" remained alive and well. The revival of interest in applied social science in the early 1970s (Nagel, 1977:9) fed the fires of this orientation. Often policy analysis was even *defined* as an effort to serve policy-makers' information needs (Quade, 1977:21). Speaking of masters-level policy program a-lumni (and master's level education which was the core of organized programs in policy analysis), MacRae (1977:164–5) wrote, "Persons trained in graduate schools of policy analysis would expect to go largely into nonacademic employment and to conform somewhat to the engineering model, supplying technical advice and skill to large organizations for otherwise given ends. In this respect graduate policy training would resemble training in engineering...." Some, like Scott and Shore (1979:204–5), vigorously argued that "Grand-scale... Lasswellian schemes in which sociologists and politicians are partners must be abandoned for less pretentious approaches that are more closely attuned to political realities and less closely tied to academic and utopian concerns."

Analysts attuned to marketing policy analysis, such as Quade, MacRae, Scott, and Shore were merely reflecting the state of existing demand. The implications of their positions, however, were far more supportive of the skills emphasis inherent in the synoptic tradition. It was inevitable, therefore, that those in other traditions have given opposing advice to the discipline. Kenneth Dolbeare (1974), for example, has sharply criticized policy analysis for excessive dependence on the goals and values of policy-makers, leading to a focus on incremental outputs rather than examination of fundamental levels of policy impact. Horowitz and Katz (1975:165) have noted the tendency of the "handmaiden approach" to undercut to traditional and vital roles of criticism played by universities. Also undermined, they note, is a systematic approach to policy analysis as a coherent interdisciplinary movement. Others, like Cohen and Rakoff (1978) of the University of Illinois' Chicago Circle campus, have sought to orient their public policy masters' programs toward just this more critical orientation, emphasizing contextual training reminiscent of that advocated by Lasswell (though of different political approach). Each of these criticisms of the "handmaiden approach" raised important issues about policy analysis as a social science—issues anticipated by Merriam and Lasswell years earlier.

The relation of policy analysis to social science is much in dispute. Some have seen in policy analysis not a diversion of energies but a real opportunity for scientific advancement. MacRae (1977:152), for example, has contrasted the "closed character of individual disciplines" with the flexibility of interdisciplinary policy research. Though it is true, he acknowledges, that disciplines select dependent variables according to theoretical interest and in policy analysis choice is dictated by valuative priorities, the difference is not as great as it might appear. Valuative discourse, he argues, can be systematic and operational causal research.

Certainly causal research must be at the heart of a social science of policy analysis. The failure to test causal theories has, however, been noted by Dye (1976:78) and others as a common shortcoming of policy analysis as an emerging discipline. The shift of the Law Enforcement Assistance Administration toward greater funding of causal research, as well as the work of MacRae, Dye, and others, has given encouragement if not optimism to the view that policy analysis will evolve centered on causal theory.

Dye himself, however, is not optimistic that government-funded policy research will generate causal social science theory. In a review of "why governmental agencies do poor policy research" (Dye, 1976:97–98), Dye notes many problems. These include resistance of agencies (particularly those whose function is symbolic) to evaluation, the bias to show positive impact, vested interests in current programs, time pressure displacing study and evaluation, lack of value consensus on criteria for judgment, unwillingness to consider experimental designs, and dependence (funding and information) of the researcher on the subject agency. Likewise Elkin (1974) notes related problems accounting for the "theoretically thin" nature of policy analysis: overemphasis on available data, underemphasis on non-local causal factors impacting local outputs, trivial conception of outputs as expenditures. Scott and Shore (1977:227) also cite the difficulty that practitioners need far simpler (hence more manipulatable) causal explanations than commonly result from conventional academic research. To this Quade adds, "The problems of public policy are likely to be 'wicked' problems. That is, they may have no definite formulation and no stopping rule to tell the problem-solver when he has a solution" (Quade, 1977:25).

Of the various problems of policy analysis, particularly government-funded policy analysis, none has caused more discussion than that of the role of values. In particular, most criticism of the synoptic tradition of policy analysis has revolved around this point, which is hardly a new one. Lippman (1955), Wengert (1955), and Appleby (1950) were among those arguing over two decades ago for the importance of public interest values in the study of public policy and administration, and Schubert (1957) was among those defending behaviorism. Writing in 1956, Herbert Kaufman saw public administration then splitting into those who saw disciplinary questions in management science terms versus those who saw them in power and value-conflict terms. Kaufman further saw the American Society for Public Administration drifting toward the former camp and the American Political Science Association toward the latter (Kaufman, 1956:1073). Later the demands for "relevancy" amid the social turmoil of the 1960s led to what Easton (1969:1052) called the "new revolution in political science"—and, for that matter, in all the policy sciences. Likewise, Trow's (1973:251) subsequent review of education at American public policy schools called for far more emphasis on the study of political contexts and organizational structures together with the values and political culture they represent.

A spokesman for this viewpoint has been Aaron Wildavsky, dean of the Graduate School of Public Policy at Berkeley. From his critiques of PPBS in his earlier work on budgeting (Wildavsky, 1964:422) to his recent collection, *Speaking Truth to Power* (1979), Wildavsky has consistently held out a vision of policy analysis as an art and craft, not a narrow science. Squarely in the anti-synoptic tradition, Wildavsky holds that "Above all, policy analysis is about improvement, about improving citizen preferences for the policies they—the people—ought to prefer" (Wildlavsky, 1979:19).

We may summarize by saying that a knowledge utilization perspective, as illustrated by writers discussed in the earlier portion of this section, leads rather directly toward the synoptic tradition. A concern with causal analysis and value issues, represented by writers discussed in the latter part, leads in the anti-synoptic direction. This is the dilemma underlying the current fragmentation of policy analysis.

THE SCOPE OF POLICY ANALYSIS: A CONCLUSION

The debate between those in the synoptic tradition and the anti-synoptic, the empirico-analytic schools and the neo-pluralist, policy analysis as a science and as an art—these tend to obscure a reasoned consideration of the proper scope of the discipline. The natural tendency is to start with the marketable skills of policy analysis and, in fact, for many analysts this is where policy analysis not only begins but ends. A more complex view argues that the analytic skills typically assume a particular procedural framework—the synoptic—and that other decision-making procedures—incrementalism, for example—must be examined equally by policy analysts. A few carry this complexity further. Fry and Tompkins (1978), for instance, propose a theoretical framework that partitions policy analysis not only by type of procedure but also by level of analysis.

As new dimensions like level of analysis are added to the original dimension of type of procedure, the complexity of theory in policy analysis escalates geometrically. This is illustrated by the relatively simple conceptualizatioin advanced by Fry and Tompkins. These authors discuss only three procedures (rational optimization, mutual adjustment, and bureaucratic routinization) and four levels of analysis (systemic, organizational, small group, and individual). This two-dimensional framework yields a twelve-place property space, each place of which is discussed by the authors in relation to existing social science literature.

Space does not permit elaboration on this useful schema except to emphasize the point that even this simple mapping forces attention on the salience to policy analysis of a *very* broad range of contributions from the literature on organization behavior and theory as well as political science and the traditional disciplines. "It can be seen," Fry and Tompkins conclude, "that a much wider set of phenomena is identified by this map than we typically find in the partial maps which characterize much of the current study of public policy" (Fry and Tompkins, 1978:311). Though the breadth of this map imposes many costs on policy analysis if it is to be covered, can anyone say that either dimension could be safely ignored or that the authors have selected too many values for each dimension?

This chapter argues that even the complexity generated by the Fry-Tompkins framework is inadequate to map the scope of policy analysis as an emerging discipline. At least six dimensions would be required to map this field. These dimensions deal not only with procedure and level but also with function, sequence, context, and normative criteria:

1. *Procedure:* This dimension may be partitioned as rational, traditional, or charismatic types (Weber, in Aron, 1964:103); rational comprehensive versus mutual adjustment (Lindblom, 1965), satisficing (Simon, 1948), mixed scanning (Etzioni, 1968), incrementalism (Wildavsky, 1964), organizational routines (Allison, 1971), polyarchy (Dahl, 1956), and many other variants.

2. *Level:* This dimension may be partitioned as Fry and Tompkins did into systemic, organizational, small group, and individual levels of analysis, to which could be added finer distinctions such as line and staff, appointed and career, or professional and nonprofessional levels.

3. *Function:* This dimension may also be conceptualized in a variety of ways, including the traditional POSDCORB (planning, organizing, staffing, directing, coordinating, reporting, and budgeting) of public administration; Bell (1973) emphasizes four functional situses (scientific, technological, administrative, and cultural) and five institutional situses (governmental, economic, academic, social, and military); and Almond and Powell (1966) utilize a more complex three-level functional typology covering system capabilities (extraction, regulation, distribution, symbolic output, responsive capability), conversion functions (interest articulation, interest aggregation into policy alternatives, conversion of policy alternatives into authoritative rules, adjudication of rules, political communication) and system maintenance and adaptive functions (political socialization, recruitment, adjustment of inputs and demands).

4. *Sequence:* A fourth dimension of policy analysis partitions analysis according to a rough sequence of stages; Lasswell (1971) was iden-

tified with a seven-step schema (intelligence, promotion, prescription, invocation, application, termination, appraisal) in which the rational-comprehensive approach was only a subset (goal clarification; trend description; analysis of causal conditioning factors; projection of developments; invention, evaluation, and selection of alternatives; selection of optimal strategies); in this dimension Jones' work is perhaps most prevalent, utilizing eleven sequential steps (perception, definition, aggregation, organization, representation, formulation, legitimation, appropriation, implementation, evaluation, and resolution/termination) (Jones, 1977:10).

5. *Context:* In this dimension the broad division is historical versus comparative analyses; analysis of economic and cultural context is another common division. This dimension was much emphasized by Lasswell in his vision of policy sciences.

6. *Normative Criteria:* In this dimension most policy analysis has been premised on criteria of efficiency/effectiveness; other essential criteria include power/control issues and equity/distribution issues. Were the latter two to become dominant, policy analysis would acquire an entirely different political complexion.

These six dimensions would require a property space of well over four thousand partitions. Obviously the simpler frameworks, such as those of Fry and Tompkins or of Jones, may be more useful precisely because they are simpler. A review of all six dimensions, however, serves to remind us that theoretical debates such as that between the empirico-analytic tradition versus the neo-pluralist take up only a very, very small part of the potential theoretical scope of policy analysis as a discipline.

In spite of the pressure of the marketplace, which places the empirico-analytic skills and synoptic approaches at an advantage, academic history suggests that in the long run the dynamic of policy analysis as a field will be toward a more and more balanced investigation and debate in *all* the dimensions which compose its scope. Lasswell long ago noted this trend in another field long associated with theoretically thin underpinnings, namely schools of business:

> Schools of business could not, however, maintain a university status without gradually coming to concern themselves with the social consequences of the business system. In short, professors of business became professional men and not shop assistants. They concerned themselves with the aggregate impact of economic institutions and enlarged the contexts of the business curriculum to include explicit awareness of the total interaction between business and the community (Lasswell, 1963:39).

Lasswell believed the same trends would occur in public administration as well.

The future of policy analysis may never achieve the idealistic synthesis represented by Lasswellian policy sciences, but neither does its future lie in the "handmaiden approach." Development of this new discipline will be toward a more and more balanced coverage of the entire range of its domain. As this development occurs, contemporary debates—such as that caricatured by Nelson's contrast of the Berkeley and Harvard, neo-pluralist and empirico-analytic approaches—will come to be seen as lesser and lesser parts of the scope of policy analysis. "Everywhere," Lasswell wrote, "the unit sooner or later searches to comprehend its role by discovering a map of the whole" (Lasswell, 1963:41).

If there are deficiencies in Lasswell's thought, at least it may be said that in his vision of policy sciences he had a map of the whole. It included not only rational-empirical procedure concerns, but deep interests in all levels of analysis from system to individual, in comparison by function, in analysis by sequential stage, and above all, in contextual and normative concerns. For years Lasswell struggled to shape a new political science that would comprehend it all and apply it to the analysis of public policy. A multi-dimensional approach to policy analysis makes this same objective still relevant today. Ironically, the way forward for policy analysis may lie in a closer examination of its past as represented by social theorists like Lasswell, Merriam, and even earlier, Weber and Marx.

REFERENCES

Allison, G. T. (1971) Essence of Decision: Explaining the Cuban Missile Crisis. Boston: Little, Brown.
Almond, G. and G. B. Powell, Jr. (1966) Comparative Politics: A Developmental Approach. Boston: Little, Brown.
Amacher, R., R. D. Tollison and T. D. Willett, eds. (1976) The Economic Approach to Public Policy. Ithaca, NY: Cornell University Press.
Appleby, P. (1950) Morality and Administration in Democratic Government. Baton Rouge, LA: University of Louisiana Press.
Aron, R. (1964) German Sociology. New York: Free Press.
Bell, D. (1973) The Coming of Post-Industrial Society: A Venture in Social Forecasting. New York: Basic Books.
Braybrooke, D. and C. E. Lindblom (1963) A Strategy of Decision. New York: Free Press.
Caplan, N. (1976) "Factors associated with knowledge use among federal executives." Policy Studies Journal 4(3):229–234.
Cohen, L. J. and R. M. Rakoff (1978) "Teaching the contexts of public policy: the need for a comparative perspective." Policy Studies Journal 6(3):319–325.
Dahl, R. A. (1956) A Preface to Democratic Theory. Chicago: University of Chicago Press.
———(1961) Who Governs? Democracy and Power in an American City. New Haven, CT: Yale University Press.
———and C. E. Lindblom (1953) Politics, Economics and Welfare. New York: Harper.

Dolbeare, K. M. (1974) "The impacts of public policy." In N. Cotter (ed.), The Policy Science Annual 1974. Indianapolis, IN: Bobbs-Merrill.

Dye, T. R. (1976) Policy Analysis: What Governments Do, Why They Do It, and What Difference It Makes. University, AL: University of Alabama Press.

Easton, D. (1953) The Political System: An Inquiry Into the State of Political Science. New York: Knopf.

———(1969) "The new revolution in political science." American Political Science Review 63(4):1051–1061.

Elkin, S. L. (1974) "Political science and the analysis of public policy." Public Policy 22(Summer):399–422.

Etzioni, A. (1968) The Active Society: A Theory of Societal and Political Process. New York: Free Press.

Friedman, M. (1962) Capitalism and Freedom. Chicago: University of Chicago Press.

Fry, B. R. and M. E. Tompkins (1978) "Some notes on the domain of public policy studies." Policy Studies Journal 6(3):305–313.

Garson, G. D. (1973) "Research on policy alternatives for America during the 1930s." Political Inquiry 1(1):50–77.

———(1978) Group Theories of Politics. Beverly Hills, CA: Sage Publications.

Horowitz, I. L. and J. E. Katz (1975) Social Science and Public Policy in the United States. New York: Praeger.

Jones, C. O. (1977) An Introduction to the Study of Public Policy, 2nd ed. North Scituate, MA: Duxbury.

Kaufman, H. (1956) "Emerging conflicts in the doctrines of public administration." American Political Science Review 50(4):1057–1073.

Lasswell, H. D. (1963) The Future of Political Science. New York: Atherton.

———(1971) A Preview of Policy Science. New York: American Elsevier.

———(1941) Democracy Through Public Opinion. Menasha, WI: George Banta Publishing Co.

Lerner, D. and H. D. Lasswell (1951) The Policy Sciences. Stanford, CA: Stanford University Press.

Lindblom, C. E. (1965) The Intelligence of Democracy: Decision-Making through Mutual Adjustment. New York: Free Press.

Lippman, W. (1955) Essays in the Public Philosophy. Boston: Little, Brown.

Lowi, T. (1967) "The public philosophy: interest group liberalism." American Political Science Review 61(1):5–24.

MacRae, D., Jr. (1977) "The social function of social science." Pp. 152–168 in S. Nagel (ed.), Policy Studies Review Annual. Beverly Hills, CA: Sage Publications.

March, J. G. (1955) "An introduction to the theory and measurement of influence." American Political Science Review 49(2):431–451.

Marvick, D., ed. (1977) Harold D. Lasswell on Political Science. Chicago: University of Chicago Press.

Merriam, C. E. (1945) Systematic Politics. Chicago: University of Chicago Press.

Myrdal, G. (1944) An American Dilemma. New York: Harper and Brothers.

Nagel, S. S., ed. (1977) Policy Studies Review Annual. Beverly Hills, CA: Sage Publications.

Nelson, M. (1979) "What's wrong with policy analysis." Washington Monthly 11(7):53–59.

Niskanen, W. A., Jr. (1971) Bureaucracy and Representative Government. Chicago: Aldin-Atherton.

Ostrom, V. (1973) The Intellectual Crisis in American Public Administration. University, AL: University of Alabama Press.

Quade, E. S. (1977) "Analysis for public decisions." Pp. 18–29 in S. Nagel (ed.), Policy Studies Review Annual. Beverly Hills, CA: Sage Publications.

Ranney, A., ed. (1962) Essays on the Behavioral Study of Politics. Urbana, IL: University of Illinois Press.

Rivlin, A. (1971) Systematic Thinking for Social Action. Washington, D.C.: Brookings Institution.

Schubert, G. A., Jr. (1957) "The 'public interest' in administrative decision-making." American Political Science Review 51(2):346–368.

Scott, R. A. and A. R. Shore (1979) Why Sociology Does Not Apply: A Study of the Use of Sociology in Public Policy. New York: Elsevier.

Simon, H. A. (1948) Administrative Behavior. New York: Macmillan.

———(1952) "Comments on the theory of organizations." American Political Science Review 46(4):1130–1139.

———(1957) Models of Man: Social and Rational. New York: Wiley.

Trow, M. (1973) "Public policy schools attuned to modern complexities." Policy Studies Journal 1(4):251.

Truman, D. B. (1968) "The social sciences and public policy." Science 160(3827):508–512.

Waldo, D. (1952) "Development of theory of democratic administration." American Political Science Review 46(1):81–103.

Wengert, N. (1955) Natural Resources and the Political Struggle. Garden City, NY: Doubleday.

Wildavsky, A. (1962) Dixon-Yates: A Study in Power Politics. New Haven, CT: Yale University Press.

———(1964) The Politics of the Budgetary Process. Boston: Little, Brown.

———(1979) Speaking Truth to Power: The Art and Craft of Policy Analysis. Boston: Little, Brown.

Zawodny, J. K. (1964) "Review of H. D. Lasswell, 'The Future of Political Science.'" American Political Science Review 58(1):121–122.

REAPPRAISING THE PROMISE OF GENERAL SYSTEMS THEORY FOR THE POLICY SCIENCES

Robert W. Backoff and Barry M. Mitnick

ABSTRACT

The core criticisms directed at the general systems movement and their relevance to policy and management science are reviewed and critically assessed. The issues examined include those dealing with the definition of "system," the holistic character of systems, the use of analogies or isomorphisms in the systems approach, the application of the systems approach to social problem-solving, and the question of complexity in the process and products of systems analysis.

INTRODUCTION

Over thirty years ago, the general system movement and the systems approach actively entered into the intellectual discourse of American scientists and managers; the ideas generated by the movement touched many fields and disciplines. The next decade, the 1960s, might well be

Policy Analysis: Perspectives, Concepts, and Methods, pages 23–40.
Copyright © 1986 by JAI Press, Inc.
All rights of reproduction in any form reserved.
ISBN: 0–89232–371–X

considered the heyday of the movement; the zealots implicitly and explicitly suggested the dawning of a new world view for science. The new approach would replace or complement the well-worn, constraining, and narrow mechanistic, atomistic, reductionistic science of the day. We social scientists can recall the curiosity the movement generated within our ranks; it offered the hope of a new means to make our subject matter more tractable and scientific. Somehow, the systems approach could salvage what the behaviorist movement had failed to deliver in applying the scientific method to the study of social, political, and economic phenomena. The 1960s also marked the introduction of new methods and techniques of rational problem-solving (or decision-making) into American government via the Department of Defense; the techniques were given the label of "systems analysis" and applied to policy planning. By 1964 they had been formally transferred to the domestic agencies for implementation by Presidential order as part of a larger package of rational resource allocation and planning (PPBS). The demise of PPBS in the Federal Government has been the subject of extensive post-mortem analysis and need not be retold here.

By the end of the 1960s, and into the 1970s, a new turn occurred for the general systems movement and its applied branches. Internal to the movement, a consolidation of original statements was followed by attempts to give substance to the early goals and promises. An outpouring of books addressed the philosophical, mathematical, disciplinary, and methodological implications of the original premises; the most relevant articles were published in the Society for General Systems Research's (SGSR) yearbooks. External to the movement the critics began to grow in number, sophistication, and stridency, e.g. Hoos (1972), Berlinski (1970; 1976), Phillips (1971; 1972; 1976) and Lilienfeld (1975; 1978). For the general systems movement, the 1970s can best be characterized as a period of both internal and external criticism of the original formulations and of attempts to elaborate and extend the initial works. From the perspective of the public policy and management sciences, one might note a parallel effort to self-consciously acknowledge the weaknesses of the early efforts at systems and systematic analysis and to repackage them in a more subtle, relevant form and under different labels, *inter alia*, decision analysis, policy analysis, organizational analysis, and contingency theory. Thus, by the end of the decade, systems ideas, concepts, and methods had diffused widely; had been criticized both in theory and application; and had been subject to many revisionist efforts. There appeared a need to review the 25 to 30 year history of the general systems movement and the application of the general systems approach. To meet this need the Society for General Systems Research commissioned a task force to report on the systems research movement; its report, *Systems Research Movement: Characteristics, Accomplishments, and Current Developments* (Cavallo, 1979b), was distributed to its membership in 1979.

Given these developments, it appears appropriate for social, organizational, managerial, and policy scientists and analysts to appraise the substance and implications of these developments. What exactly are the core criticisms leveled at the general systems movement and its core assumptions? How have the revisionists and reformers within the movement changed the original platform and do the changes meet the external criticisms? What can we conclude from these evolving arguments of relevance to our field, the policy and management sciences? In this paper, we will address these questions.

Our discussion will focus on the general systems research movement and not on applied systems analysis per se; it is the foundational assumptions that will be of interest to us. In particular, we shall review the basic criticisms of the ontological assumptions of the systems approach; these involve the existence and definition of systems and the holistic aspects of systems. Certain methodological criticisms have also been raised and addressed by systems researchers; here, we restrict our statement to issues concerning the use of analogies and the transfer of methods across subject matter.

We shall then address a core issue relating to the applicability of the systems approach to the social as well as the policy and management sciences. A core problematic concern of the systems approach is the understanding, analyzing, and managing of complexity. But how can the systems approach help the scholar, analyst, practitioner deal with a complex world when it itself tends to produce complex theories and other forms of analysis of that world? Should the rule of simplicity be a central evaluative criterion for theories, models, problem-solving methods, and other forms of analysis?

THE GENERAL SYSTEMS APPROACH REVISITED

The general systems approach, like other approaches, is a way of looking at things; it includes a basic framework or ontology, a set of goals and problems, and a collection of methods. Each of these components of the systems approach have been the target of external and internal criticism; as a result many of the vagaries of the early writers have been clarified and new contributions added. In the discussion that follows we shall highlight the most salient and significant targets of criticism and attempt to summarize the recent modifications. As a result, we hope the reader will benefit from a better understanding of the arguments posed and be in a position to draw personal conclusions regarding the merits of the arguments. As referees we have imposed some constraints in the form of selective sampling of the protagonists and added suggestions along the way concerning missing arguments or irrelevant claims, grounds, and warrants (Toulmin, 1958). In the next sections, we shall sequentially address the criticisms regarding the existence and nature of systems, the holistic quality of systems, the use of analogies, the transferability of findings and methods across subject matter domains, and the complexity of systems analyses. Throughout we have avoided detailed quotations and footnoting of pioneers in the systems movement; we believe these works are well known to most readers (if not carefully read!).[1]

If Systems Are Everywhere Are they Nothing (of Importance)?

Nothing is more damning these days among scholars than to assert that some claim, work, finding, etc., is "trivial" or commonplace. Exactly this derisive comment has been directed at the core idea of general systems thinking, namely that the world is populated with things called systems and itself is a system. This prompted (in reference to James G. Miller's early work) one of the first critics of this idea to note:

> we are indeed confronted with limitless vistas of systems. One is unable to think of anything, or of any combination of things, which could not be regarded as a system. And, of course, a concept that applies to everything is logically empty. (Buck, 1956)

The most widely cited definition of a system seems to be that of Hall and Fagen (1956:18): "A system is a set of objects together with relationships between the objects and between their attributes." A prominent external critic, Berlinski (1970; 1976:3) notes such definitions: "illuminate at low wattages. Hall and Fagen have suggested something that mathematicians would recognize as an elephantine approximation of the notion of a model." Hoos suggests that proponents of the systems approach have failed to give a precise definition of the term "system" and this produces an arbitrary eclecticism and broad inclusiveness (Hoos, 1972:17).

Turning to the SGSR report (Cavallo, 1979b) for guidance on current interpretations of the definitional issue, we find one response of system writers to the generality and impreciseness of the object of reference. Cavallo writes: "The notion system clearly means different things to different people involved in systems research. In light of the dynamic epistemology associated with systems research ... it is even reasonable to accept that a clear definition of system is not important, or maybe not possible" (Cavallo, 1979b:27). He goes on to note that the Webster dictionary definition is quite adequate (or that of James Miller) in that it captures the core ideas of "interaction" and "interdependency." He claims that a definition so defined is essentially independent of context, acceptable and relevant to problem areas of concern, and emphasizes the core foci of systems research—organization and complexity. It would appear a clear difference of view exists between the external and internal critics; the former prefer precision, even if it forces such generality as to be trivial or such specificity as to be the logical province of some more specialized domain of scientific inquiry. Within the GS movement two responses seem apparent on our reading.[2]

The first response is implied by Cavallo's statement. It is to use the dictionary or founding fathers' definitions as orienting devices and to let the ambiguity of meaning and reference allow for multiple interpretations and scientific stipulations. Thus, the would-be system researcher is given the imperative "search for things in the world which are characterized by interdependencies!" If the researcher finds them they are systems; if precision about the things and interdependencies is desired, the researcher stipulates these. The recent writers frequently suggest that systems are stipulated by the observer; it is the relationship between the observer and the observed which enters directly in the definitional (or identification) process (Weinberg, 1975; Ackoff and Emery, 1972; Kuhn, 1974).

Does this mean arbitrary eclecticism as Hoos suggests? It certainly means a linking of the subjective choice process with the objective, empirical world. As far as we can discern, the result of this approach in the recent systems research is similar to that in any science; each scholar either accepts someone else's definition as a starting premise or stipulates his or her own definitional point of departure according to the purposes of the research. As in all scientific research, various criteria to evaluate concepts and theories can be applied to assess empirical adequacy and theoretical significance.

The second response of the systems researchers has been an attempt to treat the all inclusive aspects of the definition by finding a more exact and differentiating definition. Bunge's (1979) recent work exemplifies this response. He points out that systems can be distinguished from an aggregate which is "not held together by bonds, and therefore lacks integrity or unity" (p. 4). On the other hand, a system is a complex object, the components of which are interrelated rather than loose. A system may be conceptual or concrete, but not both. Furthermore, a system must have a definite composition (a set of components), a definite environment (the set of items to which it is connected), and a definite structure (consisting of relations among components as well as among these and the environment). Bunge also acknowledges the existence of things which are only parts of some system, but not systems themselves.

On this account the range of things to be explored remains extremely broad and the difficulty of analysis is heightened—to generate components, the relevant environment, and the structure of relations between them, and orienting logical language quite exactly (set theoretically in Bunge's work). There emerges a slight conceptual distinction from earlier work; this is the emphasis on the object and its immediate environment as the final unit of analysis (or as some say the "total system" vs. the "focal system"). Furthermore, some clarity is added by Bunge and others who stipulate relations beyond mere spatial configuration. Relations of concrete systems (distinguished from mere conceptual systems or sets in mathematics) mean that one thing *acts* upon another in such a way as "to modify the latter's behavior line, or trajectory, or history" (Bunge, 1979:6).

For Bunge, then, the heroic task of the system scientist seeking exhaustive knowledge of a concrete system would involve generating the following: (1) the composition, the environment, and the structure of the system; (2) the history of the system; and (3) the laws (patterns) of the system.[3] He notes such complete knowledge is seldom attainable. This statement reflects a theme in recent system writing (see especially Churchman, 1979) concerning the gap between the ideal of inquiry and the realization in reality/practice. It reflects a continuing dilemma between the search for generality and inclusiveness as Hoos noted above and the reality of dealing with and being part of a complex natural and artificial system with limited analytical and technical tools. In the end, one has recourse to the questions: Does the ideal—however general and ambiguous—motivate the researcher? Does it produce useful results—however inadequate—relative to the ideal? Are there alternative ideals to guide us? Are there alternative ways of defining reality? If the world is not composed of systems, then what is its composition, if any? At the root, systems thinking forces us to the very boundaries of metaphysics.

The Whole Is More Than the Sum of Its Parts, Or Is It?

The early systems thinkers resurrected the idea that certain phenomena are better characterized in terms of wholes (particularly living systems) and that analytical, reductionist attempts to understand, predict, and explain them in terms of their component parts were unwise, indeed, foolish. Here we face the second ontological argument raised by the critics: Is systems theory merely the resurrection of an outdated, holistic philosophy—organicism? Does it imply a mysterious élan vital, an entelechy? Phillips (1976) has carefully sorted out different versions of holism to which systems thinkers might subscribe. There are for Phillips three versions of Holism to be analyzed:

Holism 1: Includes five theses:
  1. the analytical approach is inadequate in certain cases (e.g., biological organisms, society, and to reality as a whole)
  2. the whole is more than the sum of its parts
  3. the whole determines the nature of its parts
  4. the parts cannot be understood if considered in isolation from the whole.
  5. the parts are dynamically interrelated or interdependent (p. 6)

Holism 2: The whole, even after it is studied, cannot be explained in terms of its parts (p. 36)

Holism 3: It is necessary to have terms referring to wholes and their properties (p. 37).

Phillips concludes his analysis by suggesting what is worth redeeming of these holism claims. First, Holism 1 is inadequate except for the emphasis on the dynamic relation between the parts of an organic whole (1–(5)). Second, he agrees with holists that it is difficult to predict beforehand what emergent properties will result when new elements are brought into combination. Finally, regarding Holism 3, the introduction of new concepts is needed to facilitate the study of organic wholes. In his view, these retainable aspects of holism are not in any way antithetical to the traditional analytical method (atomistic or mechanistic). Thus, the challenge to the systems thinkers is clear; either they have nothing of merit to add on holism beyond what Phillips accepts, or what they add is quite compatible with the older tradition they had thought was to be overthrown.

In the general debate on holism and atomism/reductionism, there is a tendency to generate extreme representations of each view and attack the extremities; just so, with much of Phillip's argument. On our reading a more balanced, reasonable, and realistic view of the matter is possible. Furthermore, the recent statement by Bunge (1979), one of the handful of philosophers of science who have carefully articulated the ontology and methodology of systems science, seems to provide a clear resolution of most of the confusion. First, systems theorists of the modern bent do not deny the appropriateness, indeed, utility of the analytical methods of science. Indeed, systems scientists, too, try to understand systems by identifying their components; furthermore, as other scientists do, they attempt various forms of synthesis or recombination considering the structure of relations among components. Perhaps there is a distinction to be made regarding the modern systems scientists' focus on the relevant environmental components and their relations which goes beyond the more narrow, so-called "closed-system" or, better, "isolated system" perspective sometimes ascribed to experimental, laboratory science. To the extent, then, that the analytical scientists acknowledge the existence of systems and that they include structures of relations which are to be studied and understood, there seems to be no quarrel. As well, if they acknowledge emergent, system (collective) properties, which are different from the parts which preceded them, there, again, is no quarrel with system scientists (Holism 3 of Phillips).

We come now to the "sum of the parts" question. The system theorist does insist that systems as wholes are more than additive summations of aggregates; it is the couplings of the system's components, or the actions of some parts on others, that is of central importance (Holism 1-(5) of Phillips). The system theorist does propose to understand systems by going beyond the mere study of parts. The system cannot be fully explained by micro-laws of the parts; there are always other macro-hypotheses and data to add. By macro here we mean merely the addition of laws (pattern statements) regarding interaction among system components and among them and the system environment.[4]

Some additional, less central, sub-arguments can be quickly clarified to eliminate the vestiges of an older organicism from modern system philosophy, again drawing upon Bunge's presentation. First, systemics or systemism, as Bunge refers to his philosophy for concrete systems, does not assume the whole precedes the parts; this only occurs when a system breaks down. Further, the existence of the system may not be obvious (looking for mutual actions of parts and environment); thus, the whole cannot be taken for granted. Second, wholes do not act on their parts; rather, components of the system act on one another. Third, the system thinker does not posit some transcendental force (vitalism, etc.) outside the action of components and the environment; as a science, systemism operates on the principle of immanence. Finally, systemism does not ascribe a value judgment that the whole is better than the parts; no such ideological commitment is involved.

At this point we turn to several of the methodological criticisms of the general systems approach.

If "x" Looks Like "y", So What?

The early writers on systems proclaimed that their methodological task was to find similarities, called isomorphisms, between all or most types of systems; the isomorphisms have been variously construed as concepts, hypotheses, laws, and principles (Bertalanffy, 1968; Miller, 1972). What exactly is involved in this task, and what are its likely benefits for science and our general understanding? System critics have responded in the following manner. Berlinkski argues that isomorphisms are not new, as they have been a part of the concept of structural identity in mathematical set theory for some time; furthermore, to note that one model is isomorphic to another or mathematically similar is not a distinctive contribution of general system thinkers per se (1976:20–25). A different, but related, point concerns the non-mathematical similarities, or analogies; how are we to assess the utility of general system generated analogies (Stephens, 1976)? The point is made that no methodological criterion has been generated by general system writers to distinguish the fruitful from the sterile analogy. An additional cause for concern is the constraint placed on scientific inquiry if one focuses his/her energy on the search for similarities at the expense of differences.

Recent writing on general systems gives much less emphasis to the search for universal principles, laws, and other isomorphisms per se. The emphasis, rather, is on using analogies, and not mathematical formalisms, in scientific research as a means to create new insights, that is, as heuristics in the process of scientific discovery. As Stephens noted, there is no criterion to appraise analogies in the process of discovery, at least in the standard philosophy of science account (although recent attempts to develop a logic of discovery are clearly underway); the system thinkers are content to use the more informal criteria of science to judge the fruitfulness of an analogy—does it generate insight and understanding leading to research products judged satisfactory by more conventional criteria applied during the verification process?

A related use of analogies within today's general systems movement appears to be for the development of more integrated generic frameworks which help one to think about entire genera of entities in a variety of domains—from biology to politics. In this context they help discovery and the formulation of problems and also clarify basic ideas in many fields of inquiry. Besides the seeking of isomorphisms, the systems founders sought enhanced communication between scientists/scholars in all fields; under the current conception, there is much less interest in the direct transfer of mathematical isomorphisms useful in engineering, biology, and physics to the social and managerial sciences, and much more interest in developing empirically interpreted concepts at a high level of abstraction which have wide, but not necessarily universal, applicability (Cavallo, 1979b). Drawing on these concepts and relating them to form models of different classes of concrete systems, the systems theorist is able to quickly draw upon insights outside his or her own area of concern and use them if found appropriate. One benefit noted is the ability to synthesize diverse within-field problems drawing upon the meta-level insights from the more abstract classes of system models (Cavallo, 1979b:35).

In our reading there seems to be no agreement within the contemporary systems movement as to whether particular abstract, yet empirically referenced laws or patterns exist for wide classes of concrete systems; if they do exist they would be construed as hyper-general and not hyper-specific. To be translated, that is, interpreted for social and organizational systems, more specific theories would need to be detailed using the more general system concepts and adding subsidiary hypotheses and empirical data. These theories would then be testable; thus, the general system theory is only vicariously testable.

By this account (Bunge, 1977), general system theories (no one in the movement posits any single, all encompassing theory) have appropriate scientific status to the degree that they fit whole families of specific theories (conceptual confirmation) and help in building of specific theories that are tested in the classical manner (indirect confirmation). The theories most frequently suggested as having such potential include: the statistical theory of information, game theory, control theory, automata theory, network theory, and fuzzy set theory (Cavallo, 1979b; Bunge, 1977). These general systems theories (GSTs) are still under development themselves; thus, it is not surprising that their interpretation into more specific social and organizational theories is still in doubt.

Berlinski (1976) properly questions the relevance of many of these GSTs for the modeling or representation of social systems which he characterizes as involving unknown dynamics, high dimensionality, non-linear relations, variable coefficients, temporal dependence, adaptive control, and dynamic structures (1976:128). None of the current GSTs seems to be fully appropriate. The message is clear: policy and management scientists will have to wait a long while if they plan to use GSTs which are yet underdeveloped or not yet even conceptually created! In the meantime they have recourse to more primitive, mathematically modeled systems or simply the guiding concepts and analogies of various systems theorists.

Have Tool, Will Travel, Or Do You Have Any Tractable Problems? If Not, Redefine Them!

The most salient concern of the critics of the general systems approach focuses on the displacement onto particular methods within their larger methodology of inquiry, particularly by the applied systems analysts (Hoos, 1972). The fiascos of cost/benefit, cost/effectiveness, system dynamics analysis easily come to mind. A long list of failures in attempting applied "systematic analysis" with an overly rationalistic bias can be understood as resulting from any of the following acts of problem-solving: (1) disregarding the qualitative aspects; (2) over-emphasis on the quantitative and easily measured; (3) resort to symbols and models without substance; (4) overload of uninterpretable data; (5) dependence on easily accessible/available data; (6) neglect of subjective elements; (7) inattention to multiple objectives; (8) underemphasis on problem formulation; and (9) failure to consider the political and social "soft" factors, etc.

The basic response to all this from the active members of the contemporary general systems movement is multi-faceted. First, they note these are limitations of all rational problem-solving techniques. Relatedly, the task is to improve on these methods of analysis. The users of such methods must be competent professionals and be quite self-conscious about the limits of their work and communicate these to clients and affected publics. Furthermore, the inappropriate transfer of techniques from one field to another is to be deplored. The true general system thinker begins with the problem to be solved and after careful problem definition chooses, from a wide variety of methods and techniques, those which are clearly appropriate (Sutherland, 1975). If none is appropriate, then the researcher has to create one, if possible, or tell the client none is currently available to the best of his/her knowledge/capability. A result of this line of response has been the development of classifications of problems, systems, methods, techniques, and logics of inquiry within the newer generation of social and applied systems theorists. These taxonomies are based on the development of a criterion of "congruence" to be applied between problem, method, client, clientele, researcher/analyst/designer, and the process of problem-solving itself (Sutherland, 1975, 1977; Warfield, 1973, 1974, 1976; Mitroff et al., 1974). This is a very promising development in attempting to clarify the underlying parameters of problem-solving and acknowledging forcefully the limited domains of application of particular methods/techniques. As yet the underlying principles to help determine the extent of congruence are unclear.

Ackoff, among others, has chastised his fellow management scientists for becoming infatuated with existing tools and developing new disciplines around these; he calls for movement toward metadisciplines based on systemology. The new field would apply the system approach to what he calls problem "messes"; they would be functionally oriented to dealing with complex problem sets and not identified with particular techniques as such (Ackoff, 1973). Churchman (1979) is also critical of his colleagues and of the rationalist enterprise itself; his concerns clearly go beyond the problem of displacement to particular methods. He wants to directly face the critics of the system approach and offers two principles to guide the social system designers: (1) leave the body of rationality and put yourself in the body of one of its four enemies (politics, morality, religion, and aesthetics); experience their view of the social system; and (2) from this vantage point you can detect what is missing from the pure rational view of the social system design problem and process; in short, your own approach (including its foolishness) now becomes the object of your scrutiny from the other vantage points.

Recent proposals by social scientists complement Churchman's thoughts: it is recommended that professional social scientists and problem-solvers look beyond the rationality of cognitive, intellectual problem-solving of the individual or project team and examine the merits of studying and supporting problem-solving through the use of social learning, application of ordinary knowledge, and social interaction (Lindblom and Cohen, 1979; Wildavsky, 1979). Churchman's enemy—politics—is given renewed support through a reaffirmation of the inherent social rationality of the partisan mutual adjustment process. On the other side, the system theorist would ask: what problem does it address? Is it the appropriate problem-solving process? What methods are congruent, given the client, purpose, measures of performance, decision makers, system components and environment, planners, and implementers? And, of course, what guarantees do we have that it contributes to progress (Churchman, 1979)?

So on the applied system description and design side, we are left to face a large array of considerations, not to mention the associated uncertainty in future application. Via these methodological considerations we come face to face with the core concern of the general systems movement today, how to treat societal complexity. Fundamentally, the current systems researchers are in agreement on the label for their problem; it is called "organized complexity". As noted in the earlier discussion on system definition and holism, the systems to be studied and designed/redesigned are principally characterized as complex, not simple. The methodological ideal of the systems movement today, at least on our reading, is to generate a logic of inquiry to treat our perceived organized complexity. It is clear that the current general system research is targeted on this problem; it is also clear that there are no simple (or even complex) answers currently available for processing the problem (in contemporary systems thinking problems are no longer solved or resolved!).

If Simple Models Are Always Better, Are Systems Models Always Worse?

The systems approach has been criticized because of its propensity to produce theories, models, and other forms of analysis that are judged "complex." Such analyses seem to violate an important evaluative norm of science—the "rule of simplicity." Also known as the "principle of parsimony" or "economy" or "Ockham's razor," the rule seems to be clearly inconsistent with any analytical approach that, like the systems approach, produces complex forms of analysis. We shall argue, however, that the rule is an inappropriate criterion to apply not only to systems but to the evaluation of theories and other analyses in general. If we are correct, then the systems approach and its complex products would of course remain viable.

Because the social world is complex, a number of scholars have argued that the task of social science is to develop analytic means to handle this complexity (see, e.g., van Gigch, 1978; Brunner and Brewer, 1971; La Porte, 1975; Weaver, 1948; Quine, 1963; Rapoport and Horvath, 1959). While we shall not review the arguments that support the claim of social complexity, we note that these arguments usually identify such contributing factors as increases in size, interdependency, technological sophistication, and so on. Those who maintain the relevance of the rule of simplicity may be seen to have a greater burden, of course, if the social world is complex; they are maintaining, in effect, that simpler models do a better job of explaining complex phenomena. Social complexity can, however, be irrelevant to the evaluation of complex forms of analysis since it is the forms of analysis, not the social world, that is subject to evaluation by the rule of simplicity.

The "complexity" of systems is said to vary in "organization" (see, e.g., Weaver, 1948; La Porte, 1975; Rapoport and Horvath, 1959; van Gigch, 1978). "Organized simplicity" is characterized by linear or serial relations of elements; "unorganized complexity" features a potentially infinite number of elements engaging in chance interaction. In "organized complexity," however, there are a finite number of parts whose systemic interrelationships can produce properties that go beyond those deducible directly from the elements. Social systems, for which the systems approach is designed, have this character.

As "Ockham's Razor," the rule of simplicity is often associated with the fourteenth century scholastic, William of Ockham. Ockham argued that "plurality is not to be assumed without necessity" or, in a commentator's words, "Nothing is to be assumed as necessary, in accounting for any fact, unless it is established by evident experience or evident reasoning, or is required by the articles of faith" (Moody, 1967:307). Although such maxims predate Ockham, it was not until the mid-nineteenth century that they were raised to the status of a primary criterion in the evaluation of scientific work (Thorburn, 1918). Note that Ockham valued efficiency in argument not for its own sake or because it would bring us closer to a valid or truthful statement about the world. Simplicity is in rigid service to the aims of the inquiry and is sought only to reduce superfluity.

With this introduction, we shall consider critically several of the supports for using the rule of simplicity. Bunge (1961, 1963) has provided a basic critique that examines the contribution that simplicity makes to the achievement of a number of basic evaluative criteria for theories (e.g., explanatory power, predictive power, fertility, originality, and so on) and finds it of little importance. Rather than reviewing his analysis, we shall offer three additional comments on the supports for the simplicity criterion.

First, the systematization (and abstraction) and, hence, simplification, characterizing scientific inquiry provides no support for simplicity as an evaluative criterion. Just because two scientific theories are, by their nature, simpler than reality is no reason to believe that the simplest theory will be the best theory. Science requires simplification only, not the maximization of simplification. After all, even much-criticized complex systems models are always simpler than the social setting they depict.

Second, the problems that complex forms of analysis like systems models raise for human perception and information-processing cannot define the limits of those forms of analysis. Such pragmatic or subjective constraints bear little relevance to the validity of theories (though they may possibly have some bearing on the utility and degree of acceptance of a theory). They would ultimately place severe restrictions on the form and coverage of scientific theories since only a few (easily perceived) elements can then be of significance. And if the limits of complexity are to be human limits, which human's limits are they to be? Where do we draw the perceptual/subjective line?

Third, contrary to the assumptions and arguments of some scholars (e.g., Reichenbach, 1938; Kemeny, 1953), simplicity is not a means for obtaining true hypotheses or hypotheses that provide better prediction. Bunge (1961, 1963) argues that simpler hypotheses do not, in fact, tend more often to be true. He says the apparent pattern is that "The rule actually used in scientific research is not just 'choose the simplest,' but 'Try the simplest first and, if it fails—as it normally should—gradually introduce complications compatible with the bulk of knowledge' " (Bunge, 1961:143). Bunge supports this through a detailed review of several major instances of theory development in the natural sciences. Thus systems theories or models that are complex are not more likely to be false.

In conclusion, the complexity of systems models cannot be held out to be, necessarily, a disadvantage. The rule of simplicity should be seen as an editor's tool to encourage economy of expression; it is not a basic evaluative criterion for abstract scientific theories, an ultimate bound for (subjectively perceived) analytic approaches, or a necessary road to truth. The systems approach, moreover, was developed explicitly to deal with situations of organized complexity.

CONCLUSION

In spite of the barrages of critics such as those discussed earlier, the systems approach has continued to develop and, on occasion, even to prosper. On balance, many of those criticisms have either been addressed in later work in systems or been found lacking in substance. Problems in systems definition have been met by increasing precision in subjective definition and/or by development of more exact and differentiating definitions. Problems in the holistic character of systems have been shown to be of no concern; systems approaches both recognize the existence of constituent parts and of some system-level interaction among system components and environment that sets it apart. The superficial use of isomorphisms in systems approaches has yielded to their use as heuristics and as an aid in developing abstract, high-level concepts and models. The misuse of systems-based technologies has led to recognition of the contingent appropriateness or inappropriateness of use of given models in given settings. And the fault of complexity in systems approaches has been shown to be "in the stars" of analysts and critics rather than in the approaches themselves.

This is not to say that criticism of the systems approach can henceforth be disregarded. In fact, systems models have not yet (and may never) achieve the early claims made for them. The constraints of users and of settings for application remain real and nontrivial. But those constraints are now acknowledged. The task of modern and future systems analysts will be to recognize and incorporate—systematically—the contingencies presented by a real and complex world.

ACKNOWLEDGMENTS

The authors wish to thank Tom Saaty, Luis Vargas, and Vasant Dhar for their comments. An earlier version of this paper was presented at the 1980 Annual Meeting of the American Political Science Association, The Washington Hilton Hotel, Washington, D.C., August 28–31, 1980. For an application of the systems arguments in this paper to university management, see Backoff and Mitnick (1981). For an extension of the arguments regarding complexity, see Mitnick (1981).

NOTES

1. The reader in quickly perusing the foundational works will find the following authors quite helpful: Buckley (1968), Bertalanffy (1968), Ashby (1952; 1956), Weiner (1948), Emery (1969).

2. The major recent works in general systems research which we have drawn upon in developing our analysis here and later in the paper include the following in chronological order: Buckley (1967); Bertalanffy (1968); Berrien (1968); Churchman (1968); Klir (1969); Emery (1969); Segasti (1970); Churchman (1971); Ackoff (1971); Laszlo (1972); Klir (1972); Miller (1972); Warfield and Hill (1972); Ackoff and Emery (1972); Ackoff (1973); Pattee (1973); Sutherland (1973); Warfield (1973); Segasti (1973); Kuhn (1974); Warfield (1974); van Gigch (1974); Weinberg (1975); Sutherland (1975); Jantsch (1975); Beer (1975); Warfield (1976); Sutherland (1977); Boulding (1978); Miller (1978); Sutherland (1978); van Gigch (1978); Cavallo (1979a,b); Churchman (1979); Bunge (1979).

3. A related approach is taken by Saaty (1980) who argues, with respect to Hall-and-Fagan systems definitions, that "a much richer definition of a system can be given in terms of its *structure*, its *functions*, the *objectives* set for it in the *design* from the *perspective* of a particular individual or group (hence the possibility for conflict), and finally the *environment* (the larger surrounding system) of which it is a subsystem" (Saaty, 1980:5). Systems are said to possess an inseparable *structure* and *function* which compose "the reality we experience" (Saaty, 1980:5).

4. Thomas Saaty's work on analytic hierarchies illustrates the potential gains from taking a holistic systems view. Saaty has developed a method for structuring and analyzing complex decision problems through construction of hierarchies (including hierarchies of systems that exhibit feedback). One feature of his approach is its capability of determining to what degree evaluations in a hierarchical goal or preference structure are consistent overall, with obvious applications in facilitating group or organizational choice and action. Of particular interest is that degrees of inconsistency can not only be detected but can be shown to be tolerable (below a certain level, i.e., 10 percent). Detection of such inconsistencies (and resulting prescriptions for organizational or group action and development) is a result of a holistic perspective on the hierarchy and could not necessarily be achieved through attention only to the separate components of the hierarchy (see Saaty, 1980).

REFERENCES

Ackoff, R. L. (1971) "Toward a system of systems concepts." Management Science 17(11):661–671.
——(1973) "Science in the systems age: beyond IE, OR, MS." Operations Research 21 (May/June):661–671.
——and F. E. Emery (1972) Purposeful Systems. Chicago: Aldine.
Ashby, F. R. (1952) Design for the Brain. London: Chapman and Hall, Ltd.
——(1956) An Introduction to Cybernetics. London: Chapman and Hall, Ltd.
Backoff, R. W. and B. M. Mitnick (1981) "The systems approach, incentive relations, and university management." In J. Wilson (ed.), Symposium on Higher Education and Management Science, New Directions for Higher Education. San Francisco: Jossey-Bass.
Beer, S. (1975) Platform for Change. New York: Wiley.
Berlinski, D. J. (1970) "Systems analysis." Urban Affairs Quarterly (September): 104–126.

———(1976) On Systems Analysis. Cambridge, MA: MIT Press.

Berrien, F. K. (1968) General and Social Systems. New Brunswick, NJ: Rutgers University Press.

Bertalanffy, L. V. (1968) General System Theory. New York: Braziller.

Boulding, K. (1978) Ecodynamics. Beverly Hills, CA: Sage Publications.

Brunner, R. D. and G. D. Brewer (1971) Organized Complexity: Empirical Theories of Political Development. New York: Free Press.

Buck, R. (1956) "On the logic of general behavior systems theory." Pp. 223–238 in H. Feigl and M. Scriven (eds.), Minnesota Studies in the Philosophy of Science, Vol. 1. Minneapolis, MN: University of Minnesota Press.

Buckley, W. (1967) Sociology and Modern Systems Theory. Englewood Cliffs, NJ: Prentice-Hall.

———, ed. (1968) Modern Systems Research for the Behavioral Scientist. Chicago: Aldine.

Bunge, M. (1961) "The weight of simplicity in the construction and assaying of scientific theories." Philosophy of Science 28(2):120–149.

———(1963) The Myth of Simplicity: Problems of Scientific Philosophy. Englewood Cliffs, NJ: Prentice-Hall.

———(1977) "The GST challenge to the classical philosophies of science." International Journal of General Systems 4:29–37.

———(1979) The Treatise of Basic Philosophy, Vol. 4: Ontology II: A World of Systems. Hingham, MA: D. Reidel.

Cavallo, R. E. (1979a) The Role of Systems Methodology in Social Science Research. Boston: Martinus Nijhoff.

———, ed. (1979b) "Systems research movement." Society for General Systems Research, General Systems Bulletin, Special Issue 9(3):1–131.

Churchman, C. W. (1968) The Systems Approach. New York: Dell.

———(1971) The Design of Inquiring Systems. New York: Basic Books.

———(1979) The Systems Approach and its Enemies. New York: Basic Books.

Emery, F. E., ed. (1969) Systems Thinking. Baltimore, MD: Penguin.

Hall, A. D. and R. E. Fagen (1956) "Definition of system." General Systems Yearbook 1:18–28.

Hoos, I. (1972) Systems Analysis in Public Policy. Berkeley, CA: University of California Press.

Jantsch, E. (1975) Design for Evolution. New York: Braziller.

Kemeny, J. G. (1953) "The use of simplicity in induction," Philosophical Review 62(3):391–408.

Klir, G. J. (1969) An Approach to General Systems Theory. New York: Van Nostrand Reinhold.

———, ed. (1972) Trends in General Systems Theory. New York: Wiley.

Kuhn, A. (1974) Logic of Social Systems. San Francisco: Jossey-Bass.

La Porte, T. R., ed. (1975) Organized Social Complexity: Challenge to Politics and Policy. Princeton, NJ: Princeton University Press.

Laszlo, E. (1972) Introduction to Systems Philosophy. New York: Harper and Row.

Lilienfeld, R. (1975) "System theory as ideology." Social Research 42(3):637–660.

———(1978) The Rise of Systems Theory. New York: Wiley.

Lindblom, C. E. and D. K. Cohen (1979) Usable Knowledge. New Haven, CT: Yale University Press.

Miller, J. G. (1972) "Living systems: the organization." Behavioral Science 17(1):1–182.

———(1978) Living Systems. New York: McGraw-Hill.

Mitnick, B. M. (1981) "A brief for beards in an age of Ockham's Razor: complexity and the rule of simplicity." University of Pittsburgh, Graduate School of Business Working Paper Series.

Mitroff, I., F. Betz, L. Pondy and F. Segasti (1974) "On managing science in the systems age." Interfaces 4(3):46–58.

Moody, E. A. (1967) "William of Ockham." Pp. 306–317 in Paul Edwards (ed.), Encyclopedia of Philosophy, Vols. 7–8. New York: Macmillan and Free Press (1972 reprint).

Pattee, H. (1973) Hierarchy Theory. New York: Braziller.

Phillips, D. C. (1971) "Systems theory—a discredited philosophy." Pp. 55–64 in P. P. Schoderbek (ed.), Management Systems, 2nd ed. New York: Wiley.

———(1972) "The methodological bias of systems theory." Academy of Management Journal 15(4):469–477.

———(1976) Holistic Thought in Social Science. Stanford, CA: Stanford University Press.

Quine, W. V. O. (1963) "On simple theories of a complex world." Synthese 15(1):103–106.

Rapaport, A. and W. J. Horvath (1959) "Thoughts on organization theory." General Systems 4:87–91.

Reichenbach, H. (1938) Experience and Prediction: An Analysis of the Foundations and the Structure of Knowledge. Chicago: University of Chicago Press.

Saaty, T. L. (1980) The Analytic Hierarchy Process: Planning, Priority Setting, Resource Allocation. New York: McGraw-Hill.

Segasti, F. (1970) "A conceptual and taxonomic framework for the analysis of adaptive behavior." General Systems 15:151–160.

———(1973) "A conceptual 'systems' framework for the study of planning theory." Journal of Technological Forecasting and Social Change 5:379–393.

Stephens, J. (1976) "A perspective on the development of general systems analysis: problems, changes, and prospects." Proceedings, North American Meeting, Society for General Systems Research: 95–105.

Sutherland, J. W. (1973) A General Systems Philosophy for the Social and Behavioral Sciences. New York: Braziller.

———(1975) Systems. New York: Van Nostrand Reinhold.

———(1977) Administrative Decision-Making. New York: Van Nostrand Reinhold.

———, ed. (1978) Management Handbook for Public Administrators. New York: Van Nostrand Reinhold.

Thorburn, W. M. (1918) "The myth of Ockham's razor." Mind 107(July):345–353.

Toulmin, S. (1958) The Uses of Argument. London: Cambridge University Press.

Van Gigch, J. P. (1974, 1978) Applied General Systems Theory, 1st and 2nd eds. New York: Harper and Row.

Warfield, J. (1976) Societal Systems. New York: Wiley.

———(1973) An Assault on Complexity. Battelle Monograph No. 3. Columbus, OH: Battelle Memorial Institute (April).

———(1974) Structuring Complex Systems. Battelle Monograph No. 4. Columbus, OH: Battelle Memorial Institute (April).

Warfield, J. and J. D. Hill (1972) A Unified Systems Engineering Concept. Battelle Monograph No. 1. Columbus, OH: Battelle Memorial Institute (June).

Weaver, W. (1948) "Science and complexity." American Scientist 36.

Weinberg, G. M. (1975) An Introduction to General Systems Thinking. New York: Wiley.

Weiner, N. (1948) Cybernetics. Cambridge, MA: MIT Press.

Wildavsky, A. (1979) Speaking Truth to Power. Boston: Little, Brown.

CRITICAL THEORY AND PUBLIC POLICY

Fred R. Dallmayr

ABSTRACT

In the confines of the study of politics, public policy analysis involves a shift from pure to applied research, a shift which intensifies the problem of the fact-value split inherited from positivist behavioralism. While early public policy literature concentrated on empirical policy-making processes bypassing moral criteria, some recent writings have elaborated on policy-making and policy evaluation as a type of normative inquiry; significant steps in this direction have been undertaken by Duncan MacRae and especially by Jürgen Habermas in the context of "critical theory." According to Habermas, policy evaluation requires a critically reflective "practical discourse" open not only to experts or policy analysts but to the public at large. The paper argues that such discourse is a valuable remedy against the technical-instrumental bent of applied science, but that recovery of a fully non-instrumental "practical" judgment presupposes an evaluation not only of concrete policies but of the status of "policy" itself.

Policy Analysis: Perspectives, Concepts, and Methods, pages 41–67.
ISBN: 0–89232–371–X

41

INTRODUCTION

For a long time now, the study of politics has been in search of itself—
in search of its characteristic premises, its proper procedures, and its
distinctive focus of inquiry. During the modern era, this search has had
all the earmarks of a farflung journey if not an aberrant odyssey. Machiavelli's writings, appearing at the threshold of that era, were still
steeped in the older legacy of practical political wisdom, a wisdom nurtured by historical erudition and the "topical" common-sense of the
rhetoricians; but his recommendations to the "Prince" were leaning more
in the direction of expert counsel or of carefully calculated "policy"
advice. With the rise of modern science, both common-sense and applied
expertise tended to be subordinated to the formulation of relatively
abstract, explanatory frameworks constructed *more geometrico*—an approach evident, to some extent, in Hobbes' *Leviathan*. The preference
for theoretical constructs persisted even after the geometrical model was
replaced by, or coupled with, empirical investigations of sensory experience and after the concepts of "state" and "sovereignty" were reduced
to marginal constraints on market exchanges and economic interests.
Yet, explanatory frameworks remained elusive in the face of haphazard
social and political customs; the full sway of rationality required the
"rationalization" of actual life patterns. It was chiefly concern with the
gap between theory and practice or between theoretical models and social
conditions which, in the nineteenth century, triggered a broad-scale "turn"
toward applied knowledge and "social engineering," a turn entirely faith-
ful to scientific imperatives and exemplified mainly by utilitarianism,
Saint-Simonism and, at the beginning of the next century, by (strands
in) American pragmatism.[1]
    The motive of recalling historical precedents is not simply antiquarian
curiosity. As it seems to me, such recollection can provide helpful background for present dilemmas in at least two respects. First, one can (and
I shall) argue that, in its recent shift to a "policy" orientation, the study
of politics has undergone a similar turn as had been experienced by the
study of "society" and political economy over a century ago, in the transition from Enlightenment rationalism to utilitarianism. Second, and
perhaps more important, historical recollection brings back into view
the notions of common-sense and practical wisdom, notions which became almost apocryphal after Machiavelli. Meandering through the collective memory of the discipline of "politics" (or "political science") there
is still the legacy of a tripartite division between types of inquiry inaugurated by Aristotle: the division between "theoretical," "technical" and

"practical" knowledge. While the first type was meant to provide knowledge for its own sake (and thus is distantly but awkwardly related to modern "pure" science), and while the second supplied knowledge needed for the "making" of artifacts (thus paving the way to modern applied science and technology), the category of "practical" thought was reserved for insights garnered through life experience and through practical conduct preferably in public affairs.[2] I intend to invoke these memories and precedents in the following discussion of the present state of the study of politics construed as the study of "policy." I propose to approach this topic successively from three angles. After initially delineating the recent rise of policy studies and the meaning commonly attached to "policy analysis," I shall, in a second section, sketch diverse reactions provoked by these developments among prominent students of "politics" or the theory of politics. In the last section, turning to the issue of "policy evaluation" and legitimation, I intend to discuss arguments advanced in this domain both by some American policy students and (especially) by Jürgen Habermas, the leading contemporary representative of a "critical theory" of society, adding, by way of conclusion, some of the reasons which lead me to believe that policy evaluation needs to be expanded into a critical evaluation of the very meaning and status of "policy."

THE RISE OF POLICY STUDIES

Within the larger context of the study of politics, the contemporary preoccupation with policy issues constitutes a departure from an earlier consensus which, during preceding decades, had unified professional practitioners (particularly in America) and which had insisted on the primacy of theoretical frameworks capable of explaining and predicting political conduct seen as empirical "behavior." As a broad professional reorientation, the departure obviously resists rigid periodization. Nevertheless, despite the diffuseness of the change, there is an event in recent memory which, I believe, handily pinpoints something like the "birthdate" of the policy movement (and simultaneously the birthdate of what has come to be known as the period of "post-behavioralism"): this was the presidential address delivered by David Easton in 1969 at the annual meeting of the American Political Science Association, under the title "The New Revolution in Political Science." The address, one may recall, came at the height of intense intellectual ferment in the social sciences and also in the midst of widespread social and political unrest in the nation. Noting these troubled conditions, Easton found unsatisfactory the focus on abstract explanatory schemes, characteristic of the prevailing consensus, or the simple cultivation of science for science's sake. As he observed, the wellspring of the "new " or "post-behavioral revolution" was not hard to discern: "It consists of a deep dissatisfaction with political research and teaching, especially of the kind that is striving to convert the study of politics into a more rigorously scientific discipline modelled on the methodology of the natural sciences." In light of the noted dissatisfaction and of the steadily "increasing social and political crisis of our time," Easton's address urged a radical or "revolutionary" realignment of the discipline, namely, a shift of attention which would channel professional energies toward the solution or amelioration of the major social and political problems of the time—although problem-solving in his view was bound to honor "the findings of contemporary behavioral science."[3]

Easton's counsel to the profession, offered in his presidential role, was not without delicacy or irony, given the fact that he had been one of the main spokesmen of the erstwhile consensus and one of the chief advocates of the conversion of the study of politics into a "more rigorously scientific discipline" modelled on natural science canons. As is well known, his earlier writings had been influential in promoting a macro-framework for political analysis termed "systems theory," a framework translating the behavioristic "stimulus-response" model into the more holistic terminology of systemic "inputs" and "outputs." Despite the stress placed in this scheme on the "authoritative allocation of values" and despite a complex differentiation between types of "outputs" and between outputs and "outcomes," Easton's perspective at this point had paid only scant attention to the formulation and implementation of "policies" and to the assessment of policy alternatives. In fact, one of his major studies, entitled *A Framework for Political Analysis* (published in 1965), had disclaimed any direct concern with policy questions. "My approach to the analysis of political systems," he wrote at the time, "will not help us to understand why any specific policies are adopted by the politically relevant members in a system. Furthermore, the capacity to adapt (to system needs) does not thereby dictate that any specific, successful way of doing so is morally better or worse than any other if, under the circumstances, someone might prove that it was a necessary and, therefore, inescapable condition of persistence." The same study also had put forth a list of basic assumptions and priorities characteristic of "behavioralism" or the behavioral consensus (a list which subsequently became known as something like a "behavioral creed"). As one central assumption the list stressed the priority of "pure science" over applied research, predicated on the fact that "the understanding and explanation of political behavior logically precede and provide the basis for efforts to utilize political knowledge in the solution of urgent practical problems of society."[4] Viewed against this background, Easton's presidential address signaled in essence a reallocation of priorities: a move from pure to applied science.

Easton's call for a "new revolution" or a realignment of priorities, one can say in retrospect, was heeded by the profession more eagerly than he could possibly have anticipated—and heeded not because it was issued in a presidential address (a type of statement customarily ignored by practitioners). Clearly, despite the author's prominence, the address would have been entirely ineffectual if it had not somehow meshed with powerful intellectual and social-political trends operative during the past decade. By themselves, the notion of applied research and the need for political "relevance" were not completely absent or overlooked even during the ascendancy and predominance of "pure" behavioralism; in fact, the first steps toward the conversion of the study of politics to scientific methodology were accompanied by efforts to maintain or salvage the applicability of professional expertise. Thus, in 1927, at the time when Charles E. Merriam and other members of the so-called "Chicago School" spearheaded endeavors to create a new, empirical "science of politics," the American Political Science Association officially established a national "Committee on Policy" charged with the tasks both of clarifying the organization's role in the public domain and of fostering professional involvement in the resolution of urgent "policy" problems. However, apart from issuing a number of hortative reports and of assuaging the lingering "progressive" conscience of many practitioners, the Committee failed to exert a significant impact on the discipline and ceased functioning within less than a decade. During the Second World War, many social and political scientists served governmental agencies in an advisory capacity; but for most the experience was a short-lived interlude and only intensified concern with the refinement of scientific methodology. The postwar years saw the emergence of a professional "Committee on Citizenship Participation in Politics" and of a national "Citizenship Clearing House" designed to acquaint political scientists with the needs and dilemmas of "practical politics"; yet, initiatives of this kind were hardly more than marginal glosses on the consolidation of the behavioral consensus during that period.[5]

Thus, irrespective of Easton's persuasiveness, the recent change in the direction of policy issues must be traced to a set of conditions congenial to this move; in my view, both "endogenous" or internal-professional factors and environmental or social-political motives must be taken into account. Among the latter, primary emphasis should probably be placed on the manifest or immediate predicaments of the past decade, that is, on the "increasing social and political crises" mentioned by Easton. At the time of his address, these predicaments derived mainly from the experiences of the Vietnam War, racial tensions, and urban riots; subsequent years brought to the fore a host of additional problems and crisis conditions: problems revolving around economic stagnation, energy shortages, and unemployment—not to mention the "Watergate" episode and the disclosure of corruption in high governmental circles. On the whole, the turbulence and agitation of the Vietnam era has given way to a time of scarcity and austerity, a situation which tends to place a heavy premium on pragmatic "problem-solving" and on the efficient handling of urgent public needs. The mentioned dilemmas, I believe, can and should be seen in conjunction with more pervasive or long-range trends of our age. As was suggested before, contemporary developments in the study of politics find a distant parallel in the earlier transition from Enlightenment rationalism to utilitarianism and also from classical economics to post-classical and Keynesian economic analysis. In large measure, the delay or retardation in political inquiry can be ascribed to the marginal or subsidiary status of politics during the era of laissez-faire liberalism. In our own time, the progressive amalgamation of the "polity" and the economy has as one of its consequences the absorption of the former by the distinctive rationality and concrete "rationalization" processes characteristic of modern social-economic evolution; epistemologically and methodologically, this absorption entails the alternate (and sometimes combined) predominance of pure and applied science or, in Aristotelian language, of "theoretical" and "technical" knowledge.

In terms of endogenous or internal-professional factors, some attention should be given to theoretical antecedents or precursors. There is ample evidence to indicate that the present policy focus is not a sudden innovation but was prepared and nurtured by analytical and methodological initiatives, on the levels of both macro- and micro-analysis, stretching back over the last several decades. On the level of macro-frameworks, one may point to the progressive replacement of static equilibrium models by models stressing effective systemic "steering" and crisis management, a change evident, for example, in Gabriel Almond's shifting emphasis from the description of systemic "functions" to the stipulation of basic "capabilities" seen as required "output" criteria for handling domestic crises and environmental challenges; the same trend was also manifest in the emergence of political "cybernetics," a perspective which, according to one of its leading spokesmen, was meant to capture "a shift in the center of interest from drives to steering, and from instincts to systems of decisions, regulation, and control."[6] On the level of micro-approaches or models, one must mention especially the so-called "decision-making" framework which, in past decades, was developed both along the lines of an empirical scrutiny of decision-making

processes and in the direction of a more formalized "rational choice" or decision theory. As it seems to me, the cited approaches bequeathed to policy analysis not only their respective strengths or merits, but also all their quandaries and ambiguities. One such quandary concerns the status of "politics" or political practice—notions which tend to be submerged, on the one hand, in general management categories and, on the other, in the dimension of individual or social psychology. More directly apparent is the ambivalent character of "steering," "control" and "decision"—labels which, in professional usage, hover precariously between causal "behavioral" processes and voluntary-purposive activities; the "decision-making" model in particular leaves hazy the import of "intentionality" and the role and range of human "rationality." All the listed frameworks are beset by the positivist "fact-value" dichotomy and its implications, especially the unresolved query whether choices and decisions are amenable not only to empirical testing and prediction but also to normative evaluation and judgment.

Given its inherited quandaries and dilemmas, contemporary policy analysis is not an entirely homogeneous enterprise but makes room for different accents and formulations; like the earlier behavioral consensus, the post-behavioral realignment signals not so much a rigid doctrine as a broad intellectual tendency or outlook. Yet, despite internal flexibility and variations, it is not impossible to pinpoint a common denominator or shared thrust linking adepts of this outlook: in my view, this thrust consists in a primary concern with "outputs," with pragmatic problem-solving, and with applied knowledge. Without venturing too far afield, this affinity is readily evident from a quick glance at some of the literature which inaugurated the policy focus, writings which appeared roughly at the time of Easton's address. Thus, in a book entitled *The Study of Policy Formation*, Raymond Bauer (in 1968) defined "policy" as a "course-setting involving decisions of the widest ramifications and longest time perspective in the life of an organization," decisions designed to cope with internal or environmental problems of any kind. Similarly, Charles Lindblom's *The Policy-Making Process* treated "policy" as the outcome of decision-making processes set in motion in response to existing stimuli or challenges. What is immediately obvious in these examples is the lacking distinction between politics and non-politics or between political and general managerial policies; equally manifest is the nondifferentiation (or obscure relation) between empirical behavior and purposive action, as both Bauer and Lindblom relied chiefly on social-psychological categories. Even where the first issue is partially attended to, incidentally, the second dilemma may still persist. Thus, in his *Public Policymaking Reexamined*, Yehezkel Dror concentrated more strongly on political aspects, defining policy as the "direct output of public policy making"; but

as in the other examples the subject matter "reexamined" were essentially behavioral processes. All three studies demonstrated the effects of the positivist legacy: the focus on empirical behavior for all practical purposes barred normative inquiry.[7]

Perhaps, to gain a stronger sense of the policy focus and its quandaries, it may be advisable to take a somewhat closer look at one of the most widely used texts in the field: Thomas R. Dye's *Understanding Public Policy* (first published in 1972). From its opening pages, the text illustrated the concern with "outputs" and with the treatment of prevailing social-political ills. In Dye's definition, "public policy is whatever governments choose to do or not to do"; additionally it involves "why they do it, and what difference it makes." As he acknowledged, the preoccupation with policy issues was promoted by mushrooming domestic and international problems; however, in contrast to "many of the currently popular approaches to policy questions" like "rhetoric, rap sessions, dialogue, confrontation, or direct action," policy analysis was identified (in the subtitle of the first chapter) as "the thinking man's response to demands for relevance." According to the text, such analysis was not an entirely "new concern of political science"; however, in the past the main stress of the discipline had "never really been on policies themselves, but rather on the institutions and structures of government and on the political behaviors and processes associated with policy making." Actually, regarding the historical development of the discipline, the study delineated two prior phases, labeled respectively "traditional" and "behavioral" periods. Traditional political science was said to have concentrated "primarily on the institutional structure and philosophical justification of government" and, in terms of governmental performance, on "the *institutions* in which public policy was formulated." Modern behavioral political science, on the other hand, was described as concerned chiefly with "the processes and behaviors associated with government"; although intent on analyzing "the *processes* by which public policy was determined, it did not deal directly with the linkages between various processes and behaviors and the content of public policy." Deviating from preceding approaches, the text noted, "today the focus of political science is shifting to *public policy*—to the *description and explanation of the causes and consequences of government activity*."[8]

Despite the suggestiveness of this periodization, its plausibility was offset by the last cited sentence. Given the stress placed on causal explanation of decisions, the text shared the ambivalence of earlier volumes regarding the relation between empirical behavior and intentional action; the recommended policy focus thus amounted not so much to an abandonment as an application of the behavioral model (or to an "applied behavioralism"). Dye's study also—and in a deliberate fashion—

actions were sharply divided. For some, the dawn of policy research signaled an advance to professional maturity, that is, a breakthrough from inept speculation to applied expertise; in the eyes of others by contrast, the innovation heralded trouble for the discipline and even the potential corruption of the genuine study of politics.

To exemplify the first approach one need not look far: no one has been a more fervent champion of the new focus than Eugene Meehan, a political theorist drawing his inspiration mainly from modern empiricism, pragmatism, and utilitarianism. His attitude toward policy research—seen as a springboard for large-scale "social engineering"—results clearly from an essay published in 1972 in a book on *The Post-Behavioral Era*, entitled "What Should Political Scientists be Doing?" As the author emphasized right away, the answer to his question could not be derived from any presumed "essence" of politics nor from the administrative structure of contemporary academic disciplines, said to be based on "guild membership"; rather, the yardstick had to be found in social utility, just as the standard of medicine was effectiveness of remedies: "The physician learns to justify his interests by referring to impact on the patient; the social scientist must learn to do likewise." For Meehan, cognitive investigations in all fields were ultimately prompted by man's precarious condition in a complex and frequently threatening world and by his effort and need to master environmental challenges. He wrote:

> The point of departure for my own approach to inquiry is the human need to cope with the external environment (which includes other humans, of course) using human capacities to create instruments for achieving human needs and purposes. For survival is predicated on man's capacity to anticipate events in the environment, to control events in the environment, and to make choices (i.e., adopt policies) from among the alternative situation states that can be achieved in the environment through human intervention.[11]

Several aspects, I think, should be noted in the preceding formulation: first of all, the reliance on "human needs and purposes" and the connection of both with imperatives of "survival"; second, the stress on the human capacity to "create instruments" and tools or on man's quality as *homo faber*; and third, the focus on man's ability to "control" the environment by means of his instruments and through the adoption of effective choices or strategies. Regarding the first aspect, the essay pointed (validly enough) to the importance or desirability of linking empirical and evaluative or "explanatory and normative dimensions" of political inquiry; however, the proposed manner of effecting the linkage implicitly reduced the latter to the former. On the whole, in referring to "needs and purposes" the author's assumption seemed to be either that both are pre-given and self-explanatory or else that "purposes" are derivable from factual "needs" and equally governed by survival standards. As he pointed out, concern with survival "requires man to make and justify propositions asserting what is the case, what can be expected under given circumstances, and what should be preferred in particular situations"; thus, "man must organize what he perceives and use it to forecast changes in the environment, to explain changes in ways that allow intervention to inhibit or further them, and to express preferences or make value judgments." Some additional light on the proposed linkage can be gleaned from the second aspect relating to *homo faber*. According to Meehan, pursuit of survival needs and their cognitive elucidation presupposed a combination or convergence of instrumentalism and pragmatism. "Two assumptions," we read, "are needed to bridge the gap between observation and choice or expectation: instrumentalism—the doctrine that concepts, explanations, value judgments, and so on are tools created by man for dealing with the environment; and pragmatism—the belief that the quality of the instrument is measured by its use in the environment to achieve purpose." The two assumptions or yardsticks were said to be equally applicable to empirical and normative questions: "In normative inquiry, human purposes are construed as tools for the betterment of human life, and evaluated by comparison with other purposes that might have been pursued in the same situation with different effect."[12]

The core of the essay, however, was clearly the third aspect: the achievement of human "control" through instrumental implementation of needs and purposes. Meehan asserted:

> Systematic inquiry springs from, indeed cannot exist without, a desire to modify the environment; it consists in a search for dimensions of the environment that need changing and for the most efficient (least costly in normative terms) means of achieving such changes. The principal tasks of social science are social criticism and social engineering.

Past professional performance of these tasks, in the author's view, was dismal and uninspiring; not only had social scientists "thus far failed miserably," they "failed even to try": "For the most part, they have fled from policy making, eyed social criticism with distaste, and studiously refused to accept the principle that inquiry should be directed to the solution of human problems." Only recently was there a noticeable disenchantment and hence movement away from "scholasticism"; Meehan's own contribution was meant to accelerate this change:

> We need to identify the conditions in society that can and should be altered (or maintained), determine the available alternatives and find means of assessing their respective costs, develop priority structures for allocating resources to deal with them, and create the tools that can bring them about as efficiently as possible. The

goal is simply maximization of reasoned control over the environment, including its human dimension.[13]

A few words should probably be added regarding the notion of "social criticism" which occurs in preceding passages. As employed by Meehan, the notion stands entirely in the service of policy-making and social engineering: its critical edge is directed against useless or inefficient human pursuits or against conditions obstructing instrumental control. In his essay, the phrase clearly does not serve as a synonym for "critical reflection" or for critical moral and political "judgment," as these terms are used in the philosophical tradition. Actually, Meehan's posture toward reflection and philosophy varied from indifference to open contempt. "The questions posed by traditional philosophy," he asserted, "bear little relation to the kinds of questions for which social scientists must have answers—most particularly, what reasons can be given for preferring to live in one situation rather than another, where both are attainable and the choice is real." The trouble with much philosophical literature, however, was not only that it was irrelevant but that it was detrimental and obnoxious: "The fact is that the traditional philosophers have made an awful mess of normative inquiry without being subjected to criticism, despite the amount of destruction that has taken place in the scientific and epistemological areas of traditional philosophy." Among reflective or philosophical orientations Meehan reserved his most cutting and devastating remarks for non-instrumental or non-utilitarian types of speculation or—in his words—for "those who indulge freely their soaring imaginations": "Prophets and poets, utopians and idealists, ultras of every persuasion, share an utter unwillingness to be bound by the limits of fact and logic. At their worst, the result is mysticism, anti-intellectualism, prophecy, affect manipulation; easily destroyed by argument, though with little observable effect on the speculator."[14]

Meehan's distaste for philosophical reflection was displayed even more forcefully in a subsequent essay entitled "Philosophy and Policy Studies" (published a year later in the *Policy Studies Journal*). The central query raised in the article was what contributions, if any, philosophy in its various branches could make to the nascent field of policy analysis. The reply was blunt and unambiguous. "With some relatively minor exceptions," we are told, "those involved in the study of public policy will find little or nothing in philosophy, either substantive or procedural, that can be used productively in their work and much that is actually misleading and counterproductive." As before, the main defect of philosophical reflection was seen in the lack of a consistently technical-instrumental orientation; for, "when the products of philosophy are measured against human needs, and particularly against the need for a body of cumulable,

testable, transferable, and useful knowledge that can tell us when and
how to go about changing the world—which is what policy studies *must*
have—their irrelevance is unmistakable." In lieu of traditional speculation or " 'philosophic' activities of a scholastic sort," the author advocated
concrete problem-solving or an approach designed to produce "specific
solutions to specific situations." Properly defined and pursued, he affirmed, "knowledge supplies man with the capacity to anticipate events
in the environment and in some degree to control them by his own
actions. By doing so, it forces man to solve the normative problem of
choosing one world from among those worlds he has the capacity to
bring about. Policies I take to be the instruments to make such choices."
Toward the end of his paper, Meehan's irreverence lost its occasionally
humorous quality and began to show its teeth; the yardstick of environmental and social "control" shaded over into a plea for thought-control:
"There are some few signs that a weary population is demanding to
know why society should provide an unending feast for a horde of
unproductive locusts."[15]

Although provocatively formulated and hardly typical even of committed policy analysts, Meehan's views have been discussed here at some
length—for a reason: I think it is instructive to savor in detail the tenets
and implications of an unabashed instrumentalism. To be sure, among
professional political scientists his posture has not gone unopposed. To
the extent that it is identified with "social engineering," policy analysis
has been severely denounced by practitioners concerned both with the
integrity of "politics" and the integrity of the academic study of politics.
At this point, in order to illustrate this opposing outlook, I want to glance
briefly at important counter-arguments articulated by Theodore Lowi,
a political scientist known for his contributions both to the elucidation
of contemporary politics and to the non-instrumental study of public
policy. In a splendid essay on "The Politics of Higher Education" (published also in *The Post-Behavioral Era*), Lowi resumed and reformulated
the basic theme of Julien Benda's *Betrayal of the Intellectuals*, by castigating
not so much or not only the "politicization" as rather the "technocratization of the intelligentsia," that is, the inroads of technocratic engineering into academia and its progressive sway over theoretical reflection
and reflective judgment. "Technocratization," he stated, "takes the organized disciplines and turns them toward a direct problem-solving and
policy-oriented *relationship* to the society." This relationship, moreover,
was not simply an innocuous liaison, but was prone to lead to subservience: "With technocratization, the university enmeshes itself with regimes. This means purposive social action, master-servant relationships,
rather than merely the older functional relationship expressing the needs
of a given social class." The detrimental effects of an instrumental re-

lationship were bound to be particularly evident in the case of an "applied" political science; for, "technocratic education focuses on real social problems" and thus produces "a high degree of consonance between the scholar and the policy maker." This consonance, in turn, diminishes the accountability both of politics or politicians and of students of politics: "To help the policy maker solve problems is to make the conduct of his responsibilities a good deal more comfortable. And the problem and the solution are made more legitimate by virtue of the academic help rendered him. But most importantly, *it means that the intellectual agenda of the discipline is set by the needs of the clientele, not by the inner logic of political science.*"[16]

Proceeding from a critique of technocratization, Lowi's essay attacked instrumentalism with all its connotations: including its glorification of *homo faber* and its fusion of knowledge and "control." Taking his cues from Lord Acton's dictum, the author exposed the corrupting effects of academia's flirtation with technocracy: "Technocratization involves a power that also corrupts, but this power corrupts in a culturally more important sense. It involves a corruption of the intellect, of the purpose of academic freedom," because it embroils "the academic with the immediate and the concrete; corruption means a blurring of the difference between theory and rationalization." The main warnings of the essay, however, were sounded against the perils accruing from instrumentalism for the integrity of the study of politics. Lowi's arguments on this count are important and eloquent enough to deserve a longer quotation. He wrote:

> A political science dedicated to better solutions to society's problems cannot in the long run be radical *or* science, because it will be too closely tied to the very regimes whose roots it must constantly question. There is danger in realism. There is danger in problem solving. There is certainly danger in setting up an entire curriculum that stresses problem solving. There is danger in defining science as nothing more than a collection of rigorously stated individual hypotheses aimed at manipulating the real world. There is danger in these because each one tends to reduce the autonomy of political science as a learned society. We need look no further than public administration to find a mature example. Each of these dangers is a virtue of technocratization that tends to reduce the alienation and the detachment of political science from the society which sustains it.[17]

To ward off the cited dangers, Lowi's essay relied on the force of "radical," that is, non-instrumental reflection and of non-utilitarian judgment; only critical reason or reflection, he asserted, can salvage academia from subservience. Like any other discipline, we read, political science "is radical or conservative by virtue of its conceptual apparatus rather than by virtue of the distribution of individuals and substantive attitudes. It is radical insofar as it is out of mesh with society, rather than insofar as the individual member of the discipline may feel or act in a personally radical way about certain social issues." For Lowi, the remedy to techn-ocratization derived "from theory, not from practice," at least not from instrumental practice. If the theoretical insights or conceptions of the discipline are "energetic and relevant," he added, teachers of political science are bound to create "a generation of students who simply do not think like their older policy makers. This is deeply radical"—provided the latter term is interpreted as having to do with the foundation of the discipline: Such students "will not be necessarily radical in the sense of being dedicated to cutting out the old roots. The important thing is that the capacity to deal critically with the roots of the polity is a capacity without which political science would indeed be nothing but a handmaiden."[18]

POLICY EVALUATION AND CRITICAL THEORY

Lowi's strictures against instrumentalism, in my view, are cogent and salutary in their main thrust—although the remedies are perhaps not very clearly delineated in the discussed essay. Thus, one may wonder how a commitment to professional "detachment" and even "neutrality" can simultaneously yield theories which are "energetic and relevant"; likewise, the wholesale aversion from "practice" seems far-fetched and not readily compatible with Lowi's own concern with policy research. However these quandaries may be resolved, the author's arguments clearly point beyond the confines of technical rationality and beyond the re-duction of normative issues to problems of environmental adaptation. Along the latter lines, the need for "policy evaluation"—in the sense of a non-instrumental assessment of policy goals or preferences—has been explicitly stressed by Lowi on other occasions. In a wide-ranging review of "policy-making" literature, he noted that an approach focusing ex-clusively on means-ends questions and policy procedures "becomes es-sentially technocratic and instrumental in values, in analysis, and in ultimate impact. When one assumes that 'policy making is policy *making* is decision making' and therefore does not enter into *a priori* analysis of the character of the choices being made, one almost inevitably becomes incrementalist and manipulative." The tendency was reinforced by the positivist legacy of fact-value segregation: "When the goals of policies are not questioned because they are the values which must be kept separate from facts, the analyst becomes committed to the value context of those policies even if his political ideology would not support them if he looked more carefully at them."[19]

In the meantime, efforts have been undertaken by numerous scholars to overcome the most glaring defects or limitations of policy analysis noted by Lowi. In the domain of policy evaluation, one of the most significant developments has been to resort to the notion of normative or "valuative discourse" as a correlate and possible antidote to a narrowly empiricist or procedural approach. In the following, I intend to illustrate this development by reference to two examples: one taken from the American, the other from the Continental European setting. In the first context, the concept of "valuative discourse" has been articulated primarily by Duncan MacRae in a series of writings, beginning in 1971 and culminating in a study published in 1976 under the title *The Social Function of Social Science*. As it seems to me, the study constitutes one of the major contributions to social science literature during the past decade and certainly one of the most searching and thoughtful publications in the field of policy analysis. MacRae's point of departure in his study was the "post-behavioral" malaise in the social sciences, especially the widespread dissatisfaction with the conception—characteristic of the behavioral consensus—which viewed the social disciplines as self-contained analytical or "nomothetic" enterprises governed by the motto "science for science's sake." In contrast to more ambitious recent ventures trying to banish or exorcise behavioral "scientism" altogether, his proposal was in essence to correlate and reconcile empiricism and "valuation." Bypassing both positivist and radical anti-positivist formulas, the study noted:

> there is another path to follow; that reliable scientific knowledge of man and nature is an important resource for policy choice but can coexist with rational ethical discourse; that some of the values of science may be transferred to this ethical discourse; and that scientific propositions and ethical assertions, while clearly distinguishable, may be fruitfully combined in academic disciplines concerned with the study of man and society.[20]

According to MacRae, the combination of scientific knowledge and valuation was particularly desirable and appropriate in the field of policy analysis construed as an "applied" social discipline. To implement its tasks, such a discipline could not limit itself to the investigation of empirical conditions, but had to probe normative questions; it had to be guided by the conviction "that science should serve human welfare, not simply scientists' satisfaction or the discovery of truth as an end in itself." While advocating the strengthening of "applied" inquiry, one should note, MacRae's study held no brief for technocracy and was careful to differentiate its proposals from an instrumental model of "social engineering." Positivism and academic specialization, he observed, had produced either an infatuation with "pure science" divorced from values and intentional purposes, or else a narrowly technical or instrumental type of applied analysis. In the latter case—where research was typically the handmaiden of economic or political organizations—ends or values were treated as fixed or given and thus removed from critical scrutiny and discussion. As the author commented (echoing some of Lowi's concerns), the engineering model was damaging both to science or academic inquiry and to politics, especially to democratic politics. Operating instrumentally science betrayed its own rational ethos by subservience to non-rational dictates: "To separate valuative questions from science is perhaps to strengthen science, but also to weaken applied science by making it totally dependent for its guidance on unreflective standards and modes of valuation. The values that guide the application of science are thus deprived of the rational component that is so essential to science's own internal functioning." At the same time, definition of values by client organizations—or by such organizations in conjunction with experts or applied scientists—encouraged elitist and undemocratic proclivities, in particular the tendency to bypass the views of "informed citizens" described as "the ultimate decision makers in a democracy."[21]

Despite the concern for democratic participation, MacRae's study did not entrust the formulation of values and policy goals entirely to the "educated public" or to generally informed citizens. In order to overcome the opacity and "sluggishness" of public opinion and to facilitate the rational resolution of policy issues, ethical argument in his view had to partake of some of the qualities of scientific discourse. It was at this point that his conception of the "function of social science" came most clearly into view: social scientists were accorded a special role in the discussion of values both because of their empirical knowledge of social conditions and because of their attachment to rigorous canons of inquiry and communication. The specific recommendation of the study was "to transfer to valuative discourse some of the norms that a well-organized scientific community imposes on its own communications." With the exception of empirical testing, the norms of ethical argument were said to be "analogous to those that govern the discussion of scientific theories and hypotheses." The central yardstick of valuative discourse, as delineated in the study, was "that before anyone enter into ethical argument he first render his own ethical system clear, consistent, and general— modifying it in detail if necessary." Apart from stipulating standards for each individual participant, MacRae also outlined a set of rules governing normative debate: first, that such debate be conducted between proponents of "ethical systems" or "ethical hypotheses" which are "specified in writing in advance"; second, that "each discussant (shall) have equal opportunity to argue for his own system, and against the opposing one, by pointing out presumed shortcomings in the other system"; and third, that after each exchange "the proponent of the ethical system under criticism (shall) decide whether he wishes to alter his ethical system or make the choice dictated by it."[22]

In my view, MacRae's study was distinguished by numerous impressive qualities: including its interdisciplinary outlook, its sober and careful mode of presentation, and the cogency of many of its proposals; one of its strongest virtues was its appeal to the "common good" as ultimate yardstick of policy choice, in lieu of the separate interests either of (detached) academics or of politicians and client groups.[23] Unfortunately, such merits were marred by several drawbacks or limitations besetting the argument—drawbacks affecting both the status of ethical discourse and the range of public deliberation. In stressing the affinity between science and ethics and the role of "ethical hypotheses," the study injected into policy evaluation some of the contingent qualities of empirical research: treated as heuristic frameworks, normative propositions can yield at best hypothetical, not "categorical" obligations. Deference to science, I think, also colored the notion of application. By treating policy analysis as an "applied" discipline implementing the canons of scientific research (canons which themselves are rarely open to debate), MacRae's approach courted the danger of instrumentalism—a peril which was reinforced by his own ethical preference for utilitarianism, a doctrine traditionally associated with instrumentalist premises and convictions. The preference for utilitarianism or efficient utility calculations may also have something to do with the study's deemphasis of citizen participation in favor of social-scientific discourse. As John Ladd has noted at one point: "Like utilitarianism, policy studies often operate with a very limited picture of what morality and politics are all about; namely, they conceive of morality and politics as principally concerned with the production and (just) distribution of *consumer goods* for society." In Ladd's view, such a conception easily encourages moral "paternalism," that is, a "functional division" between moral producers and consumers: "A clear understanding of the relationship of the individual to public policy, not as a receiver (consumer), but as an active moral agent seems to me to present the most important challenge to policy studies from the point of view of morality."[24]

Many or most of the mentioned drawbacks, I believe, are remedied in the second example taken from the Continental setting: the version of "critical theory" articulated by Jürgen Habermas in a series of writings during the past decade. To some extent, the central thrust of critical theory was anticipated or intimated in Lowi's reference to a type of theorizing which is "out of mesh" with society and yet "energetic and relevant." Broadly speaking, Habermas' perspective parallels MacRae's approach with respect to the juxtaposition or combination of empirical science and moral evaluation; the parallel extends to the stress on disciplined normative deliberation, termed by Habermas "practical discourse." By contrast to MacRae's focus on application or applied analysis, however, Habermas intensifies and broadens the significance of practical-moral argument vis-à-vis empirical-scientific inquiry. While empirical science, in his view, is ultimately geared toward the goal of human mastery or "control" of the environment and thus guided by a "technical interest," ethical evaluation is rooted in interpersonal contacts and communicative interactions which, in turn, are governed by a "practical interest" in mutual understanding and in the maintenance of just or justifiable norms of conduct. As used in this context, incidentally, practice and practical interaction are not synonyms for a blind activism opposed to thought, but rather are closely linked with the capacity for radical "reflection" and self-reflection—a capacity described in Habermas' earlier writings as man's interest in "emancipation" and later as the basis and mainspring of rational "discourse."[25] In the present context, instead of surveying Habermas' sprawling opus, I intend to concentrate on two studies particularly relevant to policy issues: *Toward a Rational Society* (first published in 1970) and *Legitimation Crisis* (whose English translation appeared in 1975).

The first volume is a collection of essays not all of which are equally pertinent here. Taking its cues from Lord Snow's "two cultures" theme, an essay on "Technical Progress and the Social Life-World" explores the complex relationship between empirical science and cultural understanding and self-understanding fostered by the humanities. In our technological era, Habermas observes, this relationship is "only one segment of a much broader problem: *How is it possible to translate technically exploitable knowledge into the practical consciousness of a social life-world?*" What emerges in this question is a "true life-problem of scientific civilization" which can be couched in these terms: "How can the relation between technical progress and the social life-world, which today is still clothed in a primitive, traditional, and unchosen form, be reflected upon and brought under the control of rational discussion?" Following a review of historical antecedents, the essay applies this problem chiefly to the life-world of politics, particularly democratic politics, where it yields this query: "How can the power of technical control be brought within the range of the consensus of acting and transacting citizens?" In probing this query, Habermas rejects as too facile two customary responses: that science and technology are the automatic harbingers of democracy, or else that technology necessarily destroys democracy. He writes:

> Today, in the industrially most advanced systems an energetic attempt must be made consciously to take in hand the mediation between technical progress and the

practical conduct of life in the major industrial societies, a mediation that has previously taken place without direction, as a mere continuation of natural history.

To accomplish this mediation, it suffices in his view by no means that society matches "the conditions of technical rationality"; for, "even if the cybernetic dream of a virtually instinctive self-stabilization could be realized, the value system would have contracted in the meantime to a set of rules for the maximization of power and comfort; it would be equivalent to the biological base value of survival at any cost, that is, ultra-stability." Thus, the contemporary "challenge of technology cannot be met with technology alone"; rather, it is a question of "setting into motion a politically effective discussion that brings the social potential constituted by technical know-how into a rationally defined and controlled relation to our practical knowledge and will."[26]

Another essay in the same volume probes the relation between the "scientization of politics" (what Lowi called "technocratization") and democratic "public opinion," starting from the premise that if such "scientization" is not yet a reality, it is today "a real tendency for which there is evidence": "It is only recently that bureaucrats, the military, and politicians have been orienting themselves along strictly scientific guidelines in the exercise of their public functions—indeed this practice has only existed on a large scale since World War II." Three theoretical accounts or construals of the relationship are discussed in the paper: a "decisionistic model" dating back to Hobbes and Max Weber; a "technocratic model" deriving from Bacon and Saint-Simon; and a practical-dialectical (or "pragmatistic") model. Whereas in the first account the politician is the ultimate authority making arbitrary political choices while employing technical expertise only in the selection of means, in the second construal "the dependence of the professional on the politician appears to have reversed itself" with the result that the latter "becomes the mere agent of a scientific intelligentsia which, in concrete circumstances, elaborates the objective requirements of available techniques and resources as well as of optimal strategies and steering regulations." Habermas' own preference is clearly for the third model in which "the strict separation between the function of the expert and the politician is replaced by a critical interaction" and where the transposition of technical recommendations into practice is "increasingly dependent on mediation by the public as a political institution." As he recognizes, the feasibility of this model today is hampered by numerous obstacles, including the erosion of the "public sphere" and the pervasive collusion of bureaucracy and expertise. The integration of technology into social self-understanding and thus the interpenetration of "political will" and scientific rationality, he argues, could be effectively pursued only "under the ideal conditions of general communication extending to the entire public and free from domination." The emphasis on unconstrained communication recurs also in a third essay which distinguishes "two concepts of rationalization," a symbolic-communicative and a truncated technocratic type. "At the level of subsystems of instrumental action," we read, "scientific-technical progress has already compelled the reorganization of social institutions and sectors, and necessitates it on an increasingly larger scale." On the other hand, *rationalization at the level of the institutional framework* can occur only in the medium of symbolic interaction itself, that is, through *removing restrictions on communication*." In the latter context, "public, unrestricted and unconstrained discussion of the suitability and desirabilty of action-orienting principles and norms in the light of the socio-cultural repercussions of developing subsystems of instrumental behavior—such discussion at all levels of political and repoliticized decision-making processes is the only medium in which anything like (genuine) 'rationalization' is possible."[27]

Public discussion of alternative courses of social action, one should add, is meant here to entail not only the stipulation and confrontation of hypothetical maxims, but the articulation and clarification of valid or categorical yardsticks—whose binding character, to be sure, derives not from dogmatic acceptance but from the cogency of a "practical discourse" yielding a rational consensus among all participants. Elaboration of the character and implications of such discourse is one of the central themes of Habermas' *Legitimation Crisis*. As he points out, norms have obligatory effects and thus raise validity claims, claims which cannot be redeemed on a strictly empirical or voluntaristic basis. For, "if only empirical motives (such as inclinations, interests, or fear of sanctions) sustain an agreement, it is impossible to see why a party to the contract should continue to feel bound to norms once his original motives change"; the same situation obtains if reliance is placed on arbitrary will. In general terms, he notes, "we cannot explain the validity claim of norms without taking recourse to a rationally motivated agreement or at least to the conviction that consensus on a recommended norm could be brought about *with reasons*." Consequently, the "model of contracting parties" merely enacting preferences or heuristic maxims is inadequate: "The appropriate model is rather the communicative community of those affected, who as participants in a practical discourse test the validity claims of norms and, to the extent that they accept them with reasons, arrive at the conviction that in the given circumstances the proposed norms are 'right.' " The "rightness" or validity of norms, from this perspective, is predicated on the rational structure of the validating discourse—its openness to all affected parties and the absence of extrinsic constraints:

> Discourse can be understood as that form of communication that is removed from
> direct contexts of experience and action and whose structure assures us that possible
> validity claims of assertions, recommendations or warnings are the exclusive object
> of discussion; that participants, topics and contributions are not restricted except
> with reference to the goal of testing validity claims; and that no force is exercised
> except that of the better argument.[28]

Critical theory as formulated by Habermas—and especially his notion of "practical discourse"—undoubtedly goes a long way toward overcoming the pitfalls of technocracy and toward giving policy evaluation its proper due. Yet, I cannot conclude these comments without adding a further consideration or proviso. There are reasons for holding that critical evaluation should extend not only to the assessment of substantive policies, but to the status and role of "policy" itself. Despite the stress on interaction, Habermas' arguments at various junctures still carry overtones of instrumentalism. The connotation is evident in his commitment to broad-scale "rationalization" and a "rational society"—notwithstanding the distinction between symbolization and technological progress. The aspect is also manifest in the frequent emphasis on human (though not purely technical) "control"—an emphasis illustrated by the cited references to the need to "bring under control" the traditional relation between technology and social life-world. As it seems to me, primary preoccupation with rational action and goal-oriented human designs cannot entirely avoid instrumentalist effects; even when endorsed by a consensus of participants, such designs are liable to reduce the environment—and potentially other human beings—to the level of means. Against this background, political scientists should be reluctant to submerge their discipline in policy analysis or to identify "politics" with policy-making. In a radical sense, non-instrumental action must be construed as action unconcerned with outcomes or goal attainment and even receptive to (what one may call) the inroads of "non-action" into purposive designs.

Some guidance along these lines may be obtained from Michael Oakeshott's study *On Human Conduct*, a book which has been poorly received by students of politics but probably deserves another look.[29] In his study, Oakeshott differentiates between two main manners or aspects of human conduct: namely, substantive conduct or performance concerned with the pursuit of substantive goals or satisfactions; and rule-governed practices in terms of which particular goals are pursued and among which the most important are non-instrumental or "moral" practices. Building on this distinction, the volume further opposes two modes of interpersonal relationships, termed respectively "enterprise association" and "civil association" or *civitas*. While in the first case agents are "related in the joint pursuit of some imagined and wished-for common satisfaction," that is, in the pursuit of "some common purpose, some substantive condition of things to be jointly procured, or some common interest to be continuously satisfied," members of the second type (termed *cives*) are "not partners or colleagues in an enterprise," nor are they "individual enterprises related to one another as bargainers for the satisfaction of their individual wants"; rather, they are related in terms of a non-instrumental practice "which has no extrinsic purpose and is not related to procuring any substantive satisfaction." Correlated with these modes of association is the difference between "policy" and "politics." In a joint enterprise, Oakeshott observes, "the associates are related in terms of their choice to pursue a common purpose and of their continuous agreement upon a 'policy'; that is, upon 'managerial' decisions concerned with the actions and utterances in which, from time to time, this purpose shall be pursued." Politics, by contrast, has to do with the maintenance or modification of the "practice of civility"; it is "concerned with determining the desirable norms of civil conduct and with the approval or disapproval of civil rules which, because they qualify the pursuit of purposes, cannot be inferred from the purposes pursued."[30] Whether or not one agrees with Oakeshott's separation of the two associational types (or with his dichotomy of matter and form), the distinction between substantive pursuits and a non-purposive matrix permitting such pursuits seems worth pondering. What the distinction suggests is that the "good life" or "good society" is not simply a goal to be implemented, but depends on, or is intimated by, an ongoing cultivation of civility.

NOTES AND REFERENCES

1. The story of the progressive submergence of politics in the "social realm" during the modern era has been eloquently told by Hannah Arendt in *The Human Condition* (Garden City: Anchor Books, 1959), esp. pp. 23–69.

2. On the legacy of practical wisdom, seen against the background of the rise of scientific explanatory models especially in the American context, see Bernard Crick, *The American Science of Politics: Its Origins and Conditions* (Berkeley: University of California Press, 1964); on the Aristotelian tradition compare Wilhelm Hennis, *Politik und praktische Philosophie: Eine Studie zur Rekonstruktion der politischen Wissenschaft* (Neuwied: Luchterhand, 1963).

3. David Easton, "The New Revolution in Political Science," *American Political Science Review*, vol. 63 (1969), pp. 1051, 1057.

4. David Easton, *A Framework for Political Analysis* (Englewood Cliffs, NJ: Prentice-Hall, 1965), pp. 7, 89. In a larger companion volume published at the same time, "policies" were briefly mentioned in the discussion of "outputs" and defined mainly as "associated statements" indicative of "the more general intentions of the authorities of which any specific binding output might be a partial expression"; see Easton, *A Systems Analysis of Political Life* (New York: Wiley & Sons, 1965), p. 358. Regarding the "behavioral creed" compare also Albert Somit and Joseph Tanenhaus, *The Development of Political Science, From Burgess to Behavioralism* (Boston: Allyn and Bacon, 1967), pp. 176–179.

5. Regarding the "Committee on Policy" and the "Citizenship Clearing House" see

Somit and Tanenhaus, *The Development of Political Science*, pp. 97–99, 195–99. Professional service during World War II is mentioned by Robert A. Dahl as one of the factors contributing to the sway of behavioralism; compare his "The Behavioral Approach in Political Science: Epitaph for a Monument to a Successful Protest," *American Political Science Review*, vol. 55 (1961), pp. 763–772.

6. Karl W. Deutsch, *The Nerves of Government: Models of Political Communication and Control* (New York: Free Press, 1963), p. 76. As Deutsch added (pp. 77–78), "cybernetics suggests that steering or governing is one of the most interesting and significant processes in the world, and that a study of steering in self-steering machines, in biological organisms, in human minds, and in societies will increase our understanding of problems in all these fields." Regarding structural functionalism compare especially Gabriel Almond, "A Developmental Approach to Political Systems," *World Politics*, vol. 17 (1965), pp. 183–214.

7. See Raymond A. Bauer and Kenneth J. Gergen, eds., *The Study of Policy Formation* (New York: Free Press, 1968), p. 2; Charles E. Lindblom, *The Policy-Making Process* (Englewood Cliffs, NJ: Prentice-Hall, 1968), p. 4; Yehezkel Dror, *Public Policymaking Reexamined* (San Francisco: Chandler Publishing Co., 1968), p. 35. The neglect of normative questions did not mean the absence of (unexamined) normative preferences or priorities. Thus, as Dror stated with regard to industrialization processes (p. 39): "The goal of industrialization is accepted in some of the developing countries as the dominant value for policy-making; effects on traditional family structure and culture, which are regarded as more expendable, do not have to be heavily considered by the policy-makers in evaluating the industrialization policy."

8. See Thomas R. Dye, *Understanding Public Policy*, 2nd ed. (Englewood Cliffs, NJ: Prentice-Hall, 1975), pp. 1–3, 7.

9. Ibid., pp. 4–6.

10. See Yehezkel Dror, "Some Features of a Meta-Model for Policy-Studies," and Robert L. Bish, "The Assumption of Knowledge in Policy Analysis," *Policy Studies Journal*, vol. 3 (Spring 1975), pp. 248–250, 256. In Dror's essay, the clarification of politicians' values was to be effected through "value analysis," that is, through "methodologies designed to structure the judgment field and to explicate value dimensions in a way that permits more conscious, comprehensive and explicit judgment by the legitimate value judges" (p. 250). According to Bish (pp. 256–257), estimation of citizens' values was relatively easy in market analysis through reliance on consumer preferences; but in the public domain "preference revelation is much less specific," with the result that "knowledge of the value of the service to citizen-consumers may never be directly revealed."

11. See Eugene J. Meehan, "What Should Political Scientists Be Doing?" in George J. Graham, Jr. and George W. Carey, eds., *The Post-Behavioral Era: Perspectives on Political Science* (New York: McKay Company, 1972), pp. 55–56.

12. Ibid., pp. 56–58, 60. To implement his recommendations in the empirical and normative fields, Meehan proposed the development both of an "adequate inventory of existing social conditions" and of an instrumental value or priority system (pp. 62, 65): "An agreed value system, a priority schedule for allocating resources, is also required, and a social technology would have to be developed that could translate normative standards into meaningful social conditions."

13. Ibid., pp. 58–59.

14. Ibid., pp. 61, 70.

15. Meehan, "Philosophy and Policy Studies," *Policy Studies Journal*, vol. 2 (Autumn 1973), pp. 43–44, 47. Philosophy's inadequacy was said to be manifest in both empirical and normative domains (pp. 44–45): "To be honest about it, philosophy has about as much relation to empirical inquiry as Aristotelian science has to modern physics.... Yet by reference to the needs of the policy-maker, what philosophers have to offer with respect to

normative matters is far more pernicious and misleading than their contributions to empirical affairs."

16. Theodore J. Lowi, "The Politics of Higher Education: Political Science as a Case Study," in *The Post-Behavioral Era*, pp. 29, 32.

17. Ibid., pp. 33, 35.

18. Ibid., pp. 34–35.

19. Lowi, "Decision Making vs. Policy Making: Toward an Antidote for Technocracy," *Public Administration Review*, vol. 30 (May-June 1970), pp. 318–319. Regarding his own contributions to policy research, most well known is probably his delineation of three main types of public policy—distributive, regulatory, and redistributive—in "American Business, Public Policy, Case Studies, and Political Theory," *World Politics*, vol. 16 (1964), pp. 677–715.

20. Duncan MacRae, Jr., *The Social Function of Social Science* (New Haven, CT: Yale University Press, 1976), p. 5. For some of MacRae's earlier writings see "Scientific Communication, Ethical Argument and Public Policy," *American Political Science Review*, vol. 65 (1971), pp. 38–50; "Normative Assumptions in the Study of Public Choice," *Public Choice*, vol. 16 (1973), pp. 27–41; "Justice, Normative Discourse, and Sociology," *Contemporary Sociology*, vol. 2 (1973), pp. 129–132; and "Policy Analysis as an Applied Social Science," *Administration and Society*, vol. 6 (1975), pp. 363–388. For a more detailed review of *The Social Function of Social Science* compare my "Knowledge and Commitment: Variations on a Familiar Theme," *Polity*, vol. 12 (1979), pp. 291–302.

21. MacRae, *The Social Function of Social Science*, pp. xi-xii, 52.

22. Ibid., pp. 51, 80, 87, 92–93.

23. "The social function of social science," the conclusion stated, "is thus not simply to serve the interest of any particular class in a given period of history, nor is it to serve the interests of academics themselves. Rather, it is to provide guidance to society, through research, reasoned discourse, and education as to what interests should be served in particular circumstances and as to the means to do so." Ibid., p. 306.

24. John Ladd, "Policy Studies and Ethics," *Policy Studies Journal*, vol. 2 (Autumn 1973), pp. 42–43; compare also his "The Ethics of Participation," in J. Roland Pennock and John W. Chapman, eds., *NOMOS XVI: Participation* (New York: Atherton Press, 1975), pp. 98–125.

25. Regarding the theory of cognitive interests compare Jürgen Habermas, *Knowledge and Human Interests*, trans. by Jeremy J. Shapiro (Boston: Beacon Press, 1971); for the turn to "discourse" see "A Postscript to *Knowledge and Human Interests*," *Philosophy of the Social Sciences*, vol. 3 (1975), pp. 157–189. The broader relevance of "critical theory" for public administration is discussed in William N. Dunn and Bahman Fozouni, "Toward a Critical Administrative Theory," in *Administrative and Policy Studies Series*, vol. 3 (Beverely Hills: Sage Publications, 1976).

26. Habermas, *Toward a Rational Society: Student Protest, Science, and Politics*, trans. by Jeremy J. Shapiro (Boston: Beacon Press, 1970), pp. 52–53, 57, 60–61. As he adds (p. 61): "The substance of domination is not dissolved by the power of technical control; to the contrary, the former can simply hide behind the latter. The irrationality of domination, which today has become a collective peril to life, could be mastered only through the development of a political decision-making process tied to the principle of general discussion free from domination."

27. Habermas, "Scientization of Politics and Public Opinion," and "Technology and Science as 'Ideology,'" Ibid., pp. 62–64, 66, 68, 75, 118–119.

28. Habermas, *Legitimation Crisis*, trans. by Thomas McCarthy (Boston: Beacon Press, 1975), pp. 104–105, 107–108.

29. Michael Oakeshott, *On Human Conduct* (Oxford: Clarendon Press, 1975). The study has been reviewed and strongly criticized by Hanna F. Pitkin, Sheldon S. Wolin, and David Spitz in *Political Theory*, vol. 4 (1976), pp. 301–352.

30. *On Human Conduct*, pp. 59, 112, 114, 122, 160, 174.

TECHNOLOGY ASSESSMENT, FACTS, AND VALUES

Alex C. Michalos

ABSTRACT

There are good theoretical and practical reasons to avoid any appeals to a fact-value distinction in the assessment of technology. In the assessment of technology, or in any other area of policy analysis, one should avoid any appeals to an ontological fact-value division, since these appeals will be at least useless and at most dangerous and self-defeating.

1. INTRODUCTION

The central thesis of this paper may be put thus: There are good theoretical and practical reasons to avoid any appeals to a fact-value distinction in the assessment of technology. Alternatively, one could say that in the assessment of technology any appeals to a fact-value distinction will be at least useless and at most dangerous and self-defeating.

The structure of my defense of this thesis is as follows. In Section 2 I draw an ontological distinction between facts and values, and in Section

Policy Analysis: Perspectives, Concepts, and Methods, pages 69–91.
ISBN: 0–89232–371–X

3 an epistemological distinction between facts (truths) and falsehoods is drawn. In Section 4 I present five illustrations of types of arguments that are frequently used to draw erroneous conclusions as a result of confusing the two distinctions drawn in Sections 2 and 3. In Section 5 I consider possible, but by no means necessary, methodological advantages of distinguishing facts and values (i.e., making the ontological distinction). Then I briefly outline six theories of value (in Section 6) in order to show that one cannot simply talk about values as if everyone meant the same thing. The idea of a value, like the idea of a fact, is a theoretical idea, and a very controversial theoretical idea at that. In the light of the discussion in Sections 5 and 6, I believe it is fair to say (in Section 7) that appeals to a fact-value distinction in the assessment of any technology will be useless because of the controversial status of all theories of facts and values. What's more, such appeals will be practically or strategically dangerous or self-defeating because (a) the confusion in Section 4 will probably not be avoided; (b) the appeals usually involve unwarranted appeals to authority (credentialing); (c) the appeals encourage belief in an epistemological handicap for all evaluations which is only warranted with some theories of value; (d) the appeals encourage belief in an epistemological robustness for all alleged factual judgments which is only warranted for some; (e) the appeals encourage unwarranted self-certification of allegedly factual claims. For all these reasons, then, I recommend that in all decision-making, including all decision-making involving technology assessment or any policy-making, one should avoid any appeals to an (ontological) fact-value distinction.

2. FACT AND VALUE: ONTOLOGY

Sometimes people talk about questions of fact, factual issues, or factual matters in order to classify the questions, issues or matters prior to attempting any answers or other assessments. For example, among all the issues related to the development and use of energy from alternative sources (e.g., coal, oil, gas, uranium, water, biomass, wind, etc.) there are supposed to be some straightforward factual matters such as how much energy is obtainable from a given amount of one of these sources, using a certain technology in a certain period of time. Even those of us who don't know the answers to such questions are willing to grant that these sorts of questions are factual, if indeed *any* questions are factual.

To say that a question is factual, involves an issue or matter of fact, is obviously not to say that the question is true. It is logically impossible for questions to have truth values, to be true or false. Normally, but not always the same is true of exclamations (e.g., "Whoopie!") and commands (e.g., "Close the door.") I say "normally, but not always" because exclamations like "Fire!" may be regarded as doing at least double and possibly triple duty. One who yells "Fire!" may be regarded as asserting that there is a fire, expressing fear and deep concern, and urging listeners to do something—run for their lives, call the fire department or whatever. Only a linguistic purist would insist that "Fire!" cannot do all these jobs at once, and I doubt that many people would believe the purist.

It is not some sort of defect in questions, exclamations, and commands that they don't or normally don't have truth values. They have their own unique linguistic jobs to do. Declarative sentences do have truth values, and this is their distinguishing feature. Nevertheless, to say that a declarative sentence involves a factual matter or an issue of fact is not to say that the sentence is true. While it is logically possible for such a sentence to be true, saying that the sentence involves an issue of fact is not the same as saying that it's true. It is merely to classify the ontological category (ball park, pigeon hole) of the sentence. For example, the sentence "Canada has seven operating nuclear reactors" involves a factual matter but the sentence may be false. Similarly it may be false that the United States has fifty-four nuclear reactors, although the issue of the existence or non-existence of the reactors is a factual issue.

At least since Hempel's classic paper "Problems and Changes in the Empiricist Criterion of Meaning" in 1950 it has been known that there is not and is not likely to be any generally acceptable criterion of empirical meaningfulness. In other words, there is not and is not likely to be any rigorous criterion to apply that will allow one to decisively categorize sentences as empirically factual, sentences about matters of empirical fact or, briefly, factual sentences. We need not review Hempel's review of the demise of the verifiability, falsifiability, confirmability, etc., criteria. Before most of us, Hempel too was a teenage logical positivist. It troubled him as much as anyone to discover that nothing worked, that finally we had intuitions and hunches separating factual matters from metaphysics, theology, ethics and other things that frightened logical positivists. Still, that's where that story ends. You will not see a criterion of empirical fact. You will only see examples of sentences about empirical (sometimes logical) facts or factual matters. Here, as elsewhere, we can often agree on what or what not to do without being able to agree on why or reasons for doing it.

One may also talk about questions of value, evaluative issues, or evaluative matters in order to classify the questions, issues, or matters prior to attempting any answers or other assessments. For example, one may raise the question, "Is thermal energy from nuclear fission or burning coal more desirable from the point of view of site attractiveness?" That is, are coal-burning facilities more or less esthetically attractive than nuclear reactors?

Again, to say that a question is evaluative, involves an issue or matter of value, is obviously not to say that the question is true. It is merely to classify the ontological category of the question. A declarative sentence like "Nuclear reactors are esthetically more attractive than coal furnaces" involves an evaluative matter, but again the truth or falsity of the sentence doesn't follow from the mere fact that it involves an evaluative issue. Some people believe that such sentences are pseudo claims, that although the sentence is formally declarative, it cannot function as a declarative sentence (cannot have a truth value at all). However, even on this extreme view, to say that a sentence is evaluative, involves a matter of value or an evaluative issue, is still not to say that the sentence is true or false. Indeed, on this extreme view, it is logically impossible for the sentence to be true or false.

In short, according to some common usage, issues of fact may be contrasted with issues of value in a purely ontological classificatory sense. In this sense, truth or falsity is not at issue. Classifying a matter in this sense is not asserting the truth or falsity of the matter. Classifying an issue in this sense is logically prior to the question of truth or falsity, and the latter question may not even arise. For example, the question will not arise if one is only interested in getting a question classified as factual or evaluative, and the question will not arise when an evaluative declarative sentence is asserted and its assessor holds the extreme view that such sorts of sentences cannot have truth values.

3. FACT AND FALSEHOOD: EPISTEMOLOGY

Sometimes people use the term "fact" and its cognates as a synonym for "true." For example, people say things like "As a matter of fact there are several operating nuclear reactors in Ontario"; "It is a fact that there are nuclear reactors in Ontario"; and "In fact there are nuclear reactors in Ontario." The last sentence, for example, just means "In truth there are nuclear reactors in Ontario." The two before that may be expressed as "It is true that there are nuclear reactors in Ontario." Such usage of the term "fact" is not ontological but epistemological. The term is used not to designate an ontological category, but to designate an epistemo-logical assessment or appraisal.

In the epistemological usage of "fact" it would be self-contradictory to talk about factual matters that were false. Factual matters in this epistemological sense are true, i.e., the sentences about the matters are true. For example, it would be self-contradictory for someone to say "In fact there are nuclear reactors in Ontario and it's false that there are nuclear reactors in Ontario." If in fact there are nuclear reactors in Ontario then it is true that there are such reactors there and it cannot also be false. Similarly, if in fact John is five feet tall then it would be self-contradictory to say "In fact John is five feet tall but he's not five feet tall."

Thus, in the epistemological sense of "fact," facts are contrasted with falsehoods, or, more precisely, factual sentences are contrasted with false sentences because "factual" is regarded as synonymous with "true." In this sense of "fact" to say "In fact nuclear reactors are visually more attractive than coal furnaces" is to affirm the truth of the claim that nuclear reactors are visually more attractive than coal furnaces. Clearly, those who believe that evaluative sentences cannot have truth values would insist that a sentence like "In fact nuclear reactors are visually more attractive than coal furnaces" must be self-contradictory. That is, if "in fact" is regarded as synonymous with "in truth" and evaluative sentences cannot be true or false, then it is self-contradictory to claim that it's true that nuclear reactors are more attractive than coal furnaces *and* it's not true or false. If it's not true or false, than it's not true.

It is the epistemological sense of "fact" that is intended when people talk about gathering relevant facts or undertaking a fact-finding investigation. If, for example, a journalist is sent out to dig up all the facts he can find about Cleveland's mayor, no one will expect the journalist to return with old shoes, chairs and hubcaps. Nor would anyone expect to see the journalist bring a pick and shovel to work. What would be expected is a search for true relevant propositions or sentences about the mayor. In an ontological sense of the term, the mayor's shoes, chairs and auto hubcaps are facts in his life, literally the furniture of his world. But gathering the facts about his life does not imply gathering up such furniture. (Anyone who wants to make something out of the difference between "facts in" and "facts about" is free to do so.)

It would be nice if we had a generally acceptable criterion of truth. There seems to be general agreement that Tarski's formal definition is sound: i.e., a sentence represented by "p" is true if and only if p; e.g., "John is sick" is a true sentence if and only if John is sick. As a meaning analysis of a common notion of truth, this seems to be unexceptionable. But it's obviously worthless as a criterion for determining which sentences are true and which are false. From the meaning analysis we don't find out how to prove that John is or isn't sick. (The problem is roughly analogous to knowing what it means to bake a cake, but not knowing how to do it.) To solve the criteriological problem of truth, I think one must appeal to some notion of coherence. Nicholas Rescher's *The Co-*

herence Theory of Truth is the most recent attempt to carry out such a program. It's not the sort of program one can expect to just carry out as one carries out the garbage. However, Rescher has taken significant steps forward.

4. FROM ONTOLOGY TO EPISTEMOLOGY

Given the two common ways of talking about factual matters, an ontological way in which facts are contrasted with values and an epistemological way in which facts are contrasted with falsehoods, the stage is set for unwarranted inferences. It is easy to move from the assumption that an issue is a factual matter in the ontological sense of the term "factual" to the quite different assumption that the issue is factual in the epistemological sense of the term. In such cases, one starts with an issue that is ontologically factual and converts it into an epistemological fact, i.e., a truth or true claim, or a falsehood. Whether the conversion is intentional or not, the fallacy of equivocation is committed. One logically cannot derive epistemological appraisals of truth or falsity from mere ontological categorization.

As Edgar Bergen might have asked Mortimer Snerd, "How could anyone be so stupid?" And as Mortimer might have replied, "Wal, it's a lot easier in a crowd!" The fact (truth) is that several common ways of talking and thinking (in English at least) conspire to drive people to equivocate on the ontological and epistemological uses of the term "fact." For example, it often happens that when a group meets to discuss a problem, say, the development of an energy source, one or more members think it will be helpful to share some factual matters. If there is a thin edge of the wedge leading to complete consensus in a group decision-making situation, so the assumption goes, it must be at or near the factual side of things. So, by all means, let us lay out some of the facts as soon as possible. The move from factual matters to facts here can be a move from ontology to epistemology. Because factual matters (ontology) tend to be relatively unproblematic (relative to evaluative matters), the assumption goes, and factual matters are going to be discussed first, facts (epistemology) are going to be introduced first. The mere description of a claim as factual in the ontological sense tends to soften the path toward its acceptance as factual in the epistemological sense.

As a second example of how the equivocation arises, consider the case of expert advice given by scientists. Suppose it is granted that there really are experts on matters of scientific fact, e.g., chemical facts, physical facts, economic facts, etc. At a minimum that means that there is a body of factual (ontology) claims about which so-called experts know more than non-experts. To be an expert in, say, chemistry is just to know more about the factual claims of chemistry than most people know. Apart from the question of the truth or falsity of any factual claim of chemistry (or any chemical issue or problem for chemistry or matter of chemistry), most people I guess would be willing to grant that it is usually possible to distinguish such claims from many others. If I say, for example, that sugar is water-soluble, no one is going to quarrel about describing that as a fact of chemistry rather than a fact of sociology, economics, or arithmetic. Granted that these disciplines have fuzzy edges and no knock-down criteria of identification, it's not likely that the water-solubility matter is going to be resisted as a matter of chemistry. However, because there are some factual matters that clearly are in the province of chemistry (an ontological point) and there are experts on such matters, it is possible for the expert chemist to claim to assert chemical facts in the epistemological sense of "fact" and get away with it. The *non sequitur* runs: Smith is a chemicial expert. x is a matter of chemical fact (ontologically speaking). So, if Smith claims that x is a chemical fact (ontologically yet) then x is a fact (epistemologically speaking, true). In short, Smith's credentials are doing the job (invalidly) that Smith's evidence should be doing (validly). We often tell students of introductory logic courses to beware of people with credentials in one field making claims in another field. We should also tell them to beware of people with credentials using those credentials instead of evidence to warrant claims in the field where the credentials are held.

There is another way in which an equivocation on the term "fact" occurs related to judgments that something is a matter of scientific fact. When one judges that some issue is scientific or is a matter of science, one might base the judgment on one's knowledge that there is a body of scientific literature about it. For example, one might think that the question of the thermal energy of coal is a scientific question because there is a recognized body of physical science literature dealing with precisely this question and related questions. The same person might think that the question of the visual attractiveness of a coal furnace is not scientific because there is (as far as he knows) no recognized body of science dealing with precisely this and related questions. Now he can reason invalidly: Science deals with facts (ontology). There is no science of visual attractiveness. So, there are no scientific facts (epistemology) of visual attractiveness. Thus, whatever one says about visual attractiveness cannot have the status of a scientific fact (truth). Whatever claims about visual attractiveness are, they cannot be true.

Besides noticing that the argument just presented involves an equivocation, it ought to be noticed that the criterion of scientific significance used in the preceding paragraph is far from rigorous or decisive. There could be no new sciences if the criterion of scientific significance required every allegedly scientific claim to have a recognized body of scientific literature devoted to it already. The scientific enterprise could never have begun if that had been the criterion of selecting scientific claims. Nevertheless, I don't doubt at all that many people do use such a criterion as a rough and ready guide to judgments about what is scientific. Since I have already said that there are no generally accepted, decisive criteria of scientific significance, I have no objections to people using rough and ready criteria. I only object if people use such criteria to pronounce all evaluative claims as in principle unscientific and hence untrue. After all, in such cases the principle is known to be defective and the inference is invalid.

A fourth way in which an equivocation on the term "fact" occurs is related to a defective argument for distinguishing empirical facts from values. It is sometimes argued that facts must be different from values because it is possible to get complete agreement on the facts of a situation (event, person, thing) but still have disagreement about its value. For example, we would be able to get complete agreement from virtually everyone watching me present this paper that I have a nose. The fact that I have a nose is literally as plain as the nose on my face. We could get agreement on its size, color, shape, physiological structure and so on. Nevertheless, the argument runs, it would still be possible to have disagreement about the physical attractiveness of my nose. Some people would say it's a nice nose, others that it's ugly, or plain, superb, classical Greco-Roman, and so on. In short, unlike the fact of my nose, the esthetic value of my nose is open to a variety of opinions. The fact (truth now) that I have a nose can be established beyond reasonable doubt, but the esthetic value of my nose remains doubtful forever. The preceding sentence is crucial. What is being contrasted in that sentence is not two ontologically distinct types of things. Rather, it is the epistemological status of factual claims that is being contrasted with evaluative claims. The issue is now one of truth versus something less than the truth.

To appreciate the weakness of the argument in the preceding paragraph, consider the following analogue. Values must be different from facts because it is possible to get complete agreement on the value of something but still have disagreement about factual aspects of it. For example, long before there was agreement on the facts about things like rainbows, sunsets, mountains, waterfalls and clouds, most people found such things not only attractive but often awe-inspiring. It would have been possible for two ancient Greeks (or two contemporary folks) to agree that a particular rainbow was beautiful while disagreeing on its origin, color, size, and shape. Anyone familiar with the history of science can probably multiply such cases easily. Anyone at all can probably think of many more cases in which complete agreement in evaluative issues comes at least as easily as agreement on facts. For example, we would be able to get complete agreement from virtually everyone watching me present this paper that I don't have a moral obligation to cut off my nose during the presentation. Similarly, nobody in his right mind would think that I would be physically more attractive at this minute with a bloody hole in the middle of my face instead of a nose. Nobody thinks I would look pretty with three noses, or four, and so on. Clearly there are as many evaluations or judgments of value as there are judgments of fact about which one can get virtually complete agreement. In principle there must be an infinite number; e.g., everyone will agree that I don't have two noses, three, etc., and everyone will agree that I would not be prettier with two noses, three, etc. There does not seem to be any ontological lesson to be learned about facts and values from counting heads regarding things people agree or disagree on readily. With a little thought one can cook examples to suit oneself.

While I am on this subject of agreement, I should take a few lines to address the frequently made assumption that if people cannot readily identify a good reason for some judgment, agreement, or disagreement, then there must be an evaluation involved. In brief, people often argue: There is apparently no good reason to assert p is the case. Therefore, the assertion that p is the case must involve an evaluation, a value, a value judgment or some such thing.

Instead of leaping to such a conclusion, one should at least consider the following seven other possibilities. The judgment that p is the case may involve (a) a perception that is not clearly identifiable; (b) an idea that is vague or open-textured; (c) principles or rules of inference that are obscure; (d) so many complicating factors to aggregate that, although one can intuit an appropriate judgment, one cannot clearly support it; (e) some premises that one cannot identify; (f) a mistake about some rule or premise; (g) a disagreement about facts difficult to discern.

A fifth and final way in which an equivocation on the term "fact" occurs is related to standard textbook treatments of rational decision-making or action on the Bayesian or estimated utility model. Briefly, according to this view decision-makers are confronted with a set of mutually exclusive and exhaustive possible future states of affairs and courses of action. Each combination of state of affairs and action yields an event with a particular value or utility. By quantifying these values, multiplying these quantities by the probabilities of the events that may occur and summing the products of every event attached to every action, one can obtain the estimated value of performing that action. A rational actor then is supposed to perform the available action that has the highest estimated value.

What seems to be built into the Bayesian procedure as just described is the assumption of a fact-value dichotomy in the form of a probability-value dichotomy. Rational decision-making and action on this model requires an amalgamation of two apparently ontologically distinct kinds of entities, namely, values and probabilistic facts or factual probabilities of some sort. But if probabilities have some sort of factual status and values do not, then there is a tendency to regard values as epistemological nonstarters. Probability assessments, the assumption goes, may be more or less accurate or true, but evaluations are simply given or not. The latter is especially the case when the values used in the model are based on revealed preferences which are uncritically given and accepted. Again, then, we have the unwarranted move from an ontological to an epistemological use of "fact."

On top of the objectionable equivocation just described, it should be noticed that it is a mistake to assume that probability assessments do not require evaluations and that evaluations do not involve probability (factual) assessments. I have discussed these connections in other places and will therefore be very brief. In order to measure any probabilities one must make decisions concerning one's universe of discourse, its appropriate description, the appropriate subset of the total universe to be used for any given problem situation, and the appropriate methods to be used to make all these decisions. These and other decisions involve assessments of the benefits and costs attached to alternative decisions; i.e., the decisions involve evaluations. Similarly, the evaluations required on the other side of the Bayesian model require epistemological assessments. For example, in order to form a preference for apples over oranges one must know something about both. Without building some sort of information or knowledge component into evaluation, it becomes impossible to distinguish the proverbial Fool's Paradise from Real Paradise. Conceptually, the difference between the two is either that the fool does not have any good reasons for valuing or preferring his Paradise while someone in a Real Paradise would, or that there are good reasons for believing the Fool's Paradise is not what he thinks it is; it is not, that is, the Real Paradise he thinks it is. For example, heavy smokers who believe they can go on smoking without damaging their lungs can only have the pleasure of a Fool's Paradise. In short, uninformed evaluations are worthless.

5. FROM ONTOLOGY TO METHODOLOGY

I think that one of the reasons people believe that the so-called fact-value distinction is very important is that they have not distinguished the fact-value distinction from the fact-falsehood distinction. They believe that by determining the correct ontological status of an issue, as factual or evaluative, the truth status of the issue has also been settled. Given the particular views that some people have about evaluative issues (e.g., the people I characterized as having extreme views), evaluative sentences don't have any truth values. Hence, for people with such views, the ontological categorization of an issue as evaluative has the epistemological consequence that the concepts of truth and falsity will not be applicable at all. Against such extremists, it is pointless to try to establish the truth or falsity of an evaluative sentence. It would make as much sense as trying to establish the truth or falsity of a sneeze or a glass of beer. For these folks evaluative sentences, by definition, logically cannot have truth values. The sentences are epistemological non-starters and that's that.

If one is not an extremist on evaluative issues, then—unless one is a metaphysician interested in determining the ontological structure of the world—there is probably little of interest in the fact-value distinction. One the other hand, the fact-falsity, or better, the truth-falsity distinction is fundamental. If one can't distinguish truth from falsity, true sentences from false ones, then one runs the risk of eating stones, swimming in molten lead and making love to ostriches. Being able to distinguish truth from falsity really does have survival value in ways that being able to distinguish facts from values doesn't. So why fool around with the metaphysical question?

One answer is that it might be the case that if we got an issue correctly categorized ontologically, then we could address it with the right method. At any rate, we might be able to eliminate some methods as useless. For example, if one holds an extreme view of evaluative sentences, then once one knows that a sentence is evaluative, one knows that there is no method that can establish the truth or falsity of the sentence. This is indeed an extreme case, but it illustrates how one can use ontological knowledge to make methodological decisions. In this extreme case, the decision is simply to admit the inapplicability of every method. Given one's definition of evaluative sentences, no method is relevant to establishing their truth or falsity.

Suppose that you do not hold an extreme view. That is, suppose you believe that categorizing a sentence as factual or evaluative leaves the truth status of the sentence undecided but not undecidable. The question is: Can it help your epistemological task to know that the sentence involves an ontologically factual or evaluative claim? It might. It depends on the particular claim, your methodological resources (time, energy, strategy, money, logico-mathematical sophistication, etc.), your epistemological beliefs, and your value theory, to mention only a few salient variables. I wish there were a short answer. The only relevant short answer I can think of now is that correct ontological classification into the categories of matter of fact or value is no panacea. No one should imagine that a solution to the ontological-metaphysical problem would constitute a major epistemological breakthrough.

Consider some examples in support of the previous sentence. (1) The ultimate matter of the world is wave-like rather than particle-like. (2) Every innocent human infant should be tortured to death before the age of four months. (3) A human being wrote these sentences. (4) A morally good human being wrote these sentences. It seems to me, though this is not a knock-down demonstration, that sentence (1) is a factual claim whose truth is extremely difficult if not impossible to decide; (2) is an evaluative claim whose falsity will be granted by all but extremists and crazies; (3) is a factual claim as uncontroversial as (2); and (4) is more controversial than (3), less controversial than (2) and probably not as controversial as (1).

All I want to do with these four sentences (1)-(4) is illustrate and lend some support to my claim that solving the ontological status problem may leave one with enormous epistemological problems, depending on the particular claim to be assessed. I also said it depends on your methodological resources. For example, consider (5) It is wrong to torture all living babies to death and (6) The negation of a conjunction is logically equivalent to the disjunction of two negations. (5) is an evaluative sentence whose truth will be granted by virtually everyone who reads it, while (6) is a logical factual sentence (a sentence stating a logical fact or logical truth) whose truth will not be recognizable by everyone or even most people. Depending on one's training and methodological resources, the evaluative (5) and the factual (6) will be more or less easy to assess epistemologically.

Epistemological beliefs have a crucial role to play in determining how useful correct ontological categorizations can be. I can't review the history of epistemological skepticism here. Suffice it to say that some folks believe there can be no certainty concerning the truth or falsity of empirical sentences. They may rest their case on so-called arguments from dreams, from illusions, from limited sense perception, from peculiar definitions of complete verification, and so on. If they are thoroughgoing skeptics, then there's no hope. They will regard empirical claims as inherently unjustifiable and hence doubtful. Alternatively, they may be less-than-thoroughgoing skeptics, holding that one might have complete certainty concerning empirical claims although such claims are inherently fallible. For example, they may say that sentences like "There's only one doctor in this town" can be known to be true with complete certainty, but they are still liable to be falsified. They are still fallible or corrigible but not doubtful. Although I find this view satisfactory, some folks don't. It depends on how one defines key epistemological terms like "knowledge," "certainty," "complete verification," and so on.

The last important variable I mentioned that determines how useful correct ontological categorization would be in determining the truth status of any sentence is one's theory of value. With some theories of value, the truth or falsity of evaluative sentences is a routine matter, provided that one is not a thoroughgoing epistemological skeptic. With other theories, as I have already suggested, "truth" and "falsity" just don't apply. In the next section I will review some basic alternative views of the nature of value.

6. THEORIES OF VALUE

Before I begin my review of value theories, a couple of preliminary remarks will be helpful. In the first place, one must distinguish *things that have value* from *the value that things have*. Although virtually anything may be regarded as a thing that has value (or, briefly, a thing of value or a valuable thing), many people (especially social scientists) seem to focus on things like personal freedom, political efficacy, honesty, and self-esteem as examples. That's okay, as long as one remembers that strictly speaking sticks and stones and telephones, and anything else, may be regarded as valuable things in some sense of "value."

Just as theories of molecules, electricity, and democracy have as their subject matter molecules, electricity and democracy, respectively, so a theory of value has value as its subject matter. Just as in molecular theory one gets meaning analyses of basic terms, measurement procedures, working principles and lawlike statements, a theory of value may be expected to have a similar battery of features. I have reviewed alternative views of the structure of scientific theories elsewhere. So here it is enough to say that there are over half a dozen views about what scientific theories ought to look like, ranging from mere unrestricted universal generalizations to axiomatic systems with logical and empirical vocabularies, rules for formation and transformation, and so on. Depending on what one means by the terms "theory" and "science," there have been more or less fully developed scientific theories of value. Perhaps the most fully developed theory we have had is that of Ralph Barton Perry in his classic, *General Theory of Value* (1926).

The alternative views of the nature of value that will be outlined below should be regarded as central features of possible (and more or less plausible) theories of value. Generally speaking, I describe the sort of meaning analysis that might be adopted for each view, and briefly suggest some of its salient strengths and weaknesses. I can't, of course, provide a thorough analysis and appraisal of any theory. Moreover, I do not try to press my own preference for any of the views. For the points to be made in the following section, it does not matter what theory of value one adopts. It only matters that one appreciates the variety of theories available.

When people say that something is valuable or good, just how should their remarks be understood? For example, how should one interpret remarks like "Jesus was a good man," "Clean air is valuable," and "There is some value in friendship"? We could, of course, retreat to a handy dictionary and get a standard lexicographer's definition of the key terms "good," "value," "valuable," and so on. But that would be an inappropriate response to the question. What we want is not merely correct English usage, but a more or less systematic or theoretical account of the meanings of these key words, and an account of the things referred to by these words—if there are such things.

Generally speaking, seven distinct kinds of answers have been offered to our question, each one suggesting a different view of the nature, essential being, or *ontological status* of value. The names used by different authors to refer to these seven different views vary a great deal, to put it mildly. Hence, it is vitally important that as you read this section, you must try to get each view fixed in your mind without becoming dogmatic about the labels used for the view. You should also not be surprised to find some people combining some of these views or elements of some of them to obtain hybrid forms.

The relations between the seven views are illustrated in the following diagram, which will be discussed in the remaining paragraphs of this section.

The first distinction to be drawn is that between cognitivism and non-

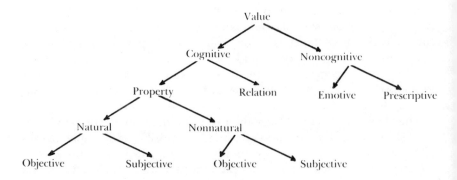

cognitivism. In the *cognitivist* view the terms "value" and "good" designate something which is identifiable and namable, but not necessarily describable. Things that have value or goodness are thus similar to things that are yellow or sweet insofar as one can identify and name the qualities they possess, but cannot necessarily describe them in other words. In the *noncognitivist* view the terms "value" and "good" do not *designate* anything at all. Things do not have value or goodness on this view any more than "Such" is the name of something, or "Help me, please" describes any state of affairs.

As you can see from the diagram above, there are two species each of cognitivist and noncognitivist views of the nature of value. Since the division of noncognitivist views takes us to the *infimae species* or rock-bottom of the righthand branch of our family tree, while the division of cognitivist views does not, I will consider the latter next.

Supposing that it is granted that "value" and "good" do designate something which is identifiable and namable, one might ask: Is value or goodness a property or a relation? From an ontological point of view, the difference between properties and relations is important. Consider, for example, the sentence "John is standing to the left of Frank." John and Frank do not seem to exist the way the relation designated by "is standing to the left of" exists. The *particular* relation seems to obtain (exist) when and only when John is standing to the left of Frank. Some people think that the *universal*, abstract entity, type or sort of relation designated by "is standing to the left of" has its own mode of existence, which Bertrand Russell called "subsistence" to distinguish it from ordinary existence.

I can't settle the old philosophical problem of the existence of abstract entities (Platonic forms, if you like—almost). But on a *relational* view, value may be thought of as a relation obtaining between at least two things (usually a person and a valued thing) *and* the relation may be regarded as a concrete particular or an abstract type of entity. I have not put two branches below "relation" on the diagram above in order to simplify the diagram. Strictly speaking, however, two branches could be drawn, one for the view that "value" designates particular relations and one for the view that "value" designates an abstract entity or universal relation. Similar divisions could be made for the view that "value" designates a property.

Whether value is regarded as particular or universal, insofar as it's regarded as a relation one will not be able to pick it out the way one picks out the terms of the relation. For example, suppose "Clean water is valuable" is taken to mean something like "There is a relation between clean water and people in virtue of which it is correct to say that clean water is valuable." We may be able to observe the clean water and the people (the two terms of the relation), but we can't observe the relation. Moreover, on this view, it is precisely that relation that provides the warrant for the attribution of value to clean water. Obviously, then, people who hold that value is a relation have special problems of characterizing the relation and given criteria for identifying it. Here the ghost of David Hume looms large, because causal relations are prime candidates to figure in relational theories of value and Hume argued forcefully that such relations are nothing more than human artifacts, products of human imagination. Thus, relational theorists will have special problems establishing the truth or falsity of evaluative sentences. If they happen to be commited to abstract entities, they are even worse off. Or, turning things upside down, if one were an epistemological nominalist (believing there are no abstract entities) and if one became convinced that "value" designated an abstract entity, a relation-type, then one would be stuck with the view that value doesn't exist. For such people sentences like "Clean water is valuable" might be false or maybe meaningless, but certainly not true.

In contrast to a relational view, one might hold a quality or *property* view according to which "value" and "good" designate some sort of a property. On this view, value belongs to things roughly the way other properties belong to things, e.g., the way height, weight, triangularity, etc., belong to things.

Supposing it is granted that "value" and "good" designate a property of things that is identifiable and namable, one might then ask: Is value or goodness a natural property of the world or not? On the *naturalistic* view of value or goodness, this property or quality is as natural as water, mountains, headaches, and itches. Just as one does not have to design or make trees and toothaches, one does not have to design or make value or goodness. It just grows naturally, the way some tadpoles naturally become frogs and people naturally grow old, if all goes well.

On the *nonnatural* view ("supernatural" would do as well) of value or goodness, these qualities do not just emerge or evolve like flowers and snowflakes. They are somehow outside, above, or beyond the natural stream of things. They have roughly the same status relative to the world of nature that God and other supernatural spirits are supposed to have. One need not believe that there are any nonnatural or supernatural things in order to understand the point of view, I think. Nonnaturalists just happen to believe that value or goodness is not finally rooted in or grounded on anything in the physical, natural, or material universe.

There are two species of naturalism and nonnaturalism (supernaturalism) that merit attention. I will consider each in turn.

Naturalistic Objectivism

On what may be called a *naturalistic objectivist* view of the nature of value, to say that something is good or valuable is to say that something has some natural property in virtue of which the predicates "is good" or "is valuable" may be appropriately applied to it. For example, suppose one says that it is good to be kind to people, that kindness is worth a lot, or that kindness is a valuable characteristic for a person to possess. On the naturalistic objectivist view, such remarks have the status of genuine truth claims, i.e., they must be true or false. Moreover, they are true if and only if whatever is referred to by the subject of each remark has some property or attribute named by the predicate of the remark. Thus, for example, it *is* good to be kind to people if and only if kindness has some special property called "goodness." Similarly, Jesus was a good man, on this view, if and only if he possessed the particular property of being a good man. Accordingly, being good, having value or worth, on this view, is precisely analogous to being triangular or having the property of triangularity. Just as polygons can be triangular whether or not anyone knows or cares about it, someone or something can be good and valuable whether or not anyone knows or cares about it. Again, just as mountains can have snow and teeth can have cavities whether or not anyone knows or cares about it, someone or something can be good or valuable whether or not anyone knows or cares about it. Furthermore, it is true to say that something is triangular or good just in case that thing has the special properties named by "is triangular" and "is good," namely, the properties of being triangular and being good.

Naturalistic Subjectivism

On what may be called a *naturalistic subjectivist* view of the nature of value, to say that something is good or valuable is to say that somebody has some natural attribute, characteristic, or feeling in virtue of which it is appropriate to apply the predicates "is good" or "is valuable" to something. The term "somebody" might designate a single person, a small group, a culture, a nation, everyone in Western Civilization, or just human beings in general. As one moves from a single individual (i.e., naive egoism) to human beings in general, one's naturalistic subjectivism tends to become more plausible, but that is a long story that need not detain us now. The attributes, characteristics, or feelings possessed by the subject of one's naturalistic subjectivism might be, say, feelings of approval, satisfaction, pleasure, or favorable interest of some sort. Hence, for example, to say that kindness is worth a lot is to affirm something like the fact that Canadians approve of kindness, most people in the world approve of being kind, or that everyone you know approves of kindness. Supposing that one can recognize acts of kindness when one sees them, it would be true to say that they are good or valuable just in case Canadians do approve of them, most people approve of them, or everyone you know approves of them. It depends on how you specify the subject for your naturalistic subjectivism. If goodness or value is determined by, for example, ninety percent of Canadians having an empirically discoverable feeling of approval toward something, then that thing is good or valuable when and only when ninety percent of Canadians have such a feeling about it.

In short, then, naturalistic subjectivism and objectivism are alike insofar as both views hold that judgments of goodness, value, or worth are *genuine truth claims*, i.e., they are in principle determinably true or false. They are different views insofar as subjectivists locate the properties that justify evaluations in people while objectivists locate the justifying properties in whatever is claimed to be good or valuable. One way to keep the two views separate is to think of them as roughly analogous to two properties of sugar, namely, mass and sweetness. When one says that sugar has mass (ignoring relativity theory), one is talking directly about a property located in sugar. On the other hand, when one says that sugar is sweet, one is talking directly about the sensation of sweetness that is in people having the sensation, rather than in the sugar. "Sugar is sweet" is an indirect or roundabout way of referring to how sugar is perceived by people, while "Sugar has mass" is a direct way of referring to how sugar is. Just so with values. For naturalistic objectivists, "Sugar is valuable" is a direct way of referring to how sugar is, while for naturalistic subjectivists it's an indirect way of referring to how sugar is perceived or apprehended.

Nonnaturalistic Objectivism

On what may be called a *nonnaturalistic objectivist* view ("supernaturalistic objectivist" would do as well) of the nature of value, to say that something is good or valuable is to say that something has some nonnatural property in virtue of which the predicates "is good" or "is valuable" may be appropriately applied to it. The nonnaturalistic objectivist accepts everything that the naturalistic objectivist accepts about value judgments *except* their justification in natural phenomena. Things really do have goodness or value in them, but these are nonnatural or supernatural qualities inexplicably existing or, perhaps, existing by the will of God. The qualities do not just emerge like snowflakes and they are not natural the way my appetite for apple pie is natural. They are *something else*, and that's all there is to it!

Nonnaturalistic Subjectivism

On what may be called a *nonnaturalistic subjectivist view* of the nature of value, to say that something is good or valuable is to say that somebody has some nonnatural attribute in virtue of which it is appropriate to apply the predicates "is good" or "is valuable" to something. The nonnaturalistic subjectivist accepts everything that the naturalistic subjectivist accepts about value judgments *except* their justification in natural phenomena. It is the spiritual aspect of human beings that is the locus, ground, or origin of value in the world. Value exists insofar as people have feelings, attitudes, likes and dislikes, but human feelings, attitudes, likes and dislikes are not just natural phenomena like the pains or itches of cats and dogs. Human beings, on this view, have something in them that is not quite natural. Although the view does not logically entail theism, those who have spoken of the image of God in man have shared this view of the extraordinary status of human beings.

Again, nonnaturalistic objectivism and subjectivism are alike insofar as both views hold (1) that value judgments are genuine truth claims, and (2) that values are not grounded in natural phenomena. They are unlike with respect to where they locate the nonnatural properties that justify evaluations.

Before moving on to a discussion of the two kinds of non-cognitive views of value, some comments are in order about the strengths and weaknesses of the four views just considered. First, if objectivist views could be sustained then there would be a universal, objective, or absolute basis for evaluations. That would be marvelous indeed. It would mean, for example, that when people say things like "Abortion is wrong" or "Jesus was a good man" that anyone who doesn't agree with these judgments is seriously out of step with the structure of the world, either the natural or the supernatural world. Such a person would be mistaken in roughly the same way that someone who ate stones for nourishment would be mistaken. If one were a nonnaturalistic objectivist, then one would have special problems of characterizing the property designated by "value" and explaining how natural beings can have access to it. If one were a naturalistic objectivist, then one would have special problems explaining the fact that different people at different places or the same people at different times have quite different views about what is or is not valuable. (Recall the discussion in section 4 above.)

If subjectivist views could be sustained, life could be better or worse, depending on the views. Naive egoism makes every person his or her own court of last appeal, which would probably make life lonely, nasty, brutish, and short. It is also a consequence of this view that two people would not be affirming the same proposition if each judges that something is good or valuable, and they would not be affirming contradictory propositions if one judged that something was valuable while the other judged that it was not valuable.

G. E. Moore's famous "open question argument" was intended to undermine all naturalistic theories of value, but it could also be used against all forms of subjectivism. In either case, as Frankena showed some years ago, the argument is question-begging.

Emotivism

On what may be called an *emotivist* view of the nature of value, to say that something is good or valuable is not to affirm anything at all, but merely to express a feeling or attitude. Emotivists depart radically from all cognitivists because on the emotivist view assertions of goodness, value, or worth are not genuine truth claims, i.e., they cannot (logically) be true or false. Moreover, they cannot be true or false because they have the logical status of exclamations, not of declarative sentences.

Let us consider the view more carefully with the help of an analogy. Suppose I step on your toe. You might say "You're hurting me," or "Ouch," or you might just pull your foot out from under mine. If you just pull your foot back then you have made no claim that might be true or false. Similarly, if you just scream "Ouch!" or "Eeaah!" you have made no claim. On the other hand, the declarative sentence "You're hurting me" must be true or false, though for our purposes it does not matter which. What the emotivist view amounts to then, is just this: Sentences that appear *formally* as declaratives in which some property, namely, goodness or value, is being affirmed of something are *functionally* exclamations in which nothing at all is being *affirmed*, though something is being *expressed*. Thus, for example, when one says "Clean air is valuable," one should be understood exactly as if one were exclaiming "Hooray for clean air!" or "Whoopie! Clean air!"—neither of which is true or false. Therefore, and most importantly, it would be foolish to try to find any property in virtue of which the predicate "is valuable" may be appropriately applied because there is no such property. Since the sentence "Clean air is valuable" is not functioning as a declarative sentence, the predicate "is valuable" is not functioning as the name of some attribute in people or air or anything else. The fundamental assumption of all cognitivists is, according to the emotivists, just plain wrongheaded. Value judgments are not genuine truth claims at all; so it is pointless to ask why some are true and some are not.

Prescriptivism

On what may be called a *prescriptivist* view of the nature of value, to say that something is good or valuable is not to affirm anything at all, but merely to recommend or prescribe something. Like the emotivists, prescriptivists also depart radically from cognitivists because on the prescriptivist view assertions of value are not genuine truth claims. On this view such assertions have the logical status of commands, not of declarative sentences. Just as the prescription "Take two aspirins and go to bed" does not have a truth value, the sentences "It is good to be healthy" and "Better to be healthy than sick" are supposed to be without truth values. Apparent declaratives like "It is good to be healthy" should be interpreted functionally as prescriptions like "Promote healthiness," "Take care of your health," "Prefer health to illness." Again then, as is the case for emotivists, according to prescriptivists the fundamental assumption for all cognitivists is just wrongheaded. Value judgments are not genuine truth claims at all; so it is pointless to ask why some are true and some are false.

The nice thing about noncognitivist views is that they provide an explanation for the apparent fact that people have not been able to discover and display the properties in virtue of which things are said to have or lack value. If "value" and "good" are not the names of any properties, there were none to be found. Noncognitivist theories also have the virtue of reminding us that evaluations often if not always are used as expressions of emotion and as prescriptions. Even if one rejects pure noncognitivism, it's difficult to reject these insights of the noncognitivist position. Evaluative sentences frequently seem to do double or even triple duty.

7. RATIONAL DECISION-MAKING

Two sections ago I raised the question: Can it help your epistemological task (the task of deciding which sentences are true and which are false) to know that a sentence in question involves an ontologically factual or evaluative claim? I answered that it might, and spent some time unpacking that answer. It might have been comforting to be able to say straightaway that yes, by God, once we know if we're confronted by facts or values we know where we are. At the very least some methodological roads are closed. Some kinds of answers will never be forthcoming, and so on. It might have been comforting, but it would not have been true.

The truth is that for some epistemological and evaluative views, the fact-value distinction is problematic and the gap between facts and values is logically unbridgeable. For thoroughgoing epistemological skeptics, the gap, insofar as it is recognized at all, is as serious as a pimple on a malignant tumor. For people holding a naturalistic theory of value, whether it is of an objectivist or subjectivist variety, there is no ontological distinction between facts and values. There are merely formally and functionally different ways to talk about and deal with facts, empirical or logical facts.

What I want to do in this final section is to suggest a useful procedural rule of rational decision-making. The rule is not, as far as I can tell, derivable in a strict sense from the preceding discussion. But it has emerged fairly directly in my own mind as a consequence of that discussion. The rule is just this: Forget about the fact-value distinction. It's almost always a red herring.

Whether the question at issue is epistemological, ontological, or axiological (i.e., a question of truth, being, or value) one is almost always wiser to tackle the question directly rather than to try to cut one's ontological pie into facts and values. Martin Luther King said that the trouble with resorting to violence is that then the issue becomes violence. I think that the trouble with resorting to metaphysics is that then the issue becomes metaphysical. Instead of fighting battles about whether something is true, good, or worth doing, one finds oneself fighting battles about credentials, either the ontological credentials of the issue before one (Is that a matter of truth or goodness or action?) or the credentials of the disputants. Instead of pressing the question "Are there good reasons for believing, preferring, or doing this or that?" the red herring question is raised "Is this a matter of values or facts?" The red herring question can have the effect of silencing voices and eliminating points of view that might happen to be right, or giving too much ground to those who are wrong. Neither error has to be risked if one insists that debate must focus on the issue of truth or falsity, or on what is to be done. Either one can substantiate one's case to satisfy most people or not. How one classifies the type of argumentation used is, I think, quite beside the point.

In the area of energy development decision-making in particular, I think that what we have been witnessing for the past few years is an attempt by some folks to have a greater voice in such decision-making. If one describes this effort as an attempt to get some values into energy policy development, then one may be drawing an imaginary line that some people will never be able to cross. On one side will be hardheads with the facts and on the other side will be softheads with values. It would be strategically wiser to describe the effort as an attempt to get a wider spectrum of issues considered or voices heard. Given our fuzzy understanding of facts and values as ontological categories, we have a stronger epistemological and moral warrant to describe the effort in this way. There will be facts and values (whatever both of these are) that everyone regards as relevant, some that everyone regards as irrelevant, and some about which people will disagree. If we can get agreement on what is true, good, or ought to be done, who but a metaphysician cares if we're agreeing on something factual or valuable or both? On the other hand, if we can agree that something is factual or valuable or both but can't agree on whether it's true, good, or ought to be done, then who but a metaphysician cares about that? In short, it seems to be a good idea for everyone but metaphysicians to forget about the fact-value distinction and get on with the pursuit of truth and the performance of good deeds.

8. CONCLUSION

In a roundabout way I think that all I have been arguing for here is humility in the interests of rational decision-making. I do not expect anyone to stop talking about facts and values as if I had laid these beasts of burden to rest. Indeed, I do not expect to stop talking about facts and values either. If I have managed to make it more difficult for some people—whether technology assessors, science policy analysts, or others—to use the terms glibly, and more difficult for them to be certain of the strengths of their own positions and the weaknesses of other people's positions, that will be enough.

ACKNOWLEDGMENT

This paper was originally published in P. T. Durbin and F. Rapp (eds.), *Philosophy and Technology*, pp. 59–81. Copyright © 1983 by D. Reidel Publishing Company, Dordrecht, Holland. Reprinted with permission.

THE CULTURES OF SCIENCE
AND POLICY

Erve Chambers

ABSTRACT

Although policy analysis is a relatively new social science discipline, it has been around in one form or another for a long time. The general relationship between policy analysis and values appears constant, even though often highly variable in its particulars. An approach to policy analysis can be effective only if, beyond its confirmed virtues, it enjoys the additional virtue of being situated securely within the sensibilities of the society in which it occurs. A public science is ultimately built more on trust than mystique, although a little of the latter probably helps.

INTRODUCTION

In his remarkable study of the ritual and ecology of the Tsembaga, a primitive New Guinea farming people, anthropologist Roy Rappaport describes ritual as a qualitative way of signaling quantitative changes in the ecosystem. A significance of many Tsembaga rituals is that they are

Policy Analysis: Perspectives, Concepts, and Methods, pages 93–110.
ISBN: 0–89232–371–X

both analytic and communicative. They summarize and to some extent interpret the Tsembaga's complex relationship to their environment in such a way that neighboring groups not privy to the "raw data" can understand what is going on—thus providing ritualistically "coded" information necessary for the maintenance of an equally complex set of relationships between the Tsembaga and other peoples occupying this piece of New Guinea territory.[1]

Although policy analysis is a fairly recent phenomenon as a disciplined, identifiable and popular branch of study, it has been around in one form or another for a long time. In whatever form it has taken, the relationship between policy analysis and values appears to be constant, even though often highly variable in its particulars. From the simplest of terms, an approach to policy analysis can be effective only if, beyond its confirmed virtues, it enjoys the additional virtue of being situated securely within the sensibilities of the society in which it occurs.

In this essay I have attempted to indicate on at least two levels both the utility and pitfalls of applying a values perspective to current policy analysis. My first objective is to demonstrate that assumptions about how values operate, particularly in their relationship to behavior, have a fairly direct effect on the analytic and predictive strength of our explanations of specific human circumstances. In this demonstration I rely heavily on the experience of anthropologists, who have devoted an appreciable amount of their energy to the study of values. My second objective is to suggest that it is not only important to understand that values affect policy analysis, on several levels, but that policy analysis—and the relationship between science and politics which it draws from—also has a compelling effect on public values.

POLICY ANALYSIS, SCIENCE AND POLITICS

Policy analysis develops in a state of continual multiple jeopardy: it is accountable to the aims of general science, to each of the disciplines from which it arises, to the state of its particular arts, and to its clientele (including the public, special public and corporate interests and their representatives, and the contractors or purchasers of policy research). Policy analysis is, in other words, *public* science, and does not typically enjoy the same milieu of independence, mystery and often begrudging respect accorded to other uses of science. Though the trappings of policy analysis (including its unavoidable "elitist" tendency toward levels of expertise which cannot be shared by the layperson) may be very similar to those of general science, the social and political environment in which policy researchers operate casts their efforts in an entirely different light.

Most importantly, policy analysis is shaped by the intentionality of the policy process, by the fact that policy analysts are generally called upon to test the effectiveness of a given range of alternative implementations of policy rather than to actually test the full range of assumptions which underlie policy.

This is not an unreasonable restraint. An "experimenting society" needs different kinds of science, not only in method but in purpose. A prospective society, subject and committed to change, requires the means of both challenging the directions of change and of fostering the implementation of change once the basic directional signals have been decided upon. To some extent, these processes of independent and collaborative inquiry must exist independently, and perhaps often antagonistically, if we are to maintain the delicate balance between chance and predictability that a complex society seems to require.

Unfortunately, the antagonisms that exist between policy analysis and general science too frequently result in mutual avoidance rather than in the sort of dynamic tensions that help us see, if even in fleeting terms, the relationships between policy and society, or the interstices between intention and its impact on the lives of people.

This essay explores what might be considered a third or intermediary mode and purpose of inquiry which seeks its primary justification in the investigation of values in public policy. In this context, human values are not viewed in a static sense, but as they arise from critical public events, such as might be discovered in the policy process. My focus is not so much on the empirical reality or practical significance of values, on the likely clustering of different value "codes" into minority or special interest groups, or on the impact of values on decision making. Rather, my emphasis tends to nearly the opposite query: How do circumstances like social research and public decision making impact human values? My primary interest is with the way a society creates and recreates itself— the manner in which intentional social inquiry and action regularly and sometimes capriciously change our ideas of what is meaningful, what is to be valued, and ultimately lead us to evaluate and reevaluate the worth of particular styles of response to public policy problems vis-à-vis other possibilities of response.

This approach, which finds its major justification in phenomenology and interpretative social science, requires acceptance of the possibility that "human science is never finished,"[2] and, perhaps more to the point of this paper, that policy problems are never fully resolved. In this respect, science and politics are united with other styles of endeavor; regardless of their claims for objectivity (science) or for equity and impartiality (politics), neither endeavor simply reflects or responds to what is "out there"; both actively participate in the constant revision of meanings by which any society or segment of society makes sense of its circumstances. This striving to make sense (not from nothing, but from present circumstance and prior meanings and the symbols which mediate both) is, I suggest, the material from which values derive and to which they are repeatedly subjected. In complex societies, the struggle for clarity appears to derive in no small part from the interaction of scientific and creative political processes, with increasingly larger and more important roles being played through the delicate craft of policy analysis.

THE TROUBLE WITH VALUES

Few social or behavioral scientists actually study values these days. There is a clear preference for studying behavior and from there, if necessary, imputing values. This preference reflects a long-term and subtle change in the *moral* paradigms of social inquiry. The shift is largely from an ethical philosophy embedded in early European ideology (maintaining that thoughts are morally equivalent to behavior even if they are sublimated or otherwise not directly acted out in human relations) to a seemingly more pragmatic but equally ethical philosophy of behaviorism (holding that behavior alone matters and that values are of explanatory significance only as they can be identified with actual behaviors). One of the disciplines closest to the actual study of values is social psychology, with its perennial concern for the relationship between belief, attitude and behavior. But even here the usual test is to link specific values to corresponding behaviors—an artifact of the primitive casual epistemology of behavioral experimentalism. Even though our current emphasis on behavioral realism reflects a reasonable suspicion of the prior association of values study with early European theology, the cost in terms of accurately relating values to behaviors is high. We have simply traded one bias for another.[3]

I doubt any social science discipline has recently come closer to the deliberate study of values than has anthropology. There was a time, a few decades past, when it appeared that anthropology was about to become a science of the study of human values. A worthwhile lesson could be learned from the notion of cultural relativity and the recognition of widespread cultural variability in human beliefs. The objectives of this special concern within anthropology were clearly as humanistic as they aimed to be scientific: a better understanding of the worlds' peoples would be achieved if culturally specific behaviors could be explained on the basis of their unique value systems; understanding in its turn would encourage a greater tolerance of human differences. There is little in our present circumstances to refute this reasoning; except that the ideology of tolerance, where it has been broadly accepted, has almost always preceeded understanding.

Where United States anthropologists fell short was not in perceiving the importance of values, but in generally failing to recognize and trace their essential mutability. In the main, anthropology moved very quickly from a quasi-radical perspective which counseled relativism and understanding in the face of intolerance, racism and cultural genocide (a view that it retains) to include a conservative perspective which emphasized cultural differences and focused on value systems almost exclusively in their capacity to persist even beyond the social and cultural circumstances which had helped shape them.

This is not difficult to understand if we note the circumstances of United States anthropology during these periods of its growth. From the 1890s through the 1940s, anthropology served primarily to chronicle the human territories of Western expansion, first among the Indians of North America, and then rapidly throughout the world. During the 1940s, anthropology assumed a new mission as some anthropologists were called upon to advise government in development related problems. Here, the values perspective which had worked so well in counseling tolerance in the face of widespread ignorance of the worlds' peoples began to assume the tenor of a somewhat forced wisdom. In their new role, closely related to the United States' growing influence in the affairs of lesser developed countries, anthropologists were generally expected to explain why a Western innovation introduced into a traditional society (such as an "improved" water supply system or a new variety of crop) was not accepted.[4] Their response, almost invariably, was that the peoples' values precluded acceptance. Anthropologists counseled gradual change and the continued tolerance of custom. This counsel was also more moral than scientific: anthropologists still could not explain to anyone's lasting satisfaction why, in the face of nearly identical cultural and economic circumstances, one village might accept and the other reject a particular innovation, or why an innovation might prove disastrous to one traditional people and have little or no deleterious effect on a similar people.

In many respects, a serious critique of the development of values research in anthropology has never been offered.[5] Rather, events seem to have conspired to pull the discipline up short. The anthropologists' view of culture as an isolate of *shared* behavior and beliefs, an essentially closed system tied closely to their concept of values, started to fall apart during the 1950s as increasing numbers of anthropologists began to look to the more complex and heterogenous social settings of modern nation states, including those of their own society. The increasing popularity of a dialectical social science and the radical challenge of the American

1960s dealt a powerful, though certainly not yet conclusive, blow to that
sense of anthropology which sought to serve in moral arbitration between
Western society and native or "minority" custom. In retrospect, one event
of the period seems conclusive at least in its symbolism: during the 1973
meetings of the American Anthropological Association, a group of young
American Indians stood up to accuse anthropologists of attempting to
preserve the obscure traditions of native American life at the expense
of the developing identity of the Indian as an eager and equal participant
in United States society.[6]

The object of this partial digression into the development of anthropology is to suggest that the ways in which values are studied can lead
to different social consequences, especially as they affect public policy.
The argument that human values arise from particular cultural and
historical circumstances is a useful one. The idea that values tend to
assume a character of endurance which transcends their circumstance
is a dangerous assumption, and a discipline which focuses on validating
such a notion at the expense of equally plausible interpretations runs a
perilous course.

Other assumptions about how values work in a society have equally
important consequences: the idea of "core values," developed during
the 1940s;[7] the continued emphasis on the distinctiveness of value orientations based on ethnic or group criteria as opposed to any significant
interest in value similarities between groups and value differences within
groups;[8] the notions of social equilibrium and stasis implied in anthropology's tendency toward a functional view which holds the parts of
society to be a equal measure in maintaining cultural solidarity and social
harmony; the concept of "cultural lag";[9] and flirtation with the concept
of "subculture," which accords class and ethnic populations within a
larger society the distinction (and onus) of remaining conceptually apart
from the mainstream.[10] These contributions, derived in large part but
not entirely from the anthropology of recent decades, have been assim-
ilated into the ethos of much of this country's public policy process. The
concepts have encouraged the recognition of alternative values and consideration of their impact of public policy; they have also lent a conservative flavor to many of our ideas of policy and value change, counseling
patience and caution at the expense of programs aimed at rapid social
reform.[11]

PLURALISM

The increasingly popular concept of pluralism departs from the anthropologist's earlier view of culture as a relatively closed system, and

thereby permits an approach to social and cultural differences which centers on the character of relationships between groups. Further, the kinds of relationships that adhere between groups in different plural societies are determined to have different degrees or types of political incorporation, leading to important distinctions between cultural, social and structural pluralism.[12] The notion of biculturalism, whereby some individuals and groups can be seen as moving back and forth between different cultural settings, is another important characteristic of some pluralistic thought, and an improvement over the more static concept of subculture.[13]

On close inspection, however, the ideas associated with pluralism and their application to policy problems are prone to many of the same problems discussed above: they tend to emphasize the differences between groups, partly because such differences do exist but also partly because the documentation of differences is crucial to the demonstration of the concept. On the other hand, differences within groups are often ignored or underrated,[14] as are similarities between groups whenever those similarities depart from the most obvious ties of economic and political interdependence.[15]

In line with the general drift of the social sciences, advocates of pluralism have had little to say about values per se; they have tended to press on almost exclusively to discussions of institutional separateness and structural inequities within plural societies. The gesture has been an important corrective to the earlier view which, in the end, tended to depict the inhabitants of traditional societies and modern subcultures as the victims of their values rather than of their circumstances. At the same time, much of the rigidity implied by the earlier view remains in the concept of pluralism. It is difficult, for example, to escape the temptation of associating social and cultural differences with gross indicators such as race and social class.[16] This is especially true in practical application to policy problems where, for example, racial and ethnic differences are often the important high visibility criteria for the policy decision maker—whereas, in fact, they may not always be the important or the most factual criteria in explaining the distribution of cultural or value orientations in particular circumstances of social conflict.

Pluralism also tends to solidify (in our minds, not necessarily in reality) the sorts of relations we might expect to occur between and among groups, as we can observe in the following quotation from van den Berghe:

> A society is pluralistic to the extent that relations *between* groups are segmental, utilitarian, nonaffective, and functionally specific, and to the extent that relations *within* groups are total, nonutilitarian, affective, and diffuse.[17]

The only way the above statement can be fully accepted is to retreat once again to the notion of a society of atomistic groups steeped in their particular behaviors and values, dependent upon and exploitative of the other, but forever exclusive in most of those aspects of existence which might be said to foster values.

The idea of pluralism extends beyond its analytic context. It is also a potent expression of contemporary politics and governance, a persuasive but still flawed metaphor for the pursuit of equity in human relations and opportunity. The flaw results in part from a tendency for political and legal priorities to become uncritically replicated in the terms of science. Policy analysis is especially vulnerable to this transfer due to its close relation to public sentiment and ideology. What is tempting is to try to make ideological statements "behave" like theoretical or hypothetical statements, which they are not.[18]

The fallout of a gradual departure in United States' domestic policy—from a "melting pot" to a pluralistic standard of public performance—has profited social science and policy analysis. Regardless of the extent to which pluralistic models for decision making have or have not resulted in more effective social programs, it is certain that the variables and standards for measuring and evaluating social change have multiplied, thus increasing the demand for sophisticated social analysis.

Still, despite the benefits of pluralistic thinking, its translation to operational and implementative terms finds pluralism to be as vulnerable to distortions in *practice* as I have argued it to be as a concept. One significant indication of such distortion would be the degree to which pluralistic policies encourage program emphasis to be put on the (often stereotypic) distinctiveness of groups at the expense of a consideration of value and behavior differences within politically defined social groupings, or consideration of similarities between such groups. An aim of policy analysis, which at its best helps mediate the interests of science and politics, ought to be to continually test the effective reach and limits of practical pluralism.[19]

VALUES AND THEIR INTERPRETATION

Anthropology is not alone in having difficulty with the concept of values, or problems in applying the study of values to the analysis of social activity—which would be to link what people do with an explanation of why they are doing it. The social and policy sciences seem to have been driven into a corner from which their practitioners are becoming increasingly content to simply explicate what people do. The rarely discussed assumption in this maneuver is that there must be a reasonably strict correspondence between actual behaviors and the values that are associated with these behaviors: people act in different ways because they have different values. What is left out here, among other things, are those common exceptions whereby people act in *essentially similar ways but on the basis of strikingly different values, or act in dissimilar ways but on the basis of quite similar values.* In other words, there is no convincing evidence (many of our assumptions to the contrary) that behavior is a consistently reliable indicator of values, or vice versa.

If what I have suggested is true, then why study values at all? It is behavior that ultimately matters—actions, not beliefs or values, are the solid indicators of civil unrest and strife and most of whatever else unsettles a society. In this respect, the retreat of much contemporary social inquiry from the study of values to the study of behaviors would seem to make sense; it would seem so, however, at the expense of our awareness that behaviors still invariably exist *in relation* to values and that the only possible explanation (as opposed to description) of an event or social phenomena is one which is basically an interpretation of those values which provide the explanatory key to behavior.

But if specific values do not strictly correspond to specific behaviors, then how can their significance to behaviors be studied? It is as fruitless to study values apart from behavior as it is to study behavior alone. The clue is in the circumstances in which values and behaviors collide.

This is not to say that students of values have up to now totally ignored the real world from which values might be abstracted. Anthropologists, for example, have consistently insisted on maintaining a close connection with the contexts from which they draw their information. The problem lies more in the basic rules or assumptions by which values have normally been interpreted—in the relationships which values are held to have with circumstances. There are at least five major assumptions concerning how values are manifest in society that can be called to question.

The first assumption is that values exist as *systems* prior to and independent of the particular circumstances through which they relate to behaviors. The expectation here is that reasonably orderly value systems exist *in* the cultural patterning of people and groups—implying, among other things, that behaviors could be predicted if we understood the value systems.' I suggest that truly a priori value systems (which would have to include rules as to how to select from conflicting values and how to deal with alien values) exist largely in the heads of those who attempt to analyze values. In turn, I suggest that the systematic nature lies within the circumstances in which they are drawn into play—that values are systematized by circumstance and can be expected to vary with circumstances. Thus, for example, the rules by which conflicting values are selected for or against are primarily rules imposed by the systemic nature of the circumstance, rather than by the workings of a previously existing system of values.

The second assumption which I hold to be misleading is the close association of values with group identity. Unique values and identifiable sets of values certainly do exist in this sense; the problem is one of emphasis, whereby groups (whether they be ethnic minorities, "mainstreamers," special interests, scientists, bureaucrats, or whatever) have come to be the effective domain of almost all our rhetoric concerning values. One difficulty with this approach is that we are, in the main, working with group delineations which have arisen from observations, expectations and stereotypes concerning behaviors, not values. (Even greater problems occur in policy analysis where, beyond the bias toward behavioral definition, we are also faced with delineating the significance of groups on the basis of policy priorities and political criteria.) My suggestion here is that we look again to the historical circumstances in which individuals and groups come together for providing the locus of value study. What we actually study at this level are the processes by which values are exchanged and, in some instances, created. In other words, circumstances increase the repertoire of values beyond those which any individual or group brings to the circumstance. Decisions and behaviors arise out of this mix of values and its increase. "The whole," anthropologists like to say, "is greater than its parts." We might also be prepared for the whole to be significantly different from its parts.

The third assumption is that values are best understood in their normative sense—indeed, in some cases, the concepts of values and norms seem to become indistinguishable.[20] Among anthropologists, this assumption has arisen partly from their devotion to research among relatively small and presumably homogeneous peoples. But the tendency to limit the search for values to the normative (that is, to shared *standards* of behavior) is also common practice outside anthropology and is closely linked to a preference for dealing with values in relation to group identities. My suggestion is that while norms are obviously constituted of values, a collection of normative statements does not adequately describe the mix of values in a complex society, or even in a single complex social situation—that is, in any circumstance where there is a potential for values conflict. Neither are norms necessarily the most significant values for understanding social behaviors; they simply happen to be those which are usually most easily identified because they usually conform to, and often derive from, our perceptions of the value significance of seemingly alien behavior.

I have introduced the fourth assumption at the beginning of this section—this is the assumption that there is a rather strict correspondence between actual values and behavior, implying that specific values signify certain kinds of behaviors. My preference is to suggest that values stand in relation to behavior, but that the translation of values to behavior results only from the circumstances which bring people and their values together. There are several extensions of this reasoning. Different circumstances might give rise to different value-related behaviors on the part of the same individual or group. The people who participate in a particular circumstance are, in turn, a part of the uniqueness of that circumstance. Circumstances not only systematize the preexisting values that are brought to bear on them; they also provide the impetus for creating and introducing new or previously unidentified values, or new ways of selecting from among conflicting values. Most importantly, circumstances permit people to change their minds, a luxury which (were we to take it more seriously as a condition of inquiry) might prove to be near the crux of social behavior.

A final assumption I want to call to question is that of value relativism— the idea that values, which are assumed to arise from particular cultural experiences, can be understood and evaluated only on the basis of that cultural experience. This notion is an important corrective to the ethnocentricity apparent in attempts to evaluate the values of an alien group against a preference for one's own values. Unfortunately, the assumption shares with those above the temptation to reify and gel our sense of both culture and values and leads us dangerously back again to the acceptance of cultures and their "value systems" as closed systems. The interpretation of complex historical circumstances as the source of nearly all significant value expressions, and of present and future circumstances as the creative fodder of altered and new relationships between values and behavior, suggests that values assume meaning largely when they are called into play. This play often occurs as values are placed in jeopardy, when behaviors clash, or when relationships between values and behaviors signal dissonance. Circumstances find whatever resolution they will in that rich territory where the bearers of values struggle with real events and even with their prior selves for such things as respect, gain, reason, and tolerance.

This is too brief a discussion to adequately explore the practical significance of the ways values have and have not been approached in social research. But two observations can be made. The manner in which values have previously been approached as an object of study has not proven very helpful in predicting behavior or promoting effective social change. Dissatisfaction with this state of affairs has led, actually over centuries of inquiry, to an increased emphasis on the study of manifest behaviors (which can be easily observed, categorized and usually counted), and an almost proportional lack of interest in the study of values. As a result, we find ourselves with a surfeit of neat and "clean" data, but very little of the ingredient which might permit us to put it together.

It may be the time for a reexamination of our own circumstances. To some extent, a second look has already begun.[21] One thing seems clear. Science is most likely to progress on those occasions in which scientists are willing to reach into two pots at once—first into the phenomenal world itself, and second into the impositions of their own minds.

THE CULTURES OF SCIENCE AND POLICY

Earlier in this paper I suggested that general science and policy analysis differ in a fundamental way—general science is geared to test assumptions within the domain of scientific knowledge, and the goal of policy analysis is largely to test the effectiveness of given policy assumptions (whether these are tested in the real world or hypothetically is beside the point). The differences between general social science and social policy analysis are primarily differences of authority and criteria of inference; it is a question of who has the right to determine a line of inquiry, and from what base of experience the phenomena of inference are to be identified.

I have also promised to describe a third mode and purpose of inquiry based on the investigation of values in public policy. I consider this an intermediary mode in that its primary aim is to note the effect of science and policy on values—that is, to indicate how the presence of particular kinds of inquiry in a society contribute to the circumstances from which values arise. This is quite a different question from asking how values influence policy and science. What I am suggesting is that the ways in which a society inquires into and tests its intentions are powerful shapers of that society's values. It is important, then, to approach the circumstances of science and policy from the extent to which they form a significant part of the *foreground* of social and cultural process in contemporary complex societies.

We can look to politics as having to do essentially with authority. Science enters politics on the basis of its authority—just as a politician might be elected to and retain office on the basis of his ability to attract a following, command resources, claim respect, keep detractors at bay, and so on. The authority of science is invested in its relation to the policy process and is largely independent of its particular goals, which are related to its claims to discover "facts," generate useful hypotheses, develop theoretical and data-based statements, and in general to solve the problems presented to it. The way the authority of science is invested in the policy process is through its values, in its perceived virtues as opposed to its methods, and in its ability to convince its constituencies that those values are desirable and worthy of support.

It is important to maintain an analytic separation between the authority and goals of science, at least for the purpose of anticipating the onslaught of two likely counter claims. The first is the claim that science's only basis of authority is its goals. This is the purist claim which argues that science progresses solely on the basis of how well it produces what it claims to produce. The second claim is that science is simply the servant of larger societal and cultural tendencies. This is the radical argument which asserts that science derives its authority on the basis of its conspiracy or cooperation with powerful ideologies.

Neither of these claims reasonably afford us the possibility of viewing science and the process of "sciencing" as active stimili to the creation and recreation of what we come to value. Science, whether it is considered to be pure or tainted, is traditionally viewed as being passive and reactive. (A similar claim, of course, exists within the mythology of politics, whereby politicians permit themselves to view their activities as resulting from the "will of the people.")

This is not to deny that science might, in particular instances, accomplish many of its goals; such an argument is simply beside the point as we seek to understand how science actually exhibits and maintains its authority in society. The belief in the assumption that science does reach its goals, and does so in the way prescribed by the rules and norms of doing science, is important in this sense; its demonstration in fact is not. Our question is what happens when science has the opportunity to flex its muscle: when enough people believe they are being informed by science; when science confronts other bases for public authority; when scientists confront each other; and as science becomes a part of the circumstances on which it reflects.

In these respects, policy analysis is more than a mechanical variant of general science. This can be demonstrated to some extent by returning to our earlier considerations of how values and circumstance play on each other.

Policy analysis is possible in our society because enough people who are not professional scientists believe that a scientific approach to problem solving will lead to better decision making. This is a different kind of statement than the usual justification, which implies that policy analysis is a necessary response to societal complexity. A values perspective suggests that particular manifestations of policy analysis are a luxury of societal belief, not a necessity of societal process, and hints again that the values of science probably contribute as much to the complexity of modern society as they do to the resolution of problems arising from that complexity. In effect, the first basis of authority for policy analysis is symbolic: it has a major role to play in the ceremonial processes of a society steeped in scientific values. The activities of policy analysts (besides whatever else they might be or lead to) are in part ritualistic, and their support derives in a significant part from their role in both preserving and asserting those scientific values which we have come to take almost for granted and which appear to be vital to our particular sense of social order and purpose.

An extent to which scientific explanation is valued in our society can be seen in recent arguments in several states concerning the teaching of creationism as an alternative to evolution in public schools. Most positions arguing for the introduction of the concepts and evidence supporting creationism in the public schools are deliberately (albeit carelessly) couched in the terms of science and rest on the argument that creationism is a scientific "theory" above and beyond its acceptance as a belief. Scientific authority is often appealed to, as in the creationist's claim that a good many scientists support their view (and some do). As we observe these and similar debates from a values perspective, we discover that the public value accorded scientific explanation can easily exist well beyond the actual demonstration of its rules of inquiry.

Policy analysis is a public science. The special role of policy analysis (vis-à-vis general science and in relation to society at large) is developed in part from its confrontation with other bases for public authority. The major claim of science to public activity is the belief that the kind of understanding to be derived from scientific investigation contributes to better decision making. Vital to this claim, however, are the transient and mutable values which provide the basis from which we decide what is "better."

Every society struggles with this sort of problem and "better" is variously defined in terms of such explicit criteria as survival, cost effectiveness, efficiency, and equity; as well as implicit criteria serving special class interests, values favoring material or other measures of well-being, and so on. Science is both a victim and participant in this struggle. For example, the effects of science on public decision making have included, in many cases, an appreciable lengthening of the decision making process, trading the value for deliberate and decisive action (which in bureaucratic circles often comes to simply mean *fast* action) against the value for reflective action based on a more comprehensive understanding of the effects of particular actions. Even the widespread acceptance of an empirical base for public decision making is a value derived largely from science.

The values of scientists, as opposed to those of science, have also had significant effects on public decision making. When, for example, United

States archeologists succeeded in their support of legislation which would make the protection of archeological resources an important criterion in the administration of the U.S. National Environmental Protection Act, they did so on the basis of their appeal to the belief that these resources had value, not on a scientific demonstration of that value.

The constraints on science also have considerable effect on public decision making. The social effects of cost-benefit analyses as a mode of decision making can, for example, be argued on the basis of *what* is being measured, which leads us quickly to a consideration of what *can* be measured given an accepted criteria of measurement. The attention given to measurable (or even simply preferred) variables of correlation and clues of causation obviously lead to an emphasis on these variables and hunches in policy research, which lead in turn to their being more highly *valued* not only as acceptable criteria of measurement but eventually as acceptable criteria of human progress. (It has long been fashionable among critics of science to regard this as an error of the scientific approach, which it clearly is not. The error is in how carelessly the products of science are often utilized.)

In the public role, policy analysis confronts the problem of authority and struggles for virtue from the ethics of both discipline and profession. The special interests of science present a paradox here. A healthy scientific discipline requires a critical dimension whereby the values, assumptions and instruments of that discipline are held up to careful and skeptical scrutiny. On the other hand, a scientific profession depends on more than the obvious (or, just as often, not so obvious) merits of its works, but also relies on the confidence of its clientele and, in even more consummate terms, on the *faith* of the public. Disciplines generally thrive on diversity within their ranks while professions tend to seek a united front. The question is sometimes as simple as: how much of his art does a ritual priest divulge to those who rely on his performance?

Science cannot escape its debt to the values of those who practice science; neither can it escape the peril of its humanness. The values which have encouraged scientists to enter the public arena are in turn threatened by their emergence in the public view. One of the great present dilemmas of many policy analysts derives from their growing recognition that the public justification of science rests in large part upon an outmoded and at least partly inappropriate view of the relation of science to society. The kind of thinking and the sorts of values which gave rise more than a century ago to the alluring promise of what was held to be a virtually foolproof escape to *scientific decision making* are now open to several lines of contention, not the least of which arise from a more experienced scientific community. If the public's increased faith in science is to be maintained into the future, it is quite possible that scientists will have to assume an active role in reorienting the values that are normally associated in the public mind with scientific work, acquainting their clientele with the limits as well as the potentials of the craft.

One aspect of this reorientation might have to be to distance science from decision making without severing the relationship. Science certainly can inform judgment, but it cannot replace it. Another important aim will be to publicly acknowledge (indeed, publicize) the manner in which science and scientists struggle along with the rest of the world with issues of values and circumstance. A public science is ultimately built more on trust than mystique, although a little of the latter probably helps.

Neither of these two aims can be accomplished without paying attention to a third—the continued development of a science which is able to view its own tremendous impact on society with continual inquiry, suspicion and occasional good humor. Some of the humor might well derive from the uneasy recognition that, once the investigator agrees to be included in the investigation, he or she begins to understand the sense of unreality and awkwardness others have felt under such scrutiny. Thus might we enter yet another tier of investigation, on the heels of our nervous laughter.

ACKNOWLEDGMENTS

I would like to thank Gilbert Kushner, William Dunn and Debra Schumann for their helpful responses to an earlier version of this essay. I am also grateful to H. Russell Bernard, who has through several discussions helped stimulate my thinking on these topics.

NOTES AND REFERENCES

1. Roy A. Rappaport, *Pigs for the Ancestors: Ritual in the Ecology a New Guinea People* (New Haven, CT: Yale University Press, 1968), pp. 233–37.

2. Stephen Strasser, *Phenomenology and the Human Sciences* (Pittsburgh, PA: Duquense University Press, 1963).

3. This is not an argument against the methodology of the scientific experiment, but rather an attempt to underscore how a single-minded search for simple casual relationships might lead to a distorted view of the phenomena under investigation, and thereby preclude other avenues of inquiry. The same, of course, is true of any approach which limits its view of the terms of the world to the terms of its necessarily restricted epistemology— which includes *any* approach I can imagine, and makes it incredibly important for us to be continually alert to the biases inherent in any encroachment on the phenomenal world.

4. See, for example, George M. Foster, *Applied Anthropology* (Boston, MA: Little, Brown and Company, 1969).

5. Munro S. Edmonson, "The Anthropology of Values," in W. W. Taylor, ed., *Culture and Life* (Carbondale, IL: Southern University Press, 1973), pp. 157–97, does offer a

critique of the work of Clyde Kluckhohn, one of the leading proponents of values study in anthropology.

6. American Indian History Society, *Anthropology and the American Indian* (San Francisco, CA: The Indian Historical Press, 1973).

7. See, for example, Cora DuBois, "The Dominant Value Profile of American Culture," *American Anthropologist*, LVII (December, 1955), pp. 1232–39.

8. See Evon Z. Voget and Ethel M. Albert, *People of Rimrock: A Study of Values in Five Cultures* (Cambridge, MA: Harvard University Press, 1966); Florence R. Kluckhohn and Fred L. Strodtbeck, *Variations in Value Orientations* (Evanston, IL: Row, Peterson and Company, 1961).

9. For a critique, see Charles J. Erasmus, *Man Takes Control* (Minneapolis, MN: University of Minnesota Press, 1961), pp. 309–32.

10. See Oscar Lewis, *La Vida* (New York: Random House, 1968), pp. xlii-lii; for critiques see Charles A. Valentine, *Culture and Poverty* (Chicago: University of Chicago Press, 1968), and Eleanor Burke Leacock, ed., *The Culture of Poverty: A Critique* (New York: Simon and Schuster, 1971).

11. The work of anthropologist Oscar Lewis offers a classic example of this dilemma. Lewis' concept of the "culture of poverty" (*La Vida*, op. cit.) was rooted in the idea that the condition of poverty led to deep-seated value orientations which encouraged their bearers to remain in poverty. Thus phrased, one would expect cycles of poverty, replicated through generations of poverty experience, to be difficult to break. Many policy advisors of the 1960s were attracted to this and similar notions (cf. Nathan Glazer and Daniel Patrick Moynihan, *Beyond the Melting Pot*, Cambridge, MA: The M.I.T. Press, 1963; Edward Banfield, *The Unheavenly City*, Boston, MA: Little, Brown 1970). Poverty-related programs of the period had the tendency to seek a remedy through long-range programs of value change, such as early childhood training. Criticism of Lewis' view (Valentine, *Culture and Poverty*, op. cit.; Leacock, *The Culture of Policy*, op. cit.) stressed structural and political problems as a more appropriate root to the poverty problem, and suggested that values would change rapidly if poor people were simply given the *opportunity* to maintain a reasonable standard of existence. To some extent, policy emphases of the late 1960s and the 1970s reflect these views in their tendency toward programs to end employment discrimination, programs directed to job training, and so on.

12. M. G. Smith, "Social and Cultural Pluralism," in V. Rubin, ed., *Social and Cultural Pluralism in the Caribbean* (New York: Annals of the New York Academy of Sciences 83, 1960), pp. 763–77.

13. Carol B. Stack, *All Our Kin* (New York: Harper & Row, 1974), pp. 124–29.

14. Barbara Luise Margolies, *Princes of the Earth* (Washington, DC: American Anthropological Association, 1975), pp. 140–44.

15. For example, pluralism helps explain some differences between Black and Anglo Americans in the United States, but to my knowledge has not developed the analytic sophistication to help explain such things as the depth of cooperation between Jews and Blacks during the early years of the Civil Rights Movement, or for that matter the cooperation between Blacks and Anglos.

16. Peggy R. Sanday, "Cultural and Structural Pluralism in the United States," In P. R. Sanday, ed., *Anthropology and the Public Interest* (New York: Academic Press, 1976), p. 61.

17. Pierre L. Van den Berghe, "Pluralism," in J. J. Honigmann, ed., *Handbook of Social and Cultural Anthropology* (Chicago: Rand McNally and Company, 1973), p. 966.

18. Subtle aspects of the relationship between ideology and science are explored by Clifford Geertz in his "Ideology As a Cultural System," in which he suggests:

> Where science is the diagnostic, the critical, dimension of culture, ideology is the justificatory, the apologetic one ... That there is a natural tendency for the two to

clash, particularly when they are directed to the interpretation of the same range of situations, is thus clear; but that the clash is inevitable and that the findings of (social) science necessarily will undermine the validity of the beliefs and values that ideology has chosen to defend and propogate seems most dubious assumptions. An attitude at once critical and apologetic toward the same situation is no intrinsic contradiction in terms (however often it may in fact turn out to be an empirical one) but a sign of a certain level of intellectual sophistication. (In *The Interpretation of Cultures*, New York: Basic Books, 1973, p. 231.)

19. A good example of such a test is found in Patricia Lee Engle, "The Language Debate: Education in First or Second Language," in P. R. Sanday, ed., *Anthropology and the Public Interest* (New York: Academic Press, 1976), pp. 247–72.

20. David Bidney, "Normative Culture and the Categories of Value," in D. Bidney, *Theoretical Anthropology* (New York: Schocken, 1967), pp. 400–32.

21. Kenneth Prewitt, President of the Social Science Research Council, has for example, recently called for greater emphasis on values-related research:

to explain behavior, events, structure, and change in a manner that takes full measure of past history and present setting, of human meaning and value, as well as attitudes and behaviors. The social sciences need this capacity to "tell a story," to narrate the meaning of class conflict in Manchester in the 19th century, to unfold the significance of the work ethic in Protestantism to uncover the latent functions of persisting structures. (In "Annual Report of the President," *Social Science Research Council Annual Report*, 1978–1979, p. xxi.)

CLINICAL POLICY ANALYSIS

Baruch Fischhoff

ABSTRACT

An analogy is drawn between policy analysis and the somewhat older profession of psychotherapy. Both offer a variety of techniques designed to help people function in a difficult and uncertain environment; both developed rapidly, sustained by at least moderately coherent underlying theories and anecdotal evidence of having helped some clients. Over the past half century, psychotherapy has faced a series of crises concerned with its transformation from an art to a clinical science. These include testing the effectiveness of various forms of therapy, validating elements of treatment programs and of the assumptions underlying therapy, improving the clinical skills of individual practitioners, and considering the broader political, social, ideological and ethical issues raised by psychotherapy. It is hoped that by considering the issues that a related profession has identified, the approaches it has developed to study those issues, and the (partial) conclusions it has reached, we can facilitate the development of policy analysis.

Policy Analysis: Perspectives, Concepts, and Methods, pages 111–128.
Copyright © 1986 by JAI Press, Inc.
ISBN: 0–89232–371–X

INTRODUCTION

Enormous progress has been made in developing methods, models, and computational aids for policy analysis. These range from "soft" heuristics for judgment and decision making, which make modest claims of being better than nothing, to "hard-boiled" procedures like decision analysis and cost-benefit analysis, which are often accompanied by claims to have characterized and solved the policy makers' problem. Mastery of these procedures occupies a major portion of the aspiring policy analyst's schooling.

When it comes time to apply these tools, however, policy analysts must more or less rely on their own wits. There is no codified body of knowledge telling them when to use formal models and when to rely on intuitive judgments, how to approach decision makers and how to coax from them their true problems, which elicitation methods to use and when to trust their results, which parameters should be subjected to sensitivity analysis and what range of alternative values should be used, how to make certain that the assumptions and conclusions of an analysis are understood and heeded, or when a given method is likely to improve the understanding of a decision problem and when it may cause more trouble than it is worth. Such knowledge as does exist regarding these topics is largely anecdotal. It is acquired by trial and error in the field, perhaps aided by apprenticeship with a veteran practitioner (Polanyi, 1962).

In order for the application of policy analysis methods to progress as rapidly as their theoretical developments, a systematic basis is needed for these practical skills. We need to know what works where and how well in order to evaluate the work of experienced analysts and to guide the professional training of aspiring ones. Creating such a fund of knowledge will require both empirical and theoretical work, the former to validate our techniques and the assumptions underlying them, the latter to understand how, in principle, these tools relate to particular settings. In essence, the application of policy analysis must be transformed from a clinical art to a clinical science.

How does one structure this complex task? The approach adopted here is to examine the patterns that have emerged from a related profession undergoing a similar transformation. The profession chosen is psychotherapy, the broad collection of theories and procedures designed to help people live their lives better. Like policy analysis, these approaches attempt to help clients understand their world, their desires and their options. They acknowledge that indecision and bad decisions are due at least in part to the complexity and constraints of the world in which their clients live and that a precondition for effective action is explicitly facing difficult issues, like uncertainties and motives. Although the clients of policy analysts, if not the analysts themselves, might back off from the analogy with psychotherapy, the similarities between these two "helping" professions seem sufficiently strong to hope that psychotherapy research might provide a preliminary organization of the topics policy analysis must face, as well as some germane substantive results.

The transformation of psychotherapy began some 50 years ago with therapists' realization that they could not satisfy either critics or their own critical sense with evidence like "my clients say it helps them" and "the theory makes intuitive sense to me." Nor were they comfortable with sending their students out into the world with a bag of tricks and the admonition to use them wisely. The tale of their attempts to systematize their realm is not one of unremitting progress. Like other scientific endeavors, it has produced its share of dead ends, misconceptualized issues and misleading results. From the present perspective, one can identify a number of issues that have proved to be both critical and fruitful for psychotherapy and might serve the same role for decision analysis. These are: (a) Does it work? (b) How valid are its assumptions and assessment procedures? (c) How can the personal skills of practitioners be improved? (d) What are the bases of resistance to treatment? (e) How is the effectiveness and appropriateness of the approach limited by the social, political, psychological and ideological world in which the client lives?

DOES IT WORK?

The ideal way to evaluate a technique is through a controlled experimental design. Potential clients would be randomly divided between two groups, one receiving the treatment of interest (policy analysis, psychotherapy), while the other receives no treatment at all or an alternative treatment. In a sophisticated design, the alternative would be a placebo treatment, some form of advice that sounds useful but which should (from the analyst's or therapist's perspective) have no systematic impact on decision-making effectiveness.

It is hard to imagine a situation in which such rigorous control would be possible. For example, both proprietary and ethical considerations might prohibit one from assigning clients to "policy analysis" and "no help" conditions. Moreover, when people really want help and can afford to pay for it, they will typically get something for their money. In such situations, evaluation might still be possible through the use of quasi-experimental designs in which statistical control substitutes for unobtainable experimental control (Campbell and Stanley, 1966; Riecken and Boruch, 1974). Instead of comparing analysis against nothing, one could compare forms of analysis, perhaps characterizing what policy makers do on their own according to the procedures it most closely resembles.

The fact that psychotherapy as a profession worries about evaluating itself is certainly to its credit. Failure to develop an evaluation methodology would have suggested that it had something to hide. The absence of a competent methodology would have left therapists prey to the ad hoc methods used by outside evaluators, who may be muddle-headed and malicious.

However, the existence of a methodology and a commitment to its use does not guarantee the steady accumulation of wisdom. In articles reviewing research on the effectiveness of such diverse treatments as marathon encounter groups, sensitivity training, drug abuse reduction, marriage therapy, and behavior modification for juvenile deliquents, one finds a litany of methodological criticisms: lack of a control group, inappropriate control groups, impressionistic statistical analysis, biased data collection, lack of follow-up observations, failure to check observer reliability, unrepresentative samples, inappropriate outcome measures. Poor methodology often tends to produce results prejudiced against therapies whose efficacy is being tested. Sloppy research increases error variance (noise) and makes it hard to detect differences between groups (Perloff, Perloff and Sussna, 1976). Although most policy analysts may have little interest in the results of studies on marathon encounter groups, these methodological pitfalls are relevant to anyone interested in evaluating analysis.

Psychotherapy researchers have found specific effects that may mask the actual degree of success or failure encountered by a treatment:

1. The fact that practitioners have been trained in a method and claim to be carrying it out is no guarantee that they are. Assessing the fidelity of implementation is crucial for knowing what is being evaluated.
2. A well-designed therapeutic program may fail because of the tenacity of the client's problem or unanticipated and uncontrollable changes in the client's world. Thus "good therapy" does not necessarily imply "good outcome."
3. Many people who apparently benefit from treatment would have improved anyway, due to changes in their life circumstances or outlook. Thus "good outcome" does not necessary imply "good therapy."

4. The success of some treatments may be less due to their substantive, theory-based message and manipulations than to the atmosphere they create. These "nonspecific treatment effects" include suggestion, reduced apprehension, increased self-confidence and heightened attention to the problem.
5. Unsubstantiated evaluations by practitioners are not to be trusted. Even dispassionate clinicians of high integrity may see treatment effects where statistical analysis shows random fluctuations (Jones, Weinrott and Vaught, 1978), a record of past success which is exaggerated (Fischhoff and Beyth, 1975), or proven treatment programs where there are but folklore and bandwagon effects (Schectman, 1977).
6. In some cases, defining a "good outcome" is far from trivial, for example, when one must weigh short-term and long-term well-being.

To draw a few of the possible parallels with policy analysis, some products labeled "policy analysis" hardly rate the name, and the craft should not be judged by their performance. The vicissitudes of life may "reward" well-analyzed decisions with unfortunate outcomes. Nor can it be presumed that everyone who seems to have done well after analysis would have floundered without it; good habits, luck and situational pressures would have "spontaneously" produced some good decisions. Analysis may help a decision maker simply because the analyst's deskside manner helps the decision maker focus attention and resources on the problem, and not because of the specific techniques used and their axiomatic justification. Although it is reassuring to hear clients say that one's efforts help them, such claims are insufficient evidence. It may be obscurant to invoke unmeasurable benefits, like enhanced peace of mind or self-confidence, when one lacks concrete proof of efficacy.

The possibility of treatments not being implemented as their designers intended raises a thorny problem for the evaluator. Obviously, it would be unfair to detract from analysis on the basis of crude, ineffectual analyses done by poorly trained individuals or under severe time constraints. Or would it? If the treatment "package" cannot be employed regularly by most practitioners, there is little point to it. If only a selected few can master the craft and the masters do little to monitor those acting in the craft's name, then its usefulness is limited. Its role is further limited if the experience is so unpleasant or expensive that few clients ever get the full treatment. A program with a relatively high drop-out rate but great success with those who complete it will not be highly regarded, particularly when one considers that people who stay in treatment are those most susceptible to persuasive messages of any kind (Bandura,

1969). Since all the resources (computer time, analyst fees, decision-makers' attention) needed for a full, proper analysis will seldom be available, a critical evaluation question becomes: Does analysis degrade gracefully? A partial analysis is obviously not as good as a full-blown one, but is it better than none at all?

No clear overview of the current state of analysis now exists. Such an overview might, however, be achieved by reviewing a random sample of recent analyses and subjecting them to questions like those in Table 1. If the reviewer has opinions about the quality of the analyses or the competence of the analysts, such judgments can be related to these criteria to see what good reports contain and what good analysts do.

Watson and Brown (1978) have pioneered an alternative, reflexive evaluation strategy using analysis to analyze past analyses. Perhaps foretelling the difficulties awaiting such efforts, in two of the three case studies chosen by Watson and Brown (1975), the greatest benefits of the

Table 1.   Criteria for Analyzing Analyses

Are the assumptions of the analysts listed?

Are the assumptions of the clients listed (e.g., those implicit in the way the problem was formulated)?

Are any of these assumptions tested, or is supporting evidence from other sources cited?

Are probabilities used? If so, is any justification given for the particular procedure by which they are elicited?

Are probabilities or utilities measured in more than one way?

Are values elicited from more than one person?

Are sensitivity analyses conducted, for probabilities, for utilities, with more than one factor varying at once?

Are interactions between impacts considered?

Is more than one problem structure used as a cross check?

Are possible alternatives given by the client or created with the client?

Are gaps in scientific knowledge noted?

Is a bottom line figure given, and if so, how is it hedged?

Is the public involved, and if so, at what stage?

Is there consideration of political feasibility or legal constraints?

Is there external criticism of the report, and if so, has the analysis been redone in its light?

Is there indication of when the analysis should be redone to consider possible changes of circumstance?

Is an attempt made to evaluate the analysis or to indicate how interested parties might do so on their own?

How much did the analysis cost?

---

analyses seemed to come not from the decisions they recommended, but from their contribution to organizational processes (reduction of controversy and improvement of communication), considerations left out of Watson and Brown's formal model for the sake of simplicity.

HOW VALID ARE ITS ASSUMPTIONS AND ASSESSMENT PROCEDURES?

When technical difficulties preclude validating entire treatment programs, one may still be able to assess the validity of the theoretical assumptions upon which the programs are based and the effectiveness of their component techniques. Such research can also point to what the treatment's strengths are and how they can be improved. In the context of pscyhotherapy, the most valuable results have emerged from attempts to test previously unquestioned theoretical assumptions, e.g., stable personality traits exist; feedback facilitates learning; psychopathology is related to unconscious libidinal and aggressive wishes; self-awareness is necessary for improvement.

As might be expected, the divide-and-conquer approach to evaluation has appealed to some students of policy analysis. For example, decision analysts (or their critics) have tested whether people accept the normative assumptions upon which the technique is based, finding (with varying degrees of definitiveness) that people often do not wish to accept Savage's independence axion (Slovic and Tversky, 1974), that people occasionally want their judgments to be intransitive (Tversky, 1969), and that people may not know whether they are risk prone or risk averse vis-à-vis particular problems (Fischhoff, Slovic and Lichtenstein, 1980; Tversky and Kahneman, 1981). Much less is known about the appropriateness of other assumptions: Are probability and utility judgments independent? Can we acceptably resolve inconsistencies in people's preferences due to theoretically irrelevant differences in elicitation procedure? Will people reply honestly to our questions about their values and, if not, can we spot their lies or "strategic responses?" Is it possible for the analyst to act as a neutral agent when eliciting judgments (Fischhoff, Slovic and Lichtenstein, 1980, Fischhoff, Slovic, Lichtenstein, Derby and Keeney, 1981).

The development of assessment procedures has long been a growth industry in psychotherapy. With the possibility of measuring every feasible personality and behavioral trait, psychologists produce over 3000 books, chapters and journal articles on assessment per year (Goldberg, 1974). Unfortunately, there is no generally accepted characterization of the universe of traits and the relationship between seemingly similar traits (e.g., honesty and straightforwardness). As a result, it is difficult to know what conclusions to make from comparisons between studies.

By contrast, analysts are primarily interested in the assessment of two fairly well-defined quantities, beliefs, and values, perhaps operationalized as probabilities and utilities. Although the quantity of research here is perhaps one percent of that in personality assessment, the cumulative progress is probably greater. We know quite a lot about probabilities (e.g., they tend to reflect overconfidence, although their validity depends heavily on context; Lichtenstein, Fischhoff and Phillips, 1982). Somewhat less is known about eliciting values, although studies (Fischer, 1976; Vertinsky and Wong, 1975) that compare a variety of methods using evaluative criteria drawn from the sophisticated methodology of psychometricians show great promise. Relatively little is known about another topic which could be considered an assessment problem: determining the structure of a decision maker's problem (Merkhofer, Robinson and Korsan, 1979).

Psychometricians have discovered two threats to the generality of assessment procedures that should concern analysts. One is that the people's feelings about a particular object and the numbers they assign to those feelings can vary greatly with arbitrary features of the elicitation procedure, such as the order in which alternatives are presented, the heterogeneity of the set of alternatives, the contrast established between the first two alternatives, whether the response scale is bounded, and the respondents' preconceptions about how the numbers are supposed to be used (Fischhoff, Slovic and Lichtenstein, 1980; Poulton, 1968, 1977). The second threat is that it is not tests but responses which have validities and reliabilities. Thus, the adequacy of an elicitation procedure in one context with one particular set of individuals is not a guarantee of universal applicability.

Once we understand the flaws of our assumptions and procedures, we need an error theory to tell us what their cumulative impact is. As Fischer (1976) notes, without an error theory, we cannot know to what extent violations of assumptions and lack of robustness in responses threaten the results of an analysis. Important steps toward developing such a theory (or theories) are:

1. Fischer's (1976) work with multidimensional utility models.
2. von Winterfeldt and Edwards' (1982) finding that with continuous decision options (e.g., invest X dollars) some inaccuracy in individual probabilty and utility assessments will not produce terribly suboptimal decisions.
3. Lichtenstein et al.'s (1982) demonstration of how moderate mis-

calibration in probability assessment can substantially reduce expected utility with discrete options (e.g., operate/do not operate).

4. von Winterfeldt and Edwards' (1975) identification of the ease
   with which dominated alternatives can be selected through improper problem modeling.
5. Aschenbrenner and Kasubek's (1977) finding that two different,
   only partially overlapping, sets of attributes produced similar results in a multiattribute utility analysis.
6. Kastenberg, McKone and Okrent's (1976) discovery of the extreme sensitivity of risk assessments to the treatment of outliers.
7. Tihansky's (1976) finding that errors in different estimates were
   positively correlated and, therefore, would not tend to cancel one
   another out.

These are but pieces of an error theory. Particularly useful additions
would be guidelines to the way in which uncertainty from varying sources
(people not knowing what they want, people being affected by choice
of questioning procedure, people being confused by instructions, random error, etc) is compounded. Until an adequate theory is developed,
we will have to be very generous in performing sensitivity analyses for
errors arising from judgmental sources.

HOW CAN CLINICAL SKILLS BE IMPROVED?

However powerful their measures and theories may be, clinicians realize
that in the last analysis, they, themselves, are their own major tool. They
must instill confidence in clients, choose the appropriate questioning
procedures to elicit sensitive information, handle crises, understand what
is not being said, avoid imposing their own values and perceptions, and
cooperate in creating solutions. To this end, clinical psychologists receive
3–4 years of supervised practice, psychiatrists spend 1–2 years in in-
ternship, and psychoanalysts undergo 4–8 years of psychoanalysis to be
fully aware of how they see and interact with others.

Such training assumes that the finer points of the craft can be learned
only in the clinic of a master. To expedite this training, many researchers
are attempting to discover just what it is that makes masters. Since these
studies consider the interaction between therapists and clients with serious personal problems, one should use caution in drawing inferences
regarding the interactions between policy analysts and corporate executives or government officials. One result that seems likely to generalize
from the psychotherapeutic context is the extent to which one individual
can shape another's responses by such subtle measures as appreciative

grunts and nonverbal communication (posture, facial expressions, etc.). One can readily imagine an analyst subtly pressuring a client to change a probability assessment to a value the analyst believes to be more acceptable (analyst seems displeased; client thinks, "Well, you're the expert on probabilities. Maybe what I meant was . . .") or an analyst and client "agreeing" that the latter's preferences on different attributes are really independent, making the elicitation procedure considerably less arduous. Slovic and Tversky (1974) showed how direct pressure can induce clients to accept normative principles. Further possibilities for influencing judgments emerge when the analyst works with groups. For example, the fact that group discussions tend to polarize opinions (Myers and Lamm, 1975) suggests that the analyst can exert some control over the group's decision by deciding if and when the group should meet. Plott and Levine (1978) demonstrated the extent to which group decisions can be manipulated by varying the order in which issues are considered. These effects must be understood if the analyst is to restrain, control, or exploit them.

In general, however, we have little concrete evidence regarding clinical skills in analysis and their improvement. One place to start would be a taxonomy of decision situations indicating which techniques to use where. Several such guides have been derived from formal properties of the decision situation (e.g., Emelyanov and Ozernoi, 1975; Fischhoff, 1984; Keeney and Raiffa, 1972; Pearce, 1976). Additional efforts might look at more subjective aspects: the public visibility of the issue at hand; how articulated people's values are; how much freedom the analyst and decision maker have to construct alternatives; and whether any evaluation of the analysis is planned. Such a guide should tell us, among other things: When, in order to avoid misplaced precision, should all resources be invested in problem structuring and none in attaching numbers? Can high-priced analysts be replaced by paraprofessionals? When is it advisable to acknowledge the poorly developed nature of people's preferences and the limits on their information-processing abilities and to sacrifice axiomatic rigor for less demanding procedures (Edwards, 1977)? Psychological theories have been likened to box cameras, which take pretty good pictures because they require subjects to be at a great distance, in the sun and immobile (Zuniga, 1975); is the same true of policy analysis?

WHAT CAUSES RESISTANCE TO TREATMENT?

Resistance to treatment takes many forms, all threatening its success. The client may reject the approach because it is not expected to work, because its procedures (e.g., talking openly about sensitive matters) are threatening, because it is too expensive, because of objections to its underlying philosophy, or because of reluctance to admit that there is a problem. The client who accepts the approach may resist its recommendations because they require assuming too much responsibility for a situation, because it seems easier to stumble along than to undertake the needed action, or because the analysis mandates acknowledging one's own fallibility, desires, and uncertainties.

Even if the client is willing and able to adopt the approach and its directives, treatment may fail when the time comes to implement it in a hostile, unaccepting world. Classic failures of this type have been encountered by the T-group (or organizational development) movement, which tries to improve communication in a work setting by involving some workers and managers in intensive group experiences stressing openness and sensitivity. All too often, however, the behavioral changes induced by the pressure of the group situation and the manipulation of the group leader vanish when group members return to their hierarchic work settings. Although one might argue that it is not the client but the client's world that is "sick" and in need of help, the result is still a frustrating failure likely to reinforce old, bad habits.

Variants of all these problems seem possible with policy analysis, particularly when it is first introduced into organizations accustomed to less rigorous methods. In such contexts, its greatest potential advantages may prove to be stumbling blocks. Analysis typically requires explicit statement of problems. This, however, may produce great discomfort. Its computational procedures greatly relieve the decision-maker's mental load; however, for those unfamiliar with its logic, its recommendations may appear to be the output of numerical mumbo-jumbo with no intuitive appeal. Even when procedures' logic is theoretically grounded, as with decision analysis or cost-benefit analysis, for uninitiated superiors, subordinates, and constituents, abandoning the comfortable old maxims (e.g., "This is the way we've always done it") may come quite hard.

Resistance within the organization may come from people who feel that they have not been involved early enough and completely enough in the analysis. Like staunch believers in due process by law, they may believe that the decision-making process is more important than its product. Others may resist because they do not like the resultant recommendation. To achieve their ends, they may fight hard and dirty, questioning every fact and assumption in the analysis and casting aspersions on the integrity of its analysts, however well the analysis is done and however much its conclusions are qualified (Barrager, Judd and North, 1976; Fischhoff, Slovic, Lichtenstein, Derby and Keeney, 1981). Analysts who believe in their work may face an uncomfortable choice between orphaning their analyses and adopting an advocacy role for the analysis and, thereby, for the recommended alternative.

Some of these problems are due to the fact that the idea of systematic policy analysis is as new as some of the problems to which it is applied. As a result, the social forms needed to incorporate it are either missing or in a state of flux (Wichelman, 1976). Westman (1977), for example, complains that the legal mandate given regulators entrusted with improving U.S. water quality precludes their adopting the most cost-effective methods. Often projects are held up so long and altered so extensively in legal and administrative proceedings that their accompanying analyses become antiquated. Majone (1976) has argued persuasively that alternatives are almost never adopted as proposed; rather, they are subject to continuous negotiation and alteration by the parties concerned.

Acknowledgment of these difficulties might lead to redirection of an analysis. Brown (1975) proposes that analysts treat action options as events and directly assess the uncertainty surrounding the form in which they will be realized. The preferred alternative might turn out to be one with dominated consequences but a better chance of being implemented. Another response would be for analysts to decide that feasibility is both a relative and mutable thing and append to each alternative a discussion of how it is likely to be waylaid en route to implementation and what needs to be done to keep it maximally intact.

In the long run, though, the adaptation should be mutual, with society and its component entities realizing the need to accommodate formal procedures. Toward this end, the educational potential of each analysis should be exploited. Broad participation should be viewed as an opportunity, not a burden. In some ways, it may be more important to build the analytic capacity of a society or organization than to guarantee the adoption of particular, desirable alternatives.

HOW DO POLITICS, IDEOLOGY AND ETHICS IMPINGE UPON ANALYSIS?

Attempts to shape and direct others' lives cannot be value neutral. The practitioner who is "only trying to help" has at least made the evaluation that there is a situation needing help. The practitioner who is "only trying to do what is best for the client" cannot avoid at least some subtle hints at what that "best" is. Even client-centered therapists, whose goal is to reflect and clarify their clients' own thoughts, are still promulgating the world view that people are responsible for their own predicaments and can extricate themselves if they understand themselves sufficiently well. Indeed, the very search for lasting solution to problems implies that the client's universe has more orderliness than may be the case.

The ideological biases of many therapeutic interventions are familiar intellectual topics: the mechanistic image of people projected by behaviorism and its potential for control, the ethnocentrism of psychoanalysis, the narcissism of many contemporary therapies, the general tendency to treat clients as objects rather than colleagues in therapy, and the fatalism induced by approaches that teach people to accept their own life crises as inevitable.

Even when a therapy's philosophical basis is acceptable, it may be resisted because of ethical problems or political bias in the way it is used. Much opposition to behavior modification arose from its use in institutional settings (prisons, asylums) in which free, informed consent for treatment by the patient is impossible. A frequent problem for practitioners is determining who the true client is, the patient or someone else (e.g., a hospital administrator) interested in maintaining order. Other therapies have lost their credibility because therapists have become so dependent upon government and the politically powerful for their livelihood that they have lost the ability to make independent criticism, others because they can be afforded only by the rich, still others because they seem to be applied mainly to coerce the poor.

At first blush, the image of people and society fostered by most policy analysis seems to be a highly flattering one. With proper coaching, people are cable of understanding and expressing what they know and what they want. Acknowledging their own information-processing limitations, people will prefer to have their values and beliefs combined by some mechanical scheme and then will take seriously the resultant recommendation.

There may, however, be problems with this seemingly innocuous perspective. One is that it may create an illusion of analyzability for problems that are insoluble, contributing to the mystique of science and "technical fixes." Because it asks us about everything important, it may lead us to believe that we have and should have beliefs and opinions about everything. We may be forced, for the sake of answering the analyst, to create preferences that are only superficially understood. Forcing people to have (necessarily shallow) opinions about many things may be an excellent way to guarantee that they have articulated views about nothing. Persistent questioning about poorly formulated beliefs may lead to responses designed to make the elicitor happy and to overreliance on easily measured and justified standards such as monetary values.

In the public domain, the very reasonableness of policy analysis is based upon a political-ideological assumption: that society is sufficiently cohesive that its problems can be resolved by reason and without struggle. Although this "get on with business" orientation will be pleasing to many, it will not satisfy all. For those who do not believe that society is in a fine-tuning stage, any technique that fails to mobilize public consciousness and involvement has little to recommend it.

Like therapy, if analysis is not biased at its core it can be biased in its application. For example, most applications to societal problems seem to foster the transfer of decision-making power to a technical elite by offering little opportunity for effective citizen participation (Sewell and O'Riordan, 1976). Although this trend seems inevitable due to the highly technical nature of the issues studied, in principle, it might be countered by a concerted effort by analysts to go beyond the narrow dictates of their analytical mandate. The theoretical problems of aggregating group opinions need not forestall efforts to elicit them. To take another example, most analyses ignore the issue of equitable distribution of good and bad consequences. Although this is not a necessary feature of policy analysis, repeated omission of equity considerations will suggest a lack of interest in such issues, or even evasiveness, on the part of analysts and those who hire them.

When analytic resources are limited, the analyst must take cues from someone about how to restrict the alternatives and consequences considered. That someone is likely to be the one who commissioned the study. If commissioners come consistently from one sector of society and consistently prefer (or reject out of hand) particular kinds of solutions or consequences, a persistent bias may be produced. Such bias would also determine what issues are never analyzed and how results are presented. If the commissioners are public officials, there may be a predisposition toward reports that bury uncertainties and delicate assumptions in sophisticated technical machinations and masses of undigested data (Fischhoff, 1977).

Psychotherapy's response to charges of ideological bias has been fairly minimal, with the most dramatic proposals within the profession being to encourage truth-in-packaging (e.g., providing potential clients with a description of the assumptions and procedures of an approach). Its response to charges of improprieties in therapeutic interactions has been more extreme. Clinical psychologists, for example, have organized as a guild with rigorous standards for entry, state and national licensing, censure mechanisms (albeit not often used), external review of research proposals and papers, and a strict code of ethics. That code addresses issues like recognizing and acknowledging the limits to one's competence, protecting clients' confidentiality and policing one's colleagues (American Psychological Association, 1977).

Whether a guild structure is needed or appropriate for policy analysis is a moot point. Certainly, all that calls itself policy analysis does not glitter. However, the costs of controlling incompetent analysts might be substantial, draining the efforts of qualified analysts, discrediting the profession by unrepresentative public quibbling and raising prices through restraint of trade. Perhaps more modest steps might be appropriate, if any are needed at all:

1. Setting up a "public interest policy analysis group" similar to that set up by the largest accounting firms in the United States in order to "give accounting away."
2. Insisting that some fixed amount of funds (say, 10 percent) in all analysis contracts be allocated to independent external review, following the lead of a National Research Council (1982) Panel recommending practices for the survey research industry.
3. Establishing a professional norm of participating in voluntary review networks.
4. Teaching students to conduct and document enough sensitivity analyses to satisfy a report's most skeptical critics.
5. Adopting informal guidelines like those proposed by Fairley (1977) for experts called upon to assess probabilities of rare accidents.

Because it functions in the public domain, as well as in the private sector, policy analysis faces ethical dilemmas at least as challenging as those faced by psychotherapy. For example, the American Psychological Association's ethics committee (American Psychological Association, 1977) was unable to agree on how to revise their standards regarding confidentiality (leaving them unchanged from 1964) even without having to consider (as the analyst might) the additional problems of what to do with proprietary information or information that could cause public panic if released. Therapists may find themselves forced to treat a delinquent when they should be treating the family. Similarly, analysts may get well into a problem before realizing that the wrong problem has been attacked, or that the wrong information has been provided, or that they are being set up to produce an advocacy rather than an honest analysis. Therapists often face the problem of how to assure informed consent by psychologically incompetent clients, whereas analysts are often asked to pursue their craft on behalf of clients, perhaps a whole society, judged by someone to be technically incompetent.

CONCLUSION

The analyst's job is extremely difficult. Confronting the issues raised above will make it even more difficult. However, the fact that they can be explicitly identified is in some sense a tribute to the clarity and comprehensiveness of the best forms of analysis and its potential for development. As a result, I believe that efforts to implement a research program exploring these problems in the context of policy analysis would be rewarding. Some of these issues have obvious pecuniary importance for the long-term prosperity of the field and its practitioners (e.g., proving its effectiveness and buttressing its foundations). Others, such as examining ideological and ethical questions, will be intellectually stimulating. Still others, though, will seem like exercises in validating what common sense knows to be true (e.g., that there is more to decision analysis than putting on a good act). However, study of even these issues may have merit, for common sense may be superficial or wrong, and may vary across individuals, as psychotherapy's concerted effort to test and refine common sense has shown. Furthermore, examining the obvious can help convince others that we are right, improve our confidence in (and willingness to act upon) our knowledge, and help us learn why we were right all along.

ACKNOWLEDGMENT

An earlier version of this paper appeared as "Clinical Decision Analysis," *Operations Research* 28 (1980):28–43.

REFERENCES

American Psychological Association (1977) "Revised ethical standards for psychologists." APA Monitor 8:22–23.

Aschenbrenner, K. M. and W. Kasubek (1977) "Convergence of multiattribute evaluations when different sets of attributes are used." In H. Jungermann and G. deZeeuw (eds.), Decision Making and Change in Human Affairs. Amsterdam: D. Reidel.

Bandura, A. (1969) Principles of Behavior Modification. New York: Holt, Rinehart and Winston.

Barrager, S. M., B. R. Judd and D. W. North (1976) "Decision analysis of energy alternatives: a comprehensive framework for decision making." Palo Alto, CA: Stanford Research Institute.

Brown, R. V. (1975) "Modeling subsequent acts for decision analysis." Decisions and Designs, Inc. Technical Report 75–1, MacLean, VA.

Campbell, D. T. and J. C. Stanley (1966) "Experimental and quasi-experimental designs for research in teaching." In N. L. Gage (ed.), Handbook of Research on Teaching. Chicago: Rand McNally.

Edwards, W. (1977) "How to use multi-attribute utility measurement for social decision making." IEEE Trans. Systems Man and Cybernetics 7:326–340.

Emelyanov, S. V. and V. M. Ozernoi (1975) "Decision making in multi-objective problems: a survey." Problems of Control and Information Theory:51–64.

Fairley, W. B. (1977) "Evaluating the 'small' probability of a catastrophic accident from the marine transportation of liquified natural gas." In W. B. Fairley and F. Mosteller (eds.), Statistics and Public Policy. Reading, MA: Addison-Wesley.

Fischer, G. W. (1976) "Multidimensional utility models for risky and riskless choice." Organizational Behavior and Human Performance 17:127–146.

Fischhoff, B. (1977) "Cost-benefit analysis and the art of motorcycle maintenance." Policy Science 8:177–202.

———(1984) "Setting standards: a systematic approach to managing public health and safety standards." Management Science 30:823–843.

Fischhoff, B. and R. Beyth (1975) "I knew it would happen: remembered probabilities of once-future things." Organizational Behavior and Human Performance 13:1–16.

Fischhoff, B., P. Slovic and S. Lichtenstein (1980) "Knowing what you want: measuring labile values." In T. Wallsten (ed.), Cognitive Processes in Choice and Decision Behavior. Hillsdale, NJ: Erlbaum.

Fischhoff, B., P. Slovic, S. Lichtenstein, S. Derby and R. Keeney (1981) Acceptable Risk. New York: Cambridge University Press.

Goldberg, L. R. (1974) "Objective diagnostic tests and measures." Annual Review of Psychology 25:343–366.

Jones, R. R., M. Weinrott and R. S. Vaught (1978) "Effects of serial dependency on the agreement between visual and statistical inference." Journal of Applied Behavior Analysis 11:277–283.

Kastenberg, W. E., T. E. McKone and D. Okrent (1976) "On risk assessment in the absence of complete data." UCLA Report No. UCLA-ENG-7677 (July).

Keeney, R. and H. Raiffa (1972) "A critique of formal analysis in public decision making." In A. W. Drake, R. L. Keeney and P. M. Morse (eds.), Analysis of Public Systems. Cambridge, MA: MIT Press.

Lichtenstein, S., B. Fischhoff and L. D. Phillips (1982) "Calibration of probabilities: the state of the art to 1980." In D. Kahneman, P. Slovic and A. Tversky (eds.), Judgment under Uncertainty: Heuristics and Biases. New York: Cambridge University Press.

Majone, G. (1976) "Choice among policy instruments for pollution control." Policy Analysis 7:589–613.

Merkhofer, W. M., B. E. Robinson and R. J. Korsan (1979) A Computer-Aided Decision Structuring Process. Menlo Park, CA: SRI International.

Myers, D. G. and H. Lamm (1975) "The polarizing effect of group discussions." American Scientist 63:297–303.

National Research Council (1982) Survey Measure of Subjective Phenomena. Washington, DC: The Council.

Pearce, D. (1976) "The limits of cost-benefit analysis as a guide to environmental policy." Kyklos 29:97–112.

Perloff, R., E. Perloff and E. Sussna (1976) "Program evaluation." Annual Review of Psychology 27:569–594.

Plott, C. R. and M. E. Levine (1978) "A model of agenda influence on committee decisions." American Economic Review 68:146–160.

Polanyi, M. (1962) Personal Knowledge. London: Routledge and Kegan Paul.

Poulton, E. C. (1968) "The new psychophysics: six models for magnitude estimation." Psychological Bulletin 69:1–19.

———(1977) "Quantitative subjective judgements are almost always biased, sometimes completely misleading." British Journal of Psychology 68:409–425.

Riecken, H. W. and R. F. Boruch (1974) Social Experimentation: A Method For Planning and Evaluating Social Intervention. New York: Academic Press.

Schectman, F. (1977) "Convention and contemporary approaches to psychotherapy." American Psychologist 32:197–204.

Sewell, W. R. D. and T. O'Riordan (1976) "The culture of participation in environmental decision making." Natural Resources Journal 16:1–21.

Slovic, P. and A. Tversky (1974) "Who accepts Savage's axiom?" Behavioral Science 19:368–373.

Tihansky, D. (1976) "Confidence assessment of military air frame cost predictions." Operations Research 24:26–43.

Tversky, A. (1969) "Intransitivity of preferences." Psychological Review 76:31–48.

Tversky, A. and D. Kahneman (1981) "The framing of decisions and the psychology of choice." Science 211:453–458.

Vertinsky, I. and E. Wong (1975) "Eliciting preferences and the construction of indifference maps: a comparative empirical evaluation of two measurement methodologies." Socio-Economic Planning Science 9:15–24.

von Winterfeldt, D. and W. Edwards (1975) "Error in decision analysis: how to create the possibility of large losses by using dominated strategies." University of Southern California, Social Science Research Institute, Los Angeles, CA, SSRI Research Report 75–4.

————(1982) "Cost and payoffs in perceptual research." Psychological Bulletin 91:609–622.

Watson, S. R. and R. V. Brown (1975) "Issues in the value of decision analysis." McLean, VA: Decisions and Designs, Inc. Technical Report 75–10.

————(1978) "The valuation of decision analysis." Journal of the Royal Statistical Society, Series A 141:69–78.

Westman, W. E. "Problems in implementing U.S. water quality goals." American Scientist 65:197–203.

Wichelman, A. F. (1976) "Administrative agency implementation of the NEPA of 1969: a conceptual framework for explaining differential response." Natural Resources Journal 16:263–300.

Zuniga, R. B. (1975) "The experimenting society and radical social reform." American Psychologist 30:99–115.

PART II

CONCEPTS

DEMOCRATIC INFORMATION SYSTEMS:
POLICY INDICATORS AND PUBLIC STATISTICS

Duncan MacRae, Jr.

ABSTRACT

The values embodied in policy indicators as one form of public statistics are notions of the common good or equity. They vary from specific to general and from partial to more inclusive, with general intrinsic values (end-values) as central ingredients of a policy-indicator system. If general end-values can be measured and used in public debate, they can facilitate the trade-offs and reconciliation of values that democratic political processes must make. Indicators of such values, and policy models suggesting manipulable causes, must be intelligible to the public.

INTRODUCTION

Political communities—nations, states, cities, and other decision units—need information to aid their collective decisions. An important contribution toward meeting this need is the design of systems of public statistics, available to the public from governmental and other sources, and

Policy Analysis: Perspectives, Concepts, and Methods, pages 131–168.
Copyright © 1986 by JAI Press, Inc.
All rights of reproduction in any form reserved.
ISBN: 0–89232–371–X

including social, economic, and environmental information. In this design process, we must choose[1] concepts, measures of them, and modes of presentation in view of their usefulness and of the costs involved.

These choices require as explicit as possible a consideration of the potential uses of the statistics in guiding action, and of the values that these uses will serve. Some of these values are matters of private taste or demand, as in the case of most market purchases, and do not require justification by the actor to other persons. In contrast, "ethical" values, involving notions of rightness or of the good, can be used in justifying one's acts to others. Ethical justifications are especially important in democratic regimes where public debate influences policy choices. Some ethical values involve notions of the general welfare or public interest, as well as of equity, and play a distinctive part in the justifications we offer for proposed policies in public debate. Such justification is more likely when the actor claims that a policy will benefit others rather than himself alone.

The public statistics with which we are concerned overlap with the field of "social indicators." As this latter field has developed during the past two decades, definitions of it have been ambiguous (E. S. Dunn, 1974:103), diverse (Carley, 1981:Ch. 2), and changing. One early proposal was that social indicators be statistics "of direct normative interest," i.e., that they measure values relating to the good of the society or political community generally. An indicator statistic was expected to be chosen "such that, if it changes in the right direction, people are 'better off' " (HEW, 1969:97); examples are statistics concerning health, education, and public safety. Time series of such statistics have been published in social reports, census publications, and elsewhere, and are often used in public policy debates.

Although many of the variables used as bases for these statistics, reflecting areas of public concern, are still extensively used in current research on social indicators in the United States, this normative justification for them has become less frequent. Writers on social indicators have increasingly contended that these statistics have little direct relation to policy choice or evaluation. Researchers in this field, especially sociologists, have instead emphasized the criteria of scientific research: that the variables in social indicator series be reliably measured over time and that they enter into theoretical models of social change (Sheldon and Parke, 1975:696–97).

These two domains—public statistics relevant to policy choice, and social indicators relevant to models of social change—are logically distinct in spite of their overlap in content. The normative domain, with which I am concerned here, requires a clearer definition and rationale that it can receive if mingled with the purely scientific under a common title. I thus propose that we deal separately with a domain of "policy indicators,"[2] which differs from that of social indicators centered on social change in several ways:

a. Its nature and use are principally defined by the values in terms of which its policy uses are justified; scientific methods and theories are important but secondary considerations. The generation of information in this domain is not considered a mere adjunct of basic research, which is then to be "applied"; rather, the choice of variables and the development of relevant models centers about the practical needs of policy choice within a political system. These models may overlap with models of social change and draw on contributions from basic science, but they center about possible policy intervention rather than the explanation of social change. Land (1975:20–21, 33) has defined a related domain of "social policy models," closely related to "social indicator models" developed through basic scientific research; but we shall distinguish more sharply between the needs of policy and of basic scientific research.

b. We consider an "indicator" to be a measure of a concept, usually characterizing individuals, in distinction from a statistic based on such a measure. Thus the presence of a disease in an individual is a concept related to health; a record of a case of a disease, a health indicator; and an aggregate count of such records for a population, a health indicator statistic for that population. This distinction is necessary in order to draw together the concepts and measures used in reporting, on one hand, with those used in policy analysis and choice, on the other; the same concepts and measures can fruitfully be used in both, though often applied to distinct populations and analyzed with different methods. An "indicator" is then defined as a measure justifiably used as a basis for public statistics, but it can also be used in relevant analyses of special populations for the study of causation.

c. It does not emphasize the distinction between "social" and "economic" as the social indicators movement has done; rather, it includes in a common framework any useful measures of human conditions and related variables whether derived from economics, other social sciences, natural science, or sources outside basic disciplines. We thus use the term *policy indicator* without the qualifier "social," to refer to a measure justifiably used in a public statistical system to aid policy judgments made in view of ethical values.

Because the subject matter of "policy indicators" is not simply the social system under observation, but the provision of information to the members of a political system, we must broaden the scope of "policy indicators" to consider various sorts of political systems and ways of providing information. Thus for the most general definition of this field we should not restrict it to national statistics but should treat sub- (and possibly supra-) national systems. It can thus also extend to organizations and non-democratic systems, so as to permit comparison with the information systems of management and of centralized planning. Moreover, the information it provides need not be disseminated through published social reports issued at intervals of a year or more, but can involve other intervals of observation and methods of dissemination (e.g., weekly information disseminated through computer data facilities). Though we cannot treat these dimensions of variation in detail here, they illustrate the scope of the field.

My aim here is to show how the development of this domain of statistical information, centered about anticipated use and guided by public values, would lead us in different directions from the currently dominant (United States) approach to social indicators as regards the choice of concepts and indicators, the dissemination of information based on them, and related research.

TYPES OF ACTION AND OF INFORMATION USE

The distinctive feature of policy indicators (as defined here) is that they are useful for collective decisions aimed at the general welfare or equity. This is by no means the only way in which public statistics are used. They are in fact used for several different sorts of purposes, all of which are relevant to the planning of an entire statistical system, but only some of which relate to policy indicators. The types of action that may be aided by this information differ from one another as regards who ultimately decides (Is the actor acting alone or participating in a collective decision?)[3] and as regards the motive for action (Is it done in private self-interest, or for ethical reasons?). If the actor *claims* to be seeking the public interest, his need for statistics in justification will be much the same regardless of whether the claim is sincere or hypocritical.[4] Diverse notions of the public interest will call for diverse sorts of statistics, but at this point we group them together.

On these bases we distinguish four types of action as shown in Table 1. We shall discuss cells a, b, c, and d in turn; the last of these will correspond to "policy indicators."

a.   Information may be used in private market or nonmarket transactions (*"economic" actions*), in which the actor acts alone, seeks self-in-

Table 1. Types of Decisions and Motives

	Locus of Decision: Actor is:	
	Acting Alone	*Participating in a Collective Decision*
Motive — *Self-interest (private interest)*	a. "Economic" actions	b. Pursuit of particular interests through collective decisions
Ethical (general welfare or equity)	c. Private altruism	d. Pursuit of ethical values through collective decisions

terest, and thus makes no effort to justify the action ethically. An increase in crime may lead individuals to buy burglar alarms or exercise caution in walking at night; an expected economic downturn may lead firms to reduce their inventories. These private decisions usually involve adaptation to the conditions revealed by the statistics, rather than efforts to change these conditions through collective action.[5] The statistics themselves may relate not only to *generally* valued or disvalued conditions, but also to conditions that different people value differently; a prediction of rain may be useful to farmers for planting and to vacationers for rescheduling their trips (Biderman, 1970:227). Those who use this information need also to know causal relations to predict the consequences of their actions, but the models of these relations that they need for adapting to a given state of affairs are usually simpler than those involved in public policies for changing it.[6]

b.   Actors can use information to pursue their *particular interests* (private, non-ethical values) through *collective decisions* such as the formation of public policy. A decline in the real wage of an employee group may lead to their advocacy of public support for wage increases. A decline in the economic position of a domestic industry may lead to an appeal by the industry for price supports or tariffs.[7] A voter facing a choice about a town budget may "want only to understand 'What's in it for me?' " (Lindblom and Cohen, 1979:59). The Census Bureau's success in measuring the unemployment rate has depended in part on relations with opposed constituencies—business and labor—who use this information to serve their disparate interests (de Neufville, 1975:70–86). Public officials may also respond to indicator statistics in seeking private goals such as material gain or reelection. Johnson and Lewin (1984) have proposed that municipalities publish periodic reports with specific attention to the interests of diverse user groups.

These private actions affecting public policy may or may not further the general welfare or equity. Exploitation of the public purse by public officials or private groups will presumably not do so. But when a group argues persuasively that it is needy or deserving or has been treated unfairly, and is supported by others who recognize this claim, we may have difficulty in classifying its action. Market-like competition and exchange by diverse interests in politics have also been seen by some as means for furthering the general welfare (Coleman, 1970).

Groups seeking to advance their particular interests through politics may provide internal justifications for their actions that are shared by their members ("It will benefit us"); but when they seek to persuade outsiders in public terms rather than by private bargains, they must invoke the general welfare in their arguments (Dibble, 1962). The use of these arguments moves them nearer to cell d of Table 1.

c.   Actors acting alone and seeking to benefit others without increasing their own well-being (*private altruism*) may also make use of information. Information about poverty may increase charitable donations. Knowledge of an impending disaster may lead to community aid. Information on discrimination in employment can aid private as well as public efforts to remedy it. Those who act in this way may justify their action to others by ethical arguments including references to the public interest; but this persuasion is directed toward individual action rather than toward voting or other participation in binding collective decisions. In this respect scientific communities, universities, and foundations can make choices affecting the general welfare, aided by information, independently of public policy. Their internal decisions may, however, be collective and in this sense fall in cell d.

d.   Finally, information can be used by actors in their pursuit of *ethical values* such as the general welfare or equity, through *collective decisions*, e.g., through public policy. This use of information concerns what should be done for the good of society or as right action, in more or less general terms. In specific terms it can relate to particular values that are widely accepted in the community (e.g., traffic safety). In general terms it calls for comparisons or trade-offs in terms of more inclusive values, among various particular values (how much health is worth how much education?) and groups (what benefit to the non-poor is equivalent to a given benefit to the poor? What benefit to those now living is equivalent to a given benefit to the next generation?). These trade-offs, in addition to extensive causal information required, complicate the calculations required relative to those needed in cell a.

When public policy choice aimed at ethical values is involved we shall refer to public statistics that are useful for this choice as *policy indicator statistics.*[8] The choice among possible public policies, like all the other types of action discussed here, requires not only information on valued conditions but also causal knowledge as to how to promote them. Causal models, whether based on research or not, are therefore an indispensable accompaniment of policy indicator statistics; we shall discuss such models below.

TYPES OF POLICY INDICATORS

We then take as a starting point for the design of policy indicator systems those values espoused in the name of the general welfare or equity for the political community for which the systems are being designed. We shall now use the term "values" to designate conditions valued in terms of these public, ethical values rather than individual tastes; "value concept," a concept widely believed to correspond to welfare or an aspect of it; and "the general welfare," any of a variety of concepts referring to the collective welfare of members of a political community. We may come to criticize some of those values; they may represent the interests of a community at the expense of outsiders; or some may be unnecessarily specific, having blind spots that reflect the interests of dominant groups in the community. But as an initial basis for choice of indicator variables, these claims to serve the general welfare can often be operationalized and converted into statistics on the community's well-being.

The value concepts most often used as bases of social indicator systems—measures of which may be possible policy indicators—are those corresponding to "social goal areas" (Carley, 1980:185–190), such as the list of "areas of social concern" proposed by OECD (1976): health, development through learning, employment and quality of working life, time and leisure, personal economic situation, physical environment, social environment, personal safety, and social opportunity and participation. Most of the values in such lists are not ends in themselves (even if widely treated as such) but means to other ends: employment can be a means to economic and subjective well-being, and environmental quality a means to health and subjective well-being. Some such values are ends in themselves ("end-values") but not inclusive enough to stand alone as complete notions of welfare. Health, example, even if defined in terms of subjective well-being or economic production, does not exhaust the possibilities of realizing either of these latter variables; and aesthetic appreciation, often included in such lists in the form of enjoyment of the arts, is similarly not a complete notion of welfare. Statistics based on items in such lists have also been referred to as aspects of the "level of welfare" (Drewnowski, 1970); and Land (1975:17, 23–24) proposes a similar list as "end products of social processes" associated with social institutions.

In view of this possible reexamination of relations between means and ends, and between more and less inclusive values, we may distinguish three types of value concepts that may be measured by policy indicators:

a.   Inclusive notions of intrinsic value, which we shall call "general end-values." When these concepts are used in public debate they are not usually defined precisely enough to provide a basis of measurement; in choosing measures for them we may have to compromise by narrowing their meaning somewhat (Johnston and Carley, 1981:224). Yet we shall eventually recommend three types of general end-values as bases for aggregate statistics playing a central part in policy indicator systems: income (with its aggregate, national income, equivalent to the national product); subjective well-being together with its duration; and the distribution of the first two among population categories, including aspects of equity.

b.   Less inclusive end-values, such as health or aesthetic appreciation.

c.   Causes of these general end-values, which will be called "contributory variables."[9]

The operational measures of value concepts will be called "value measures." Conceivably there might be policy indicators that were not value measures, i.e., measures of non-valued concepts; but because the function of policy indicators has been defined to relate to public policy choice, those contributory variables that are value measures appear to have priority for presentation in policy indicator statistics.

In discussing policy models below, we shall illustrate value concepts in the relatively specific and contributory social goal area of education. Ultimately, however, we shall seek more general criteria for comparing or trading off such variables and thus comparing policies that affect diverse social goals. The choice and measurement of these more general values is then a *first* major concern of this paper; but it will be postponed until near the end of the paper, after we analyze the use of information in a pluralistic democracy.

Even if we can measure the changes in a value (i.e., a valued condition) over time, we may still need other information in order to act on it. We need, of course, to know how our policies are likely to affect that value. Moreover, the policies we make may have their effects indirectly, and we may wish to monitor intermediate variables that are affected by policies and that in turn affect the value. Nonmanipulable variables may also affect the value in question; these effects need to be set aside statistically both in defining problems and in monitoring progress. Policy indicator systems may thus contain measures of some contributory variables—those that are policy-manipulable or that intervene between policies and end-values—including some social goal variables but also more specific contributions to well-being. They may also include analytic indicators, such as age-standardized rates, incorporating other contributory variables as statistical controls.

By our concern with public policy and values, we imply an interest in variables that can be changed through policies. The models of interest to us thus overlap only partly with those studied in academic or "basic" social science. Some types of contributory variables that may be of special interest are:

a. Direct transfers of money or goods to persons in need, whether through the private or the public sector. These include the aid of families to their dependent members; unemployment insurance; income maintenance; and restitution or insurance to victims of crime.

b. The provision of services, or the availability of physical facilities, to individuals and groups (e.g., to promote health, education, or justice), and the amounts spent on them. The efficiency of these services and facilities, however, is often uncertain, and precise measurement of their efficiency can be hindered by the resistance of those who provide them. Categories (a) and (b) together include program outputs, but also include the supply of the same outputs from nongovernmental sources.

c. The prevalence of private cooperative behavior that furthers the purposes of public programs; Whitaker (1980) has referred to this as "coproduction." Examples are protective activities to reduce criminal victimization, transportation accidents, or lung cancer attributable to smoking. This sort of activity may be either modifiable by public policy or relevant as a statistical control. The resources spent on it are also relevant.

Among the contributory variables may be quite specific administrative characteristics such as pupil-teacher ratios in schools, details of the administration of food stamp programs (Rich, 1981:66), or measures of organizational performance. Such variables may be of special value at the local level where citizens can understand them better. These variables may not seem general enough to include in national social reports (Johnston and Carley, 1981:243); but the transition from general to specific variables, and from citizen to administrative audiences, is so gradual that we would be well advised to consider all these sorts of variables as possible parts of a functioning indicator system (Garn et al., 1976). Indeed, the effective choice of policies includes following them through the state of implementation, in which factored problems (Allison, 1971:80–81) and specific measures of process and outcome are more important than at the stage of enactment. But even while we focus attention on highly specific program goals, we must remember to link them to the more general values that the programs were designed to serve.

The models of causal relations implied by the term "contributory" may be derived from scientific research; or they may be judged to exist on the basis of experience, expert opinion, or public opinion generally. Thus for health as a value concept, both health services and environmental conditions are included in indicator systems as contributory variables, even though our scientific knowledge of their effects is limited. For crime reduction as a value concept, police budgets, the skills and numbers of law-enforcement personnel, and community crime-protection activities are treated as relevant even though their effectiveness is sometimes uncertain. I include contributory variables about which our knowledge is uncertain, not to make a virtue of uncertainty, but to stress that we normally work with imperfect knowledge and cannot wait for scientific certainty.

POLICY INDICATORS AND THE PUBLIC RECONCILIATION OF VALUES

We have defined policy indicators as measures that can justifiably be used in public statistics. How, then, can some be justified more than others? Two functions performed by argument within political systems can make use of these statistics: (a) identifying problems, and (b) guiding public choice among alternative policies. The second function, guiding policy choice, involves relative judgements among alternative policies, and often includes trade-offs among particular values or disvalues that these policies produce. These trade-offs can require especially inclusive values and indicators of them.

Both these functions depend on the participants' assigning some shared meaning to the common good or equity, underlying both shared problems and shared criteria for policy choice. Two major criticisms have been made of such assumptions of consensus: first, that societies and political systems are characterized by conflict rather than consensus; and second, that no operational meaning can be attached to the public interest. As regards the existence of consensus, it is never complete and its prevalence varies greatly among political systems over time. I have chosen to emphasize this particular use of statistics because I believe (as early advocates of social indicators did) that there is ample opportunity for it in the contemporary United States. The critics' argument also suggests that apparent common values may well be those of a dominant group rather than genuinely public values; we should be alert to this possibility. As regards the difficulty of defining the public interest, policy indicators have the distinct feature of proposing precise measures of it. We may not all agree that these measures are ethically valid, and some may prefer to have no measures rather than the ones I shall propose; but at least I shall propose specific definitions. The proposal of such measures must, of course, reflect some degree of consensus in the polity as well as among the experts who devise measures and causal models; it is not and cannot be merely personal.

Political systems—and especially those systems having some internal consensus, which we shall call political communities—typically make policies by transforming a set of diverse particular values into a single choice. The political processes that lead to such choices may involve the imposition of one set of values on persons who do not subscribe to it; they may involve bargaining or vote-trading, in which the only appeals are made to others' self-interest; or they may involve justifications in terms of ethical values. Policy indicators can be useful for this last sort of reconciliation of values.

The gross national product (GNP) or the measure of economic welfare developed by Nordhaus and Tobin (1972), for example, directs our attention to an aggregate to which particular policies can contribute. At a lower level of aggregation, the net economic benefit (benefit minus cost) from a particular project is the contribution of that project to the GNP. The net benefits from different projects can be compared if their benefits and costs can be estimated in monetary terms; thus efforts to improve health, education, safety, and other valued conditions can be compared.

Trade-off procedures need not be limited to monetary valuation, however. If we were interested in equality of educational achievement between races, for example, we might use a measure of this equality as a criterion for comparing two policies aimed at equality, such as school desegregation and redistribution of funds among schools. If we were interested in safety as a criterion, we could use it to compare effects of using a given amount of resources for fire prevention and for automobile inspection. In either case if we could predict the effects of the alternative policies through knowledge of causal relations, and if we could measure the effects in comparable terms, we could compare the benefits of the two policies.

Policy indicators can play two roles in these trade-offs. One is the encouragement of the public to define the problem in inclusive terms, by calling their attention to general values. The other, more directly relevant to trade-offs, is the relation of such a general variable separately to each of the more specific variables (such as program outputs) under comparison; this depends on using a common general variable in relation to each, but not necessarily on using aggregated public statistics based on this variable.

This function of comparison or reconciliation is suggested in an assessment of indicator validity by OECD (1976:25–26), which proposes:

> The most valid indicator is the one that is able to compare the effects of as many instrumental variables as possible on the concern under consideration. In the health area, for example, an indicator that could be taken as a criterion for the effects of both a cancer detection programme and a new technology for treating heart attacks would be more valid than indicators which could not compare these two influencing factors with respect to a common unit....

It is important to seek more inclusive value concepts and measures, not only for philosophical reasons, but also because of decisions that any political community must make about the allocation of scarce resources. If our value indicators deal with a set of incommensurable intrinsic values, they can aid the community only up to a certain point in allocating these resources.

The policy choices that face a political community range, in terms of the indicators involved, from the specific to the general, and from means and immediate goals to more inclusive ends. Some of our measures of problems and accomplishments are indeed quite specific. The manager of a public program may monitor that program's achievement of its specific goals (e.g., providing services). When that program is evaluated he is likely to welcome "formative" evaluation that tells how to improve the program in the same specific terms.

In a slightly more general approach, the director of a health agency charged with controlling a particular disease might examine indicators of the incidence of that disease and of the conditions that affect it, in order to compare alternative policies for controlling it. Those indicators would permit the comparison of various programs such as preventive measures, personnel training, and the use of drugs. But a government agency concerned with overall health policies might make use of mortality rates or patients' capacity to function, in order to compare the effects of different diseases and choose among policies affecting them. Similarly, for choices among policies affecting various types of crimes, we might compare the public's judgments of the seriousness of various types of crimes (Sellin and Wolfgang, 1964; Rossi et al., 1974).

We might wish to make still more general choices, however, and to assess the relative value of health policies and crime-reduction policies. Comparisons of this sort are typically the task of a higher level of government than the particular substantive agency—the chief executive or its budgetary agency, the legislature, or the citizens themselves. For this purpose we would need more general bases of comparison. To make comparisons of this sort among social goal areas, we commonly rely on the "partisan mutual adjustment" (Braybrooke and Lindblom, 1963) of groups and organizations, each of which seeks its specific goals, and on the interest aggregation that political groups and parties provide; we might make these judgments more systematically through respondents' weighting of the importance of various particular goals, or through multiattribute utility calculations (Keeney and Raiffa, 1976); but we can be more explicit about our reasoning if we try to reconcile them in terms of a more general end-value.[10] We shall examine indicators of such end-values in further detail below.

General end-values can be useful both for calculating policy trade-offs and for clarifying definitions of social goal variables. But insofar as general values are measured and used in these ways, they are considered by some to be a threat to democratic processes. Benefit-cost analysis, for example, implies a different intellectual approach from that of a politics driven by the demands of interest groups. Rather, it implies "fine tuning"—the assumption of a social welfare function and the allocation of our scarce resources so that at the margin, each unit of resources is used to produce the greatest contribution to total social welfare. This "fine tuning" approach is at odds, not only with the play of interest groups (though this has been also considered at times to produce a fine-tuned "resultant"), but also with the ideas that support large coalitions of groups, and that unite social movements, in the more dramatic types of politics that we know. It seems to imply an "end of ideology"—pronounced prematurely to have occurred in the early 1960s. On the one hand there seems to be a politics of experts, of calculation, of incremental trade-offs at the margin; on the other a politics of drama, of meaningful symbols, of struggle, and of public participation. It might be argued that the politics of benefit-cost analysis—and of abstract trade-off indicators generally—is bloodless and elitist.[11].

Yet a "politics" of general values such as net economic benefit, or quality-adjusted life years, can never exist by itself; it can, at most, be an ingredient in a larger political process. As we consider *various* definitions of the public interest, the differences among these definitions themselves contribute to democratic politics. Moreover, even if one such definition should prevail, it would be at most a damping influence on the normal oscillations of democratic politics—an effort to introduce trade-offs and optimization more into public debate and to reduce the fluctuations of policy from one side to the other.

In examining this question it is useful to study the role of economics in benefit-cost analysis. This technique has risen greatly in importance in the last three decades (Haveman and Margolis, 1977:Introduction) but is far from the dominant criterion for governmental policy choice even in areas where its calculations can be made validly. Its recommendations are open to criticism, but broad and intelligent criticism requires clear presentation as well as widespread citizen education. The necessary criticism and review require clarity, and openness to examination, of the entire process by which data are gathered, analyzed, and presented (Hanke and Walker, 1977:352). A central problem in the use of benefit-cost analysis is in fact not that it distorts democracy, but that political interests distort the numbers that are purported to result from its reasoned calculation (Hanke and Walker, 1977).

The example of applied economics shows that a community of experts can center substantial areas of research about values. As long as these values are not obviously aligned with the interests of one segment of society, they can be taken as noncontroversial in public debate. Conceivably this same possibility could exist for a potential expert community concerned with the quality and quantity of life. If this end-value were detached from direct alignment with partisan claims, research on ways to influence it might leave the expert community more united and might reach a wider audience in the political community. This research should be open to public criticism, but it could still serve to narrow the range of dispute and suggest desirable policies. At the same time, the additional dimension in public debate that would result from consideration of subjective as well as economic well-being would fulfill some of the initial hopes of the social indicators movement.

The acceptance of the GNP as a policy indicator statistic, and of benefit-cost analysis as a corresponding basis for trade-offs, have not depended on their wide understanding by the public. Consensus on the part of economists as to the theoretical meaning of the GNP and the technical procedures for estimating it, together with acceptance by other elite groups, have contributed to this acceptance. The prestige of a discipline can sometimes forestall criticism and support the use of a less intelligible indicator for policy purposes.

We conclude that economics has provided a policy indicator that is used for trade-offs; that the discipline is genuinely influential in defining problems for the nation as well as in recommending policies; and that this influence extends considerably beyond the sector of the public that understands its reasoning. It therefore provides a useful example for both emulation and caution.

POLITICAL COMMUNITY AS CLIENT OR AUDIENCE: VALUES AND ROLES

If we are designing indicator systems for collective decisions, we must first identify the political community[12] to be served by decisions based on them. We must also recognize (or choose) the loci of decisions about the generation and use of information—e.g., the legislative, administrative, or judicial organs of central or local government—and the points of contact between ourselves and the decision processes. Different systems may require different sorts of information and require us to take different roles.

A political community that needs information about itself is likely to have at least a certain minimum size; a single family does not need indicators of its own well-being, nor does a small community in which all members know one another well. If it is to use policy indicators, it must also possess a certain degree of skill and objectivity on the part of those who produce and use the statistics, and support by citizens and leaders for statistical quality. Indicator information can lead to embarrassing questions and controversial conclusions, which would sometimes be easier to suppress. If we believe in knowing the truth about ourselves,[13] we must be prepared to tolerate and even support the messenger who brings bad tidings.

Stability is also a necessary condition for the regular collection and use of indicator statistics. Continuing data series require continuing political support; in a pluralistic democracy with diverse possible majorities, this means a broad consensus. Zapf (1972:249) has characterized the political orientation of the social indicators movement as "liberal incrementalism." Insofar as indicator systems merely define problems in terms of departures from a previous situation, they can involve the bias that problems are seen as temporary and the previous situation as essentially satisfactory (Sharpe, 1978:309–310). But an incremental approach to the use of indicators, presuming some constancy in the framework for decision, can be employed in socialist systems as well (Osipov and Andreenkov, 1979).

When the collective choices under consideration are to be made democratically, we shall refer to information systems that aid them as "democratic information systems." The proper use of information in a democracy, and its relation to indicator choice and development, is thus a *second* major concern of this paper. By dealing with "information" rather than simply with indicators in the conventional sense of social reporting, we can enlarge our perspective and consider other possible forms of information besides annual published statistical series. Not only possible new items of information, but their relation to preexisting information, must become part of our analysis.[14]

In the management of business and government there is an extensive literature on "management information systems." Managers occupy roles in an organizational hierarchy, and can presumably be more effective by using better information about the organization. In a democracy, however, the departure from hierarchy is essential. Even though government officials need accurate information on the state of their society and economy, they are not a unified hierarchical leadership; they operate within an environment of mutual influence among agencies and branches of government, to which different groups bring diverse goals and values. The information they need and the policies based on it must also be subject to public criticism. The task of developing information systems that contribute to reasoned analysis by the public of issues and policies is far more difficult than the design of management information systems, because the public is more diverse in its values and capacities. This task requires that we reconcile the calculations of specialists with the intelligibility of their reasoning to the public—at least to group leaders and to others who are especially involved and informed (Hanke and Walker, 1977:352). In this sense the phrase "democratic information systems" implies an inescapable tension between expertise and democracy (MacRae, 1976a:ch. 2).

The choice of indicators, or of modes of information, suitable for democratic policy decisions thus involves different criteria, not only from those of the scientific approach to indicators of social change, but also from those used to choose policy indicators in a hierarchical political system. The initial normative concern of the social indicator movement must remain important insofar as democracy requires justifications in terms of the public interest and not merely the play of private interests. Reliability and theoretical validity of variables, stressed in the scientific approach to social indicators, also play a part, but they cannot be the sole criteria for the choice of policy indicators. A connection with manipulable policy variables is also essential to any indicator system designed to guide choice and action. Intelligibility and communication to a wider public are necessary, not only for the use of policy indicators, but because the public and its leaders have a part to play in the institutionalization and termination of these indicator series.

Let us then assume (temporarily) that we have chosen to serve a democractic political community as an ultimate client, recommending policy indicators or related causal models. We shall then face questions about its collective values and our own roles—questions that concern applied research generally and not merely the design of policy indicators. If we intend simply to serve this "client" we have taken an "outsider" role, in which we provide expertise (means) and the community provides values (ends). Often we choose part of a community as a client, thereby making ethical choices similar to those we make in choosing to work with the community in the first place. In either case, after choosing that service role, we forego the right to participate further as a citizen.

This "outsider" role, which takes the community as client, may be chosen by social scientists on the basis of either philosophy (positivism) or prudence. Prudence may dictate their keeping a certain distance from current controversies in order to sustain longer-run values concerning method and theory, or to further the viability of the institutions that generate information.[15] The "outsider" role is occupied of necessity by foreigners (Brewer and Brunner, 1975:10–11); it is usually also the stance of paid consultants or employees, who by taking pay commit themselves to serve the client's or employer's goals.

If we are merely outsiders in this sense, regarding the political community as a client, we face the problem of choosing or identifying the values that we shall serve among multiple more or less explicit values in the community. Just as evaluation researchers often have problems in discovering the "true" goals of the programs that they seek to evaluate (Weiss, 1972:26–30), the consultant to a political community has problems that are similar but greater. That community, unlike an organization or program, is rarely founded for a purpose. Its culture often embodies dominant values, but in a free society a respect for diversity is also encouraged. If government is to sponsor the continuing collection of information, then the various groups in the community must have broad consensus to support the gathering of this information, as we have noted. This consensus, if it does not exist on every particular value, may be built through bargaining or logrolling so that multiple clienteles, each seeking its own values, nevertheless agree to sustain the whole enterprise.[16] Such a consensus requires cultivation if it is to last. It may also require the limitation of public support for information that might exacerbate major conflicts within the community.

I have spoken of the political community as an ultimate client; we may not be dealing with its members directly. We cannot do so easily in a large community; typically we deal with government officials or group leaders as immediate clients. We may think ideally of the citizens as the primary users of indicator information; but in actuality information systems for urban or national planning are used primarily by public officials.[17] An information system in Cologne in the early 1970s, for example, required permission from the responsible department before someone outside that department could use it (Beresford et al., 1976:303). The acceptance and support of indicator systems can also depend importantly on bureaucratic politics (Rich, 1981). The public's participation may then depend on the initiative of active group members or of the media, seeking out statistics, selecting and publicizing them.

The government officials with whom we deal may, as we have noted, be moved by personal motives or by specific, factored aspects of public problems as well as by concern for the general good. So, too, may be the academic or professional who advocates the collection of indicator data so as to favor the activities of experts from his own specialty. If we regard the political community rather than the present government officials as our client, we may wish to deal with persons who are dedicated to its long-run well-being. We may also wish to promote wider participation in the decision as to the choice of indicators. Even if we (as professionals) could choose variables that reflected the true interests of the community, without participation we could still risk lack of support for the indicator system we proposed. Thus participation can provide a sort of parallel information system, in which dissent or difference of opinion can reveal alternative values.[18]

Even if we could bypass government officials and deal with the public, the problem of representatives would not be automatically solved. The groups that can most easily pay us as consultants or understand our technical language, and those that use statistics most, are not necessarily those most in need of help. Political systems that are officially democratic can never represent all groups with exact equality, and the group systems in those polities often reflect the same "bias" as the officialdom. One approach to even-handedness has been proposed by Coleman (1980:346–47), who suggests a style of "pluralistic policy research" serving not a single client but a variety of interested parties in society. Presumably a designer of indicator systems might do likewise, seeking to increase and diversify their use. This role would maintain some of the detachment characteristics of academic research, taking a position near the "truth" end of Price's (1965:Ch. 5) "spectrum from truth to power." Alternatively, we might consider setting ourselves against the bias of the system, taking underrepresented groups as our clients, but at the same time risking no longer aiming at a general public interest as well as becoming less effective.

The option of choosing and advocating particular values and policies, however, suggests another role we may occupy besides that of the "outsider"—that of an active member of the community. Citizens and leaders of the political community can take the initiative, try to persuade others, and need not simply listen for the composite preference of other citizens. This opportunity exists by right for citizens of a democracy, and is not merely insinuated into the relationship as it is for a consultant with a client.

I have addressed the reader so far as though "we" are social scientists— whatever other roles we may occupy. Those who are also active members of the political community may be elective officials or candidates for office, seeking to lead their constituencies and not simply to follow them. They may be government officials, trying to facilitate their work, coordinate it with that of other agencies, and respond to the public directly or through its representatives. They may be citizens, organized in groups, seeking not merely to increase consciousness of an issue by publicizing conditions such as unemployment, illness, illiteracy, or inequality, but also to monitor possible progress toward reducing such conditions. Regardless of which of these roles we ourselves occupy, all of them must be involved ultimately in any successful indicator system. Public officials or private organizations must administer the information-gathering system and others must be among its users. Citizen groups must provide continuing political support and criticism. Experts are necessary to monitor the quality of the information presented and to relate it continually to their theoretical understanding of causal relations. The interrelations among such groups have been an essential condition for the institutionalization of indicator series (de Neufville, 1975:Ch. X). This process has been slow but may be speeded by use of the prior experience of other political communities.[19]

These active roles in the community may simply happen to be occupied by persons who are also social scientists. A person who thus combines the two may compartmentalize his or her activities into those undertaken as citizen and as scholar. Yet it is also possible for the two types of roles to be combined. One relatively active role is that of "public interest science" (Nelkin, 1979:114–16). Some natural scientists, who feel social responsibility for the uses of their specialized knowledge in relation to their notions of the public interest, have joined in groups to analyze public issues and take stands on them. Social scientists have done likewise (MacRae, 1976a:75). Such roles are not, however, always consistent with the "neutral expert" role that is more characteristic of scientific communities. In practice, those who take this role and become involved in controversies risk belittlement by their fellow citizens of their claim of scientific expertise, especially if they are social scientists. Such public judgments may extend to their disciplines as a whole.

The combination of scientist and citizen roles by social scientists thus faces practical limits, especially when the viability of a science-based institution is affected. Governmental agencies that generate continuing statistical series face this problem, which may thus be more acute for policy indicator design than for the development of policy models. The role played by economists in influencing the content of public statistics again suggests itself as a possible compromise, in that an expert group can espouse values that are widely supported in the political community but that also enter into its own conceptual scheme.

Because of the difficulty of combining these roles, some social scientists may wish to treat the political community simply as an audience, disseminating their findings by making them generally available. They may thus seek to have information related to their work placed in censuses, books, periodicals, newspapers, or data facilities.

These means of dissemination assume, however, that users seek out information by interrogating a data source (e.g., telephoning or querying a computer), going to a library, or buying a periodical or book. Users may also obtain statistical information as part of a bundle of information-type goods (buying a newspaper, subscribing to a cable television service). But if newspaper headlines alert readers to problems, newspapers and their reporters must seek out the information first. Similarly, if a public official is to use indicator information to call the public's attention to a problem, the official or a staff member must first seek out that information. In the utilization of evaluation research, Patton (1978:Ch. 4) has stressed the importance of having a strongly motivated client who needs and seeks the information.

To define problems for a political community, we need means for bringing signals of warning or of progress[20] to the attention of relevant publics; and we need to define special social roles such that persons in them may attend to such signals for the community (like forest rangers in observation towers), thereby enhancing the observation capacity of the public through a two-stage dissemination process. The use of statistical information for public decisions thus depends on the identity and motives of those who seek it out and interpret it.

These specially motivated users may be journalists, public officials, political candidates, party or group leaders, staff assistants of such leaders, scholars, or interested citizens. They include, in other words, the active members of the political community whom we have mentioned above. Their motives can range from personal advancement—for a news scoop or a telling campaign issue—to a concern for the general good, or a mixture of the two. They are often led, however, to interpret information in terms of the general good because of their need to gain the attention or support of uncommitted citizens. Conflicts between interested parties are often enlarged in scope by the involvement of the spectators (Schattschneider, 1960:Ch. 1).

The dissemination of information to *motivated* users may be different from dissemination to the general public. It may require periodically updated data facilities that can be accessed quickly for the user's purpose, disaggregated (within the limits that respondents' privacy permits), and shaped in different ways for different users (Johnston and Carley, 1981:252). In this respect, even apart from questions of time scale, information may well be disseminated in the form of data facilities and not simply in books.

To a limited extent, analyses and interpretations of these data can also be made available in the same way as the data themselves (Mare, 1981:111–112). Like scholarly publication, however, the preparation of these analyses can cause delays in relation to the needs of decision. Moreover, various groups of users might require different sorts of screening of these analyses in terms of quality, intelligibility, and valuative bases; and "official" interpretations must not attempt to resolve controversial issues prematurely.

The appropriate channels and styles of dissemination of data and interpretations thus differ among user roles. We can recognize three types of motivated users in terms of the values they represent: (a) representatives of groups with particular interests in policy outcomes; (b) persons who advocate policies in view of notions of the public interest— a category that partly overlaps the first; and (c) neutral experts who present information and interpretations with only minimal advocacy or espousal of controversial values. In the area of overlap between (a) and (b) are advocates of groups or of value-positions who argue in terms of distinct notions of the public interest. Their system of communication is more like that of weekly or monthly journals of opinion, published for limited and self-selected audiences, than that of newspapers or television. Among the neutral experts are journalists who, when governed by a code of objectivity, seek out information to observe and tell, but not to recommend; somewhat similar are teachers who use indicator statistics (Johnston, 1978:294). The data-facility user who is an analyst for a group, and the reporter who allows the reader to become a citizen-analyst, thus represent alternative role-types of central importance; they closely resemble alternative roles for social scientists which we have discussed above. The problem of how social scientists should be involved with the political community cannot be escaped by treating the community as an audience.

CHOOSING CONTRIBUTORY VARIABLES: MODELS OF CAUSATION

In discussing the uses of policy indicators, I have assumed that a major function of indicator series is to define problems facing a political community. But the definition of problems is of no value unless it can lead to action to deal with them.[21] But ultimately, the value of information systems lies in the actions they permit us to choose and in the consequences of those actions (Raiffa, 1968).

Thus the design of information systems should rest on the improvements in well-being (or other values) that are expected to result, either directly or indirectly, from the use of that information. The information we provide should aid citizens to advocate policies, after comparing alternatives with regard to their expected effects. If, as is usually the case, policies affect the relevant values only indirectly, we may need to assess whether the policies affect intervening contributory variables. We may seek to improve the level of health, but work through health services or environmental conditions; or seek to increase competence in production and citizenship, but work through schooling. In addition, we must be able to set aside statistically the effects of non-policy contributory variables that affect the values in question. To some extent our choice of contributory variables as policy indicators depends not on scientific research but on causal relations that are believed by the public to be true. We thus choose these contributory variables in part to enlighten public debate, and not simply because of their status in scientific discourse.[22]

This process of choice of contributory variables, and changes in our choice, can be illustrated in the social goal area of elementary and secondary education in the United States. We shall take as an illustrative value the educational achievement of students—recognizing that this may be only a means to the student's later production, consumption, opportunity, and citizenship, but treating it as our goal.

The first contributory variables related to education on which data were gathered were measures of inputs—expenditures, numbers and qualifications of teachers, facilities available, numbers of pupils and years they spent in school. This information was needed for administrative purposes, but was also accepted by the public as related to education as a social goal. As concern increased in the 1960s about racial equality in the public schools, the "Coleman Report" (Coleman et al., 1966), a cross-sectional study of over 645,000 public-school pupils, was commissioned by Congress and shifted public attention to outcomes as measured by students' test scores. The results of the study also cast doubt on the efficacy of the conventional inputs and placed special emphasis on the mix of students in the school and on teachers' skills. The finding that student mixture seemed to promote achievement by minority students supported the decision of the Supreme Court to require racial desegregation, and the racial mix in schools became an important contributory variable. Indeed, without completely conclusive and replicated findings about its effects on achievement, racial desegregation came to be valued somewhat independently of its effects on achievement. It was a direct object of policy (a manipulable variable) and found its principal justification in the Court's judgment that it was required by the constitutional provision for "equal protection of the laws."

The 1966 Coleman Report had a significant influence on the demand for indicator statistics on student mixture and students' achievement, even though the report itself was not based on time series or on "indicators" in the sense in which they later came to be defined. Such a relation between "indicator" statistics and "non-indicator" research often exists, however, and the links between them are *policy indicator variables.* Our choice of contributory variables for our causal models (and perhaps for policy indicators) must rest on whatever reasonable causal inferences we can make, regardless of whether they are based on time series of national data.

Two succeeding reports having Coleman as the senior author threw further light on contributory variables in education. Coleman, Kelly, and Moore (1975) studied a possible side effect of school desegregation: the departure of white pupils from desegregated public schools, through either transfer to private schools or change of the parents' residence. They concluded that such an effect existed, undermining the aim of improved achievement. This finding provoked considerable controversy among sociologists studying education, but eventually some consensus developed that it held under certain conditions.

My purpose in citing this second report is not to state its specific conclusions, but to suggest its conceptual separation from the concerns of the earlier report. Migration, desegregation, and the role of private schools were all presumably contributory variables that should figure in a more general model relevant to educational policy. The second report, however, dealt with only one segment of the model; it did not try to assess the net effect of desegregation, which might have been positive as well as negative. What is more unfortunate is that there seems to have been little effort on the part of the social-science community to incorporate these findings in more general models concerned with educational achievement.

A third report by Coleman, Hoffer, and Kilgore (1981) dealt with differences in educational achievement of students in public and private schools. This, too, stimulated widespread controversy; but some of the criticism of the report was facilitated by the prompt availability of the "High School and Beyond" data set—the first wave of a longitudinal study—on which the report was based. Like the second report, this focused on a particular aspect of the overall educational process—the differences in achievement between different types of schools. Like the second, it dealt with the issue of segregation but did not examine the effects of segregation on achievement. And again, like the second, it encountered controversy about its specific findings and recommendations, but this debate seems to have drawn little scholarly attention to the building of cumulative, inclusive, research-based causal models relevant to educational policy.

How can we devote more coordinated effort to developing such policy models? We cannot, of course, ask that each piece of research that contributes to them deal empirically with all the questions that would enter into such a model. Rather, this linkage must take place in the literature and in the relevant communities of researchers, through the justifications that are offered for the importance of each particular contribution. If this guiding principle is accepted, the introductory statement of the problem in a research report will then refer to the contribution the particular research makes to general educational policy models—*not* simply to a current policy debate or to the basic theory of a discipline. The literature cited in the report will then also be chosen so as to link the particular work with this larger model-building enterprise. And, equally important, the researchers trained to participate in this effort must recognize that it is something other than the pursuit of basic disciplinary theory—that it does not lie fully either in the world of the individual discipline or in the world of action (Coleman, 1972), but lies in a terrain between them that we need to cultivate.

Social scientists can indeed change the public's conceptions of causal relations through research. Contributory variables need not always be chosen on the basis of common-sense models of causation alone, since common sense is influenced in the longer run by science. But in this case and perhaps in others, the building of policy-relevant models may well be hindered by academic social scientists' insufficient recognition of the need for policy-related causal models as foci for research. Social scientists are not motivated toward the steady development of these models either by the policy debates of the moment, or by the prestige attributed to general theoretical work within particular disciplines. The development of general models of the educational system, of the crime and justice system, or of the policy system for dealing with poverty and welfare, has not been perceived as equal in importance to contributions to the basic theories of the disciplines. These models may draw on basic theory, and the work that is done on them may at times contribute to that theory; but because they are usually interdisciplinary and their development is driven by the needs of practice, they do not emerge automatically from basic disciplinary research.

Thus in addition to simply testing hypotheses offered in public debate, social scientists and policy analysts can ask broader questions as to what values are being sought and whether they are being sought appropriately. They—and natural scientists as well—can give higher priority to the development of "policy models" centered about policy indicators. Some such models might derive from evaluation research, others from social experiments or studies of time series. The results might be not simply direct policy recommendations, but also proposals to measure on a larger scale and more regularly those contributory variables that were found to be effective in studies of special populations.

The choice and use of contributory variables then depends on developments in two parallel communities: the political community that makes policy decisions, and the various scientific or technical communities (MacRae, 1976b) that assess the quality of measurements and the validity and significance of causal relations. Developments in both communities must be incremental and capable of correction. The political community may change its immediate focus of attention, but can still benefit from the longer-run continuity of measurements that may guide future decisions. The indicator and information systems of various political communities may well differ from another, as Scott (1973) has recommended for indicators of development. At the same time, however, there are gains from sharing information through comparability of indicators among systems, requiring interchange and coordination such as has been carried out by OECD (1976).

GENERAL END-VALUES

The values that I have used for illustration so far have been ones conventionally used in social indicator systems; health, educational accomplishment, and the like. The acceptance of variables of this sort as central ingredients of policy indicator systems depends on their recognition as important by broad segments of the public (including social scientists in their citizen roles), and by professionals who either deliver related services (physicians, educators) or analyze their properties (biostatisticians, educational testing specialists). These are not, however, necessarily intrinsic values in a philosophical sense. In relation to a more general end-value such as general well-being, they may be means—fairly general contributory variables, but not intrinsic values. Alternatively, they may be intrinsic values but more specific than general well-being. To show these relations, we shall propose a general end-value that will supplement net economic benefit, and then analyze the relations between two conventional social indicator variables—social mobility and health—and more general end-values.

Economic benefit-cost analysis provides an example of a more general value: the maximization of a social welfare function, the national product or income.[23] The increment that a particular program makes to the national product is considered to be its net economic benefit. It then serves as a general value in terms of which the relative contributions of other more specific values can be assessed (traded off), so that in principle we can tell how much of our resources should be devoted to each. In addition, if we are willing to accept the national product as an end-value, it may guide us toward the relevant aspects of more specific values, such as aspects of health that contribute to productivity, and help us to refine their measurement. These advantages would result from benefit-cost analysis even if data on the GNP were not published.

We must next ask whether other end-values could permit similar general choices. The social indicator movement has represented a protest against the values involved in economic indicators. It has resulted in a proliferation of indicator variables, some noneconomic and others (such as work force data) bordering on the economic. It has not, however, provided alternative general values in terms of which more specific social goals can be compared. The task remains, therefore, of retaining the general tradeoff capacity of the GNP but exemplifying it in other types of values—stressing, for example, well-being that is not associated with money and possessions, and providing for greater equality among persons in the counting of well-being.

One such general variable would combine two components already familiar in the literature on social indicators—subjective quality of life and duration in time. In principle, each interval of time for each person could be weighted by the quality of life experienced during that interval. Formally analogous weightings of time by the value of time have been proposed by Fox (1974:54) and by Juster et al. (1981:76) as components of social accounting systems; but the development of such systems is not a prerequisite for the use of this variable.

In connection with the evaluation of health policies, Weinstein and Stason (1976, 1977) have proposed that we not only consider the aggregte length of life that various policies will produce, but also include in that aggregate a weighting factor for the quality of those life years. The result would be a total of "quality-adjusted life years" (QALYs). In particular choices of health policies, patients would be asked to compare their life experiences when under medication with those of "full health," and judge what fraction of a year of full health would be equivalent to a year under medication. More generally, techniques that have been developed for the measurement of subjective well-being (Campbell et al., 1976) might be adapted to weighting of life years by their quality. Such measurements are far from ready for policy application at present; questions such as the difference between happiness and satisfaction, the cardinal properties of such indices, and the interpretation of aggregate trends over time (Rodgers, 1982), remain to be resolved. Moreover, special care will be required to estimate amounts of suffering; homeless people, mistreated children, and institutionalized persons are among those who risk underrepresentation or departures from valid measurement.

If, however, the measurement of QALYs should become a central concern for those developing policy indicators, it might provide a basis for comparison and criticism of more specific indicators and a philosophical alternative to benefit-cost analysis. Unlike economic measures, it places value directly in experience rather than in the satisfaction of preferences in the market. In addition, it is based on time, which is more nearly equally available to all than money, and might thus circumvent some of the inequity of weighting the demands of rich and poor in dollars in valuing the GNP.

Suppose, then, that the concept of quality-adjusted life years was accepted as a general value variable to be incorporated in indicator statistics; how would we do this? Let us acknowledge that there are problems of measurement, and concentrate on the problems that would arise if we had good measures of subjective well-being as well as of its duration. The social indicator literature already contains information on quality of life as well as on death rates by age and on life expectancy; how would we combine them?

An annual publication based on a one-time interview could not directly measure the sum over time of QALYs over a year, for example, unless we relied on retrospection. Apart from weekly or seasonal fluctuations, however, the distribution of satisfactions and dissatisfactions experienced by the respondents at one time might represent those experienced over a year. If the population remained constant, therefore, the available data on subjective well-being would be a useful surrogate for statistics on QALYs.

We wish to know simultaneously, however, whether the quantity as well as the quality of life is changing. We must first set aside in a separate statistic the size of the population as a whole; by doing so, we can compare populations of different sizes, as well as consider separately the ethical question whether twice as many lives, all other things being the same, are twice as desirable. This might lead us to seek a measure, for a single "average life," of "quality-adjusted life expectancy." As indicator of this sort, based on capacity to function rather than subjective well-being, has been proposed by Chen et al. (1975:80–84). Such a calculation for subjective variables, however, seems at present to require too many gratuitous assumptions about the constancy over a lifetime of relations between personal characteristics and satisfaction.

A further problem is that our data on length of life, based on death records, do not necessarily pertain to the same individuals who report the quality of their lives. We are therefore forced to deal with population subgroups, further subdivided by age, and to present data for each such subgroup on quality of life and on probability of survival through the year. For general reporting purposes, it is these data that I suggest we present. But for analysis of particular policies, we may be able to follow particular populations over time and collect data on both survival and quality of life.

Such statistics, even in the approximate form in which they are now available, could be useful in providing an alternative measure of value in contrast to the economic standard. Descriptively, they could show what segments of the population were experiencing high or low quality of life relative to what would be expected from their incomes; we know already that the assocation is far from perfect. They would treat more equally persons who were paid unequally (by race or sex) or who were not producers for the market (the elderly). They might illuminate possible trade-offs between quality and quantity of life, where public resources can be used to increase one at the expense of the other. And especially in studies of the elderly, they might throw light on the social benefits of our efforts to prolong life, as they affect not only the elderly themselves but also those around them. These sorts of studies reflect the important uses of policy indicators for particular policy judgments, and not only for national social reporting.

We thus propose that two general end-values constitute the central core of a policy indicator system: economic benefit (the GNP or national income) and quality-adjusted life years. Together with these two variables, we must also consider their distribution over population groups as a measure of aspects of equity or of needs.[24]

This brief proposal has numerous implications, however. First we must note in examining economic equity that the distribution of production and income, and of income and consumption, are not the same. Production and consumption by individuals, especially within the family, involve components that are not priced in the market. For a full exploration of the distribution of individuals' consumption, and of the resources and obligations that affect individuals' production, consumption, and well-being, we need to measure and study noneconomic contributory variables even if our value variable is economic. These include family relations and that aspect of health related to a person's capacity to function, as well as the models of educational effectiveness discussed above.

We must also recognize that many of the causal relations by which contributory variables affect quality-adjusted life years remain to be determined. Variables affecting the duration of life itself are better known, as they draw on the knowledge of the biological and health sciences. The determinants of subjective well-being may lie closer to the individual, in intimate relationships, and farther from public policy than are economic variables. They may also relate to the individual's symbolic environment, and thus be affected by hopes and fears engendered by political and private discourse; for this reason, some may distrust these variables as reflecting "illusory" rather than "real" well-being. But it is precisely because they represent a counterbalance to the perhaps too "real" variables of economics and the material environment that we need to examine them.

Even though we propose QALYs as a yardstick for comparison of policy outcomes among particular social goal areas, this comparison of the effects of disparate policies is more difficult for subjective than for economic variables. It depends on tracing subtle chains of causation rather than on assigning monetary values. In principle we can compare health and crime policy as they affect QALYs, but in practice much research is necessary and problems of measurement and inference must be overcome.

To see more clearly the advantages of considering general end-values, let us analyze their relation to two widely used indicator variables: social mobility and health. The concept of social mobility, as we shall see, does not have a sufficiently clear valuative connotation, but can be interpreted in terms of our proposed general end-values; in the case of health, the concept as expressed by conventional indicators is not sufficiently general to provide the sort of guidance that it might.

Social mobility was chosen as a major indicator concept in an early proposal (HEW, 1969). Early cross-national research in this area (Lipset and Bendix, 1959) was concerned with mobility both as a value (opportunity) and as a possible cause of the lack of socialism in the United States. More recent studies of the "status attainment" have aimed at predicting the occupational status reached by persons in terms of their parents' education and occupation, their own education, their group membership, and other variables.

The "status attainment" concept comes nearer to being a measure of well-being than does mobility itself. Mobility, in the literal sense, may be downward as well as upward; it may occur excessively rapidly, thus failing to make use of specific human capital (Becker, 1975); and even upward mobility may bring psychic conflict and insecurity. Perhaps the hope of advancement is itself a source of well-being or of motivation to produce, and that of fair advancement a source of social cohesion; but such connections need to be verified. Thus in place of social mobility as a value, we might better deal with the *efficiency* of occupational placement systems for overall production and consumption; the *subjective well-being* that people enjoy in their work, consumption, and other activities in relation to mobility among roles; and the *equity* with which roles and their attendant opportunities are distributed. Status attainment has some relation to the well-being that individuals receive from changes in roles; but the passage from individual to aggregate attainment may bring with it compensating disadvantages when the advancement of some persons entails losses for others (Hirsch, 1976). By considering these more gen-

eral end-values and treating aspects of social mobility as possibly contributory to them, we can clarify the relations between mobility and the
values we seek.

The choice of health as an indicator concept seems obvious in view of
its valuative importance as well as its relevance to an important segment
of production—the health services professions and industries. Indeed,
it has been considered an intrinsic value in the philosophical sense (Frankena, 1963:72). Yet health falls short of being a general end-value and
cannot be used as a surrogate for well-being.

The statistics used to measure health (or ill health) generally provide
one of two types of information—on incidence of disease, or on capacity
to function. The first of these, disease, is a disvalued physiological condition defined by medical science and usually capable of being remedied
by the health professions. Thus a handicap or the result of an accident
or crime may not come within the scope of a disease indicator, even
though it may have the same effect as a disease on a person's production,
consumption, or subjective well-being. The loss of function of one arm
from a stroke is more clearly a disease statistic than the severing of that
arm through an industrial accident. The dysfunctions of old age, insofar
as they are not easily curable and indeed seem "normal," are not so likely
to be counted in disease statistics as are the remediable or temporary
malfunctions of younger persons.

The second type of health statistic, measuring the individual's capacity
to function, should be able to include disabilities from whatever source
they arise. Examples are statistics on days of bed-disability or restricted
activity. An index combining death and disability rates into "expectancy
of healthy life" has been proposed (HEW, 1969:99–100); but in counting
death and permanent bed-disability equally, it weights disability too favorably in terms of its use of productive resources, and too unfavorably
in terms of the subjective well-being it may entail. An index considering
a larger number of levels of functioning has been proposed by Chen et
al. (1975). Indicators of this type relate health (in a broad sense) to
production—either on the job, or in "household production," which is
closely related to consumption.

Neither disease indicators nor function-status indicators, however, reflect the subjective aspect of quality of life. Some writers (e.g., Bradburn,
1969:7–8) have pointed out that mental health is closely related to subjective well-being. Subjective well-being (in the form of pain) is among
the symptoms that physicians consider, together with capacity to function, in diagnosing disease; both are more general values. But as we have
noted, this transformation of information on function *or* subjective well-
being into disease statistics can omit noteworthy variations in these general values simply because they do not fall within the diagnostic categories

used. The same sorts of omission can occur for deficiencies in subjective well-being as for function status. Pain or anxiety, if not traceable to a specifiable disease, may be relegated to psychiatric treatment or drug therapy rather than to an investigation of environmental, work, or family conditions. And even if a manipulable cause cannot easily be found, reporting of the incidence of low levels of subjective well-being may stimulate a search for additional manipulable causes.

We have suggested that conventional social indicator variables can be usefully subjected to valuative critiques in view of the more general end-values that we seek. At the same time, however, cost and the requirement of reliable measurement lead us to use indicators that are less than perfect measures of value concepts. In the health area, statistics on disease are more easily available in objective form than statistics on people's capacity to function, and these, in turn, than data on subjective well-being. For similar reasons, a national commission assessing labor force data in the United States explicitly rejected the use of indicators such as unemployment statistics to measure welfare (Adams, 1981:128). In this tension between criteria, what is important is to recognize the direction in which we would be led in the longer run, by centering indicator systems on general end-values.

SUMMARY AND CONCLUSIONS

Policy indicators differ from indicators of social change in three ways: (a) the design of policy indicator statistics centers about their use in political systems; (b) they are variables (not aggregate statistics), which are common to aggregate statistics and to the causal policy models that accompany them; and (c) they include economic, environmental, and other policy-relevant variables as well as social conditions.

Policy indicators, as defined here, are those variables that are justifiably included in public statistical systems because of their contribution to collective policy decisions guided by ethical values. To justify their inclusion we must look to the consequences that eventually flow from their use. The utility of policy indicator statistics depends on their contribution to the public's definition of problems and choice of policies, and on their cost and their other uses. Public judgments about problems and policies can be aided by causal "policy models" connecting possible policies with valued or disvalued conditions measured by indicator statistics. The dependent variables in policy models must be policy indicators, but otherwise the development of these models has no necessary dependence on indicator statistics. The contributory variables in policy models, including manipulable policy-related variables, are potential policy indicators.

The values embodied in policy indicator statistics are notions of the common good or of equity. They vary from specific to general and from partial to more inclusive, with general intrinsic values (end-values) as central ingredients of a policy indicator system. If general end-values can be measured and used in public debate, they can facilitate the trade-offs and reconciliations of value that democratic political processes must make. They can make a contribution to democratic debate, but cannot be expected to dominate it. Indicators of such values, and policy models suggesting their manipulable causes, must be intelligible to the public. The work of economists, in computing and using measures of the GNP and of net economic benefit, provides a general end-value and an example for both emulation and caution.

In parallel with indicators of net economic benefit, it may be useful to seek long-range development of statistics and models based on quality-adjusted life years—a variable used in health policy analysis but having broader significance as a general end-value. In addition, distributional equity as it affects other policy indicators represents a third major type of end-value that can guide the development of policy indicators and models.

Social scientists' roles in developing policy indicators and policy models must differ from those of basic scientific research. Although basic research can serve the development of policy indicators and models, it is insufficient alone for either of these purposes. The invisible colleges of basic research must be supplemented by "technical communities" of researchers who center their work about general policy models rather than disciplinary theory or immediate public problems. Members of technical communities must be prepared to deal with citizens and public leaders while subjecting their recommendations to quality control by fellow members. To the extent that they can reconcile the requirements of these two reference groups, they may be able to make expert contributions to democratic policy choice.

ACKNOWLEDGMENTS

This paper draws on a longer manuscript, *Policy Indicators*, prepared under the auspices of the Social Science Research Council's Advisory and Planning Committee on Social Indicators, that has been published by the University of North Carolina Press. Numerous persons have given me useful comments on that manuscript, but for comments related to this paper I am particularly indebted to Judith I. de Neufville. Useful suggestions have also been made by Otis Dudley Duncan, William N. Dunn, Kenneth C. Land, and Robert Parke. None of these readers is responsible for my errors. Previous versions of this paper were presented under somewhat different titles at the Tenth World Congress of Sociology, Mexico City, August 16–21, 1982; at the annual meeting of the American Political Science Association, Denver, CO, Sept. 2–5, 1982; and at the annual meeting of the Southern Sociological Society, Atlanta, GA, April 7–9, 1983.

NOTES

1. From an economic perspective there would be no need for us to deliberate collectively about the choice of these variables—or of other aspects of information systems—if their provision responded to a well-functioning market. The production of information for private consumption (e.g., the reporting of market prices in newspapers) can respond somewhat to demand, and privately used information can be analyzed from an economic standpoint (Machlup, 1962, 1980). Insofar as information is a collective good, efficiency may be promoted by subsidizing it; then decisions as to what to subsidize arise when we do not have a clear expression of demand. If information is needed by citizens for decisions in view of the public interest, it may be considered a merit good, so that subsidy will encourage citizens to attend relatively more to the public interest than to private interests; in this case decisions are needed not only to summarize demand, but also to judge how the public interest might be served. The choice of indicator variables for policy guidance is thus itself a policy problem, though its effects are less direct than those of many other policy choices.

2. More precisely, we define a policy indicator as a measure such that statistics based on it are justifiably included in a system of public statistics useful for choice of policies in view of public, ethical values. Aspects of this definition are discussed below.

3. The actor may be an individual, group, or organization. A collective decision is a decision taken by a collection of actors and binding on the particular actor; for our purposes the most important example is a government decision. A group as an actor may act alone, as in deciding to produce some good; or as a participant in a collective decision, as in lobbying. Our classification of motives, like that of economics, tends to omit malevolence.

4. Even though public argument derives much of its force from an interplay of private interests, those who speak for these interests often support their claims by arguing that these claims promote the general good. The quality of public discourse can be improved if we take these arguments seriously, design information systems for measuring and monitoring such concepts of the general good, and conduct research to test whether such arguments are valid. We do not necessarily try to "unmask" these arguments (Mannheim, 1949:37) by pointing to the social origins or interests of the speaker; rather, we examine their persuasiveness in their own right (Steinfels, 1977:5). In so doing we depart from political scientists' models of the "rational (selfish) voter" or economists' models of "public choice" based on maximization of individual "utility"; there may be truth in these models, but it is a partial truth. Even the most public-spirited policy analysts, however, when seeking to maintain an organization and resources, will be driven to support that organization's narrower interests (Wildavsky, 1979:Ch. 9).

5. Some governmental decisions can be adaptive, such as the response of public-school planning to demographic trends (Parke and Sheldon, 1973:107–108).

6. These adaptations can create values (or disvalues) that contribute to the overall net benefit of providing the information. The private values served may be disparate and not enter into ethical discourse; but as citizens we can aggregate them, trade them off, and use these aggregates to justify policies in terms of their contributions to the general welfare. In this respect, information policy is public policy affecting private actions.

7. The individual member of such a group is then acting in the group's interest rather than simply in self-interest, but we still refer to the motive as "private" in contrast to the wider public interest.

8. Diverse notions of the general welfare would give rise to diverse sets of policy indicators, and if the differences were reconciled this would have to be done politically (see below). In terms of the definition above (footnote 2), a variable or statistic is justified for inclusion not only by its use for this purpose, but also by its cost and other uses.

9. We use this term rather than "explanatory variables" to stress the decision-oriented character of the models that link them to value variables. Johnston and Carley note the distinction between discipline-based explanatory variables and variables more closely related to movement toward preferred future states (1981:241, 250, 253). Land (1975:17) defines "analytic indicators" as components of models of social processes which result in "values of the output indicators," but contends that models developed for scientific purposes can be transformed into policy models by the simple addition of valuative criteria (p. 33). Basic researchers, however, are not usually properly motivated to include in their models just those variables that are most useful for policy purposes.

10. The characteristics denoted by "intrinsic" and "general" are not identical; the cultivation of the arts, for example, is often considered to be of intrinsic value even though it does not subsume other social goals. The type of variable that is viewed as a general end is discussed critically by E. S. Dunn (1974:107ff.) in relation to the quest for a "grand indicator."

11. Altshuler (1965:338, 343) argues that "the profession which consolidates all the measures of its success into one immeasurably enhances its claim to be called expert in its sphere"; but notes also that "it is obviously impossible to specify technical qualifications for the *most* general evaluators."

12. For greatest generality we should speak of a "political system" and of the "affected population" to be served; this usage would apply to hierarchical organizations whose decisions affect nonparticipants and nonmembers, and to formal governmental organizations whose populations are deeply divided and feel little sense of community (such as the United Nations). By using the term "political community," however, we wish to suggest an aspect of a functioning democratic order by implying that most of those affected are participants. The term is defined by Easton (1965:177–79), but not with this implication.

13. It could be argued that some aspects of the truth are not easily grasped through statistics, or that some aspects of our well-being depend on the persistence of myths and illusions; but we assume here that science can contribute to our well-being.

14. The utility of new information must always be assessed in terms of its relation to preexisting information, in a perspective of "value added" (Lindblom and Cohen, 1979). Our discussion will center about time series of indicator statistics, however, rather than non-statistical or non-periodic information.

15. Carley (1981:125) points out that "government statistical agencies are duty bound to remain politically neutral." This does not mean, however, that their managers can afford to ignore politics, either partisan or organizational.

16. The values supported by the members of such a coalition do not necessarily represent aspects of the public interest. They may sometimes reflect alternative notions of the public interest; but they may also be values accruing to distinct groups and more appropriate to an economic view of politics as based on self-interest.

17. Sheldon and Parke (1975:695–96) refer to "goal-oriented analyses" as lying within the scope of administrators and their agencies, and only general "enlightenment" being appropriate for the public; but citizens may also engage in analysis.

18. This participation requires freedom of communication among citizens, and must not be curtailed by government through data files on individuals or through governmental

information control. At the same time we must recognize that technical information not easily understood by the public (e.g., economic or environmental) can benefit the public; and that information about a nation's environment (foreign intelligence) can sometimes be of greater benefit to the public if it is not made public.

19. The Swedish level-of-living surveys have been developed in about a decade (Vogel, 1982).

20. Warning signals may be generated by current values of indicator variables, by extrapolation of current trends, or by more complex forecasting models. Signals of progress can not merely decrease the sense of urgency of a problem, but also encourage further efforts if they show that previous efforts have borne fruit. Examples are the gradual decline of pollutants in the River Thames, and the decrease in the United States of the disparity in educational achievement between blacks and whites (Burton and Jones, 1982).

These statistics can sensitize members of the community to needs for collective action and policy formation; but even though they are useful for highlighting problems, they are not equally useful for all sorts of problems. Time series are most relevant in problem definition if our standard of comparison is an earlier condition or trend. If the standard is an external one, such as an absolute judgment or the condition of another community or group, then a single "snapshot" observation can suffice. Large, new, "strategic" problems may lie outside the domain of past indicator series. Finally, policies should not be chosen in terms of our sense of problems alone; their justification depends also on their prospective benefits and costs, as well as on moral and legal constraints. Thus some deficiencies revealed by indicators cannot be remedied except at prohibitive cost, whereas new opportunities for improvement may arise even when indicators do not reveal a deficiency (MacRae and Wilde, 1979:31–33). Moreover, the expected effects of a proposed policy depend on its political feasibility; a widespread sense that a problem exists enhances the feasibility of policies aimed at this problem, but does not assure feasibility by itself.

21. Some action, it is true, must be preceded by the growth of public concern, the mobilization of political resources, or research on the expected effects of various actions; for these preparatory steps, the defintion of problems alone may be useful. Other actions may be merely symbolic, to assert our sense of control over events.

22. W. N. Dunn (1982) places policy research within a context of public argument; but even though we recognize this as a political constraint and a democratic goal, we can still seek to improve the standards of public argument. Some of the policies we consider may be concerned with decision processes and the use of information themselves, but these are especially difficult to assess in terms of specific valued consequences.

23. The relevant published indicator statistics deal most often with the gross national product, neglecting depreciation; but in benefit-cost analysis depreciation should be considered.

24. Other general values have also been proposed. Allardt (1973:65–66) has proposed three of them—having, loving, and being. The first of these corresponds to resources that an individual can use for production and consumption, and thus approximately to things that are valued in economic terms. "Loving" refers to close personal relations, which we suggest are a major source of subjective well-being. "Being" relates to self-actualization— perhaps an aspect or an alternative definition of subjective well-being, and thus a possible intrinsic value.

REFERENCES

Adams, A. V. (1981) "The American work force in the eighties." Annals of the American Academy of Political and Social Science 453:123–129.

Allardt, E. (1973) "A welfare model for selecting indicators of national development." Policy Sciences 4(1):63–74.

Allison, G. T. (1971) Essence of Decision. Boston: Little, Brown.

Altshuler, A. A. (1965) The City Planning Process. Ithaca, NY: Cornell University Press.

Becker, G. S. (1975) Human Capital, 2nd ed. New York: Columbia University Press.

Beresford, J., P. Billot, H. Hansen, Y. Ollivier, J. Willis, G. Staack, P. Chardavoine, P. Gremion and H. Jamous (1976) Information Systems in Government, vol. 3. Marseille: Data for Development.

Biderman, A. D. (1970) "Information, intelligence, enlightened public policy: functions and organization of societal feedback." Policy Sciences 1(2):217–230.

Bradburn, N. M. (1969) The Structure of Psychological Well-Being. Chicago: Aldine.

Braybrooke, D. and C. E. Lindblom (1975) A Strategy for Decision. New York: Free Press.

Brewer, G. D. and R. D. Brunner, eds. (1975) Political Development and Change: A Policy Approach. New York: Free Press.

Burton, N. W. and L. V. Jones (1982) "Recent trends in achievement levels of black and white youth." Educational Researcher 11(4):19–14.

Campbell, A., P. E. Converse and W. L. Rodgers (1976) The Quality of American Life. New York: Russell Sage Foundation.

Carley, M. (1980) Rational Techniques in Policy Analysis. London: Heinemann.

———(1981) Social Measurement and Social Indicators: Issues of Policy and Theory. London: George Allen & Unwin.

Chen, M. M., J. W. Bush and D. L. Patrick (1975) "Social indicators for health planning and policy analysis." Policy Sciences 6(1):71–89.

Coleman, J. S. (1970) "Political money." American Political Science Review 64(4):1074–1087.

———(1972) Policy Research in the Social Sciences. Morristown, NJ: General Learning Press.

———(1980) "The structure of society and the nature of social research." Knowledge 1(3):333–350.

Coleman, J. S., E. Q. Campbell, C. J. Hobson, J. McPartland, A. M. Mood, F. D. Weinfield and R. L. York (1966) Equality of Educational Opportunity. Washington, D.C.: U.S. Government Printing Office.

Coleman, J. S., T. Hoffer and S. Kilgore (1981) Public and Private Schools. Draft report to the National Center for Education Statistics by the National Opinion Research Center. (Revised version: High School Achievement. New York: Basic Books, 1982).

Coleman, J. S., S. D. Kelly and J. A. Moore (1975) Trends in School Segregation, 1968–73. Washington, D.C.: The Urban Institute.

de Neufville, J. I. (1975) Social Indicators and Public Policy. New York: Elsevier.

Dibble, V. K. (1962) "Occupations and ideologies." American Journal of Sociology 68(2):229–241.

Drewnowski, J. F. (1970) Studies in the Measurement of Levels of Living and Welfare. Geneva: UNRISD.

Dunn, E. S., Jr. (1974) Social Information Processing and Statistical Systems—Change and Reform. New York: Wiley.

Dunn, W. N. (1982) "Reforms as arguments." Knowledge 3(3):293–326.

Easton, D. (1965) A Systems Analysis of Political Life. New York: Wiley.

Fox, K. A. (1974) Social Indicators and Social Theory. New York: Wiley.

Frankena, W. K. (1963) Ethics. Englewood Cliffs, NJ: Prentice-Hall.

Garn, H. A., M. J. Flax, M. Springer and J. B. Taylor (1976) Models for Indicator Development: A Framework for Policy Analysis. Washington, D.C.: The Urban Institute.

Hanke, S. H. and R. A. Walker (1977) "Benefit-cost analysis reconsidered: an evaluation of the mid-state project." In R. H. Haveman and J. Margolis (eds.), Public Expenditure and Policy Analysis, 2nd ed. Chicago: Rand McNally.

Haveman, R. H. and J. Margolis, eds. (1977) Public Expenditure and Policy Analysis. Chicago: Aldine.

HEW (U.S. Department of Health, Education, and Welfare) (1969) Toward a Social Report. Washington, D.C.: U.S. Government Printing Office.

Hirsch, F. (1976) Social Limits to Growth. Cambridge, MA: Harvard University Press.

Johnson, R. W. and À. Y. Lewin (1984) "Management and accountability models." In T. C. Miller (ed.), Public Sector Performance. Baltimore: Johns Hopkins University Press.

Johnston, D. F. (1978) "Postlude: past, present, and future." Annals of the American Academy of Political and Social Science 435:286–294.

Johnston, D. F. and M. J. Carley (1981) "Social measurement and social indicators." Annals of the American Academy of Political and Social Science 453:237–253.

Juster, F. T., P. N. Courant and G. K. Dow (1981) "The theory and measurement of well-being: a suggested framework for accounting and analysis." In F. T. Juster and K. C. Land (eds.), Social Accounting Systems. New York: Academic Press.

Keeney, R. L. and H. Raiffa, eds. (1976) Decisions with Multiple Objectives. New York: Wiley.

Land, K. C. (1975) "Social indicator models: an overview." In K. C. Land and S. Spilerman (eds.), Social Indicator Models. New York: Russell Sage Foundation.

Lindblom, C. E. and D. K. Cohen (1979) Usable Knowledge. New Haven, CT: Yale University Press.

Lipset, S. M. and R. Bendix (1959) Social Mobility in Industrial Society. Berkeley, CA: University of California Press.

Machlup, F. (1962) The Production and Distribution of Knowledge in the United States. Princeton, NJ: Princeton University Press.

———(1980) Knowledge: Its Creation, Distribution, and Economic Significance, vol. I, Knowledge and Knowledge Production. Princeton, NJ: Princeton University Press.

MacRae, D., Jr. (1976a) The Social Function of Social Science. New Haven, CT: Yale University Press.

———(1976b) "Technical communities and political choice." Minerva 14(2):169–190.

MacRae, D., Jr. and J. A. Wilde (1979) Policy Analysis for Public Decisions. Belmont, CA: Duxbury Press. Reprinted by University Press of America, 1985.

Mannheim, K. (1949) Ideology and Utopia. New York: Harcourt, Brace. First published in 1936.

Mare, R. D. (1981) "Trends in schooling: demography, performance, and organization." Annals of the American Academy of Political and Social Science 453:96–122.

Nelkin, D (1979) "Scientific knowledge, public policy, and democracy: a review essay." Knowledge 1(1):106–122.

Nordhaus, W. and J. Tobin (1972) "Is growth obsolete?" In Economic Growth. Fiftieth Anniversary Colloquium V. New York: National Bureau of Economic Research.

OECD (Organisation for Economic Co-operation and Development) (1976) Measuring Social Well-Being. Paris: OECD.

Osipov, G. V. and V. G. Andreenkov, eds. (1979) Issledovanie Postroeniia Pokazatelei Sotsialnogo Razvitiia i Planirovaniia (Investigation of the Construction of Indicators of Social Development and Planning). Moscow: "Nauka" Publishing House.

Parke, R. and E. B. Sheldon (1973) "Social statistics for public policy." Pp. 105–112 in American Statistical Association, Proceedings of the Social Statistics Section.

Patton, M. Q. (1978) Utilization-Focused Evaluation. Beverly Hills, CA: Sage Publications.

Price, D. K. (1965) The Scientific Estate. Cambridge, MA: Harvard University Press.

Raiffa, H. (1968) Decision Analysis. Reading, MA: Addison-Wesley.

Rich, R. F. (1981) Social Science Information and Public Policy Making. San Francisco: Jossey-Bass.

Rodgers, W. L. (1982) "Trends in reported happiness within demographically defined subgroups, 1957–78." Social Forces 60(3):826–842.

Rossi, P. H., E. Waite, C. E. Bose and R. E. Berk (1974) "The seriousness of crimes: normative structure and individual differences." American Sociological Review 39(2):224–237.

Schattschneider, E. E. (1960) The Semisovereign People. Hinsdale, IL: Dryden Press.

Scott, W. (1973) "The measurement of real progress at the local level: examples from the literature and a pilot study." Geneva: United Nations Research Institute for Social Development Report No. 73.3.

Sellin, T. and M. E. Wolfgang (1964) The Measurement of Delinquency. New York: Wiley.

Sharpe, L. J. (1978) "The social scientist and policy-making in Britain and America: a comparison." In M. Bulmer (ed.), Social Policy Research. London: Macmillan.

Sheldon, E. B. and R. Parke (1975) "Social indicators." Science 188(4189):693–699.

Steinfels, P. (1977) "The place of ethics in schools of public policy." A report from the Hastings Center Institute of Society, Ethics, and Life Sciences to the Ford Foundation (April).

Vogel, J. (1982) "The Swedish annual level-of-living surveys: social indicators and social reporting as an official statistics program." Paper presented at the Tenth World Congress of Sociology, Mexico City (August).

Weinstein, M. C. and W. B. Stason (1976) Hypertension: A Policy Perspective. Cambridge, MA: Harvard University Press.

———(1977) "Foundations of cost-effectiveness analysis for health and medical practices." New England Journal of Medicine 296: 716–721.

Weiss, C. H. (1972) Evaluation Research. Englewood Cliffs, NJ: Prentice-Hall.

Whitaker, G. P. (1980) "Coproduction: citizen participation in service delivery." Public Administrative Review 40(3):240–246.

Wildavsky, A. (1979) Speaking Truth to Power. Boston: Little, Brown.

Zapf, W. (1972) "Social indicators: prospects for social accounting systems." Social Science Information 11(3/4):243–277.

THE *SENSUS COMMUNIS:*
A FRAMEWORK FOR VALUATIVE
DISCOURSE ON PUBLIC POLICY

Guy B. Adams

ABSTRACT

The *sensus communis* (literally, "common sense") may be used to describe two features of valuative discourse: the setting of ethical standards and the receiving of ethical standards from cultural tradition. The active process of setting ethical standards may be characterized in terms of aesthetic design, while the receiving of ethical standards is evident in the meanings of equality in this and other cultures. *Sensus communis* offers a framework which illuminates the poverty of valuative discourse on public policy and the possibilities for its enrichment.

INTRODUCTION

The *sensus communis* provides a framework which can both describe and inform the valuative discourse which is the foundation, however unseen or submerged, of public policy. Used in a descriptive manner, the *sensus communis* can illuminate the standards of social and political practices in

Policy Analysis: Perspectives, Concepts, and Methods, pages 169–184.
Copyright © 1986 by JAI Press, Inc.
All rights of reproduction in any form reserved.
ISBN: 0–89232–371–X

a community. Normatively, it is the sense that founds community, and thus, is made visible in judgments about right and wrong action, becoming the sense of the right, or general good, that is found in all those who "dwell in" the community. *Sensus communis* means, literally, "common sense." I mean "sense" as something that is felt or held as a belief; and I mean "common" as the common body of the people of any place, the community or commonalty.

The essay proceeds as follows. First, I attempt to establish the need for a framework to understand valuative discourse on public policy. I suggest that the field of policy studies has neglected questions of value, and that valuative discourse is a critical element in the formation of public policy. Next, I characterize explicitly the concept of *sensus communis*, the sense of commonalty that is enacted through the practice of living together. I suggest that ethical standards, which constitute the *sensus communis*, arise from a dialectical process comprised of the active creation of ethical standards and of the receiving of those standards through the cultural tradition.

The setting of ethical standards as seen as an active, creative process, and treated as a matter of design. Design, taken as tacit, is extended to the possibility of societal design, and then linked to aesthetics.

I go on to suggest that the receiving of ethical standards is a central part of the process of acculturation; it is a part of how we learn our cultural tradition. The value, "equality," is used as an example of a received ethical standard, and is contrasted with the meaning given to equality with the ancient Greek cultural tradition.

Finally, I argue that the *sensus communis*, in its normative sense, founds community. The importance of community for social life is developed through a number of examples; and three ideals: love, mutual aid or cooperation, and altruism, are put forward as generative for valuative discourse on public policy.

THE NEED FOR SUCH A FRAMEWORK IN PUBLIC POLICY STUDIES

Inquiry about public policy has proceeded from the underlying assumption that facts and values are separated, and further, that values are to be settled on prior to the beginning of any policy inquiry.[1] The view of policy studies as "value-neutral" has, however, come under increasing criticism (Fisher, 1980). Martin Rein, in *Social Science and Public Policy*, has proposed a typology of approaches to policy studies which he portrays as follows (1976:79):

The value-critical approach provides a relatively doubtful and uncertain position because it accepts neither the advantages of a claim to pure science (the value-neutral approach) nor the moral embrace of pure ideology (the value-committed approach). It tries to submit each issue to impartial analysis, mindful that it can never altogether be successful in what it attempts.

The *sensus communis*, as a framework, falls within the value-critical approach. However, it is important to note that the *sensus communis* deals with only one aspect of public policy inquiry, namely valuative discourse. An example of valuative discourse around a public policy issue is the volume *When Values Conflict: Essays on Environmental Analysis, Discourse and Decision* (Tribe, Schelling and Voss, 1977), in which are collected a series of papers written for a symposium commissioned by the American Academy of Arts and Sciences. These papers discuss the valuative discourse underlying the public policy issue of whether or not to build the Tocks Island Dam on the Delaware River. As good as the volume is, it is primarily noteworthy as an exception in the public policy literature— an odd duck that required special funding to gain existence.

Valuative discourse is that part of public policy studies most radically neglected by mainstream approaches like cost-benefit (so-called "rational") analysis. Valuative discourse is the critical interpretation of what economists call "externalities," in an ironically revealing turn of phrase. As might be imagined for a system of discourse long considered "external," valuative discourse on public policy is a little-understood, largely tacit process. Donald Schon recognized this fact in attempting to account for what he called "ideas in good currency" (1971:123):

> Underlying every public debate and every formal conflict over policy there is a barely visible process through which issues come to awareness and ideas about them become powerful. The hidden process by which ideas come into good currency gives us the illusory sense of knowing what we must worry about and do . . . These antecedent processes are as crucial to the formation of policy as the processes of discovery in science are crucial to the formation of plausible hypotheses. But our bias in favor of the rational, the 'scientific,' the well-formed and the retrospective causes us to disregard the less visible process and to accept the ideas underlying public conflict over policy as mysteriously given.

There is a clear need for a framework that can account for the valuative processes at work in the generation of ideas in good currency; the *sensus communis* may provide such a framework.

There is an equally clear need for a framework to provide normative guidance not only in describing valuative discourse, but also in informing that discourse. Its long neglect has rendered valuative discourse on public policy into an impoverished, withered, little-heard conversation among a neglected few. However submerged, valuative discourse takes place within the cultural tradition of a society, even as it shapes that tradition.[2] The cultural tradition of our society includes American culture, Western culture, and more broadly, both the cultures and the culture of mankind. Understanding valuative discourse, and more generally, public policy inquiry, as within the cultural tradition tends to open access to historical consciousness, the lack of which has had crippling public policy implications (Rothman, 1971; 1980). Sam Bass Warner's *The Urban Wilderness*, by providing a historical analysis of the American city, shows clearly the extent to which, for example, urban policy has been uninformed by historical consciousness and the extent to which it has suffered as a result (1972: 267):

> American urban life confuses us in its intermingling of endless repetition with ceaseless change. Consider our habitual responses. We do not see in the brand-new downtown apartment towers or the freshly carpeted suburban model home the inevitable repetition of failure which surely awaits them... Since at least the founding of the Republic we have been concealing failure from ourselves with newness, and ever since we proved unable to protect our farmer and artisan forefathers from the oppressions of the workplace we have desperately sought to isolate home from work. Thus for generations we have dwelt in a self-created urban wilderness of time and space, confounding ourselves with its lusty growth and rising to periodic alarms in the night. It is no accident that we have no urban history.

The *sensus communis*, rooted in the cultural tradition of a society, can inform valuative discourse by calling up for dialogue those values within a tradition that foster community.

The cultural tradition is not only, perhaps not even primarily, an enabling phenomenon for public policy. It is also powerfully limiting. The cultural tradition often appears to act much like the legal principle of *stare decisis*, which describes the preference of courts to let a previous decision stand when an issue has been adjudicated earlier. In the cultural tradition, previous decisions do indeed stand—often squarely in our path. There can be a crushing concreteness to the social reality of the cutural tradition (Jacoby, 1975:65): "The content of the social laws is not nature but *second nature*: coagulated history. They are man made, but they also make men; they are dialectical, at once subject and object, neither totally one or the other." Nonetheless, such possibilities as we have for the creation of public policy in the service of human emancipation exist only within the cultural tradition; they are not to be created through the continued, ostensible rationalization of public policy inquiry.[3] The aim here is to characterize the *sensus communis* as a normative framework within which one can critically interpret the current valuative discourse on public policy, and thereby also inform that discourse.

THE SENSUS COMMUNIS

It should be appropriate here to convey more directly what I mean by the *sensus communis*. The term, *sensus communis*, is taken from an early eighteenth century humanist thinker, Giambattista Vico (1965; 1948). His use of the concept has been described as follows (Gadamer, 1975:22):

> Vico goes back to the Old Roman idea of the *sensus communis*, as found especially in the Roman classics which, when faced with Greek cultivation, held firmly to the value and significance of their own traditions of public and social life. A critical note, directed against the theoretical speculations of the philosophers can be heard in the Roman concept of the *sensus communis*; and that note Vico sounds again from his different position of opposition to modern science.

Moreover, for Vico, the *sensus communis* is made visible in judgments about right and wrong actions, and thus becomes the sense of the right, or general good, that is found in all, or at least in all those who "dwell in" the community (Polanyi, 1969: 160). The implications of this expansion of the concept may be expressed in the following way (Gadamer, 1975: 21):

> The main thing for our purposes is that *sensus communis* here does not mean only that general faculty in all men, but the sense that founds community. According to Vico, what gives the human will its direction is not the abstract generality of reason, but the concrete generality that represents the community of a group, a people, a nation, or the whole human race. Hence the development of this sense of the community is of prime importance for living.

The *sensus communis*, then, in its descriptive mode, may be used as an essentially valuative framework to view the ethical standards underlying the social and political practices and traditions of a community. In its normative mode, the *sensus communis* informs the valuative processes which are the base of those social and political practices. Thus, the *sensus communis* is the set of ethical standards belonging to a community and what those ethical standards might become.

Normative ethics, which is concerned with standards of moral and political conduct, is the stream of contemporary ethical philosophy most compatible with the *sensus communis*. Normative ethics is concerned with moral argument, which, rather than proceeding from abstractions, is seen as occurring within the limits and possibilities of norms and social customs. The aim of ethical inquiry becomes the exposure of the basis of normative standards and the criteria for their espousement. The way in which normative ethics differs from other contemporary approaches to ethics has been captured as follows (Dallmayr, 1976:76):

Although grounded in on-going interactions and meaning patterns, moral discourse and the justification of norms...cannot be grasped adequately either though the descriptive portrayal of prevailing practices or though the stipulation of abstract, prescriptive rules; rather their understanding requires an effort to reconstruct and explicate in a critical manner the normative standards implicit in intersubjective communicative encounters.

THE SETTING OF ETHICAL STANDARDS

In its descriptive mode, the *sensus communis* conceives of valuative discourse as a dialectical process of two moments: the active process of norm or standard setting, and the receiving and holding of the values of one's cultural tradition. The on-going tension between these two moments is the process of valuative discourse, which, construed in this manner, is analogous to the social dialectic as characterized by Berger and Luckmann (1966:61):

the relationship between man, the producer, and the social world, his product, is and remains a dialectical one. That is, man...and his social world interact with each other. The product acts back on the producer...Society is a human product. Society is an objective reality. Man is a social product.

In the case of valuative discourse, the values imbedded in the cultural tradition represent the product, which acts back on the producer, man, as ethical standards are being produced.

The process of setting and resetting ethical standards is a crucial part of man's way of ordering and organizing experience. It is, in some measure, a matter of human design; indeed the concept of design seems to capture the essence of the standard-setting process rather well. In addition, design evokes aesthetics, and this is most apt, since the aesthetic is virtually the only dimension in Western culture openly acknowledged as tacit. And the process of standard-setting is fundamentally tacit (Vickers, 1978; 1980).

The idea of design, however, has been most commonly conceived as a part of an engineered or technological order. Understanding design in this way is a part of the broader contemporary problem of our exclusive attention to problem-solving to the detriment of problem-setting. However, the crucial issues of our time center not around know-how, but rather around know-what. Problem-setting, know-what is, of course, the central focus of valuative discourse.

Design has been defined as "the conscious effort to impose meaningful order" (Papanek, 1971:3). Perhaps the most important element of this definition is the idea that design is characteristically intentional. This, of course, does not mean that design cannot be largely tacit—it often is. Intentionality here implies that man as an agent has been an active part of the process of design. One important work on design goes so far as to suggest that the process is not so much creation of form as it is successive elimination of misfit (Alexander, 1967). One knows, via a set of tacit criteria, that some particular design does not quite have it, does not quite fit. These mis-fits or mis-matches gradually guide one closer to a "fit." However, even if the design is right, even if there is a fit, we are not closer to uncovering the tacit criteria. This conceptualization of design, taken to the societal level, is particularly apt in attempting to understand the process of norm-setting.

A number of writers have concerned themselves with the concept of societal design, only two of whom will be taken up here (Friedmann, 1973; Jantsch, 1975). The first of these, John Friedmann, a planner, criticizes our current societal design (or guidance, in his terms) systems as unresponsive, inefficient and alienative. He proposes a process of societal guidance, transactive planning, that would be judged for adequacy along six dimensions: autonomy, responsiveness, innovative ability, effectiveness, efficiency, and legitimacy. He then suggests that transactive planning is compatible with an advanced view of societal change, namely, experimental evolution, in which "history appears as a process of social learning in which old knowledge yields to new as it emerges from the interplay of theory and practice." (Friedmann, 1973:23). Experimental evolution is seen as the only form of social change which can be guided by active man. One might suggest in assessing the idea of transactive planning as a form of societal design, that Friedmann has not quite escaped the problem-solving mind-set of conventional planning theory. Nevertheless, transactive planning represents a view of societal design which is some improvement over the sort of technological determinism that has held sway over this area in the past (Barrett, 1979).

A more satisfactory notion of societal design has been presented by Erich Jantsch in *Design for Evolution*. His orientation toward design becomes clear early in the book (Jantsch, 1975:6). "The human predicament is regulation—not only living in accordance with, but *designing* forms of regulation which will ensure the steering of a viable course." This formulation sounds a bit too formal and engineered; however, Jantsch tempers it with the concept of "centering." Centering has had a prominent history, especially in Eastern religious and disciplines, but has achieved a special prominence in the Quaker religion. For the Quakers, "centering down" is the principal form of spiritual meditation, or spiritual inwardness, through which one communes with God. In the more secular sense in which Jantsch uses the term, it has to do with putting one's center into oneself, or one's being, to be attuned to whatever one happens to be doing. Jantsch describes the positive effect that centering has on the human design process as follows (1975:121):

> Design implies emancipation from the grip of a rigid reality. It implies balance in motion—centering. I view such a 'floating,' self-balancing system of design processes, with no firm ground to step on, in analogy to climbing a sand dune—man linking hands with reality and with his appreciated world ... what I mean primarily, is the establishment of a closer link between consciousness and reality—'tuning in' to a dynamic reality which is not autonomous but is interdependent with man in a physical, social, and, above all, spiritual or evolutionary way.

Thus, for Jantsch, the distinctive ingredient of design is spiritual, which he identifies, interestingly enough, with evolution. The spiritual ingredient which Jantsch accords to centering seems to have something of the aesthetic to it.

The aesthetic dimension has to do with the beautiful (as opposed to the merely pleasing); in the case of societal design, it has to do with creating order *well*, hence the setting of ethical standards. Vickers has observed the extent to which design is aesthetic (1973:90):

> I believe that aesthetic judgment is the ruling passion of truly human kind; and I deliberately call judgment a passion. By aesthetic judgment I mean the passionate but patient struggle to bring significant form into being whether what we have to shape is a city, an institution, a public policy or a personal life; knowing that what makes the new form significant is itself a product of time, that the standards by which it is judged will be changed even by being realized.

The tacit standard-setting process, the process of societal design, is our way of bringing the good to light, of setting standards by which to judge our social order.

RECEIVING THE ETHICAL STANDARDS OF A CULTURAL TRADITION

An equally important element in valuative discourse is the acculturating process of receiving the values, the ethical standards, of one's community. This process is essentially the transmission of the cultural tradition. For many, it begins and continues as received knowledge. One of the central reasons why the need is so great for attention to valuative discourse, is the urgency of critical interpretation of that received knowledge. The distortions in our society will continue to resist any public policy which is not grounded in such interpretation; only a critical interpretation will yield a policy that can make any difference (Fay, 1975).

The ethical standards, the values of a cultural tradition are indeed "second nature," as it were. They are susceptible to change, yet they more often persist for generations. But the modern age is often characterized as impermanent. I think this view is less true than it seems on the surface; there is a durability, a consistency to at least parts of human existence. It is clear that what changes attracts our attention far more than what remains the same over time. This illusion of inconstancy in human affairs has contributed greatly to the loss of historical consciousness and the creation of the modern sense of alienation. The recovery of historical consciousness requires, in a profound way, an appreciation of the continuity in human existence.

It may be instructive to consider as a case in point the way in which one value, equality, has changed in meaning over time, while enduring as a concept. There is no aspiration here to provide a complete history of the concept, but simply to indicate one sense in which contemporary normative standards of equality have strengthened the value of equality and one sense in which they have weakened it. This can be accomplished by comparing contemporary standards with those held as an ideal in ancient Greek thought. Such a comparison between our modern equality and ancient Greek equality is accomplished in an article by Lynne Belaief (1975). She holds that our contemporary concept of equality, which she calls social equality, has emphasized performance-oriented stress, which she associates with the conditional love of fathers. This has the effect of diminishing the psychological security associated with the unconditional love provided by mothers. Thus, social equality, an "equality" of opportunity, has placed the emphasis on performance and achievement, on domination, not on equality. To be equal, under this concept of equality, is to underachieve. One's basic self-esteem is conditional upon performance, leading to a social ethic of domination. Belaief goes on to describe a second view of equality, human equality, which:

> is based on a self-perception which is independent of performance or achievement. It is experienced as a deep sense of the rightness of one's existence, and evolves into a basic trust in the lasting quality of this perception ... The experience itself originates in the infant's somatic perception of the mothering figure's joy in his existence, quite apart from any particular skills he may, or may not show ... The emotional and cognitive responses to these wonderful feelings of affirmation issue in what is known as basic self-esteem and a sense of given and equal worth with others (1975:32).

Human equality, it is important to point out, does not deny the validity of performance and achievement as worthy human values in themselves. Rather it seeks simply to sever the spurious connection between success and self-esteem. If people's self-esteem is well-founded and independent, one no longer has to incur guilt as an inevitable companion to

success, because of damaging another's self-esteem through out-per-
forming him.

Now, social equality describes rather well the way in which our social
order has informed the value of equality. Human equality, on the other
hand, is very similar to the ancient Greek ideal of equality (Arendt,
1958:175):

> Human plurality, the basic condition of both action and speech, has the twofold
> character of equality and distinction. If men were not equal, they could neither
> understand each other and those who came before them nor plan for the future
> and foresee the needs of those who will come after them. If men were not distinct,
> each human being distinguished from any other who is, was, or ever will be, they
> would need neither speech nor action to make themselves understood.

The way in which our modern equality, social equality, has improved
upon the Greek concept of human equality is that the former is being
extended to more and more people (however belatedly), while the latter
was the privilege of the few. What we have lost, as described above, is
the central importance of interaction between self-esteem and success.
Making either one conditional upon the other is a profound social loss.

Our received value of social equality has a powerful impact on the
valuative discourse surrounding public policies on inequality in our society. Its emphasis on performance and achievement essentially traps us
in policies of "equal opportunity." The message given to those whose
self-esteem is often already wobbly, is that they may earn esteem conditional on their performance. The lingering and pervasive inequality
in American society, after nearly twenty years of public policy initiatives
designed at least to ameliorate it, is very powerful testimony indeed to
the impoverished and even deformed character of valuative discourse
on public policy (de Lone, 1979). What would it mean to broaden the
valuative discourse on inequality to include the idea of human equality?
What would a public policy based on human equality look like? For most
of us, the answers to those two questions remain shrouded in ambiguity,
precisely because we pay so little attention to valuative discourse. Values
in public policy, after all, are either settled in advance or taken as given
(received knowledge).

THE CREATION OF COMMUNITY

The *sensus communis* in its normative mode, informs valuative discourse;
it does so to the extent that it founds and develops community. The aim
of valuative discourse, then, should be the creation of community:

the more a human group lets itself be represented in the management of its common affairs, and the more it lets itself be represented from outside, the less communal life there is in it and the more impoverished it becomes as a community. For community...declares itself primarily in the common and active management of what it has in common, and without this it cannot exist (Buber, 1958:133).

I want to suggest here several ways in which community may be founded in social life.

Vickers (1973:123) speaks, in *Making Institutions Work*, of our bonds and bondage. Our bonds are self-expectations, and what we trust others to expect of themselves; our bondage is others' expectations of us, especially when they do not match our own self-expectation. It seems to me that we can only decrease our bondage by willingly taking on more bonds—the bonds of community. This may be accomplished through a deepened and enriched view of membership in institutions, such as that afforded by Vickers (1973:14):

Those who depend so completely as each of us does on our membership of many human systems cannot afford to withhold the dues which they demand and need from us, if they—and consequently we—are to survive and function. These dues are payable not merely in money—though the money dues also will have to rise— but in all the qualities which are needed to resolve or contain human conflict; in responsibility, loyalty and mutual trust; in intellectual effort and informed debate; in extended sympathy and tolerance; in brief, in a dramatic extension of the frontier which divides self from other and present from future.

This concept of membership seeks to develop a shared appreciation for community building, and the acceptance of the responsibility for achieving it. The idea of responsible membership seems quite conducive to the nurture of a *sensus communis* in social life.

Responsible membership would seem to facilitate some kinds of action over others. As Hirschman (1970) argues, our societal options may be characterized by the concepts of exit, loyalty and voice. Exit and loyalty, while widely used in our society, do not seem to contribute greatly to community. Voice, however, may be seen as responsible membership. Voice implies commitment, something which has become increasingly imperative for change in social life and elsewhere. A commitment to responsible membership involves the activity of building and rebuilding consensus, a consensus in which we all have a voice. The voice of responsible membership speaks to the sense of community in social life.

Creating conditions in which people can once again feel "at home" is another way of fostering community. People feel most at home, feel the strongest sense of community, in small communities. The strength of this tradition comes clear in the following observation of Vickers (1976:25):

> For more than ninety-nine percent of our time on earth our species has lived in small communities, each of which had found a stable set of external relations with the surround in which or on which it lived. Its standards of order (its culture) were simple and coherent.

I do not know if we are at liberty to return to a life of small communities, but I think we must, at least, attempt to create a sense of that life in human society.

A form of social organization particularly appropriate for community-building is the Israeli kibbutz. The kibbutz, a kind of cooperative, or collective, farm is organized around the following five principles (Spiro, 1963:17–28):

1. the moral value of labor—farming the land is seen as a kind of calling;
2. public ownership of property—the nation is given deed to the land, all other property is community-owned;
3. the moral value of equality—differences in ability and skill are recognized (and treasured), but are not used as a basis for differences in privilege;
4. distribution according to need; and
5. individual liberty—the kibbutz is known as the freest society in the world.

The group, in kibbutz culture, becomes not only a means to some end, but a moral end in itself. The kibbutz represents a model which could be used in other cultures to build community.

Many of these same themes are echoed on the group level by Mary Parker Follett. For Follett, the particular kind of relations in the group represents the key to the success of the group process. She observes three ways of relating in groups: (1) domination, in which only one party gets what it wants; (2) compromise, in which no one's needs are met; and (3) integration, in which all parties' needs are met. She elaborates on integration:

> The most familiar example of integrating as the social process is when two or three people meet to decide on some course of action, and separate with a purpose, a will, which was not possessed by anyone when he came to the meeting, but is the result of the interweaving of all (1919:576).

The integrative phenomenon is the essence of what Follett calls "creative experience," which in turn is the basis of the social process, of social interaction. Community for Follett (1918:48) involves the rule of an interacting group, an "interpermeating whole." It is fostered at the group level through creative experience, which in turn fosters community.

There are several ideals which I believe are generated through the ongoing creation of community and which could enrich our valuative discourse on public policy greatly. These are love, mutual aid or cooperation, and altruism, which will be taken in order. Love has been put forward as a central ethic by many writers, especially theologians (Tillich, 1954; Buber, 1955). Gibson Winter sees love as the preeminent social value (1966:251):

> The implicit hypothesis of the present inquiry is that man's social world is more than the playing off of contrary powers in a dialectic of absurdity. Our informing perspective is that love as the power of giving, openness, and reconciliation shapes the natural, social, and cultural world toward enriched interdependence and harmony, luring man to freedom as particular being in an interdependent world.

Winter's perspective has been carried over into the institutional sphere by Harmon who views love as an essential harmony and need for unity with others (1980:196):

> if institutions are derived from the most elemental unit of human experience (the 'We-relation'), it follows that the norms used to determine the efficacy of 'institutional' conduct should themselves be derived from love, the normative expression of the 'We-relation.'

Thus, in a social context, exploitative and dominating relations are fundamentally wrong, in that they deny community.

In this book, Peter Kropotkin, the Russian anarchist thinker, develops the idea of mutual aid or cooperation, which he distinguishes from love, but which seems nevertheless akin to the sort of social love, or *agapē*, just discussed. Kropotkin says (1972:21):

> It is not love to my neighbour—whom I often do not know at all—which induces me to seize a pail of water and to rush towards his house when I see it on fire; it is a far wider, even though more vague, feeling or instinct of human solidarity and sociability which moves me.

He builds this idea of mutual aid on a biological base, in the belief that the widespread interpretation of Darwin's theory of natural selection as survival-of-the-fittest was mistaken. He claims to have observed in the animal kingdom a cooperation, a sense of solidarity, which has enabled the various species to survive. Warring and strife are quite the exception within all of the species observed by Kropotkin. He goes on to assert that the same phenomenon of mutual aid is operative in the human sphere (1972:21):

> It is the unconscious recognition of the force that is borrowed by each man from the practice of mutual aid; of the close dependency of everyone's happiness upon

the happiness of all; and the sense of justice, or equity, which brings the individual
to consider the rights of every other individual as equal to his own.

The ideal of mutual aid may be seen as reinforcing the dimension of
cooperation, of community in human society.

Closely akin to mutual aid, but more directly altruistic, is Richard
Titmuss' (1972) discussion of the gift relationship. His book is a study
of paid versus voluntary blood-doning, in which the latter is found to
be far more satisfactory. In describing "social theory," which for Titmuss
incorporates voluntarism and altruism, he states that it:

> must inevitably be concerned with the unquantifiable and unmethodical aspects of
> man . . . what unites it with ethical considerations is its focus on integrative systems:
> on processes, transactions, and institutions which promote an individual's sense of
> identity, participation, and community and allow him more freedom of choice for
> the expression of altruism and which, simultaneously, discourage a sense of indi-
> vidual alienation. (1972:224)

Thus, the "gift relationship" is one example of altruism conceived as an
informing social ideal.[4]

To summarize, the attempt here has been to develop the *sensus communis* as a framework for understanding the valuative discourse which
underpins public policy. The *sensus communis* may be used to describe
that valuative discourse as having two features: the setting of ethical
standards and the receiving of the ethical standards of the cultural tradition. The active process of setting ethical standards was characterized
by the notion of aesthetic design. The receiving of ethical standards was
illustrated by examining the meaning of the value, equality, within our
cultural tradition, and then comparing it with another culture. The *sensus
communis* may also be used to inform valuative discourse on public policy,
because it is the sense that founds community among a people. By maintaining a tension between its descriptive dimension and its informing
dimension, the *sensus communis* offers a framework which illumines both
the poverty of our current valuative discourse on public policy and the
possibilities for enriching that discourse through informing ideals.

NOTES

1. See, for example, Laurence Tribe (1972). Perhaps the most blatant statement affirming the separation of facts and values in social science inquiry is to be found in Friedrich
A. Hayek (1967).

2. For an understanding of the role and importance of the cultural tradition in human
affairs, see Hans-Georg Gadamer (1975).

3. As an example of the latter, see Edith Stokey and Richard Zeckhauser (1978).

4. See also Joseph A. Matter (1974); as well as Sorokin's many books on altruism.

REFERENCES

Alexander, C. (1967) Notes on the Synthesis of Form. New York: Pantheon.

Arendt, H. (1958) The Human Condition. Chicago: University of Chicago Press.

Barrett, W. (1979) The Illusion of Technique. Garden City, NY: Doubleday.

Belaief, L. (1975) "Self esteem and human equality." Philosophy and Phenomenological Research 36:25–43.

Berger, P. and T. Luckmann (1966) The Social Construction of Reality. Garden City, NY: Doubleday.

Buber, M. (1955) Between Man and Man. Boston: Beacon Press.

———(1958) Paths in Utopia. Boston: Beacon Press.

Dallmayr, F. (1976) "Beyond dogma and despair: toward a critical theory of politics." American Political Science Review 70:58–78.

deLone, R. H. (1979) Small Futures: Children, Inequality and the Limits of Liberal Reform. New York: Harcourt, Brace and Jovanovich.

Fay, B. (1975) Social Theory and Political Practice. London: Allen and Unwin.

Fisher, F. (1980) Politics, Values and Public Policy. Boulder, CO: Westview Press.

Follett, M. P. (1918) The New State. New York: Longman, Green.

———(1919) "Community is a process." Philosophical Review 28:569–582.

Friedmann, J. (1973) Retracking America: A Theory of Transactive Planning. Garden City, NY: Doubleday.

Gadamer, H.-G. (1975) Truth and Method. New York: Seabury Press.

Harmon, M. M. (1980) "Toward an 'active-social' theory of administrative action." In C. J. Bellone (ed.), Organization Theory and the New Public Administration. Boston: Allyn and Bacon.

Hayek, F. A. (1967) Studies in Philosophy, Politics and Economics. Chicago: University of Chicago Press.

Hirschman, A. O. (1970) Exit, Voice and Loyalty. Cambridge, MA: Harvard University Press.

Jacoby, R. (1975) Social Amnesia. Boston: Beacon Press.

Jantsch, E. (1975) Design for Evolution. New York: Braziller.

Kropotkin, P. (1972) Mutual Aid: A Factor of Evolution. New York: New York University Press.

Matter, J. A. (1974) Love, Altruism and World Crisis: The Challenge of Pitirim Sorokin. Chicago: Nelson-Hall.

Papanek, V. J. (1971) Design for the Real World. New York: Pantheon.

Polanyi, M. (1969) Knowing and Being. Chicago: University of Chicago Press.

Rein, M. (1976) Social Science and Public Policy. New York: Penguin.

Rothman, D. I. (1971) The Discovery of Asylum. Boston: Little, Brown.

———(1980) Conscience and Convenience. Boston: Little, Brown.

Schon, D. (1971) Beyond the Stable State. New York: Norton.

Spiro, M. E. (1963) Kibbutz: Venture in Utopia. New York: Schocken.

Stokey, E. and R. Zeckhauser (1978) A Primer for Policy Analysis. New York: Norton.

Tillich, P. (1954) Love, Power and Justice. London: Oxford University Press.

Titmuss, R. M. (1972) The Gift Relationship. New York: Vintage.

Tribe, L. (1972) "Policy science: analysis or ideology." Philosophy and Public Affairs 2:66–110.

Tribe, L., C. S. Schelling and J. Voss (1977) When Values Conflict: Essays on Environmental Analysis, Discourse and Decision. Cambridge, MA: Ballinger.

Vickers, Sir Geoffrey (1973) Making Institutions Work. New York: John Wiley.

————(1976) Western Culture and Systems Thinking. Unpublished manuscript. Goring-on-Thames, England.

————(1978) "Rationality and intuition." Pp. 143–164 in J. Wechsler (ed.), On Aesthetics in Science. Cambridge, MA: MIT Press.

————(1980) Responsibility: Its Sources and Limits. Seaside, CA: Intersystems.

Vico, G. (1948) The New Science. Ithaca, NY: Cornell University Press.

————(1965) On the Study Methods of our Time. Indianapolis, IN: Bobbs-Merrill.

Warner, S. B. (1972) The Urban Wilderness. New York: Harper and Row.

Winter, G. (1966) Elements for a Social Ethic. New York: Macmillan.

A VALUE BASIS FOR CONSERVATION POLICY

William Leiss

ABSTRACT

This chapter applies a particular value (caring) to the domain of social policy, specifically resource conservation policy. The argument is that our consumer society erodes the social basis for the development by individuals of a sense of well-being and personal identity, and that a conservation ethic based on the concept of caring could provide a foundation in practical morality and public policy for a viable sense of well-being.

INTRODUCTION

In Canada official inquiries into future energy supply and demand forecasts have been a feature of public policy for some time.[1] The most dramatic instance, because of the scope of the anticipated social and environmental impacts, was the dual inquiry concerning northern pipeline proposals. In 1974 Mr. Justice Thomas Berger, of the British Co-

Policy Analysis: Perspectives, Concepts, and Methods, pages 185–201.
Copyright © 1986 by JAI Press, Inc.
All rights of reproduction in any form reserved.
ISBN: 0–89232–371–X

lumbia Supreme Court, was appointed by the federal government to investigate and report on the "terms and conditions" for a pipeline down the Mackenzie River Valley. Three years later his report, entitled "Northern Frontier, Northern Homeland," appeared; in a moving document that detailed the threat of disruption to native communities and wildlife presented by the pipeline, Berger recommended a ten-year moratorium on construction and the permanent closing of the northern Yukon as an energy corridor. Shortly thereafter the parallel pipeline inquiry by the National Energy Board rejected the Mackenzie Valley route in favor of the Alaska Highway line.[2]

At the same time, Ontario, Canada's most populous and wealthiest province, was experiencing long-term bond financing pressures as a result of the electrical power supply expansion plans of Ontario Hydro, the semi-autonomous, monopoly public utility. In 1975 the Ontario government established a Royal Commission on Electric Power Planning (the Porter Commission), with a mandate to recommend long-range planning procedures for electrical energy; the Commission's final series of reports appeared in 1981. Its interim report on nuclear power, released in 1978, recommended a significant retreat from Ontario Hydro's proposed future expansion of the nuclear system, pending resolution of environmental issues such as disposal of uranium mine tailings and spent fuel wastes.

The work of the Berger and Porter commissions represents only the most publicized segment of the many studies, inquiries, hearings, reports, monographs, and conferences on Canadian energy policy that have taken place since the mid–1970s.[3] Apart from a rhetorical commitment to a greater national self-sufficiency in energy supply, the pious hope that Canada shares with some other industrialized nations, no clear consensus or policy direction has emerged. The only safe conclusion one can draw at present is that these numerous reports and inquiries will be followed by many more.

The main thrust of government initiatives so far has been the strengthening of energy supply options: stimulating explorations for fossil fuel deposits in frontier areas, developing new fossil fuel sources (especially tarsands and heavy oil deposits), providing research support for the next generation of nuclear systems, and completing the huge James Bay hydroelectric project in Quebec. All of these are large-scale endeavors requiring massive capital outlays. Opposition to them from various coalitions of environmental and public interest groups, which so far has been of little effect, has concentrated on two main themes: (1) the necessity for research and development support for alternative supply technologies (solar, wind, biomass), and (2) a far greater emphasis on energy conservation.

The reason why the opposing energy policy strategies have had so little impact to date is not hard to discern. The government initiatives favor the kind of large-scale, capital-intensive production process that is characteristic of industrial development generally. It therefore has the aspect of "business as usual" that is comforting to those who occupy positions of authority in the interlocking public and private bureaucracies in contemporary society. The opposing strategies, on the other hand, see the "solution" to the energy crisis in terms of a challenge to that dominant direction of industrial development, a reorientation toward more decentralized, smaller-scale institutional structures and a commitment on the individual level to less wasteful patterns of consumption.

This suggests that conflicts over energy policy are, at least in part, conflicts over basic values and goals in the process of social change. For the most part this has remained a hidden dimension in public debate over energy policy. The remaining pages of this paper are based on the presumption that this situation could change, and that much of the coming conflict over energy policy could involve explicit disagreements over general social values and goals.

In other words, there is the possibility that this debate will spill over the narrow utilitarian boundaries it has respected so far. For example, studies have shown that some industrialized countries, especially Canada and the United States, are much higher in their ratios of energy use to national output than are others (notably Sweden) with a comparable standard of living; and other studies have suggested that, by improving energy efficiency, the United States could reduce its energy consumption by thirty or forty percent while producing the same output.[4] Thus the net effect of conservation policies may be simply to enable us to maintain or increase GNP in the face of rising prices or supply constraints for natural resources.

Such utilitarian considerations should not be dismissed. The main point of this paper, however, is that conservation policy can go beyond the domain of resource economics. It is my contention that the present-day consumer society erodes the social basis for the development by individuals of a sense of well-being and personal identity; that this erosion represents a problem for our society; and that a conservation ethic based on the concept of caring could provide a foundation in practical morality and public policy for a viable sense of well-being. Obviously this is a large subject, and I can only sketch the argument's outlines in what follows.[5]

LIFESTYLE CHANGE IN THE CONSUMER SOCIETY

There are many accounts of what is meant by the phrase "the consumer society." As used here it means a society in which most individuals have access to large numbers of goods; in which many goods have complex characteristics; in which the characteristics of goods change quickly and frequently; and in which there is an enormous number of "messages" suggesting to individuals what should be their personal objectives in their consumption activities.[6]

The consumer society is quite new: for all practical purposes we should regard it as having emerged only in the 1950s. Thus most people born in North America before 1945 can remember a quite different kind of society; one could call it by way of comparison a "conserver society."

Most people raised in that older conserver society practiced "conservation" as a matter of habit, without being consciously aware of doing so. They took pride in prolonging the useful life of their possessions through their skills in re-using and repairing them. For example, I remember as a child carefully folding the lunch bag I had carried to school, so that I could take it home to use again. My father spent much time each evening in winter preparing the coal-burning stoves for the night, so that maximum benefit could be derived from the right amount of fuel. These may appear to be trivial examples, but I think that they illustrate a habit of mind, or pattern of behavior, that was widespread. Clothing, toys, and tools were repaired for as long as possible; as children we were admonished constantly not to "waste" anything.

Since we have become rather cynical in the intervening period, it would come as no surprise to me if the behavior described above were explained today as merely a response to poverty or economic necessity: people practiced this kind of conservation because they could not afford not to do so. We tend to find such "straightforward" explanations comforting nowadays, because they can be expressed in quantitative terms. But we should consider the matter more closely before agreeing to accept such a facile explanation.

The older conservation behavior was supported by the idea that waste was "wrong" or "immoral." This idea was often associated with formal religious teachings, but it was also sometimes presented as a nonreligious ethical principle. Obviously this principle was most meaningful to people whose economic circumstances also obliged them to be frugal in their consumption patterns. But it had a broader significance as well. I believe there is a close relationship between a "caring" attitude toward how we use material goods, and a caring attitude toward ourselves (a sense of self-respect) and toward other persons. And I believe that an adequate sense of personal satisfaction and well-being requires, among other things, this kind of caring attitude.

To anticipate some of the discussion to follow for a moment: The consumer society encourages us to discard things that are no longer "fashionable," even if those things have many remaining useful qualities.

Yet as we consume things we "invest" our own personality and feelings in them: in buying clothes or cars we believe that in part our choices "say something" about ourselves to others whose approval and friendship we seek. As many persons respond to more and more frequent fashion trends, they must become indifferent to what they have and how they use it at any particular time, since it will be "obsolete" in a short while. The personal feelings and interpersonal associations invested in their possessions are discarded along with the goods themselves, to be replaced by a new set. The consumer society encourages us to regard not only material goods, but our own states of feelings toward ourselves and others, as easily disposable items.

Individuals did not give up that older behavior pattern, with its values of thrift and conservation, simply because more disposable income became available. It is true that, over a relatively short period of time, many persons in North America were able to increase their consumption of goods and services. But in my opinion it is not primarily the *number* of goods that is important, but rather the cultural context which shapes our attitudes about using them. The cultural context in this case was a far too rapid change in lifestyle "models." This development, rather than the higher levels of material consumption, brought about the equally rapid erosion of the values associated with the older conserver society.

This was partly a matter of chance. The economic developments which made possible the higher material consumption coincided with important technological innovations in mass communications media. Television (and to a lesser extent improved color photography in magazines) brought about a huge increase in the daily exposure of individuals to the imagery employed in advertising and programming. In addition, the special qualities of visual imagery made television much more significant in this regard than radio had been. Psychological studies have shown that information or messages are conveyed far more effectively when they are associated with visual images—as opposed to being put simply into written or spoken form.[7]

During the same period, individuals were changing the kinds of daily activities on which they spent their time. The so-called "time budget" studies show in detail where the changes occurred. On average, individuals reduced the amount of time they used to spend on—for example— walking, reading, and eating meals; and about half of this time has been reallocated into watching television.[8] Both the amount of time spent watching television every day in the average household, and the special effectiveness of visual imagery in conveying messages, are significant. For individuals are now exposed, every day, to highly effective presentations of "modern" lifestyles—not only in the advertisements, but just as much (if not more so) in the background settings of the programs themselves—for example, the type of automobiles, homes, clothing, and other possessions that are owned by the characters in the soap opera programs.

Both the direct messages in advertisements, and the indirect messages in the background settings of visual media, supply the "cues" that shape values, preferences, and behavior. If we consider all the media together (television, radio, billboards, magazines, newspapers, store displays, and so forth), we can realize how many cues there are for individuals in our social environment today. The common underlying theme in these cues is the invitation to the individual to try something new, to change his or her preferences, with the suggestion that greater personal success or happiness will result. The unrecognized consequence is *the gradual loss of stable and readily-identifiable indicators of personal well-being.*

For example, the stronger ethnic ties of older generations kept alive traditional customs of dress, cuisine, and popular entertainment; the acquisition of skills in perpetuating these customs provided a stable reference-point for the sense of individual satisfaction. The "homogenized" popular culture of the consumer society continuously promotes new fashions in such matters, and the rapid turnover of new styles does not allow individuals to achieve any *depth* of experience in adjusting their tastes to them. To take another example, the choice of a particular vocation to be followed by a young person was often a matter of careful consideration in middle-class and lower-middle-class families, and as a result the person expected to derive a significant part of his life-satisfaction from performing with skill the tasks of this vocation. At present, the overriding personal imperative is to maximize one's income, and individuals are constantly urged to improve their chances in this regard by re-educating themselves to qualify for different, higher-paying jobs. In these cases, as in many others, individuals have lost the cultural guidance that once afforded them a clearly recognizable standard by which to measure their achievements and to find satisfaction in them.

The decline in stable indicators of well-being must result in increasing ambiguity and confusion in the sense of personal satisfaction. Without institutional guidance from outside the marketplace, and bombarded daily with complex, ever-changing symbols of success in the messages and cues that refer us always back to the marketplace, individuals can only keep searching for the right lifestyle "package"—and hope that it does not become obsolete before they have assembled it. Everyday life in the consumer society somewhat resembles a lottery.

VALUES AND THE SENSE OF WELL-BEING

In the restricted market society that existed until the 1950s, most families were already dependent for their livelihood on earning incomes through employment for wages. But the major difference between the restricted market society and the consumer society that succeeded it is that, in the former, the marketplace itself, and particularly consumer buying in the marketplace, was not the principal source for the formation of the sense of well-being.

Until the advent of the consumer society, the sense of well-being was formed primarily by cultural systems of values and ethics that existed independently of "economic" determinations. Definitions of roles, codes of individual behavior, and ideas about what represented "worthy" accomplishments in life were derived from ethical postulates that had evolved largely in the context of formal religious teachings, whether or not they were actually expressed as such. The dominant social values, rooted in those religious traditions, incorporated the following principles, among others: caring for one's family, defined more or less broadly, directly rather than with the assistance of public institutions; employment in a trade or profession as itself a worthy accomplishment, apart from its particular monetary advantages; maintenance of established roles, for example sex roles; continuity of family association; pride in a high degree of self-reliance in a wide variety of life skills.[9]

The most basic and profound change in the coming of the consumer society is the orientation of individuals toward marketplace activity as the source of cues for what is appropriate in tastes, preferences, and behavior generally. All specific forms of attitude and behavior patterns in the consumer society follow from this underlying orientation. These include: the extension of "fashion" consciousness to embrace so many types of products; the steady replacement of parental by peer-group influence; the attentiveness to marketing cues at an earlier and earlier point in the child's development; the greater quantitative scope and qualitative technical sophistication of persuasive communications; the linking of suggested value, role, and lifestyle changes to product messages; and the integration of diverse personal and product images into holistic "packages" that serve as general models for styles of behavior in specific segments of the consumer market.

The consumer society lacks stable reference points for the sense of well-being. Its freedom, openness to innovation, and flexibility do have many attractive features for individuals, but in the end its lack of any stability in its behavioral codes is a serious drawback. Stability need not necessarily mean rigidity, and thus it is not necessarily opposed to a considerable degree of flexibility and openness to innovation. In the absence of any stable reference-points for behavior, however, individuals cannot make judgments about priorities (since these depend on values) and instead can only adapt and adjust their preferences in response to each new wave of external cues from market-based stimuli. This process erodes the sense of personal identity, the sense of self; without a sense of self, and the associated characteristics of self-respect and self-worth, the possibilities for contentment and well-being evaporate.

The consumer society erodes the sense of personal identity and well-being because marketplace cues, by their very nature, cannot really tell us how we *ought* to act and to make choices. What a market can do, with varying degrees of success, is to adjust supply and demand factors in response to a given set of preferences. It should not be relied on to indicate what our preferences ought to be.

It is vitally important for us to begin to recognize this fundamental defect in our consumer society. It is equally important to devise a sensible way of remedying it. There is no turning back: no return to the "good old days," no reinstallation of "traditional" values is really possible, for the social infrastructure that nourished them has disappeared. There are advantages as well as disadvantages in the process of social change that led us from the restricted market society to the consumer society. It was not the material progress in that transition that gave rise to the problematic behavioral patterns I have described, but rather the far too rapid pace of the transition itself. There was insufficient time for value systems and cultural norms to adjust to economic changes, and to exert some independent authority over the individual and social consequences of those changes. Values must possess some resilience and resistance to change if they are to be values at all; they need not and indeed should not be impervious to change, but they require time to maintain some real continuity with the past while exerting their influence on a new social environment.

THE PHILOSOPHY OF CARING AS A
CONSERVATIONIST ETHIC

A value or an ethical postulate is something that is regarded as being intrinsically worthy and good. Personal honesty, for example, is a value in this respect that is widely shared in our society. When we say that something is intrinsically good, we mean that a certain course of action is to be followed no matter what the circumstances of the moment, or the probable consequences of the action, might be. This does not mean that we are entirely indifferent to the outcome: we believe that a wide-spread commitment to the value of personal honesty will result in a better society for everyone. But no value can be established by a utilitarian calculus, by adding up benefits and costs to discover whether or not they yield a net advantage. This is because our conception of benefits and costs itself is determined by the criteria we apply, i.e. by the relative weights we assign to some types of behavior as opposed to others—in summary, by our definition of a "good life."

In simple terms this means that we do not, and indeed cannot, "choose" our values in the same way that we choose our styles of clothing or automobiles. Some types of judgment are more fundamental than others, and different criteria must be brought to bear on the various levels in a hierarchy of judgments or choices. Most people recognize that their everyday choices reflect some sense of priorities in various possible courses of action, and in commonsense terms such schedules of priorities represent an operative system of values.

Liberal-democratic societies have a public attitude toward values that is different from what prevails in most other societies and different from their own past histories. In this attitude, values are said to be largely a matter of individual judgment, except in certain well-defined areas. This contrasts with the more common pattern where behavioral codes are more rigidly ordained and enforced by laws and public opinion, even in such matters as dress and appearance. This recent development coincides with, and is an essential aspect of, the consumer society, which deliberately encourages individuals to experiment with changing lifestyles.

Yet there must be an identifiable relation between a society's values and its social and economic order. Many of the values held by preceding generations are incompatible with the consumer society's orientation— for example, the level of indulgence in credit buying that is promoted by businesses, banking institutions and governments today would horrify earlier ages; yet our economic "prosperity" is unthinkable without it, given existing institutional arrangements.[10] Different social structures employ quite different mechanisms for inculcating a code of responsible behavior in individuals. Today we rely upon individuals to retain enough common sense to remain financially solvent amidst constant blandishments to indulge themselves with their credit cards. Most persons have managed so far; but the level of current consumer indebtedness creeps slowly upward.

We will still live in a consumer society for the forseeable future. Within that social framework, however, the underlying basis for the sense of well-being will have to undergo a major transformation. The consumer society will have to shift into a new, more "mature" phase. The presence of marketplace indicators of performance will still be very important, both for society as a whole and for most individuals; but the significance of those indicators for us must change. However important they remain as regulating mechanisms for our *economic* relations, they must decline in significance as direct measures of personal well-being.[11]

The first phase of the consumer society is marked, with respect to the sense of well-being, by a "turning outward" of individuals toward their social environment generally as the source of cues for approved behavior, conceptions of personal identity and self-respect, and life-styles. This represents a departure from traditional frameworks for the value systems that had once generated those cues, which had been based in extended family and community (ethnic) associations. The second, mature phase of the consumer society will be marked by a reverse development, a "turning inward." This will not be a mechanical reversal back toward those traditional frameworks, for the simple reason that they have disappeared (or are still in the process of disappearing). Necessarily this restructuring of value fameworks will result in a more diffuse, heterogeneous, and individualized pattern by comparison with those in the past; but it will have a common element in that personal identity will be much less dependent on responses to market-based stimuli.

The turning inward I have in mind must be distinguished at the outset from other recent developments that are superficially similar, namely the new "religious" cults and the personal therapy industry. Most of the former are rooted in the search for an authoritarian group identity that is the precise opposite of personal identity, since they depend in fact on the destruction of personal identity. The latter is more an expression of the first phase of the consumer society than its transcendence (at least in most cases): the individual shops around for therapy services much as one would experiment with brands of cigarettes.

What both lack is any attempt to integrate personal development with broader social concerns. This is precisely what earlier values systems, rooted in the traditional frameworks mentioned above, strove to do. The restructuring of value systems in the second phase of the consumer society must be founded on this integration of personal and social dimensions.

The philosophy of caring provides an excellent framework for this purpose.[12] It has its source and strength in the interpersonal relationships on which the traditional bonds of extended families and ethnic communities were founded. In this respect it draws upon some of the most stable and enduring wellsprings for responsible individual development that are known to human cultures. But it is also amenable to extension and reformulation in the light of contemporary experience, including a practical dimension that can respond to resource conservation issues.[13]

The philosophy of caring has two essential features: (1) caring gives one an ordering of priorities; (2) caring gives one a sense of "being in place" or "being at home" in the world. Together they provide the foundations for a stable sense of well-being.

Caring is commonly regarded as involving primarily a relation to other persons, although it is easy to see that we also extend our caring at least as far as other sentient beings, notably animals. However, it is actually broader than this. We can care for anything that we regard as having intrinsic value. Thus we can and do care about ideals, ideas, and artistic accomplishments; about reputations, honor, and integrity; about the future; about unfilled potentialities, and so on.

Since its domain is actually so broad, caring is liable to lose all clearly identifiable characteristics of its own, and to be indistinguishable from simple "concern" or "interest." We can pin down its unique properties in the following way. Caring means a concern for the "other" (person, ideal, object) *according to its own principle of being or development*. The essence of caring, therefore, is not just our own state of concern for the other, but a specific form of our concern, namely for the intrinsic integrity of the other.

The best example of caring in this sense is the relation between parent and child. The everyday expression of parental caring is in providing the best possible external environment, according to particular cultural norms: emotional bonds, nutrition, role models, education, and so forth. At a deeper level of caring, however, we look for something more than the production of a well-nourished, well-mannered, well-educated representative of a cultural type; we look for expressions of individuality, especially a capacity for individual judgment, and of qualities that have their own uniqueness and flavors. The kind of concern that makes this development possible must allow the other sufficient space for exercising faculties of judgment, including a willingness to support the other if (and especially when) we "know" he or she is making a wrong choice. Thus caring must restrain its concern, when this would conflict with the other's requirements for the autonomy that is a necessary part of its individuality.

As an example of our caring for things or objects, we might think of a family heirloom. The association with memories of other persons that are "carried" by the object make up much of its value for us, and it cannot be replaced by another object which happens to have identical physical properties. In other words, these associations become part of the object itself, so that it is possible to regard doing certain things to or with it as inappropriate (for example, replacing the picture in a frame). Later I shall suggest that we can relax this stipulation that applies caring only to objects that are heirlooms, and that we can care for objects in the absence of association with memories of other persons.

When we care for "abstractions" such as ideals, we have regard not only for our public demonstrations of adherence to them, but also for whether our everyday actions are in conformity with the "spirit" as well as the "letter" of our ideals. In other words, the ideals make demands of their own, stemming from such factors as logical consistency or historical associations, that continuously challenge our professed concern for them. For example, the ideal of equality of treatment for all persons has co-existed in ongoing tension with different social practices, which come under criticism for being—from a new perspective—inconsistent with the ideal. A powerful ideal has an inner logic of development of its own, and our caring for the ideal is in one sense precisely what allows the ideal's own development to take place.

Caring thus supplies what is most basic to any value system: a clear view of priorities and of individual responsibility. Caring can never occur as only an expression of the interests of the one who professes care; on the contrary, it must always consider the "standpoint" of the other. The state of being or development of the other is, as mentioned earlier, the central reference for caring, and this determines what is appropriate action on the part of one who cares. Caring means placing the highest priority on the realization of the appropriate state of being or development for the other.

Through caring and being cared for we achieve a sense of being in place or being at home in the world. When we care for another in the way described above, we do so on the basis of a judgment about what is most appropriate for the being or development of the other at a given point in time and space. In other words, we judge the appropriateness of our action by how it affects the relation of the other to its "environment." This type of judgment presupposes a willingness to take sufficient time and patience to understand the situation of the other in depth, and to reflect on the tensions and possibilities that characterize any situation, before choosing a course of action.

Being in place, like the concept of stability, does not entail rigidity or the notion of a pre-established order to which persons and things must "conform." It is applicable to a dynamic, changing environment as well as to one which is relatively static. Being in place refers essentially to some sense of *coherence* in the overall scheme of things, to a perception of a meaningful network of associations or relationships, where each component part has some unique properties that are valued as its contribution to the overall signficance of the whole.

Through our own expressions of caring we reveal at the same time our own need for the emergence of caring behavior in other persons. Caring orients others toward ourselves, in reciprocal movement, binding us and them in a network of associations. So long as these bonds are true expressions of caring they will not be fetters or restrictions, but rather the preconditions for our own freedom to develop our individuality. For our individuality can never result from a mere absence of any external control; without a complementary attention to the needs of others it can easily degenerate into tyranny. A network of reciprocal caring relationships gives to each participant a sense of being in his or her own place in the world.

In our society today we believe that we have a reasonably effective public commitment to the philosophy of caring, as it applies to persons. We express our commitment less and less in traditional forms, through the maintenance of extended families and ethnic communities, and more in terms of social welfare policies. We believe that we have assigned sufficiently clear mandates to public agencies to ensure that no one is denied access to the basic material necessities of existence. What is mainly lacking in these arrangements, however, by contrast with traditional ones, is any personal involvement in the process of caring for others. Thus, although our bureaucratic forms of caring are undoubtedly of real benefit to those who depend on them, they do not incorporate the two essential features of caring, namely the ordering of priorities resulting from a direct relation with the other and a sense of being in place in a network of caring relationships.

Our society has split the process of caring that was united in traditional socialization frameworks. Caring for others outside the domain of the nuclear family, in terms of basic needs, has been relegated increasingly to public agencies. At the same time, the formation of a sense of personal identity and well-being has been detached from the network of caring relationships and routed instead through the marketplace—which, I have suggested, cannot successfully perform this function.

Now I should like to apply the concept of caring to the domain of resource conservation. In its deepest sense conservation is a kind of caring, and it shares the features of caring that have been discussed earlier. A commitment to conservation yields both a system of priorities and a sense of being in place in the world.

I will discuss two examples of conservation as caring to illustrate these features: (1) using things in accordance with the priorities established by the qualities of the things themselves; (2) preserving and prolonging the useful life of things, instead of replacing them in obedience to the whims of fashion, in order to establish a "relationship" with objects that helps to form the sense of being in place.

We know that we do not make the best use of the qualities of fossil fuels when we burn them to heat our buildings and generate electricity. There is a "hierarchy of qualities" in the substance itself (e.g., petroleum) which ought to dictate, at least in larger part, its uses to us: those qualities that yield petrochemical products are more unique and more characteristic than those that produce combustion. Furthermore, the tremendous inefficiencies at all stages in the process of (for example) electrical heating of homes through oil-fired generation stations waste most of the combustible properties themselves. Our caring for the object in this case would mean a resolve to allow its intrinsic hierarchy of qualities to establish priorities for the uses to which we put it.

With objects that are family heirlooms we usually take special care; but I believe that we can and should be more caring than we now are with the ordinary range of objects, notably our personal possessions, that we encounter in daily life.[14] Many kinds of things that are not mass-produced have special qualities, for example the grain in wood, that lend the thing a uniqueness and character of its own. But even mass-produced objects can acquire a "character" if they are given the time necessary to do so, instead of being replaced with great frequency, by virtue of their "being there" during an extended period in which we have derived pleasure from them. In many ways the thing itself can undergo a process of "development" as an aesthetic object; for example, the finish on a piece of furniture can develop a patina with special qualities all its own.

Our caring for objects can contribute to a feeling of being in place, in that we associate ourselves with things that themselves have a "history": a tradition of development of their own unique qualities or of associations in memory with activities and events that have been important to us. Being in place means being accorded the treatment that is appropriate for the unique qualities of the entity. We have achieved a proper set of priorities for our own demands on the earth's resources when we structure those demands in such a way that, to the greatest degree possible, they respect the intrinsic hierarchy of qualities in those resources; similarly when we structure our uses and care of things in such a way that we allow them the time to develop their full potentialities as both useful and aesthetic objects. The more we do so, the richer is the network of meaningful associations that we allow to emerge in the world around us. And the richer that network is, the more possibilities there are for feeling "in place" in the world, and for constructing a stable sense of well-being.

In broad terms, conservation as caring can guide a reorientation of behavior away from *extensive* forms of experience, where we are primarily concerned with the range of goods and activities, toward *intensive* forms, where we are primarily concerned with the depth and fullness of our associations with persons and things. The intensive mode that is characteristic of caring encourages and supports the "turning inward," in the formation of personal identity, that will signal the beginning of the mature phase of the consumer society.

CONCLUSION

Schipper and Darmstadter state emphatically that "conservation is not an end in itself, but instead a means toward furthering economic and social goals that involve resource use."[15] Certainly conservation is a means of extending the useful life of our resources and of extracting greater tangible benefits from them by eliminating unnecessary waste. In my view, however, this is too narrowly utilitarian an interpretation of what a serious public commitment to energy and resource conservation practices could mean for our sense of well-being in the future.

One of the main presuppositions of this paper is that, in the consumer society, what our "standard of living" *means* to people is not to be judged by quantitative indicators (such as per capita energy consumption). Rather, it is largely a function of the changing network of symbolic associations that link images of happiness with goods and services. While people do derive a measure of genuine satisfaction from these symbolic associations, these associations are also ambiguous and confusing. This ambiguity, together with the dilemma of rank happiness and positional goods competition, explains why greater material affluence does not result in a firm sense of increased well-being in our society as a whole.[16]

Eventually we will have to formulate for ourselves more stable indicators of satisfaction and well-being on a personal level. A new conservation ethic can, I think, play an important role in bringing this about. On this level conservation is simply a caring attitude toward the environment from which we draw our daily sustenance. I do not think there would be much disagreement with the view that most persons derive a deep sense of satisfaction from caring for others, and from being cared for in turn by them. This has always been so on the level of interpersonal relations. And our society today acknowledges, on the level of public responsibility, a degree of obligation in this regard far higher than was the case in earlier times (even if it is often cast in impersonal bureaucratic forms).

In our fascination so far with the deceptive promises of the consumer society, with its rapid turnover of fashions and preferences, we have forgotten that this caring attitude once extended to our use of nature's resources as well. Out of those resources we make and choose the things that express in part our own identity and personality, and that reflect the qualities of our selves which we would like others to regard as being worthy of respect. These are, I suggest, the deepest and most stable sources of the sense of satisfaction, well-being and quality of life.

The caring attitude that forms the basis of the sense of personal satisfaction is now out of balance, owing to our indifference toward the carelessness with which we use our natural resources. A new commitment to a conservation ethic could help us restore the balance and enhance the quality of our lives.

NOTES AND REFERENCES

1. In this paper I usually refer to energy supply and demand issues, rather than to resource conservation more generally, in discussing a value basis for a conservation policy. This is because almost all of the public debate so far in Canada has focussed on energy, and I expect that this will continue to be the case. Energy conservation will be the decisive test case for conservation policy.

2. Thomas R. Berger, *Northern Frontier, Northern Homeland: The Report of the Mackenzie Valley Pipeline Inquiry*, 2 vols.; K. M. Lysyk, *Alaska Highway Pipeline Inquiry*; National Energy Board, *Reasons for Decision: Northern Pipelines*, 3 vols. All were published in 1977 by Supply and Services Canada.

3. The final reports of the Royal Commission on Electric Power Planning (RCEPP), published by the Government of Ontario, represent the most comprehensive quasi-official survey of energy policy issues in Canada. These reports are not included in the otherwise useful section on "Canada" (pp. 227–232) in E. J. Yanarella and A. Yanarella, *Energy and the Social Sciences: A Bibliographic Guide to the Literature* (Boulder, CO: Westview Press, 1982). An excellent independent study is David B. Brooks, *Economic Impact of Low Energy Growth in Canada*, Discussion Paper No. 126 (Ottawa: *Economic Council of Canada*, 1978). The most comprehensive government-sponsored examination of resource conservation "scenarios" is: GAMMA, *The Selective Conserver Society*, 4 vols. (Ottawa: Supply and Services Canada, 1977). The best single source is C. Hooker et. al., *Energy and the Quality of Life: Understanding Energy Policy in Canada* (Toronto: University of Toronto Press, 1980).

4. L. Schipper and A. J. Lichtenberg, "Efficient Energy Use and Well-Being: the Swedish Example," *Science* 194 (3 December 1976), pp. 1001–1013; M. H. Ross and R. H. Williams, "The Potential for Future Fuel Conservation," *Technology Review* 79 (February 1977), pp. 48–59.

5. In general this theme is related to attempts by other authors to analyze dilemmas in social values in contemporary society. Three of the best-known representative works are Daniel Bell, *The Cultural Contradictions of Capitalism* (New York: Basic Books, 1976); Jürgen Habermas, *Legitimation Crisis* (Boston: Beacon Press, 1975); and Robert Heilbroner, *Business Civilization in Decline* (New York: Norton, 1976).

6. This is developed more fully in William Leiss, *The Limits to Satisfaction: An Essay on the Problem of Needs and Commodities* (Toronto: University of Toronto Press, rev. ed., 1979); "Needs, Exchanges and the Fetishism of Objects," *Canadian Journal of Political and Social Theory*, vol. II, No. 3 (Fall 1978), pp. 27–48; "Marx and Macpherson: Needs, Utilities and Self-Development," in A. Kontos (ed.), *Powers, Possessions and Freedom: Essays in Honor of C. B. Macpherson* (Toronto: University of Toronto Press, 1979), pp. 119–138.

7. S. Kline and W. Leiss, "Advertising, Needs and 'Commodity Fetishism,' " *Canadian Journal of Political and Social Theory*, Vol. II, No. 1 (Winter 1978), pp. 5–30.

8. Tibor Scitovsky, *The Joyless Economy* (New York: Oxford University Press, 1976), pp. 161–5.

9. I am well aware that the earlier socialization patterns had many regressive aspects, that they lent legitimacy to injustice, and thus that they had an ideological function in social reproduction. I have referred to them not to suggest they represent worthy ideals per se (although they certainly had worthy aspects), but rather to make the point that the sense of well-being was largely immune from *direct* determination by lifestyle models originating in the marketplace.

10. In Canada bank loans for large consumer durables purchases (such as automobiles) were uncommon before the mid–1950s.

11. My suggestion about a transition to a new phase of the consumer society has been

informed in part by the thesis that there are internal *social* limits to social and economic "progress" as defined by the conventional, quantitatively-expressed indicators. This is the theme of Fred Hirsch's *Social Limits to Growth* (Cambridge, MA: Harvard University Press, 1976) and Lester Thurow's *The Zero-Sum Society* (New York: Basic Books, 1980).

12.   This discussion was inspired by Milton Mayeroff's fine book, *On Caring* (New York: Harper and Row, 1971).

13.   The implicit framework for this attempt to relate values to social policy is the "value-critical approach" defended by Martin Rein in *Social Science and Public Policy* (Harmondsworth: Penguin, 1976) and *From Policy to Practice* (Armonk, NY: M. E. Sharpe Inc., 1983).

14.   Cf. M. Csikszentmihalyi and E. Rochberg-Halton, *The Meaning of Things: Domestic Symbols and the Self* (New York: Cambridge University Press, 1981), esp. p. 195: "The perceptive self is one capable of aesthetic experience and can allow the intrinsic qualities of an object or situation to be fully realized in the interpretation."

15.   L. Schipper and J. Darmstadter, "The Logic of Energy Conservation," *Technology Review* 80 (January, 1978), pp. 41–50.

16.   For the idea of "rankhappiness" see Scitovsky, op. cit.; for positional goods competition, Hirsch, op. cit. Cf. R. P. Coleman and L. Rainwater, *Social Standing in America* (New York: Basic Books, 1978).

APPALACHIAN POLICY, SOCIAL VALUES, AND IDEOLOGY CRITIQUE

Herbert G. Reid

ABSTRACT

This chapter explores the historical interplay of Appalachia and America over the past one hundred years. The focus is on questions of culture and ideology, policy and values as these have been constituted in the development of our "corporate state" and its penetration and integration of the region. A careful examination of Henry Shapiro's *Appalachia on our Mind* brings to the surface many of the assumptions and values generally underlying the social and public policies binding the nation and the region. Ideological aspects in the genesis of the region as a social problem receive considerable attention. It becomes apparent that understanding Appalachia hinges on critical, historical perspectives on modern America: the liberal tradition, the technological world-view, and the politicized economy of the corporate state. The notion that "time stood still" in Appalachia (the static image) has developed in ways that deflect or obscure comprehension of the region's particular form of modernization.

Policy Analysis: Perspectives, Concepts, and Methods, pages 203–222.
Copyright © 1986 by JAI Press, Inc.
All rights of reproduction in any form reserved.
ISBN: 0–89232–371–X

INTRODUCTION

One perspective in contemporary policy theory is that public problems may best be thought of as more created than discovered. As we shall see, this view is significant in illuminating the development of social and public policies regarding Appalachia. But if it is pushed to the extreme notion that the region is nothing but a symbolic creation of "outside" forces, its utility becomes problematical. Bureaucratic intervention in Appalachian culture and mainstream efforts at the generation of meaning for these affairs have been accompanied by a history of struggle and resistance as well as appropriation and adaptation. Social history must complement intellectual history lest southern mountain people continue to be locked into romantic or negative stereotypes grounded in a static image of Appalachian time and history.

APPALACHIA:
A WEB OF RESISTANCE AND COMPLICITY

Such a history is being written and is revealing the extent to which many southern mountain people have experienced poignantly some of the most fundamental value conflicts in the development of American society. Addressing this problem, David Whisnant has suggested that the regional culture may be understood as "a web of both resistance and complicity"—a view which enables one to appreciate the continuities as well as discontinuities in the historical relationship of region and nation.[1] Consider, for example, the historical intervention of the Tennessee Valley Authority's steam coal policies, their stimulation of large-scale strip-mining and the resultant environmental devastation in eastern Kentucky.[2] In the process, from eastern Kentucky emerged not only powerful coal operators such as William Sturgill and Robert Holcomb but also courageous opponents of strip-mining such as Dan Gibson, Warren Wright, and Harry Caudill. Other episodes in the region's history may have had similar overall results, but the point is that Appalachia's "modernization" never has lacked a politics of resistance and alternative development.

Nevertheless, there has been a long-standing tendency of "mainstream" American interpretations to take Appalachia and its people as a "passive text," the most recent manifestation of which involves writing off the region as a "national sacrifice area" in terms of the alleged imperatives of "our energy crisis." This crucial aspect of national ideological images of Appalachia has a parallel in the "modernist" view of the Populist movement, as explained by Lawrence Goodwyn:

> The long inability of Americans encased in 'the progressive society' to comprehend the agrarian revolt may be taken as a fairly instructive index of the social relevance of modern political thought, sadly confined as it is by the ubiquitous ethos of the corporate state. The victims of modern culture have tried to view their personal resignation and intellectual submission as a form of sophistication and have attempted to sustain their morale by teaching the young not to aspire too grandly for too much democracy. In America the two political names for this narrowed despair are liberalism and conservatism. The language of one is grounded in civic illusion, the other in self-interested complacency.[3]

Before pursuing the problem of historical interpretation, I want to elaborate upon and reconstruct Goodwyn's theme of the confining and ubiquitous ethos of the corporate state in terms of my own working theory of American politics and society.[4] First, the "liberals" and "conservatives" involved in the mainstream politics of our corporate state have a common ideological background in the bourgeois-liberal tradition, historically oriented in terms of the perspective of competitive or possessive individualism. On the ontological-epistemological level of "world-view" as distinguished from the politico-economic plane of "ideology," we must take into account the historical institutionalization of the corporate state's dominant cultural horizon: the technological world-picture which provides a metaphysical basis for American liberal society's increasingly favored mode of knowledge, instrumental rationality. The leitmotif of this picturing of the world has been the "conquest of nature." Technocratic ideology (technocratized liberalism in the United States) is a more recent development involving the fetishization of instrumental rationality and an ideological conception of modern science. Instrumental rationality as a primary form of American liberal thought must be situated historically in relation to the subject-object dualism of the technological world-view. The historical critique of instrumental rationality (by twentieth century philosophy) provides an essential perspective on its contemporary manifestation as dualistic modes of experience structurally mediated by the corporate capitalist economy and state. These modes of experience are displayed in such social and political dialectics of American society as: privatism and bureaucratism, pluralism and patriotism, moralism and technologism, and subjectivism and scientism. (The examination of American policies in Appalachia which follows will give considerable attention to the interplay of technologism and moralism as an aspect of the region's "social problems.")

Goodwyn's herculean reinterpretation of Populism and his important point about our cultural difficulties in comprehending it may have a suggestive parallel in the way "Appalachia" has played on mainstream screens of the American mind. Henry Shapiro's recently published study of the Southern mountains and mountaineers in the American consciousness over the period of 1870 to 1920 provides much evidence to amplify the point. His book is a thorough intellectual history of American ideas or images of Appalachia, notions which were not all of a piece, and residues of which persist in the general culture as any lively Appalachian politics course will reveal. In the years just after the Civil War, a major stream of middle class consciousness was bounded by the concern "that America was, or was becoming, or ought to become a unified and homogeneous national entity, and that what characterized such an entity was a coherent and uniform national culture."[5] The basic image of Appalachia that fastened to the national mind was that of a "strange land and peculiar people." Shapiro's study suggests that the screening of "Appalachia" in the mainstream theatres of an emergent corporate state often revealed as much or more about the latter's developing cultural ethos than about the realities of mountain life. The need to reconcile Appalachian "otherness" with certain assumptions and beliefs about the nature of America and American civilization is relentlessly traced in *Appalachia on our Mind*, beginning with the "discovery" of Appalachia as a topic for literary exploitation by writers of the local-color movement. The next chapter in the story is the cultivation of the region as a field for benevolent work by the home missionaries of the northern Protestant churches. Noteworthy here is the process the author calls "the institutionalization of Appalachian otherness" and its relationship to notions of the mountaineers' "need." Shapiro patiently traces the transformations in benevolent work of the "agents of denominational uplift" from the 1860s into the 1890s, illuminating the role of nationalism, the racial compromise, the bureaucratization of sectarianism and denominational competition. After 1890, Shapiro argues, Appalachia was no longer simply the "interesting" phenomenon of a "strange land inhabited by a peculiar people." "The existence of Appalachia itself now appeared as a problem to be solved, and the apparent disparity between mountain life and the 'normal' life of Americans elsewhere in the nation as a 'social problem' to be remedied through systematic benevolence."[6]

The socioeconomic basis of this cultural development deserves particular attention. This important period in the formation of the American middle class, including the emerging "culture of professionalism" identified by Bledstein, must be better understood in order to gain critical historical perspective "on the norms against which Appalachian otherness was measured." As Shapiro delves into various efforts at solving the "problem" of Appalachian otherness, he keeps his reader mindful of the larger discussion and debate "on the nature of America, its history, its current situation, and its future."[7] However, it is Goodwyn's brilliant analysis of Populism that more sharply focuses the shapening political power and cultural authority crucial to the developing corporate economic order. The People's Party "attempted to bring under democratic control" this emerging corporate state.[8] The defeat of Populism with its movement culture focused by the vision of a corporate commonwealth paved the way for the hegemony of business elites in the South and elsewhere, for the nation's social and political life increasingly was locked into the gears of powerful new institutions of economic concentration and cultural regimentation.

Reading *Appalachia on our Mind* enables further recovery of a historical sense of this emerging national ethos based on deterministic concepts of America, especially the mystique of Progress. Capitalist motivations were combined with metaphysical dreams of technological world-domination. Economic modernization was not narrowly conceived by the prophets of Progress. Rather it was heralded for an industrialization of culture which would bring "civilization" itself. John Stephenson's essay on Charles Dudley Warner's 1889 *Harpers* "Comments on Kentucky" frames this perspective and notes its persistence in different linguistic categories.[9] Warner, who co-authored *The Gilded Age* with Mark Twain, had traveled to Eastern Kentucky and found it, given the importance of coal and iron ores, "on the eve of an astonishing development" which portended a revolutionary transformation of the barbarous human "material" to be found in the area. Three decades later, as corporate capitalism entered another phase, we find its advertising ideologues formulating mass *consumption* as a "school for freedom" and "civilizing" process. Stuart Ewen, who has documented and insightfully analyzed this development of the 1920s, provides the needed long-range perspective in stating that the "emergence of bourgeois social production meant the creation of a *social life style* over and above a work style prescribed by the conditions of the job."[10]

Shapiro's *Appalachia on our Mind* draws upon at least a critical sense of the forms of cultural production integral to the rise of industrial capitalism in analyzing the diverse ways in which the industrialization and "Americanization" of Appalachia have intertwined. For example, Chapter 9 includes some attention to the penetration by the logic of commodification of the crafts "revival" advanced by the Appalachian crafts centers of the mission schools and mountain settlements.[11] As Shapiro's study understandably gives increasing attention to regional spokesmen and their circles, to lose sight of these fundamental processes would be a mistake.

Appalachia on our Mind details the role of Berea College president William Goodell Frost whose personal and public struggle with the bothersome otherness of Appalachia led him to "invent" a type of pluralist concept of the region that continues to have strikingly ironic or ambivalent ramifications. Moreover, Frost's "invention" promoted "acceptance of Appalachian otherness as the normal concomitant of Appalachia's existence as a discrete region."[12] But the discovery around the turn of the century, first, of an indigenous crafts tradition and, next, of an indigenous folksong tradition led to an even more self-enclosed concept of the region and of social work objectives or goals.[13] Basic conceptions of population and society were turned away from hierarchical and nationalist assumptions and toward pluralist and regionalist notions by Frost and John C. Campbell. Boiling this down, Frost and Campbell helped to undermine the invidious scales allegedly measuring mountaineer "degeneracy" or "primitivism." From Frost's invention of "Appalachian America" to Campbell's work for the Southern Highland Division of the Russell Sage Foundation, Shapiro's account traces a complex series of issues, rivalries, and events culminating in what he calls "the institutionalization of Appalachian regionalism."

This precarious accomplishment of the "agents of systematic benevolence" emerged partly out of a reaction to a particular "New South" approach (ca. 1910) to "Economic Modernization and the Americanization of Appalachia," the irony-laden title of Shapiro's Chapter Seven. In this version, Appalachia was attacked as an uninhabitable land, and the solution to "our mountain problem" was said to be migration and the utilization of the mountain population as a labor force in the cotton mills. Shapiro's central point is that the benevolent workers—at least partly in response—moved toward "a commitment to maintain Appalachia as a discrete region and to assist the mountaineers in becoming in fact a distinct people."[14] Regarding the latter aspect in terms of the motto "E Pluribus Unum," it may be that Shapiro neglects the mainstream sense of "Unum" that persisted in this new regionalized version of American pluralism. As cultural regionalism in recent decades became entangled in the *political* ideology of pluralism, the mystification of Appalachian life in America grew, and perhaps especially in public policies of recent decades, insofar as they were based on concepts of a "subculture of poverty" and "regional underdevelopment."

The concluding chapters of *Appalachia on our Mind* must be read carefully. On one level, they chronicle the institutionalization of Appalachian regionalism and the "integration of the mountaineers into modern American civilization" as a "triumph of pluralism." On a deeper level, we may find a penetrating analysis of the early twentieth century processes contributing to the construction of a powerful contemporary "myth of Appalachia." These chapters deal with the folk schools, the crafts revival, and the folksong revival, but once again it is the meaning structures underlying organizational work and action that Shapiro labors to help us understand. "To the degree that mountain life was seen as a legitimately distinct pattern of life . . . the work of the benevolent agencies now became the melioration of conditions in Appalachia in such a way as to preserve the essence of mountain life."[15] Here only mention can be made of how the professionalization of benevolent work, the impact of World War I, and other factors contributed to the "normalization of diversity" and the emergence of Appalachia as a symbol of America. Shapiro leaves no doubt that some good work was accomplished on the basis of the new regionalism and pluralism, pivoting at times on the notion of a folk community not fully realized. For instance, he hints that there were promising beginnings in the 1930s, but more importantly he detects an increasing difficulty in going beyond a "mythic system" to ask fundamental questions.[16] Professor Shapiro's refusal to ape the dominant academic style by closing with an uncritical celebration of the "triumph of pluralism" merits considerable reflection. The new pluralism with its image of mountaineer "conservators of *the essential culture of America*" may conceal the "myth of a coherent culture among an homogeneous population."[17]

Cultural pluralism and political regionalism are legitimate projects of scholars in the Appalachian Studies Conference and elsewhere. Studies in this context, however, have been made problematic by the historical interplay of the basic myth of Appalachia as a *cultural region* with the political pluralist ideology legitimating the corporate state. This process has obscured the region's internal statification patterns and problems and their bases and functions in the national system of class relations, labor markets, i.e., in short, our capitalist society.

THE DIALECTIC OF TECHNOLOGISM AND MORALISM

The historical process by which southern Appalachia was unevenly and uneasily brought into the industrial capitalist system has presented enormous tasks of ideology-critique and theoretical explanation. The capitalist mode of production was established in southern Appalachia in the same period (1870–1930) that the "static image" of the region was taking hold in the American cultural "mainstream." Since 1930, this mainstream imagery has fed many projects for the "modernization of the southern mountains and their people." A major task on the agenda of Appalachian studies is comprehending how the institutionalization of certain versions of Appalachian regionalism has become functional to the ideological dynamics and structural operations of the American corporate state.

Beginning especially in the last decade, historical studies by social scientists, historians, folklorists, and others have been appearing that are essential for this task. Historian Ronald Eller's research on industrialization and social change in Appalachia from 1880 to 1930 explodes the "static image," the construction of which was discussed earlier. This is not the place to attempt to summarize Eller's study (or those by other scholars such as Green, Gaventa, Conti, Banks, Walls, and Tudiver). The fundamental point to be drawn is simply that "the persistent poverty of Appalachia has not resulted from the lack of modernization. Rather," as Eller puts it, "it has come from the particular kind of modernization that unfolded in the years from 1880 to 1930." What occurred in this period was that:

> By 1930 . . . most mountaineers whether they remained on the farm or migrated to the mill villages, timber towns, or coal camps, had become socially integrated within the new industrial system, and economically dependent upon it as well. To say the least, this dependence was not on their terms—that is to say, it was not a product of mountain culture but of the same political and economic forces that were shaping the rest of the nation and the western world.[18]

The historical roles of European immigrants, blacks, and native Americans in this new industrial system with its rural industrial workforce are also becoming better understood.

Recent scholarship discloses a number of criticisms of the perspective on Appalachia as "a region apart," because growing historical evidence indicates that much of the region has been increasingly integrated with the dominant industrial economy since the 1880s. Much of the academic and popular preoccupation with the region as an economic "anomaly" (e.g., as "backward") has missed the point, perhaps reflecting dependence upon a shallow, uncritical view of industrial capitalism's development. A valuable contribution by David Whisnant illustrates the problem by commenting on the 1964 Report of the President's Commission on the Appalachian Region.

> The root confusion of the report . . . lay in its mistaken assumption that Appalachia had problems because it was not integrated into the larger economy, when in fact its problems derived primarily (as early drafts acknowledged) from its integration into the national economy for a narrow set of purposes: the extraction of low-cost raw materials, power, and labor, and the provision of a profitable market for consumer goods and services.[19]

The problems of this "region apart," the Commission argued, would be solved only when it fully was brought into the "free enterprise orbit." Yet primary ownership and control of the region's vast resources have been in this "orbit" for a hundred years. The cultural ethos of the corporate state promotes a view of the American economic system in which "development" and "domination" must be antithetical. Yet Richard Simon has tried to show that destructive competition in the early twentieth century coal industry was "consistent with" the form of national economic growth promoted by the monopoly capitalist sector of the general system.[20] And John A. Williams has described West Virginia industrialists such as Davis and Elkins as "the agents—and . . . principal beneficiaries— of the process of national integration that accompanied industrialization."[21] It is interesting to note that while Henry G. Davis was a leader in the Democratic Party, his son-in-law Stephen B. Elkins was a leading Republican. The joint political and economic roles of these turn-of-century industrialists and others such as Johnson N. Camden (a Rockefeller associate) are historical aspects of the concept of the corporate state.

The static image exaggerating Appalachian otherness has manifested curious combinations of romantic motifs and negative stereotypes. Under the weight of deterministic notions of technological progress and market place logic, the nostalgic commonly has either given way to or passed over into the realm of cultural negation. Not only the land but also the people have been rationalized, on the "bottom line," as little more than resource objects for exploitive policies.

David Whisnant's *Modernizing the Mountaineer*, a study developed over the last decade, excavates the "substructure of cultural values and assumptions" crucially involved in the plans and programs of TVA, ARA (Area Redevelopment Administration), and the ARC (Appalachian Regional Commission). The view that more often than not has prevailed in their varied activities has alternately romanticized and denigrated 'Appalachians," operating essentially as a "cover for . . . culturally destructive . . . policies," largely implemented through the rationalization and facilitation of "conventional private development," especially corporate capitalist ventures.[22]

Consider, for example, the following from James Branscome's study of *The Federal Government in Appalachia*, where he is discussing a 1935 Department of Agriculture report on social and economic conditions in the southern Appalachians:

> The report noted authoritatively, "The Appalachian area is a reservoir of population. A reservoir is a place where supplies are stored and furnished at the right time to places where they are needed." The report recommended the "encouragement of emigration" to be accomplished "gradually." David Lilienthal, TVA director and later chairman, notes in his *Journals* that after being pestered repeatedly by James Dombrowski of Highlander Center and Mrs. Roosevelt to help unemployed miners in Grundy County, Tennessee, he had suggested to Dombrowski that the people should be moved out.[23]

Both Branscome and Whisnant note the persistence of this viewpoint among policy-makers in later decades.

A more recent example is the interest of the U.S. Forest Service in creating a "Rural Museum" near the Mount Rogers Recreation Area (in southwest Virginia) to illustrate rural life to passing tourists.[24] As corporate state policies and ventures continue to hasten the devastation of that way of life and the demise of the farmers struggling to extend it, such plans vividly exemplify what I have termed the American liberal "dialectic of technologism and moralism." In other words, this mind-set turns on the assumption of "technological imperatives" and "inevitable technological progress" leavened by the myopic morality of token preservationism. Fortunately, the latter is just one tendency or pattern in the field of cultural policy and development. Folklorists are right to remind sociologists of this fact. But the Tellico Dam/Little Tennessee River valley episode of recent years provides more evidence of the destructive aspect of public policy.[25]

To comprehend the complex structure of such policies, critical scholarship needs not only concepts of the corporate state, its capitalist market "logic" and "bandaid" reform-liberal response, but also a post-modern sense of the technological world-view. While this way of viewing the world is the dominant cultural horizon in our system of political economy and public policy, it remains in conflict with other traditional cultural worldviews and is under challenge by postmodern ecological perspectives of science and nature. The Appalachian mountaineer's continuing struggle, internal as well as external, with the technological world-picture projecting industrial progress at the cost of his/er sense of place, unveils a key issue in the global ecological crisis we face. John Opie has provided one of many discussions of the mountaineer's close relationship with the land and with nature. "The land for him is not an idea or abstraction but a sacred mystery with enormous power and durability. To change or transform it would be to destroy his sense of safety." Exaggerating somewhat, Opie adds: "What is satisfied in Appalachian life has been almost removed from mass society—a profoundly fundamental human need to have a 'habitat' and know it intimately."[26] Unfortunately, the house trailer or mobile home is an increasingly apt symbol of what is happening to this fundamental human need in Appalachia.

The empirical context of migration studies is provided by the patterns of land ownership and control of mineral resources. Beyond this critical first step, we need more studies of the ways in which class relations on the national level have impacted in southern mountain communities, and of the role or functions of local communities in the U.S. class structure, particularly through the labor market of the corporate state. Sari Tudiver's recent study of "the political economy of wage-labour migration in an Eastern Kentucky mountain community" (Breathitt County) provides a useful model for analyzing some important problems in this field.[27] These problems appear to be becoming more intellectually recognizable and accessible as we gain better historical perspectives such as we find in Ron Eller's study of the Appalachian coal barons (1880–1930) who, in general ideological orientation and business practice:

> were not unlike other industrial entrepreneurs of the Age of Enterprise. Highly ambitious men, they valued order, coveted power, and disdained labor unions. Having entered the mountains solely to exploit the region's vast mineral wealth, they undertook to wield their powers over the local communist in direct support of their business enterprises. After creating a system of closed company towns, the majority departed again from the region—their personal fortunes having been made. Motivated preponderantly by economic considerations, they had opposed "burdensome" taxes and had often justified civic improvements only as a business expense. During a critical period of social change, they had maintained a personal dominance over the affairs of the coal community which had thwarted the growth of alternative local industries, social services, and public institutions. They carried industrialization to the mountains, but they left the region ill-equipped to confront the social and economic problems of the new industrial age.[28]

As Ron Eller and Harry Caudill have indicated, this era definitely was closed out between 1927 and 1932 as the coal market sagged as never before, competition took a heavy toll among the small companies, giving added weight to the consolidated and "captive" mines and the larger corporations. Still, as Caudill's account of wartime prosperity and the heyday of the "truck mine" operations makes clear, the so-called competitive sector of the industry was revived with a significant new trend of concentration starting only after 1950.[29] The oligopoly companies clearly have become the dominant sector, especially since the efforts about twenty-five years ago of John L. Lewis's U.M.W.A. and the Bituminous Coal Operators Association to "stabilize" the industry. As James Ridgeway states:

> By 1970 it was made plain that the oil and gas and coal companies had reorganized themselves into what was called an "energy industry," and were off on a new tack. Not only had the coal industry become more concentrated with ten firms controlling more than two-thirds of all production, but also nearly two-thirds of the top fifty companies were owned by companies in other industries.[30]

More recently, John C. Wells, documenting further the conglomerates' absorption of much of the coal industry, has argued that the growing role of the energy industry in the corporate state weakens the position of the UMWA "striking against the conglomerates when only ten or less percent of their adversary's income derives from coal."[31] Considering also the well-known internal difficulties of the UMWA and developments such as the decline of its excellent health-care system raises important questions about sustaining its historic role in countering the political and social hegemony of "King Coal" in the region. Wells' dissertation synthesizes the massive evidence of the industry's pervasive political role in the region. As he puts it:

> the coal industry is tied by various arrangements and interlocks to all major decision-making bodies in the Region that might affect their enterprise. Banks, courts, school boards, law firms, elected and appointed officials, all are integrated into an extensive structure that offers protection and insulation to the industry.[32]

He also discusses what may be considered as the hegemonic role of this structure in the political culture and social life of Central Appalachia. It is this historical process of the establishment of political and cultural hegemony by industrial and business elites and their official collaborators that is the primary benchmark for evaluating strategies of political and social change. To the extent that fundamental change is being effected, counter-hegemonic projects will be involved in the development of a new public sphere not only in Appalachia but in American society generally.[33]

A value-critical approach to Appalachian policies is one important aspect of this strategy. It is timely, for as one research consultant to the E.P.A. and the A.R.C. put it in 1977: "the extensive energy resources in the Appalachian region are now of major importance as the nation seeks to cope with its growing energy problems." In the 1960s, the public was exhorted to support policies that would "aid" Appalachia. In the next decade, however, the emphasis seemed to be "going into reverse," so to speak. Not only did U.S. Senators and others proclaim Appalachia's coal vital to the nation but a few policy consultants began to invoke an image of the region as a "national sacrifice area." Whenever this term is "posted" in the United States, people had best take heed for, as C. S. Lewis once stated, "What we call Man's power over Nature turns out to be a power exercised by some men over other men with Nature as its instrument."[34] Mountain people in Appalachia have learned this in the context, for example, of resistance to strip-mining. Robert F. Gates of Charleston, West Virginia has produced a film "In Memory of Land and People" which starkly depicts the environmental havoc created by strip-mining. In one scene, Walter Franklin of McDowell County, West Virginia says: "If we lived in a country that loved the land, then we'd live in a country that loved people."

CRITIQUE OF IDEOLOGY

This paper has worked toward a critical, historical view of the Appalachia/America dialectic by sifting through the transmutations of the cultural and political problems and issues of pluralism and regionalism. These major foci of Appalachia studies and of U.S. policies for the region are encumbered by much conceptual confusion and ideological mystification. This paper has attempted to disengage theories of cultural pluralism and political regionalism (where, for example, the latter is seen as an alternative to U.S. federalism) and questions of their relevance *from* the historically convergent ideologies of cultural regionalism and political pluralism in mainstream policy. The critique of the *political* ideology of pluralism as an account of power in the United States has been extended to Appalachia with particularly forceful results by such scholars as Couto, Gaventa, Walls, and Whisnant. They have demonstrated that "Appalachian inequality is an on-going product of our society, and power plays an important role in maintaining and reinforcing inequalities within the region."[35] In the mainstream ideology of pluralism of our society, that power has been legitimated and its real functions obscured by its symbiosis with romantic images and negative stereotypes generated out of the myth of a "strange land and peculiar people."

David Whisnant's book provides examples from most of the last seven decades, including his analysis of the 1925 "Program for the Mountains" of the Conference of Southern Mountain Workers (eventually called the Council of the Southern Mountains). He documents from this statement and from the organization magazine's first issue editorial the view that the "solutions to problems in the mountains were judged to lie in integrating the region's politics and economy into the mainstream while preserving, if possible, its picturesque and nostalgic folkways and religion."[36] Fundamental structural changes were established on the forefront of the organization's agenda only around 1970, a process involving a great deal of factional dispute and interpersonal conflict. Not surprisingly, the initial version of Whisnant's interpretation published in 1974 elicited harsh criticism from some leading figures in the organization prior to its "transformation."[37]

The perspective offered by Loyal Jones merits quotation. (Jones was C.S.M. Executive Director Perley Ayer's assistant and later his successor in the turbulent 1960s.) "The Council was always in business to work with and assist those who were at a disadvantage in our economic and social system. The Council was liberal and respected in the region from the beginning." In other words, the major thrust of the C.S.M. before 1970 was liberal reform and no doubt within this generally mainstream framework "consciousness-raising" took place, while some were even "radicalized," as Jones suggests. Furthermore, he insists, the " 'new' Council is built upon the 'old.' "[38] Perhaps it is possible to grant these points and understand the Jones–Whisnant polemics within a broader critique of American ideology.

The strength of the right-wing of our "liberal society" (as compared to our weak socialist tradition) has been such that its "left-wing" (our reform liberals) for years enjoyed an unusual sense of moral or "humanitarian" ascendancy. Yet our reform liberals (e.g., Hubert Humphrey, Nelson Rockefeller, Walter Mondale) have never been anticapitalist in principle or advocates of structural change in the corporate economy. During the last fifteen years, however, liberal reform has come under severe attack, first, from the "New Left," more recently from right-wing groups whose cultural "presence" has been pervasive for decades. It is this historical perspective on the hegemony of our essentially bourgeois "liberal tradition" that helps prevent mystification of the corporate state's power dynamics generating tensions between impulses toward reform and reaction in the political mainstream. Nevertheless, one paradoxical aspect of liberal reform must be underlined: its capacity to foster (sometimes indirectly) popular tendencies with democratic potential.[39]

This historical perspective discloses the connections between what Shapiro calls the "new pluralist" version of the Appalachia myth—grounded as it usually was in cultural idealism (e.g., the notion of "Christianizing industry")—and the contradiction-laden role of liberal reform in Southern Appalachia. This "movement" of cultural regionalism has stimulated both neo-populist actions and hopes and the depoliticizing patterns of the corporate state (and in neither case is a rationalist concept of "intention" crucial). American reform liberalism is the primary ideological thread that ties together, however loosely, the missionary movement, the Conference of Southern Mountain Workers (which became the Council of the Southern Mountains), the TVA, the OEO, and the Appalachian Regional Commission (ARC). For the past several years, the *academic paradigms* associated with and utilized in the reform liberal tradition involved in Appalachian affairs have been subjected to increasingly systematic and fundamental criticism. Tensions, conflicts and changes involving the OEO, the Appalachian Volunteers, and the CSM from the late 1960s into the early 1970s constituted one political arena reflecting and giving impetus to this critical process.[40]

The liberal reform effort to establish Appalachia as a social problem in the national consciousness led to diagnoses of Appalachian problems as "regional" in nature. As David Walls has observed, this "tradition was carried forward in the 1960s by three models of Appalachian problems ... the subculture of poverty, regional development, and internal colonialism models (which) focus on the special character of Appalachian Problems."[41] These models have been thoroughly outlined and analyzed by Walls, Lewis, and others, and will not be of concern here. The first model was illuminated by the late Rupert Vance in his introduction to Jack Weller's best selling *Yesterday's People*, widely regarded as the most influential example of the model. "To change the mountains," Vance said, "is to change the mountain personality." The second model is pinned on the conventional wisdom of "underdevelopment" or, as we have seen, the "region apart" idea which means the state should build the "infra-structure" for (further) capitalist development. The colonialism model was developed in both liberal and radical versions and stresses the ex-ploitation of land and people in the region as a "colony" of absentee owners.

Eastern Kentucky lawyer Harry Caudill from the mid–1960s has been the best-known reform-liberal exponent of the colonialism model. Cau-dill, who wrote a very favorable foreword to *Yesterday's People* (1965), was joined in 1973 by Weller who had come to emphasize a view of Appa-lachia as "a mineral colony."[42] Wielding the image of eastern Kentucky as a colony, one reform plank in this group's platform has been to urge a greater return of Kentucky severance tax money to the Appalachian counties. In the shortrun, such a strategy seems quite "practical," as Americans like to say. However, the historical development of Appala-chia as an aspect of the expansion of industrial capitalism "may present," as Walls and Billings have argued, "a better example of class domination than colonial domination."[43] Another recent analysis of the development of capitalist social relations in certain Kentucky counties describes how:

> Wage labor in the logwoods, coal mines, and oil fields became increasingly important in the lives of the rural-dwelling mountain people. The region's abundant natural resource endowment was funneled out of the area by outside capitalists *and* native entrepreneurs. The local men of business formed the critical link between the heretofore overwhelmingly rural culture of the mountains and the rapidly growing urban culture of the American state . . . (For the majority) labor, previously oriented to independent farm production and bound only by family obligation and neigh-borliness, became merely another marketable item . . . that meant heavy work in the logwoods or the mines and eventually in factories outside their highland homeland. A mountain based minority with political and commercial ties to metropolitan bases formed the nucleus of a flourishing town-based culture in the region.[44]

In this perspective, the question must be asked: might it be that those whose concept of Appalachia as a "mineral colony" is coupled to *a regional "consensus" approach,* are saving the "chickens" for the "foxes" already in the "coop"?

But we have been discussing only one variant of the colonialism model. Colonialism models are conceptually grounded in different ways and vary in their forms of intellectual relationship to the "mythic system" (Shapiro). The image of Appalachia as a besieged colony has been po-litically employed in recent years for diverse purposes and with varying effects. For example, the Appalachian Alliance in *Appalachia 1978: A Protest from the Colony,* among other proposals, insisted that "coal can be mined as if people mattered," that "stripmining and mountains don't mix," and called for the condemnation "of corporate land in Appalachia for public needs such as housing." (Nevertheless, the Alliance has not developed a coherent program for fundamental change or, for that matter, anything approaching a comprehensive approach to energy policy.) During the same year (1978), Helen Lewis and her associates published *Colonialism in Modern America: The Appalachian Case* and included a final section on "Rethinking the Model." In short, there appears to be growing recognition (as David Walls' article in that section puts it) of the need for advanced capitalism models that place "less emphasis on the regional character of Appalachian problems and more on their national context." Recent studies have illuminated the fundamental view that the acquisition of land was more than its "theft." It led to the introduction of a whole new set of social relations in the region, as shown above.[45] The separation of people from the land and the development of a working class (including a large pool of migrant laborers) have constituted key components of the Appalachian phase of what Wendell Berry has called "the unsettling of America." It is too simple for regional radicals to assume that their political starting point is "two cultural traditions in conflict" (to draw Tom Plaut's phrase from the Lewis collection). Historically, the New South creed of "Progress" and cornpone Babbitry have been around in mountain culture, especially town life, for a long time. Furthermore, as Brown and Schwarzeller observed in 1969: "Cultural diversity has been absorbed by the mining communities rather than drained away, and this has fostered internal change in their social structure, making them less familistic and more like that of urban America."[46] The implication for the strategy of the regional movement for social change is that it must think nationally and globally, cultivating resources in the widest context as well as in local areas, if it seeks impacts and changes that are fundamental and long-range.

What the American mainstream mediates to us as "Appalachian poverty" reveals a larger problem of the poverty of the American political mind and of the sociological imagination, as C. Wright Mills might have put it. The Appalachian region's politics of resistance and movement for social reconstruction may have somewhat meager symbolic/conceptual resources to draw upon from much of the American political tradition. Nevertheless, it may be that the radical colonialism argument— lodged essentially in the last decade by the Peoples Appalachian Research Collective at Morgantown[47] and by Lewis and her associates—made an important "historical turn" from which there will be no going back.

Alain Touraine has stated that a "social movement is a *collective action oriented toward the control or the transformation of the system of historical action. ...it is a direct attack on the society's model of development and its* power structure."[48] The radical colonialism argument may be understood as a critical "moment" in the reinterpretation of the American liberal tradition and especially of reformism as one of its aspects. The largely middle-class missionary/professional reform "movement" to establish Appalachia in the national consciousness as a social problem area, while no small achievement, was still well within the corporate state's dynamic "system of historical action." While categories and definitions abound in social theory, it is difficult to refer to these liberal reformers as a "movement" that never developed a "mass base" or "following" (cf. Walls) when there is little evidence that most of them were interested in developing a "mass movement." On the other hand, it would be an oversimplification of history to treat this social problem movement as a purely "exogenous" development, an entirely separate matter from mountain society, as other social scientists seem inclined (cf. Batteau). The historical record will not sustain even the most sophisticated versions of the colonizers/colonized dichotomy.

But the point to be reiterated is that the radical colonialism model and the continuing debate over it has enabled a number of Appalachian activists to move beyond the paradigm (or hegemony) of the reform liberal/social problem approach. The critique of the liberal tradition tends toward questioning the instrumentally rational concept of politics as "social work" and "piecemeal reform." Moreover, when "Appalachian movements funnel themselves into demanding legislative reform, the partial remedies they win (such as concessions from the federal government)—after years of struggle—never eliminate the root problems but do dissipate the political pressure that's been mobilized.[49]

The way is rough and uncertain but there seems to be growing awareness that Appalachian history renders many themes for the critique of the corporate state and its model of development. This model includes the questionable brand of "regionalism" and underlying mythic structures I have sought to illuminate. We need models of democratic reconstruction that facilitate the emergence of a new "system of historical action," a new public sphere for the political and social development of Appalachia/America. More than fifty years ago, John Dewey observed that in America the "democratic public is still largely inchoate and unorganized." He argued that a democratic public's "outstanding problem . . . is discovery and identification of itself" and that this problem would be remedied only by reversing "the dislocation and unsettlement of local communities" and reconstructing community life through democratic modes of communication and decision generating new forms of social intelligence and public knowledge.[50] The disruption of community and family life in Appalachia is another aspect of the processes by which the corporate state has undermined the institutional bases and "strip-mined" the cultural resources for an effective, democratic public in the United States.

NOTES AND REFERENCES

1. David Whisnant, "Brief Notes Toward a Reconsideration of Appalachian Values," *Appalachian Journal* Vol. 4 (Autumn, 1976), pp. 46–48.

2. See James Branscome, *The Federal Government in Appalachia* (New York: Field Foundation, 1977).

3. Lawrence Goodwyn, *Democratic Promise: The Populist Movement in America* (New York: Oxford University Press, 1976), p. 612.

4. See my "Totality, Temporality, and Praxis," *Canadian Journal of Political and Social Theory* Vol. 2, #1 (Winter, 1978), pp. 113–135; "Toward a Post-Modern Theory of American Political Science and Culture," *Cultural Hermeneutics* II (1974), pp. 91–166; and "Critical Phenomenology and the Dialectical Foundations of Social Change," *Dialectical Anthropology* (1977), pp. 107–130.

5. Henry David Shapiro, *Appalachia on Our Mind* (Chapel Hill: University of North Carolina Press, 1978), p. xi.

6. Ibid., p. 63.

7. Ibid., p. 31, 65. See also Burton J. Bledstein, *The Culture of Professionalism* (New York: W.W. Norton, 1976).

8. Goodwyn, op.cit., p. 612.

9. John B. Stephenson's essay was contributed to the "Whose Bicentennial? Appalachia '76" Symposium in *Appalachian Journal* Vol. 4 (Autumn, 1976), 34–38.

10. See Stuart Ewen's "Advertising as Social Production: Selling the System" reprinted in Herbert G. Reid (ed.), *Up the Mainstream: A Critique of Ideology in American Politics and Everyday Life* (New York: David McKay/Longmans, Inc., 1974), pp. 130–152.

11. Shapiro, op.cit., p. 221.

12. Ibid., p. 121.

13. Ibid., pp. 130–131.

14. Ibid., pp. 131, 185.

15. Ibid., p. 215.

16. Ibid., pp. 263–265.

17. Ibid., pp. 214, 260 (emphasis added). Shapiro's treatment of Campbell in *Appalachia on Our Mind* and his Introduction to Campbell's *The Southern Highlander and His Homeland* (Lexington: University Press of Kentucky, 1969) may be compared to Rupert Vance's view in the latter's Foreword to Campbell's book first published in 1921.

18. Ronald Eller, "Industrialization and Social Change, 1880–1930: A Look at the Static Image," in Helen M. Lewis et al. (eds.), *Colonialism in Modern America: The Appalachian Case* (Boone: Appalachian Consortium Press, 1978), pp. 35–46, at pp. 41–42. Also: Eller's "Toward a New History of the Appalachian South," *Appalachian Journal* Vol. 5, #1 (Autumn, 1977), p. 77.

19. David E. Whisnant, *Modernizing the Mountaineer: People, Power, and Planning in Appalachia* (New York: Burt Franklin, 1980), p. 129.

20. Richard Simon, "West Virginia and Capitalist America," April, 1978. Paper presented to the Eastern Economic Association Meeting. See also the important study by sociologist Alan Banks, "Labor and the Development of Industrial Capitalism in Eastern Kentucky, 1870–1930," Ph.D. Dissertation, McMaster University (Ontario), 1980.

21. John Alexander Williams, *West Virginia and the Captains of Industry* (Morgantown: West Virginia University Library Press, 1976), p. 165.

22. Whisnant, *Modernizing the Mountaineer*, pp. vi-xxi, and especially Chapter 10.

23. Branscome, op. cit., p. 11.

24. Ronald Eller, "The Past and the Future of Appalachia: The Historian as Social Planner," Guest Lecture at Emory and Henry College (Va.), Oct. 10, 1978, p. 12. See also Stephen Fisher and Mary Harnish, "Losing a Bit of Ourselves: The Decline of the Small Farm," Appalachian Studies Conference paper, March 1980; and Wendell Berry's thoughtful discussion of *The Unsettling of America* (New York: Avon Books, 1978).

25. See Peter Matthiessen, "How to Kill a Valley," *New York Review of Books* XXVII (Feb. 7, 1980), pp. 31–36.

26. John Opie, "A Sense of Place: The World We Have Lost," in *An Appalachian Symposium*, ed. by J. W. Williamson (Boone: Appalachian State University Press, 1977), pp. 113–114, 117. For just one account of a current power struggle illustrating this conflict in values, see the Brumley Gap, Va. "citizens report" of their fight with the Appalachian Power Co. by Lee McDaniel and Mike Turley, "They Want the Land We Love So Dearly," in *Mountain Life and Work* Vol. 56, #4 (April, 1980), pp. 4–9. See especially McDaniel's comment on the death of her father, Ike Lilly, as it relates to the deeper issues involved. On the housing situation in Central Appalachia, the 1979 publication of the Appalachian Alliance, *National Sacrifice Area*, pp. 15–20 provides a good overview.

27. Sari Tudiver, "Country Roads Take Me Home: The Political Economy of Wage-Labour Migration in an Eastern Kentucky Mountain Community," 1977. Unpublished paper, Dept. of Anthropology, University of Manitoba.

28. Ronald D. Eller, "The Coal Barons of the Appalachian South, 1880–1930," *Appalachian Journal* Vol. 4 (Spring-Summer, 1977), pp. 195–207 at 205.

29. Harry M. Caudill, *Night Comes to the Cumberlands* (Boston: Little, Brown, 1963), pp. 165–176, 219–263.

30. James Ridgeway, *The Last Play* (New York: New American Library, 1973), p. 64. See also The Appalachian Landownership Task Force study of *Who Owns Appalachia? Landownership and Its Impact* (Lexington: The University Press of Kentucky, 1983), pp. 5, 14–40.

31. John C. Wells, Jr., "Poverty Amidst Riches: Why People Are Poor in Appalachia," Ph.D. Dissertation, Rutgers University, 1977, p. 217. See also the new study by John Gaventa, *Power and Powerlessness: Quiescence and Rebellion in an Appalachian Valley* (Champaign: University of Illinois Press, 1980) based on his doctoral dissertation presented to Oxford University.

32. Cf. Herbert G. Reid and Randal H. Ihara, "Appalachian Praxis, the Corporate State, and American Culture: Toward a Critical Theory," September, 1978. Paper presented at the American Political Science Association Annual Meeting.

33. I have deveoped this argument in "Beyond the Energy Complex: The Role of the Public Sphere," a paper with E. Yanarella, delivered at the 1981 Annual Meeting of the American Political Science Association.

34. C. S. Lewis, *The Abolition of Man* (New York: Macmillan-Collier paperback edition, first published in 1974), p. 69.

35. From Richard Cuoto's excellent essay on "Political Silence and Appalachia," *Appalachian Journal* Vol. 5, #1 (Autumn, 1977), pp. 116–124, at p. 120.

36. Whisnant, *Modernizing the Mountaineer*, pp. 8–9, 32 in Chapter 1.

37. The initial version of Chapter 1 of Whisnant's book appeared in the *Appalachian Journal* Vol. 2, #1 (Autumn, 1974), pp. 7–45. Volume 2, #3 (Spring, 1975) of the *Appalachian Journal* carried the critique by Loyal Jones (pp. 171–180), other responses by Thomas Parrish and A. H. Perrin, and David Whisnant's reply (the latter at pp. 189–191).

38. Loyal Jones, op.cit., at pp. 171, 180. Cf. Chapter 1 of Whisnant's *Modernizing the Mountaineer*.

39. See my *Up the Mainstream*, especially the introductions to Chapters 1 and 5.

40. An interesting account will be found in Bill Horton and David Walls, "The Appalachian Volunteers: Community Organizing in the Southern Mountains," forthcoming in the *Journal of Sociology and Social Welfare*. See also Peter Schrag's "Appalachia: Again the Forgotten Land," *Saturday Review* (January 27, 1968), pp. 14–18, and Chapter 7 of Whisnant's *Modernizing the Mountaineer* which deals with the Appalachian Volunteers.

41. See the Ph.D. Dissertation by David S. Walls, "Central Appalachia in Advanced Capitalism: Its Coal Industry Structure and Coal Operator Associations," University of Kentucky Sociology Department, 1978, especially chapters 1 and 7.

42. The Reverend Jack Weller's article "Appalachia: America's Mineral Colony," which my copy indicates first appeared in 1973, is available in the collection *Colonialism in Modern America: The Appalachian Case*, edited by Helen Lewis and others (pp. 47–55). See also Harry M. Caudill's *The Watches of the Night* (Boston: Little, Brown, 1976). For an interesting commentary on Weller's *Yesterday's People* and Caudill's *Night Comes to the Cumberlands* (1963), see Mike Maloney and Ben Huelsman, Scientism, and Southern Mountaineers," *Peoples Appalachia* Vol. 2, #3 (July, 1972), pp. 24–27.

43. David Walls and Dwight Billings, "The Sociology of Southern Appalachia," *Appalachian Journal* Vol. 5, #1 (Autumn, 1977), p. 134.

44. Eugene A. Conti, Jr., "The Cultural Role of Local Elites in the Kentucky Mountains: A Retrospective Analysis," *Appalachian Journal* Vol. 7, 1–2 (Autumn-Winter, 1979/1980), pp. 65, 67.

45. Cf. Richard M. Simon, "The Labor Process and Uneven Development in the Appalachian Coalfields," *International Journal of Urban and Regional Research* 4 (March, 1980), pp. 46–71, and Alan J. Banks, "The Emergence of a Capitalistic Labor Market in Eastern Kentucky," *Appalachian Journal* 7 (Spring, 1980), pp. 188–198.

46. Harry K. Schwarzweller and James S. Brown, "Social Structure of the Contact Situation: Rural Appalachia and Urban America," West Virginia University Appalachian Center Information Report #1 (June, 1969), p. 5.

47. The Morgantown collective published *Peoples Appalachia* between 1970 and 1974. Pierre Clavel has authored an interesting discussion of the group's efforts toward "opposition planning" in *Opposition Planning in Wales and Appalachia* (Philadelphia, PA: Temple University Press, 1983). Clavel contrasts official and opposition planning efforts in Wales and Appalachia and argues that the conflict facilitated an expansion of possible futures for the two regions.

48. Alain Touraine, *The Self-Production of Society* (Chicago: University of Chicago Press, 1977), p. 139. What I call the technological world-picture is fundamental to what H. T. Wilson addresses as the "American ideology." In *The American Ideology: Science, Technology, and Organization as Modes of Rationality in Advanced Industrial Societies* (Boston: Routledge, Kegan Paul, 1977), Wilson writes that this "ideology is a sustained and influential set of ideas whose joint acceptance constitutes a commitment to a rather specific world-view with serious implications for society, culture, and history," pp. 14–15.

49. Curtis Seltzer, Review of *Colonialism in Modern America*, in *Southern Exposure* Vol. 7 (Fall, 1979), pp. 120–121, at p. 121.

50. One important analytical contribution to this task is Harry Boyte's *The Backyard Revolution* (Philadelphia: Temple University Press, 1980). For an Appalachian contribution to a program for democratic reconstruction, see *Appalachia in the Eighties: A Time for Action* edited by Bill Horton and Frank Einstein for the Appalachian Alliance (1982). For John Dewey's analysis, see *The Public and Its Problems* (Athens: Swallow Press, 1927), pp. 109, 185, and passim.

PRINCIPLES OF ETHICS AND THE JUSTIFICATION OF POLICY

Frederic G. Reamer

ABSTRACT

Policy analysts frequently encounter conflicts among arguments based on ideological, empirical, and ethical statements. In the final analysis, however, only an ethical principle can proscribe immoral policies by using in a moral sense such terms as right, wrong, good, bad, just, unjust, duty, and obligation. Conclusions based on ideology or empirical evidence must ultimately serve to inform judgments that are based on ethical reasoning. This chapter provides an ethical analysis of policy issues, and examines the place of moral theory in contemporary policy debate.

INTRODUCTION

Although policy analysis as we know it today is a relatively young enterprise, the subject matter of the discipline—speculation about the design and implementation of policies that govern and guide people—extends at least as far back in history as the earliest city-state. What has

Policy Analysis: Perspectives, Concepts, and Methods, pages 223–245.

223

changed, of course, is that modern day discourse about these matters is considerably more formal and systematic. Over time we have managed to erect rather complex apparatus about us, so that policy analysis now is something one can do for a living, with the aid of sophisticated measurement tools, theories, data analysis technology, symposia, and literature. Yet despite the complexity and sophistication that characterize contemporary policy. analysis, the principal aim is roughly the same as it was in its ancient clothes: to wonder about the governance of people and how best to go about the task.

In recent years considerable attention has been paid to questions about how policy is formulated: What are the ingredients that contribute to the formation of policy? How does policy unfold? How ought we to go about designing policy? Although contemporary policy tends to be justified on many different grounds, in general these grounds can be classified as ideological, empirical, and ethical. Ideological grounds relate to beliefs that certain policies are desirable because they are consistent with a set of assumptions; these assumptions may be informed by, for instance, traditional practices, religious beliefs, or simple intuition. For example, the argument that federal spending for social services ought to be decreased may be based on an ideological assumption that American tradition has emphasized minimal government intervention. The argument that federal legislation ought to be passed to provide insurance coverage in instances of catastrophic illness may be based on an ideological assumption about the rights citizens have to basic health care.

Empirical grounds are related to science and to what is known from research about the effectiveness or likely consequences of a policy. A decision to subsidize a failing corporation may, for instance, be based on research that indicates that the long-term drain on federal funds if the corporation fails (due to increased unemployment rates, welfare costs, loss of income taxes) far exceeds the cost to the government of loaning large sums of money to help subsidize the corporation. Or, a policy designed to subsidize the cost of child care may be based on empirical evidence that mothers who have child care available are more likely to seek employment and are less likely to require aid for their dependent children than mothers without child care.

In contrast to ideological and empirical grounds, ethical grounds are those that relate to conclusions based on an analysis of what is right and wrong, or good and bad in a moral sense. That is, while empirical evidence may indicate that subsidies to failing corporations are less costly to the government than the consequences of allowing corporations to fail, the ethical principle that it would be fundamentally wrong, in a moral or ethical sense, for the state to intervene in the affairs of a private enterprise in such a fashion is viewed by some as the critical reason why such intervention should be avoided.

Despite a superficial similarity, ethical grounds and ideological grounds must be distinguished. Both include normative language that characterizes a policy as right or wrong, or good or bad. The critical difference, however, is that ethical grounds depend on a deliberate philosophical analysis of the morality of the principles upon which a policy is based, while ideological grounds do not. For example, the "aphilosophical" assertion that federal spending for social services ought to be minimized because such spending is inconsistent with American tradition is ideological because it is not, in this form, based on deliberate or systematic ethical analysis. The assertion that such federal spending would be wrong because it violates certain enumerated, carefully examined, and fundamental rights from the point of view of a philosophical critique would be ethical in nature in that it depends on a deliberate consideration of the morally relevant concepts of right and wrong (for example, related to the rights citizens have to be autonomous and free from interference by the state, and the duty of government not to interfere gratuitously with the freedom of its citizens). One might argue, for instance, that the federal government has a moral obligation to reduce spending on welfare programs because of citizens' right to freedom from interference by government in their personal affairs, regardless of the extent to which such a policy is consistent with the *ideological* assumptions of the Democratic, Republican, or whatever party. As Leonard Hunt (1978:15) has noted in this regard:

> the fundamental conflict is between those who hold that views concerning beliefs, values and their prescriptive entailments, are to be adopted arbitrarily, urged upon us by the necessity of choice and without the benefit of reason and reflection; and those who hold that the choice of beliefs and values, although prompted by the shared human predicament of being persons confronted with conflicting systems, can, and must, be taken with the guidance of reason and reflection. Therefore, beliefs and values held ideologically and those held philosophically will differ with regard to their rational status, even if to the sociologist of knowledge they present the same appearance. This is not, of course, to claim that ideological beliefs and values will be devoid of intellectual content and argument, but that it is essentially characteristic of them, precisely qua ideological, that their holders do not reckon their basic elements to . . . need . . . any kind of intellectual justification.

The degree to which ideological, empirical, and ethical grounds should serve as the primary justification of social policy has been the subject of extended debate (see, e.g., Sundquist, 1968; Kahn, 1969; and Rein, 1970). It is argued by some that despite grand ideals and normative beliefs about what is right and wrong, the "real world" is one where ideological factors (informed, for example, by political and economic conditions) prevail. Others argue that it is primarily facts, based on careful scientific inquiry, that produce informed judgments about the desirability of certain policies. And still others argue that to be guided ultimately by factors other than those based on beliefs about what is morally right or wrong, or duty and obligation, is shortsighted.

I will examine below the merits and demerits of these competing points of view. I will do so by tracing the development of a current policy debate in the social service field, that concerning the desirability of diverting and deinstitutionalizing juvenile offenders from the formal juvenile justice system comprised of police, courts, and correctional facilities. This is a policy whose relevance extends beyond the circumscribed field of juvenile justice. It raises fundamental questions about such critical values and concepts as freedom, justice, welfare, and the role of government—values and concepts whose importance certainly is not restricted to this particular area of social policy. In that the policy debate concerning diversion and deinstitutionalization centers on such compelling questions about freedom and well-being, conclusions we reach about the place of ideological, empirical, and ethical grounds in the justification of this particular policy will have important implications for the justification of social policy in general.

In the end, I will conclude that ethical beliefs about what is right or wrong must serve *in the final analysis* as the primary justification of social policy. Our task below is to develop the arguments that support this conclusion and to identify the proper place of ideological and empirical factors as determinants of social policy.

IDEOLOGICAL GROUNDS

Beliefs about how juvenile offenders ought to be treated have changed considerably over time. The first attempts to remove juveniles from the grip of formal criminal justice processing can be traced to the nineteenth century, with the founding of the New York House of Refuge in 1825 and the Lyman Reform School in Massachusetts in 1874 (Rosenheim, 1962). The inauguration of the first statewide juvenile court in 1899, in Cook County, Illinois, is commonly regarded as the event most symbolic of this nation's desire to distinguish children from adults in the eyes of the law. The development of this court enjoyed widespread support and reflected a view among those who worked with troubled youth that children were a human substance different from adults, a group incapable of criminal intent and not responsible for its mischief (Hurley, 1907).

It helped engender an unusually pure public sentiment that children were, in a phrase, "to be saved" (Platt, 1969).

Just prior to the origin of the first juvenile court, there were several public organizations supporting the view that children were to be treated kindly and uplifted rather than punished. At the Second International Penitentiary Congress held in Stockholm in 1878, it was resolved that "delinquent children should not be punished but educated so as to enable them to gain an honest livelihood and to become of use to society instead of an injury to it" (Platt, 1969:50). For those youth who needed to be removed from their homes, it was noted by the Board of Public Charities of the State of Illinois in 1879 that "the object of reformatory institutions is well stated; it is not punishment for past offenses, but training for future usefulness" (Platt, 1969:106).

Perceptions of the young offender as a child not responsible for his acts did not change dramatically during the first fifty years of the court's life (Kahn, 1953; Rosenheim, 1962). The mission of the court as conceived in 1899 was consistently defended. Criticisms addressed only the need to improve methods of court administration and services. In addition, the academic literature concerning delinquency and its causes that appeared during the first half of the twentieth century generally supported the ideological view that juvenile offenders are not responsible for their acts. In the early twentieth century, the work of the Italian positivists—Cesare Lombroso, Enrico Ferri, Raffaele Garofalo—foreshadowed a series of writings that characterized youth as compelled by physiological, psychological and environmental forces beyond their control (Quinney, 1970). In the 1920s, Burgess, Shaw, and McKay (the so-called "Chicago School") argued that ecological factors influenced delinquency rates, and in 1938 Merton presented his hypothesis that the disparity between youth's goals and the means available for attaining them accounts for much delinquent behavior (Quinney, 1970:79–92). In the late 1940s and early 1950s there was a burgeoning of psychoanalytic theories that asserted a connection between poor character formation and delinquent behavior (Berman, 1959:612–21). The literature during this era also emphasized the difficulties adolescents experience in their transition to adult status (Bloch and Niederhoffer, 1958), and the problems experienced by youth in female-dominated households (Parsons, 1947). In 1955 Cohen argued that the delinquent behavior of lower-class boys is a "reaction formation" against middle-class values, and Cloward and Ohlin (1960) elaborated upon the relationship between delinquency and environmental opportunity. As one reviews the major theoretical formulations that were developed during this era it becomes apparent that, in general, the view of the juvenile offender as a willful, calculating actor is absent. This prevailing mood was entirely consistent with that first espoused by the supporters of the first juvenile court.

The Unfulfilled Promise

In the early 1960s, a gradual but significant shift in ideology about the mission of the juvenile court began. Scholars, jurists, and practitioners began to question both the juvenile court's effectiveness in carrying out its mission and the constitutionality of certain of its procedures. In its final report, for instance, the 1967 President's Commission on Law Enforcement and Administration of Justice stated:

> In theory the court's operations could justifiably be informal, its findings and decisions made without observing ordinary procedural safeguards, because it would act only in the best interest of the child. In fact it frequently does nothing more nor less than deprive a child of liberty without due process of law—knowing not what else to do and needing, whether admittedly or not, to act in the community's interest even more imperatively than the child's. . . . [T]he limitations, both in theory and in execution, of strictly rehabilitative treatment methods, combined with public anxiety over the seemingly irresistible rise in juvenile criminality, have produced a rupture between the theory and the practice of juvenile court dispositions. While statutes, judges, and commentators still talk the language of compassion, help, and treatment, it has become clear that in fact the same purposes that characterize the use of the criminal law for adult offenders—retribution, condemnation, deterrence, incapacitation—are involved in the disposition of juvenile offenders too (President's Commission, 1967:9).

In addition, it became clear that despite rhetoric to the contrary, youth in correctional facilities were generally not receiving benign treatment:

> Whatever one's motivation, however elevated one's objectives, if the measures taken result in the compulsory loss of the child's liberty, the involuntary separation of a child from his family or even the supervision of a child's activities by a probation worker, the impact on the affected individual is essentially a punitive one. Good intentions and a flexible vocabulary do not alter this reality. This is particularly so when, as is often the case, the institution to which the child is committed is, in fact, a peno-custodial establishment. We shall escape much confusion here if we are willing to give candid recognition to the fact that the business of the juvenile court inevitably consists, to a considerable degree, in dispensing punishment (Allen, 1964:18).

The Shift Toward Diversion

The consequence of this widespread concern about the effects of processing juvenile offenders through the juvenile court and correctional institutions was a shift in ideology about how juvenile offenders should be treated. As a result there was a concerted effort to divert many youth from the juvenile justice system and to deinstitutionalize those who were in its secure facilities. Correctional programs were frequently deemed harmful and ineffective; in addition, it was widely thought that "one of the great unwanted consequences of wardship, placement, or commitment to a correctional insititution is the imposition of stigma," and that this stigma "in some ways helps to fix and perpetuate delinquency in many cases" (Lemert, 1967:92–4).

A prominent result of this shift in ideology has been a deliberate effort on the part of the federal government to promote diversion and deinstitutionalization programs. The federal effort began with the passage of the 1961 Juvenile Delinquency Act and the publication of the 1967 report of the President's Commission on Law Enforcement and Administration of Justice. The enactment of the 1974 Juvenile Justice and Delinquency Prevention Act and subsequent amendments represents the most significant federal legislation to date designed to encourage the development of diversion and deinstitutionalization programs.

As a result of this legislation and the shift in ideology, diversion and deinstitutionalization programs have been established nationwide. These programs have taken on a variety of forms and have been made available to youth at several stages in the formal processing of juveniles. In many jurisdications around the nation, both residential and nonresidental programs have been established as alternatives to formal processing by police, as alternatives to secure detention between the time of arrest and court appearance, to court intake, and to secure correctional institutions (Reamer and Shireman, 1981). The policy of diversion and deinstitutionalization has not, however, been without its critics. The proliferation of community-based programs has been accompanied in particular by persistent debate concerning the risks they pose to the community. A common concern is that caring for juvenile offenders in nonsecure settings increases the likelihood that citizens will be victimized.

Whether or not the safety of the citizens is in fact in greater jeopardy when youths are cared for in nonsecure, community-based settings appears to be a straightforward empirical question; youths who have participated in these programs either do or do not have higher recidivism rates than comparable youths who have been placed in secure institutions. We must therefore survey the results of evaluations of the effects of diversion and deinstitutionalization programs on youth's subsequent behavior and consider the extent to which they support the policy of community-based care of juvenile offenders.

THE EMPIRICAL GROUNDS

While numerous attempts have been made to evaluate the effectiveness of diversion and deinstitutionalization programs, very few of the studies have included random assignment of youth to diversion and nondiversion conditions, or to institutionalization and deinstitutionalization conditions (because of the usual and in many instances reasonable reservations judges and administrators have about the appropriateness of these procedures). However, some generalizations can be suggested based on the evaluations that are available from a series of quasi-experimental designs (Shireman and Reamer, in press).

Several studies have assessed the effects of diversion programs introduced at the point of contact with police or court intake on youth's recidivism rates. Of these studies, three report positive findings (Baron, Feeney, and Thornton, 1973; Klein, 1974; Ku and Blew, 1977)—that is a decrease in recidivism rates for youth in diversion programs; two report negative findings (Lincoln, 1976; Elliott, 1978); and eight report findings that are equivocal (Carter and Gilbert, 1973; Forward, Kirby, and Wilson, 1974; Klein, 1974; Stratton, 1975; Binder, 1976; Berger, Lipsey, Dennison, and Lange, 1977; Lincoln, Teilmann, Klein, and Labin, 1977; Elliott, 1978). Bohnstedt (1978) found similar mixed results in his review of recidivism rates of eleven diversion programs located in California. Similar results are reported by Lundman (1976) and Gibbons and Blake (1976).

The U.S. Office of Juvenile Justice and Delinquency Prevention recently funded an evaluation of an eight-state project that included programs designed as alternatives to secure detention of status offenders between the time of arrest and appearance in court.[1] The programs generally provided supervision of youth in their own homes, foster homes, or group homes in lieu of detention in secure facilities. Over a twelve-month follow-up period, there proved to be no measurable, significant differences between the effects on recidivism rates of secure detention and the alternatives to detention (Klein, 1979). The two interventions had similar effects regardless of the youth's offense histories, that is, whether they were only marginally involved in status offense behavior, were chronic status offenders, or were youth who had committed both delinquent and status offenses.

Evaluations of alternatives to correctional facilities to which youth are sent after adjudication also fail to provide evidence of a significant difference between the effects of alternative programs and secure facilities. Empey and Erickson (1972) report some reduction in recidivism as a result of an intensive, community-based "guided-group interaction" pro-

gram that included supervised employment and help with school relationships. And in an assessment of California's well known Community
Treatment Project, Palmer (1974) reports that community-based, intensive supervision and counseling appear to be more effective than institutions with some categories of youth but not with others. Yet in a report
summarizing the effects of the dramatic closing of all large juvenile
correctional institutions in Massachusetts, Coates, Miller, and Ohlin (1978)
conclude that the alternatives to institutionalization resulted in recidivism
rates little different than those following institutional care. Other reports
on the effects of alternatives to correctional institutions are inconclusive
(Empey and Lubeck, 1971; Murray and Cox, 1979; Empey, 1973).

The general conclusion, then, when the empirical evidence concerning
the effectiveness of diversion and deinstitutionalization programs is considered, is that neither alternative programs nor formal processing of
juveniles is superior when the data are considered in the aggregate. How,
then, does one translate these findings into a policy recommendation
concerning the use of diversion, deinstitutionalization, and secure confinement for juvenile offenders? Clearly, the results can be interpreted
in several ways. The data suggest on the one hand that there is no clear
benefit as a result of community-based programs over and above institutional care. These data might thus be viewed as evidence that there is
no justification for placing juveniles in institutions (except, perhaps, those
who represent an immediate danger to the community) or processing
them formally through the juvenile court. Given the evidence that community-based and institutional programs have similar effects on youth's
recidivism rates, confining youths in correctional institutions represents
only a vengeful act which is neither more effective nor humane. Alternatively, however, it might be argued that the community ought to at
least be able to express its outrage and condemn youths who violate its
laws and that institutionalization, with its punitive connotation, is therefore justifiable on this ground alone. One interpretation places primary
emphasis on the value of freedom from institutional care, while the other
places primary emphasis on the value of punishment and retribution.

The obvious difficulty with these interpretations is that they do not
provide a clear, unambiguous conclusion about the desirability of diversion and deinstitutionalization. The descriptive, empirical evidence
does not lead directly and immediately to an unequivocal conclusion
about which of these interventions ought to be preferred. This is a clear
example of what David Hume referred to in the eighteenth century as
the "is-ought" problem, according to which normative conclusions cannot be deduced directly from descriptive facts (Hudson, 1969). The fact
that the absence of significant differences between the effects of the two
forms of intervention can lead to conflicting conclusions suggests that

deciding whether to endorse the policy of diversion and deinstitutionalization may reduce to a decision based on ethical factors—factors that
relate to values such as individual freedom, justice, and social welfare.[2]
As Rein (1970) has stated: "Social policy is all about social objectives and
the values that embody the choice of social programs. These are precisely
the problems that touch the limits of social science and raise the spectre
of that ancient but still inadequately explored terrain where facts and
values merge."

ETHICAL GROUNDS

Students of social policy have acknowledged consistently the importance
of values in policy formulation (Kahn, 1969). Discussions of values in
social policy have generally included an enumeration of values considered central to the planning task, for example, the principles of promoting individuality, freedom, autonomy, self-respect, and self-
determination among those affected by social policies. Frequently these
discussions include guidelines for the conduct of individuals engaged in
the formulation of policy: "Encourage maximum participation of concerned interest groups"; "Foster democratic decision-making"; or, "Distribute resources in a manner that benefits the least advantaged." To
date, however, discussions of the normative values and ethical guidelines
considered central to the formulation of social policy have generally been
presented as if these values and guidelines are self-evident. For example,
a report prepared by the Illinois Law Enforcement Commission (1980)
concerning detention of juveniles in Illinois states: "This policy, referred
to as deinstitutionalization of status offenders, is based on several assumptions. Foremost is the belief that children should not be locked up
for nondelinquent actions. Detention of such youths was and is seen not
only as *unjust* but as potentially harmful to the child." The grounds upon
which this judgment about the injustice of detention is based are not
presented. In general, discussions of diversion and deinstitutionalization
that make similar prima facie claims tend to suffer from the same omission (Reamer and Shireman, 1981).

   In this respect, most traditional discussions of social policy that have
made reference to such normative concepts as right and wrong, justice,
and welfare have been, almost exclusively, ideological in nature. Despite
their normative language, these discussions have not been ethical ones—
in the strict sense defined earlier—in that they have not been based on
a deliberate analysis of the morality of the principles upon which a policy
is based. As we noted above, there is an important difference between
ideological statements that include normative concepts and ethical state-

ments that are based on an analysis of the merits of the normative concepts themselves from the point of view of moral philosophy.

It is reasonable to ask, then, how one moves beyond ideological statements about social policy that are not based on ethical analysis. What grounds are there for claiming that any ideological assertion in favor of a particular policy is superior to any other? In particular, if policy decisions do in fact frequently reduce to ethical judgments and choices among values, by what criteria shall our judgments and choices be guided?

Traditional Ethical Theories

Moral philosophers have attempted to justify ethical values and guidelines in a variety of ways. Their theories generally represent two major schools of thought. First, there are those who argue that certain values or actions are inherently right or wrong, or right or wrong as a matter of principle. Advocates of this school of thought are generally referred to as deontologists (Hancock, 1974). For instance, a deontologist might argue that it is inherently wrong to place a status offender, who technically is not considered responsible for his or her behavior, in secure detention. Second, there are those who claim that certain actions are to be engaged in not because they are inherently right or good, but because they are right or good by virtue of their *consequences*. Those who claim that the rightness or wrongness of an action is determined by the goodness of its consequences are generally referred to as teleologists. For instance, a teleologist might argue that it is justifiable to place certain status offenders in secure detention if other youths are deterred from being ungovernable as a result (Frankena, 1973).

Utilitarian theories, which hold that an action is right if it promotes the maximum good for everyone, historically have been the most popular teleological theories and have been used to justify many policy decisions. Utilitarian theories have traditionally been of two kinds. First, there are those that justify actions that tend to promote the greatest aggregate good. Second, there are theories, such as those proposed by Jeremy Bentham and John Stuart Mill, that justify actions that tend to promote the greatest good for the greatest number, taking into account the number of people to whom goods are distributed as well as the quantity of goods produced. The distinction between these two forms of utilitarianism is important when one considers, for example, whether to distribute a limited amount of community development funds in a way that tends to produce the greatest degree of improvement in public services (which might entail dispensing large sums of money to relatively few communities), or produces the greatest improvement in public services *for the greatest number of communities possible* (which might entail dispensing smaller sums of money to a larger number of communities). Similar dilemmas arise whenever decisions must be made concerning the distribution of scarce resources, for example, medical care, public aid funds, nursing home beds, or an administrator's time.

The choice between defining an action as inherently right (a deontological approach) and as right because of the goodness of its consequences (a teleological approach) is an important one for policy makers because decisions and policies justified on these grounds will often have substantially different effects. For instance, while a deontologist might argue that there is an inherent obligation on the part of the federal government not to subsidize a failing corporation, a teleologist might justify such a subsidy on the grounds that, in the long run, this will safeguard the welfare of those who might be harmed if the corporation fails (a desirable consequence). Or, while a deontologist might argue that it is inherently wrong to deny public aid benefits to a needy applicant who has provided partially false information, a teleologist might justify disapproval on the grounds that future applicants may, as a result, be deterred from submitting false information.

How helpful are these points of view for policy makers who face difficult ethical decisions? In particular, what do these points of view suggest about the policy regarding diversion and deinstitutionalization, given the ambiguous empirical results presented above?

One well-known problem with deontological justifications of a value or ethical guideline is that individuals will disagree about which values and guidelines are inherently right or wrong. One who does not favor diversion and deinstitutionalization may claim that punishment of ungovernable behavior is inherently right; however, one who opposes institutionalizing youth might claim that incarcerating a juvenile who technically is not responsible for his acts is inherently wrong. And there are no agreed upon standards provided by deontologists to resolve such disagreement. A second problem is that there are no clear standards available for individuals to reconcile their own vacillating judgments about what is inherently right or wrong. Though the argument that judgments about what is inherently right or wrong are never more than matters of individual taste and preference may have some popular appeal, this form of relativistic ethics by now has little appeal to moral philosophers. If ethical principles and guidelines are to be subscribed to by policy makers, they will have to be based on more than the ideologically-based selection of certain values considered to be inherently right or wrong.

Utilitarianism, on the other hand, appears at first to provide a compelling ethical guideline. One reason that utilitarianism has been used frequently as a justification of social policy is that its requirement that the greatest good be pursued appears to foster generalized benevolence. Utilitarianism thus seems consistent with our intuition about morally right action. Despite its initial appeal, however, utilitarianism has been criticized extensively since it was first introduced by Bentham in the eighteenth century. One problem relates to the difficulty of assigning quantitative values to consequences of actions that are frequently qualitative in nature. For example, how could we calculate whether the long term consequences for the broader community if status offenders are placed in secure detention are better or worse than if they are not detained? How can we go beyond the measurement of recidivism rates and compare the value of increased freedom to the value of punishment and deterrence? Concepts such as freedom and the value of punishment are hard to operationalize and quantify. Though social scientists have been trying for years to construct mathematical models to simulate the phenomena we study, and to quantify that which is considered to be qualitative, our efforts in this regard have not produced very impressive results. These are difficult problems, ones for which utilitarianism has not been able to provide adequate answers.

A related problem concerns the kinds of consequences that should be considered when one is attempting to determine the rightness of a particular act. What kind of temporal and spatial boundaries should we draw around our consideration of consequences? Should immediate consequences be assigned greater weight than consequences that will emerge only in the distant future? What is our obligation to future generations? Should the consequences of diversion and deinstitutionalization be considered only for the area within the geographical boundaries of a particular program, or for the surrounding area as well?

The problem with utilitarianism that is perhaps the most troubling is that the principle may technically permit the subordination of the rights of a few if the net result is an increase in the aggregate good. Thus, the rights certain juveniles may have not to be institutionalized may be sacrificed if empirical evidence suggests that incarceration of a small but arbitrarily selected group will deter a considerable number of other youth from engaging in illegal behavior. In its most extreme form, this principle technically permits the punishment of innocent individuals if a greater aggregation of good results. In the end, then, the implications of classical utilitarianism are rather disquieting, despite the principle's tempting premise. As Samuel Gorovitz (1971:xviii) has noted: "The principle of utilitarianism thus presents us with an ethical theory at once enchanting and enigmatic. Its surface clarity quickly gives way as we are drawn by an attempt to understand the theory into vigorously contested philosophical disputes."

Toward an Ethics of Social Policy

It is perhaps tempting to think that the difficulties moral philosophers have experienced in their efforts to develop unambiguous ethical principles should lead to the conclusion that philosophical analysis may not have much to offer those of us interested in the design of policy. Such a conclusion is not warranted, however. No one would deny that many—perhaps even most—of the debates about ethical theory and values are filled with genuine disagreement. We tend to disagree about which values are worth considering in the first place, which values should take precedence over others, and what criteria should guide our choices. But true veterans of these debates will also tend to claim that there is something valuable about the conceptual and intellectual wrestling we engage in with others, and sometimes with ourselves; the harder we think and argue, the more likely it is that we will discover and expose both the merits and demerits of our respective arguments, and this offers us the best chance we have of formulating sound, value-based policy in the end. When we construct public policy, we are engaged in far more than mere cognitive gymnastics; we are inventing frameworks that will affect people's lives, we hope for the better. Philosophical discourse tends to push us to think through in a disciplined way the ideas we are about to unleash upon the world, and it is important to identify and examine critically our differences of opinion. As Dorothy Emmet (1962) so aptly put it:

> In these days when few of us think we can look up the answers to moral problems at the back of a book, we may get further if we are prepared to take the risk of developing our powers of making moral judgments, rather than sit back and let these powers atrophy because of our uncertainties. . . . Even if the result is to drive us back on to some moral principles or values for which we can give no further reasons, there will be a difference between holding them in this way *after* a process of critical heart-searching and just asserting them dogmatically. At any rate we can learn both to see moral questions as problematic and open ended, which means that they can be thought about and discussed, and also see there are reasonable ways of going about this.

How, then, can principles of ethics—about which there will always be debate—be applied fruitfully to policy analysis? Let me offer an example of a theory that I find generally persuasive and examine its relevance to the policy of diversion and deinstitutionalization around which I have organized this discussion. The theory I will explore has been selected arbitrarily in the sense that there are dozens of others that could also be introduced here to illustrate the application of ethical theory to the formulation of policy. My selection is not arbitrary, however, in that I find this theoretical point of view compelling, especially as it pertains to the policy under discussion here.

In his *Reason and Morality*, Alan Gewirth (1978) sets out to develop an ethical principle that is compelling philosophically and that avoids many of the problems cited earlier that have plagued traditional ethical theory. Gewirth argues that an ethical principle can in fact be justified on non-arbitrary, logical grounds and in a manner that avoids some of the most serious problems of deontology and classic utilitarianism. He claims that an ethical principle must provide conclusive and determinate answers to three central questions: (1) the authoritative question: Why should one be moral and accept the requirement of considering the interests of others? (2) the distributive question: Whose interests should be considered in addition to one's own and to whom should goods be distributed? and (3) the substantive question: Which goods are to be considered important and valued, and which among them should be considered the most important? The derivation of Gewirth's overriding ethical guideline—what he refers to as the Principle of Generic Consistency—is based on what Gewirth considers to be the concept fundamental to any discussion of ethics: action. He identifies two necessary features of action: (1) voluntariness or freedom, and (2) purposiveness or intentionality. Voluntariness is defined as an action being under a responsible person's control in that he chooses to act as he does, unforced, knowing the "relevant proximate circumstances of his action." By an action being purposive Gewirth means that the person acts for some end or purpose that constitutes his reason for acting. One who is purposive is concerned with three kinds of goods: (1) basic goods: those aspects of well-being that are the necessary preconditions for the performance of any and all action (for example, life, health, food, freedom, mental equilibrium); (2) nonsubtractive goods: goods the loss of which would diminish one's ability to fulfill his purposes, for example, as a result of being stolen from, cheated, lied to, being subjected to inferior living conditions or harsh labor; and (3) additive goods: goods which enhance one's ability to fulfill his purposes (for example, education, income, knowledge, self-esteem) beyond those included under basic goods.

The derivation of Gewirth's moral principle begins with these assumptions about voluntariness and purposiveness as necessary features of action, and proceeds through a series of formal deductive steps to the Principle of Generic Consistency: (1) A responsible person is one who initiates or controls his behavior through his unforced, informed choice with the intention of fulfilling his various purposes. (2) Since he wants to fulfill his purposes he considers his freedom and well-being, the necessary preconditions of the performance of any and all action, as necessary goods. (3) As a responsible person who is in a position to act he holds that he has "generic" rights to freedom and well-being.[3] (4) Therefore he must admit that all responsible persons who are in positions to act have these rights. (5) Hence he must acknowledge that he at least ought to refrain from interfering with the freedom and well-being of others. The principle is presented formally as: "Act in accord with the generic rights of your recipients [the objects of one's actions] as well as of yourself" (Gewirth, 1978:135).

It may appear at first that this principle is a mere restatement of the most popular form of the Golden Rule, "Do unto others as you would have them do unto you." However, Gewirth argues that unlike the Golden Rule, the Principle of Generic Consistency—because it obligates one to respect the freedom and well-being of others—prohibits abhorrent acts that would be consistent with the letter, though not the spirit, of the Golden Rule (for example, in the case of a fanatic who justifies injuring others because he is willing to harm himself). Moreover, while the Golden Rule does not specify which goods individuals ought to value, the derivation of the Principle of Generic Consistency provides reasons why we are obligated to respect and promote the freedom and well-being of others. Finally, while the Golden Rule is not based on reason in the formal sense, the Principle of Generic Consistency, Gewirth claims, is derived by formal logic from premises concerning the necessary features of action; to deny the principle is to deny a principle to which all persons are logically committed (Gewirth, 1970, 1974, 1978).

Recognizing that there will always be some question about the technical derivation of Gewirth's principle, and the extent to which it provides determinate and conclusive criteria for resolving all ethical dilemmas, this principle does represent a major advance beyond other contemporary ethical theories by virtue of its carefully constructed theoretical foundation and its focus on developing criteria for resolving difficult conflicts among ethical principles and values. It also provides an example of an ethical theory that can be usefully applied to the justification of a social policy.

The Application of Ethics to Social Policy

The principal conclusion Gewirth reaches is that every responsible person has a right to freedom and well-being. On the surface, this conclusion appears straightforward; each individual has a right to act as he or she wishes as long as one's actions do not interfere with the freedom and well-being of others. We encounter difficulties, however, when we confront instances when the freedom and well-being of one individual threatens or conflicts with the freedom and well-being of another. For example, it is possible that in principle the freedom of community residents to oppose community-based care of juvenile offenders may conflict with the well-being of youth who would otherwise be subjected to the insalubrious quality of life which tends to be associated with confinement in a correctional institution. This is an example of a conflict between what the philosopher W. D. Ross (1930) referred to as *prima face* duties and *actual* duties. A prima facie duty is an action we ought to perform *other things being equal,* or independent of other ethical considerations. That is, individuals have a prima facie duty to respect other individuals' right to both freedom and well-being. However, in some instances prima facie duties (or rights) will conflict, and this forces us to decide which of the duties (or rights) should take precedence. Prima facie duties which conflict must thus give way to an actual duty.

Conflicts among prima facie duties and rights frequently occur in the formulation of social policy, and decisions about one's actual duty or right in instances when they conflict are among the most critical choices policy makers must make. These are the cases in which one must decide, for example, whether taxes should be increased despite public protest in order to augment services for the elderly and disabled, whether residents of a community should be displaced in order to rehabilitate a deteriorating neighborhood, or whether an industry which serves as the economic life line for a community ought to be closed down because of violations of environmental regulations. In each case a difficult choice must be made between the freedom and well-being of one group of individuals over another. It appears that in each case there is a conflict between two or more prima facie duties or rights which cannot be respected simultaneously. As Alan Donagan (1977) has said, "it is possible, by breaking one moral prohibition, to entangle yourself in a situation in which, whatever you do, you must break another: that is, in which you are perplexed *secundum quid.*" The difficult task, of course, is settling on criteria for resolving these baffling conflicts.

One of the implications of Gewirth's derivation is that guidelines can be formulated for resolving conflicts among individuals' right to freedom and well-being. Several guidelines can be postulated: (1) If one person or group violates or is about to violate the generic rights of another to freedom and well-being (including basic, nonsubtractive, and additive goods), action to prevent or remove the violation may be justified. Whether the action to prevent or remove the violation is justified depends on the extent to which the violation threatens an individual's ability to act in the future. (2) Since every individual has the duty to respect others' right to the goods that are the necessary preconditions of action (freedom and well-being), one duty takes precedence over another if the good that is the object of the former duty is more necessary for the possibility of action, and if the right to that good cannot be protected without violating the latter duty. (3) Rules pertaining to relations among individuals can, in particular cases, override the duty not to coerce others. Such rules must, however, meet several conditions: any coercion permitted by the rules must be necessary to prevent undeserved or unneeded coercion and serious harm; such coercion must not exceed what is necessary for such protection; the rules which permit occasional coercion must be imposed by the procedures of the method of consent (Reamer, 1982).

In the case of the policy of diversion and deinstitutionalization, we have an instance where the rights to freedom and well-being of one group of individuals (community residents) may conflict with the rights to freedom and well-being of another (juvenile offenders). Our review of the empirical evidence available concerning the effects of community-based programs indicates that caring for youths in noninstitutional settings does not, on the average, pose any greater risk to the safety and well-being of the public than does institutional care. It appears that in light of this evidence, the policy of diversion and deinstitutionalization is defensible on the ethical grounds we have just reviewed because of the greater degree of freedom it affords youths without increasing, on the average, the risk to the community. The youth's freedom can thus be enhanced without sacrificing the community's well-being and thus should take precedence. It may be that as a result certain community residents may be "coerced" into accepting noninstitutional care of juvenile offenders against their wishes (which may technically interfere with their prima facie right to freedom), but this action is justifiable because of the freedom of action it affords the juveniles without increasing the risk to the community, in addition to allowing the youths to avoid the dire living conditions which tend to exist in institutions. To do otherwise constitutes unnecessary coercion and harm to juveniles and might also jeopardize their chances of becoming meaningfully integrated in the life of the community and, hence, the likelihood that they will become responsible adults who do not continue to threaten the rights of others to freedom and well-being. This conclusion does not require us to ignore whatever desire exists among community residents to express their deeply felt resentment of youth's illegal behavior. The communication of such resentment is to be expected and is not necessarily undesirable. However, there is no evidence available to suggest that secure confinement in an institution is necessary in order to convey this message to juvenile offenders. There is, to the contrary, reason to believe that most youth (with the exception of those who have a history of particularly violent or chronic misbehavior) can be served humanely in noninstitutional settings which attempt to establish meaningful ties between each youth and his community while simultaneously communicating to the youth the fact that the community resents his mischief (Coates, Miller, and Ohlin, 1978).

THE PRIMACY OF ETHICS IN SOCIAL POLICY

The analysis of the ideological, empirical, and ethical factors related to the policy of diversion and deinstitutionalization illustrates the way in which an attempt to justify a policy in principle reduces to a question of ethics. In this instance, the ethical justification of diversion and deinstitutionalization, as I perceive it, is consistent with the tradition in practice immediately prior to and following the enactment of the 1974 Juvenile Justice and Delinquency Prevention Act, where attempts to minimize the detrimental effects of processing youth through the formal juvenile justice system have been a priority. However, the conclusion that the policy of diversion and deinstitutionalization is right, in the moral sense, does not follow merely because it is consistent with this ideological tradition. Rather, it is right because it can be justified in terms of ethical argument. Were this policy inconsistent with previous practice it would be no less right. In fact, history provides us with too many examples of practices long engaged in that have been judged later to be immoral.

What, then, is the place of ideology and empirical factors in the justification of social policy? The answer is that both types of factors are valuable and make important contributions. Ideological factors that reflect a tradition of practice often evolve for the very reason that thoughtful individuals have contemplated the ethical reasons why certain policies ought to be drafted and implemented. But we know from experience that ideology is not always based on such careful reflection. Too often it represents only intuition, political expedience, or other assumptions that are not grounded in moral judgments about right and wrong, or duty and obligation.

Empirical evidence can also be quite helpful in our attempts to shape policy. Results from carefully designed research can frequently help us anticipate the likely effects of certain policies or the success we may have in our attempts to implement them. However, empirical evidence by itself cannot be translated directly into policy. One major difficulty with basing policy decisions on the results of empirical evidence is the temptation to derive "ought" statements from "is" statements, that is where an assumption is made that statements of fact about the world can lead us directly to ethical judgments. As we saw above, there is no logical connection between descriptive statements of fact and ethical judgments. A related problem with the use of empirical evidence as the primary basis for policy decisions lies with the inevitable disagreements among individuals about the meaning of any particular set of empirical data. While such differences of opinion frequently lead to new empirical questions, there is no certainty that any empirical evidence will ever be interpreted without disagreement.

A final problem connected with the use of empirical evidence in justifying policy relates to fundamental questions about the validity and reliability of data gathered in research. These questions, frequently debated by philosophers of science, concern such issues as the ability of researchers to construct operational measures that accurately represent the concepts studied, limits on the ability of researchers to make causal inferences from data that only include correlations, and the effects of research procedures themselves which may contaminate attempts to measure empirically (Rosenthal and Rosnow, 1969; Popper, 1950).

Policy makers will do well to consider what ideology, tradition, and empirical evidence suggest about the merits and demerits of particular policies. When ideology, tradition, and empirical evidence seem to suggest a policy that is consistent with ethical justification, one will be in a position to make a persuasive argument in favor of the particular policy. When there is a conflict among these factors, one must choose to which priority will be given. In the final analysis, however, only an ethical principle can contain language that proscribes immoral policies by using such terms as right, wrong, good, bad, duty, obligation, just, and unjust in the moral sense; conclusions based on ideology or empirical evidence must ultimately serve to inform judgments that are based on ethical reasoning. By definition, ideological and empirical statements do not incorporate ethical concepts; they merely make nonmoral claims about what policies should be favored or what the data suggest about their effectiveness. Once we move to making moral claims about what one is obligated or has a duty to perform—informed perhaps by ideological convictions and empirical evidence—one has moved to the arena of ethical discourse (Reamer, 1982). While an ethical principle may not, by itself, always lead to unequivocal guidelines about which policies ought to be pursued and may not in fact prevent immoral practices, knowing that our decisions frequently reduce to ethical ones that require careful judgments which consider normative factors (as well as nonnormative ones) represents a nontrivial conclusion.

As I observed earlier, the application of one ethical theory that I happen to find persuasive to a particular social policy is in one sense arbitrary; other theories may have been used, and the one I have drawn upon can be interpreted in alternative ways. What I have demonstrated, however, is a process that someone who is committed to thoughtful analysis of policy issues can use to join the world of ethics with the worlds of ideology and empiricism, with which many of us are more familiar (and perhaps more comfortable).

It would be naive to claim that the arguments I have painted with a broad brush should necessarily convince anyone of the substantive conclusions I have reached. This would take much more detail and precision than the space here permits. Rather, my aim has been to use broad strokes to make a broad point—that it is incumbent upon us to use our intellectual capacities to explore the value and ethical implications of our policy decisions. Some of us will be moved by these considerations and some of us, no doubt, will not be. But there is something of value in stirring the moral imagination. To do otherwise would only fulfill the prophecy that the eighteenth century Spanish artist, Francisco Goya, inscribed in one of his series of etchings and aquatints, "Los Caprichos": "El sueño de la razon produce monstruos" ("The sleep of reason brings forth monsters").

NOTES

1. A status offender is formally defined as a youth who has committed an offense that would not be considered a crime if committed by an adult, e.g., running away from home, truancy, ungovernability.

2. Of course, such decisions must consider the economic and political factors that may finally determine whether a given policy is implemented. However, the decision to endorse a particular policy in principle necessarily rests on value-laden assumptions.

3. Gewirth uses the term generic to characterize rights he considers fundamental. The rights to freedom and well-being are generic, he argues, because they either "subsume other rights in that the others are specifications of the rights to freedom and well-being, or they take precedence over other rights in that the latter, if they are to be valid, must not violate the rights to freedom and well-being" (Gewirth, 1978:64).

REFERENCES

Allen, F. A. (1964) The Borderland of Criminal Justice. Chicago: University of Chicago Press.

Baron, R., F. Feeney and W. Thornton (1973) "Preventing delinquency through diversion." Federal Probation 37:13–18.

Berger, D. E., M. W. Lipsey, L. B. Dennison and J. M. Lange (1977) The Effectiveness of the Sheriff's Department's Juvenile Diversion Projects in Southeast Los Angeles County. Claremont, CA: Claremont Graduate School (mimeo).

Berman, S. (1959) "Antisocial character disorder: its etiology and relationship to delinquency." American Journal of Orthopsychiatry 29:612–621.

Binder, A. (1976) Diversion and the Justice System: Evaluating the Results. Irvine, CA: University of California at Irvine (mimeo).

Bloch, H. A. and A. Niederhoffer (1958) The Gang: A Study in Adolescent Behavior. New York: Philosophical Library.

Bohnstedt, M. (1978) "Answers to three questions about juvenile diversion." Journal of Research in Crime and Delinquency 15:109–123.

Carter, G. W. and G. R. Gilbert (1973) An Evaluation Progress Report of the Alternative Routes Project. Los Angeles, CA: University of Southern California Regional Research Institute in Social Welfare (mimeo).

Cloward, R. A. and L. E. Ohlin (1960) Delinquency and Opportunity. New York: Free Press.

Coates, R. B., A. D. Miller and L. E. Ohlin (1978) Diversity in a Youth Correctional System: Handling Delinquents in Massachusetts. Cambridge, MA: Ballinger.

Cohen, A. K. (1955) Delinquent Boys: The Culture of the Gang. New York: Free Press.

Donaghan, A. (1977) The Theory of Morality. Chicago: University of Chicago Press.

Elliott, D. S. (1978) Diversion: A Study of Alternative Processing Practices. Boulder, CO: Behavioral Research Institute (mimeo).

Emmet, D. (1962) "Ethics and the social worker." British Journal of Psychiatric Social Work 6:165–172.

Empey, L. T. (1973) "Juvenile justice reform: diversion, due process, and deinstitutionalization." In L. E. Ohlin (ed.), Prisoners in America. Englewood Cliffs, NJ: Prentice-Hall.

——and M. L. Erickson (1972) The Provo Experiment. Lexington, MA: Lexington/D. C. Heath.

——and S. G. Lubeck (1971) The Silverlake Experiment: Testing Delinquency Theory and Community Intervention. Chicago: Aldine.

Forward, J. R., M. Kirby and K. Wilson (1974) Volunteer Intervention with Court-Diverted Juveniles. Boulder, CO: University of Colorado (mimeo).

Frankena, W. K. (1973) Ethics, 2nd ed. Englewood Cliffs, NJ: Prentice-Hall.

Gewirth, A. (1970) "Must one play the moral language game?" American Philosophical Quarterly 7:107–118.

——(1974) "The 'is-ought' problem resolved." Proceedings and Addresses of the American Philosophical Association 47:34–61.

——(1978) Reason and Morality. Chicago: University of Chicago Press.

Gibbons, D. C. and G. F. Blake (1976) "Evaluating the impact of juvenile diversion programs." Crime and Delinquency 22:411–420.

Gorovitz, S., ed. (1971) Utilitarianism: John Stuart Mill. Indianapolis: Bobbs-Merrill.

Hancock, R. N. (1974) Twentieth Century Ethics. New York: Columbia University Press.

Hudson, W. D., ed. (1969) The Is/Ought Question. New York: St. Martin's.

Hunt, L. (1978) "Social work and ideology." In N. Timms and D. Watson (eds.), Philosophy and Social Work. London: Routledge and Kegan Paul.

Hurley, T. D. (1907) Origin of the Illinois Juvenile Court Law. Chicago: Chicago Visitation and Aid Society.

Illinois Law Enforcement Commission (1980) Implementation of Senate Bill 346. Chicago: Illinois Law Enforcement Commission (mimeo).

Kahn, A. J. (1953) A Court for Children. New York: Columbia University Press.

——(1969) Theory and Practice for Social Planning. New York: Russell Sage Foundation.

Klein, M. W. (1974) "Labeling, deterrence, and recidivism: a study of police dispositions of juvenile offenders." Social Problems 22:292–303.

——(1979) "Deinstitutionalization and diversion of juvenile offenders: a litany of impediments." In N. Morris and M. Tonry (eds.), Crime and Justice: An Annual Review of Research. Chicago: University of Chicago Press.

Ku, R. and C. H. Blew (1977) A University's Approach to Delinquency Prevention: The Adolescent Diversion Project. Washington, D.C.: U.S. Government Printing Office.

Lemert, E. M. (1967) "The juvenile court: quest and realities." In President's Commission on Law Enforcement and Administration of Justice (ed.), Task Force Report: Juvenile Justice and Youth Crime. Washington, D.C.: U.S. Government Printing Office.

Lincoln, S. B. (1976) "Juvenile referral and recidivism." In R. M. Carter and M. W. Klein (eds.), Back on the Street: The Diversion of Juvenile Offenders. Englewood Cliffs, NJ: Prentice-Hall.

————, K. Teilmann, M. Klein and S. Labin (1977) "Recidivism rates of diverted juvenile offenders." Paper presented at the National Conference on Criminal Justice Evaluation, Washington, D.C.

Lundman, R. J. (1976) "Will diversion reduce recidivism?" Crime and Delinquency 22:428–437.

Murray, C. A. and L. A. Cox, Jr. (1979) Beyond Probation: Juvenile Corrections and the Chronic Delinquent. Beverly Hills, CA: Sage Publications.

Palmer, T. (1974) "The youth authority's community treatment project." Federal Probation 38:3–14.

Parsons, T. (1947) "Certain primary sources and patterns of aggression in the social structure of the Western world." Psychiatry 10:167–181.

Platt, A. M. (1969) The Child Savers. Chicago: University of Chicago Press.

Popper, K. R. (1950) "Indeterminism in quantum physics and classical physics, part I." British Journal for the Philosophy of Science 1:117–133.

President's Commission on Law Enforcement and Administration of Justice (1967) Task Force Report: Juvenile Justice and Youth Crime. Washington, D.C.: U.S. Government Printing Office.

Quinney, R. (1970) The Problem of Crime. New York: Dodd, Mead and Company.

Reamer, F. G. (1982) "Conflicts of professional duty in social work." Social Casework 63:579–585.

————(1982) Ethical Dilemmas in Social Service. New York: Columbia University Press.

————and C. H. Shireman (1981) "Alternatives to the juvenile justice system: their development and the current 'state of the art.' " Juvenile and Family Court Journal 32:17–32.

Rein, M. (1970) Social Policy: Issues of Choice and Change. New York: Random House.

Rosenheim, M. K., ed. (1962) Justice for the Child: The Juvenile Court in Transition. New York: Free Press.

Rosenthal, R. and R. L. Rosnow, eds. (1969) Artifact in Behavioral Research. New York: Academic Press.

Ross, W. D. (1930) The Right and the Good. Oxford: Clarendon.

Shireman, C. H. and F. G. Reamer (in press) Rehabilitating Juvenile Justice. New York: Columbia University Press.

Stratton, J. G. (1975) "Effects of crisis intervention counseling on predelinquent and misdemeanor juvenile offenders." Juvenile Justice 26:7–18.

Sundquist, J. L. (1968) Politics and Policy: The Eisenhower, Kennedy, and Johnson Years. Washington, D.C.: Brookings Institution.

CONCEPTUALIZING PUBLIC POLICY ANALYSIS

Stuart S. Nagel

ABSTRACT

This chapter clarifies basic concepts associated with public policy analysis. These concepts are grouped into two sets which may be applied, respectively, to define the field of policy analysis and to conduct a policy analysis project. The analysis of these basic concepts can add to the conceptual framework that is being developed by many people in this relatively new, useful, and important field.

CONCEPTUALIZING THE FIELD OF POLICY ANALYSIS

Definition

Public policy analysis can be defined as determining which of various alternative public or governmental policies will most achieve a given set of goals in light of the relations between the policies and the goals.

Policy Analysis: Perspectives, Concepts, and Methods, pages 247–265.
Copyright © 1986 by JAI Press, Inc.
All rights of reproduction in any form reserved.
ISBN: 0–89232–371–X

That definition brings out the four key elements of policy evaluation which are:

1. *Goals,* including normative constraints and relative weights for the goals.
2. *Policies,* programs, projects, decisions, options, means, or other alternatives that are available for achieving the goals.
3. *Relations* between the policies and the goals, including relations that are established by intuition, authority, statistics, observation, deduction, guesses, or other means.
4. Drawing a *conclusion* as to which policy or combination of policies is best to adopt in light of the goals, policies, and relations.

Other concepts that are often used to mean the same thing as public policy analysis include policy evaluation, policy studies, program evaluation, public management-science, and policy science. One could make distinctions between those concepts as follows:

1. Policy evaluation emphasizes evaluating alternative public policies, as contrasted to describing them or explaining why they exist.
2. Policy studies includes describing policies, explaining their existence, and evaluating them.
3. Program evaluation emphasizes evaluating a specific program like a halfway house in Chicago in 1984, as contrasted to developing general principles of how to evaluate.
4. Public management science emphasizes decision-making that is involved in implementing broader decisions, generally made by legislatures and agencies that have quasi-legislative authority.
5. Policy analysis emphasizes systematic analytic methods which can be quantitative or qualitative.
6. Policy science emphasizes quantitative methods.

Methods of public policy analysis refer to:

1. How to draw a conclusion as to which policy to adopt from information on goals, policies, and relations.
2. How to establish the relations between policies and goals.
3. How to determine what policies are available for adoption and what goals are appropriate to consider.[1]

Sources of Elements

A frequently asked question in public policy analysis is where do the goals, policies, and relations come from. The main sources are authority, statistics, observation, deduction, and sensitivity analysis.

Authority involves consulting one or more persons, books, articles, or other entities that are considered knowledgeable as to what the relevant goals, policies, or relations might be.

Statistical or *observational* analysis involves analyzing specific instances in order to generalize as to what the goals, policies, or relations might be.

Deduction involves drawing a conclusion from premises that have been established from authority, observation, and/or intuition.

Sensitivity analysis involves guessing the goals, policies, or relations, and then determining what effect, if any, the guessed values have on the bottom line of which policy is best.[2]

Types of Rationality

There are three types of rationality in public policy analysis. They consist of rationality of intentions, consequences, and procedures.

Rationality of *intentions* refers to people trying to maximize benefits minus costs in whatever they do. That is a tautology or an occurrence that is true by definition. Benefits minus costs is a synonym for net satisfaction, and net satisfaction refers in a circular way to what people are trying to maximize. Although that kind of rationality is present by definition, it is still a useful concept in providing an initial premise at a high level of generality for many examples of policy analysis.

Rationality of *consequences* refers to being successful in maximizing benefits minus costs in reaching decisions. That is impossible to always do for two reasons. One is that although very little information is often needed to make optimizing decisions, sometimes even the minimum of accurate information is lacking with regard to goals, policies, and/or relations. Second, many policy decisions are based on averages or probabilities of success that may not be so present in a given situation. For example, a decision-maker may choose to go ahead with a project because it truly has a .90 probability of success. The decision-maker, however, may be unlucky enough to hit that one-in-ten chance in which the project fails, and the decision-maker may not get ten chances or even one more chance to come out even.

Rationality of *procedures* refers to developing a set of procedures that will maximize benefits minus costs if one does have adequate information

and average luck. Those procedures in turn refer to such methods as
benefit-cost analysis decision theory, optimum level analysis, and allocation theory, as defined below in Section II-A. Those are the kinds of
procedures with which systematic or rational polcy analysis is concerned.[3]

Objections to Feasibility

There are three major objections to the feasibility of procedural rationality in public policy analysis. They refer to subjective goals, missing
information, and multiple goals/alternatives.

The goals in public policy analysis are generally highly *subjective*, difficult to measure, and on different dimensions as compared to the goal
of maximizing income minus expenses in business analysis. This objection can be dealt with by a variety of methods for handling non-monetary
benefits and costs such as norming the raw scores of each alternative on
each goal by calculating part/whole percentages. The raw scores are thus
put on a 0 to 100 percent scale, and the raw scores on each goal sum to
100 percent.

Information is more often *missing* or unreliable in public policy analysis
than it is in business analysis. The probabilities of risky events are often
especially unknown or unreliable. This objection can often be handled
by determining the probability or other score above which one alternative
wins and below which another alternative wins. One can then decide
whether the true score is above or below that threshold score.

There frequently are *many* goals and policies to consider in public
policy analysis. A typical optimum level of mix problem may involve an
infinite number of alternatives, such as ways in which a budget could be
allocated among various activities or places. Goals, however, can be com-
posited or aggregated even if they are nonmonetary. Likewise multiple
policies can be reduced through processes of elimination and by treating
allocation problems in terms of the finite number of objects to which
resources are being allocated rather than in terms of the infinite number
of alternative allocations.

Another objection is that the mathematics of systematic policy analysis
may be too *complicated* for the average person to deal with, as contrasted
to elementary business calculations. One is not likely, however, to need
anything more complicated than an inexpensive hand calculator, a
knowledge of the substance being dealt with, and the codified common-
sense which the policy analysis field is developing.[4]

Trends

Systematic decision-analysis in the public sector began in the 1970s.
Trends which have already emerged include the following which relate

to goals, means, methods, and the public policy-evaluation orientation or profession.

As for *goals*, there is a trend toward more taking of goals as givens and then attempting to determine what policies will maximize or optimize them, rather than taking policies as givens and then attempting to determine their effects. Policy analysts are also becoming more sensitive to social values, with more questioning of goals in evaluating alternative policies.

As for *means*, there is a trend toward showing increased sophistication with regard to the political feasibility of policies being adopted and the feasibility of alternative delivery systems or implementation systems after they are adopted. Policy evaluation is also becoming increasingly interdisciplinary in drawing upon a variety of disciplinary sources as to means or policies for achieving goals. This includes economics, political science, sociology, and psychology among basic disciplines, and includes business administration, planning, public administration, law, social work, and education among applied disciplines.

As for *methods*, policy evaluation research has been building on business analysis especially with regard to maximizing benefits minus costs. It has, however, been developing its own methodology especially in matters of a measurement, equity, negative social indicators, and administrative psychology. Policy evaluation is also developing increased precision with its methods, but at the same time it is increasingly recognizing that simple methods may be enough for many policy problems. Policy evaluation is also becoming increasingly pro-active or pre-adoption rather than reactive or post-adoption. That distinction partly corresponds to deductive modeling as contrasted to empirical before-and-after analysis.

As for the policy-evaluation *orientation*, it has undergone substantial growth in training programs, research centers, funding sources, publishing outlets, and scholarly associations. It is also becoming increasingly used by government at the federal, state, and local levels, and in the executive, judicial, and legislative branches. This is indeed an exciting time to be in the field of public policy analysis in view of its growth and vitality.[5]

CONCEPTUALIZING A POLICY ANALYSIS PROJECT

Methodological Form

There are various ways of classifying the forms of policy analysis. An especially useful classification is in terms of the methods for drawing prescriptive conclusions. There are five main categories consisting of optimum choice, risk, level, mix, and timing analysis.

Optimum *choice* analysis or basic benefit-cost analysis involves lump-sum alternatives that do not allow for adopting a fraction of an alternative or more than one of the same alternative. The object is to pick the alternative that maximizes benefits minus costs.

Optimum *risk* analysis or decision theory also involves lump-sum alternatives, but the extent to which they produce benefits or costs is contingent on the occurrence of one or more probabilistic or risky events. The benefits and the costs thus have to be discounted or multiplied by the probability of their occurring.

Optimum *level* analysis involves a policy which can take many positions along a continuum, but doing too much or too little is considered undesirable. The optimum position is the one that (1) maximizes benefits if all the effects have been stated positively, (2) minimizes costs if all the effects have been stated negatively, or (3) maximizes benefits minus costs if some effects are positive and some negative.

Optimum *mix* analysis or allocation theory involves multiple policies, places, activities, persons, or other entities to which a budget, time, or other scarce resources are to be allocated. Part/whole percentaging (as mentioned for norming nonmonetary goals) can be helpful here for calculating allocation percentages with different weights for different goals.

Optimum *timing* analysis is sometimes referred to as a fifth methodology, although it frequently uses optimum choice, level, or mix analysis. It can be defined as the development of principles for deciding how to minimize time consumption by efficiently controlling the ordering of events, arrival rates, processing rates, critical paths, and other time-relevant items.[6]

Potential Usefulness

There are three major uses to which policy evaluation models can be put. Those uses relate to making, influencing, and predicting decisions. Other important but less frequent uses of policy evaluation models include measuring decisional propensities and deducing motives.

For *making* decisions, the basic approach involves determining the goals to be achieved, the policies available for achieving them, and the relations between the goals and the policies. In benefit-cost terms, this means determining the benefits and the costs for each policy. The benefits and costs are goals to be increased and decreased, respectively. The quantity of benefits or costs which a policy is predicted as achieving is a measure of the relations between the policies and their goals. From that input data, one should be able to draw conclusions as to the policy or combination of policies that should be adopted or decided upon for maximizing the goals, or for maximizing benefits minus costs.

For *influencing* decisions, the basic approach involves starting out with a decision that is considered socially desirable, or desirable from the perspective of whoever is seeking to influence decisions. That decision can be considered as the rightdoing decision, and its opposite as the wrongdoing decision. One should then seek to change the reality and the perceptions of the benefits and the costs so as to encourage more rightdoing. This means drawing conclusions as to how to (1) increase the benefits of rightdoing, (2) decrease the costs of rightdoing, (3) increase the costs of wrongdoing, (4) decrease the benefits of wrongdoing, and/or (5) increase the probability that the benefits and costs will be received.

For *predicting* decisions, the basic approach involves determining what the benefits and costs are considered to be by the relevant decision-makers, as contrasted to what they might actually be. One also needs to determine how those benefits and costs are likely to change or might change. One then draws conclusions as to how the decisions are likely to change in light of various changes in the benefits and costs of the alternative policies, programs, or decisions.

For *measuring* decisional propensities, the basic approach here is to determine a model that relates decisional outcomes to the perceptions of the benefits and costs of alternative courses of action. Ask people whose decisional propensities one is seeking to measure how they assess the various benefits and costs, instead of asking them directly about their decisional propensities. From data provided by their answers and from the model that relates decisions to benefits and costs, draw a conclusion as to their decisional propensities. The conclusion might be expressed in the form of a threshold probability above which they are likely to decide in one direction and below which they are likely to decide in the opposite direction. The conclusion might also be expressed in the form of a threshold benefit/cost ratio where the questions have mainly dealt with perceptions as to certain facts occurring, rather than questions asking about their values.

For deducing *motives*, the basic approach is to try to be able to determine what a decision-maker's goals are from knowing what decision he or she reached plus other information. If the information is in the form (1) X decision was reached and (2) the decision-maker perceives that the only effect of X is Y, then we can conclude that if the decision-maker (DM) adopts X, the DM must want to achieve Y. If, however, the DM perceives that X causes Y, but also perceives that X causes Z, then the DM's motivation might be to achieve Z. One can develop a similar pair

of rules for deducing the DM's causal perceptions (rather than motivations) if the information is in the form (1) X decision was reached and
(2) the DM favorably values Y and only Y. Other rules can be developed
which involve combinations of decisions, perceptions, and motivations
whereby one can or cannot deduce one of the three elements by knowing
something about the other two.[7]

Actual Utilization

Table 1 helps to see the concept of research utilization as being a
continuum concept, rather than a yes/no concept. Utilization at its lowest
level involves doing a policy research project that is not in any way
referred to by the people who make policy in the subject matter area.
Nor is there any evidence that the policy makers were aware of the
project, even though they did not explicitly cite it. That is clearly non-
utilization. At the other extreme or the highest level of utilization, the
research project converts the decision-makers from being negative to
being positive or vice versa on an issue. That is an extremely rare occurrence and may never even occur for controversial issues.

At the next to highest level is research that reinforces preconceived
decisions. This is reasonably common. Some skeptics of the value of
systematic policy analysis consider that occurrence not to be utilization.
Policy researchers should, however, be quite pleased if their research
accelerates a worthwhile decision which otherwise might not be made
for awhile. An example might be the research that showed more defendants could be released prior to trial without increasing the no-show
rate, provided there is some systematic screening to determine who is
to be released. Liberals found support in such studies since they wanted
to see more defendants released in view of the presumption of innocence.
Likewise, conservatives also found support in such studies since they
wanted to see a reduction in the expensive jail burden on the taxpayers.
That kind of reinforcement did accelerate the presumably desirable
occurrence of increased pretrial release with a constant or lower no-show
rate.

At the next to the lowest level is research that is referred to by the

Table 1. Degrees of Utilization of a Policy Research Study

Not Even Referred to	Referred to	Reinforces Values or Decisions	Converts Values or Decisions
(1)	(2)	(3)	(4)

0 —— 100

policymakers orally or by being officially cited. The citing could be by either the majority group among the decision-makers or the minority/dissenters. Either kind of citing is an example of low level utilization, even if the research cited was not on the winning side, and was not influential enough to convert decisions or even reinforce preconceived decisions. This is also a common occurrence. People who are skeptical of the value of policy research tend to emphasize how common the first two categories are of no citing or citing but no influence. One should, however, recognize that progress in dealing with policy problems may require many unutilized research projects before a research project is developed that does get well used. The policy research system is still a success if only one in ten projects gets used, but that one tends to produce benefits which outweigh the costs of the other nine.[8]

Adoption

Table 2 shows the relation between the concepts of policy research utilization and policy research adoption. Utilization here is divided into a *yes* category and a *no* category. The *yes* category includes categories 2, 3, and 4 in Table 1. That means a research project is considered utilized if it has been cited. One could, however, define the *yes* category in Table 2 as only including categories 3 and 4 from Table 1 or even as only including category 4. Common usage, though, would consider a policy research project as having been utilized by the Supreme Court if the Supreme Court cites it, especially since it is relatively easy to determine whether a project has been cited, but relatively difficult to determine whether the project has been influential.

Policy adoption refers to whether the recommendations of the research project have been adopted by the policy-makers, regardless whether

Table 2. Relations Between Utilization and Adoption

| | | Utilization (Referred to by policymakers or other evaluators) | |
		No	Yes
Adoption (Recommendations adopted, regardless whether referred to)	*Yes*	A Middle (#2)	B Best (#1)
	No	C Worst (#4)	D Middle (#3)

the project was referred to. Like utilization, adoption can be thought of as occurring in degrees, and not just as being present or absent. There is more adoption if the federal government or all 50 states adopt a policy than if only one state does. There is more adoption if a policy becomes part of the Constitution, rather than just part of a statute, an administrative regulation, or a judicial opinion, in that order. One can also talk about degrees of adoption in terms of the size of the favorable vote which the policy received in a legislature or other decision-making body without being vetoed or nullified by a chief executive or a high court. A policy is also more meaningfully adopted if a bigger appropriation or enforcement/administrative apparatus is provided along with the adoption. For the sake of discussion, however, we can talk in terms of the presence of adoption as meaning the proposed policy was officially adopted by some governmental body. Adoption of a policy, of course, does not necessarily mean successful implementation.

Given those definitions of utilization and adoption, it is possible to be *yes* on both (Cell B), *no* on both (Cell C), or *yes* on utilization in the sense of being cited, but *no* on adoption in the sense of not being adopted (Cell D). It is also possible to be *no* on utilization in not being referred to, but yet the bottom-line recommendation was adoption in spite of (rather than because of) the research project, or the adoption and the research project were unrelated (Cell A).

One can treat Table 2 not just as a four-cell table that shows four alternative ways of combining two dichotomous variables. The table can also be treated as a payoff matrix, in which we indicate the relative net benefits of each outcome. The best outcome from the perspective of a policy research is to have one's work cited and to have one's recommendations adopted. The worst outcome is to not be cited and to not have one's recommendations adopted. In between, one could say that Cell A is more desirable than Cell B because getting one's recommendations adopted should be more important than being cited, especially if one is working directly or indirectly for a government agency or interest group. Thus, a *no* on utilization accompanied by a *yes* on adoption should be worth more than a *yes* on utilization accompanied by a *no* on adoption.

A four-cell table can have at least three purposes. One purpose is to show how the categories on two variables can be combined together. That is the main purpose of Table 2. Such a four-cell table can be referred to as a combinations matrix. They generally only have letters or words in the cells, like yes-yes or yes-no. A second purpose is to show for each combination its relative or absolute value in comparison to the other combinations. That kind of table is referred to as a payoff matrix. They have numbers in the cells that indicate rank orders, relative values

Table 3. Cross-Tabulating the Values of Policy Evaluators and Policy-Makers

		Policy Evaluator		
		Reject or Terminate	Adopt or Retain	
Policy-Maker	Adopt or Retain	6 (30%)	72 (90%)	78
	Reject or Terminate	14 (70%)	8 (10%)	22
		20 (100%)	80 (100%)	100 Policy Research Studies

on a zero to 100 scale, dollar values, or other evaluations of the four outcomes. The third purpose is to show for each combination how often it occurs out of a set of possibilities. That kind of table is referred to as a cross-tabulation matrix. Table 3 is such a table. It involves a sample of 100 hypothetical (but realistic) policy-research studies. In each study there was a key policy proposed for adoption or a key policy that had been adopted.

Of the 100 studies, the policy evaluators concluded in 80 instances that the policy should be adopted or should be retained. In 20 instances, they concluded the policy should be rejected or terminated. Of those 80 instances, the policy-makers voted to adopt or retain 90 percent of the time and voted contrary to the evaluations 10 percent of the time. Of the 20 instances of the negative evaluations, the policy-makers voted to adopt or retain 30 percent of the time, and voted in accordance with those evaluations 70 percent of the time. Those hypothetical findings could be converted into a regression equation of the form $M = .30 + .60(E)$. That equation means that when the evaluator moves from a zero score of reject to a 1 score of adopt, then the probability of the policy-maker adopting moves from a base of .30 up to. 90. The reason for the close relation, however, is probably because both the policy evaluators and the policy-makers are responding to the same stimuli or social forces, and not because the policy evaluators are causing the policy makers to adopt when they otherwise would reject.[9]

Validity

Table 4 shows the relation between the concepts of policy-research utilization and policy-research validity. The utilization concept has the

Table 4.   Relations Between Utilization and Validity

		Utilization	
		No	Yes
Validity (More Important)	Yes	A Middle (#2)	B Best (#1)
	No	C Middle (#3)	D Worst (#4)

same meaning as in Table 2. There are four key elements in policy-evaluation research which lead to four aspects of policy-research validity. The four elements are:

1. Goals to be achieved, including normative constraints and relative weights for the goals.
2. Policies, programs, projects, decisions, options, means, or other alternatives that are available for achieving the goals.
3. Relations between the policies and the goals, including relations that are established by intuition, authority, statistics, observation, deduction, guesses, or other means.
4. Drawing a conclusion as to which policy or combination of policies is best to adopt in light of the goals, policies, and relations.

Validity in general refers to being accurate. In the context of policy-evaluation research and its key elements, validity refers to:

1. The internal consistency of logically drawing a conclusion that follows from the goals, policies, and relations.
2. The external consistency with empirical reality in describing the relations between the alternative policies and the goals.
3. The policies being considered should encompass the total set of feasible alternatives and only feasible alternatives. Feasibility in this context refers to being capable of being adopted and implemented by the relevant policy-makers and policy-appliers.
4. The listed goals include all the major goals and only the goals of the relevant policy-makers in this context.

Validity (like adoption and utilization) can occur in degrees, or at least invalidity can. A valid study meets all four of the above requirements. An invalid study fails to meet at least one of the four requirements. A study is even more invalid if it fails to meet more than one of the requirements, or fails to meet a requirement by a large margin. Validity in policy evaluation is thus like equity where equity is defined as providing a minimum benefits level for all relevant persons, groups, or places. Thus, if that minimum level is met, equity is present although equality may not be present. There can, however, be degrees of inequity depending on the size of the individual deviations from that minimum level and the number of people involved, as is the case with non-validity.

In relating utilization to validity, there are four possible combinations when utilization and validity are both dichotomized. The best possibility is for a study to be both utilized and valid. If validity is more important than utilization as it should be, then the next best possibility is for one's research to be valid even if it is not utilized. The *yes* row on validity thus dominates the *no* row on validity in Table 4, just as the *yes* row on adoption dominates the *no* row on adoption in Table 2. Unlike Table 2, however, it is better to be *no* on both variables in Table 4 than it is to be *yes* on utilization and *no* on validity. This is so because the worst combination is to have an invalid study utilized in view of the harm that such a study could have if utilized. In other words, utilizing invalid studies worsens the situation, rather than improves it.

One could create a table like Table 4, in which adoption rather than utilization is related to validity. The relative value of the cells would be the same since utilization and adoption are associated by virtue of the fact that adoption is sometimes a high degree of utilization, although one's policy recommendations can be adopted without one's research being utilized or referred to. The absolute value and disvalue of the cells, however, would be different with adoption substituted for utilization. Cell D would still be the worst cell, but the harm might be even greater since one can get a *yes* on utilization by merely being cited, but a *yes* on adoption means the proposed policy has become an actual or promulgated policy. One should, however, distinguish between the validity of the research study and the validity of the proposed policy. The research study may be invalid for any one of the four reasons mentioned above. The policy might nevertheless be valid in the sense of being capable of achieving the desired goals, even though the research study involved faulty deductive logic in drawing a conclusion and/or faulty inductive statistical inference in determining the relations between the policies and the goals.[10]

Importance

Table 5 shows the relation between the concepts of policy-research utilization and policy-research importance. The concept of importance can be defined in two ways:

Table 5. Relations Between Utilization and Importance

		Utilization	
		No	Yes
Importance	Yes	A Middle (#2.5 to #1)	B Best (#1)
	No	C Worst (#4)	D Middle (#2.5 to #4)

1. Does the research deal with issues in which there are big societal benefits minus societal costs being analyzed? Thus research on avoiding nuclear war is more important than research on whether tbe city of Champaign should have a strong mayor form of government or a city manager.
2. Does the research deal with a subject matter or a set of causal hypotheses that potentially have broad explanatory power? This is theoretical importance, as contrasted to policy importance.

There can be degrees of policy importance depending on the product of the total benefits times the total costs that are at stake. That benefits-*times*-costs criterion make sense in judging the relative importance of two research projects even though benefits-*minus*-costs is the criterion for judging which of two investments or alternatives policies to adopt. In other words, if one research project deals with benefits of 100 units and costs of 150 units, and a second project deals with benefits of 10 units and costs of 8 units, then the first project is more important (15,000 versus 80) given the size of the benefits and the costs, even though the second project would be a better or more profitable investment (-50 versus $+2$). We would not want to *add* benefits to costs to judge importance since they are likely to be measured in different units which cannot be meaningfully added, but in this context, different units can be meaningfully multiplied.

Table 5 shows that policy research is best which is both important and utilized. Policy research is worst which is neither important nor utilized. In the middle are the no-yes and yes-no combinations. We could also have a middle row on importance that covers the gray area of research that is neither obviously important nor obviously unimportant. We could likewise have a middle column on utilization that covers "just being cited" (category 2 in Table 1). On the right could be "being influential" regardless of whether one is cited (categories 3 and 4). On the left could be "being both uncited and uninfluential" (category 1).

Some policy researchers would say that it is better for one's feelings of satisfaction to do research that is important but not utilized, than it is to do research that is trivial but does get utilized. Other policy researchers would say that research which is not so important (meaning small societal benefits minus costs), but that gets utilized is better than research on achieving the ultimate societal happiness, but does not get utilized for anything. In other words, they would say that unutilized research is useless, just as a tree falling in Siberia with no one to hear or see it makes no noise or visual display. Given the differences of opinion on the relative value (at least to the researcher) of small scale research that is utilized versus large scale research that is not utilized, Table 5 shows those two middling positions as being close to tied, unlike the related Table 2 which deals with utilization and adoption.

In spite of that, one could still argue that doing important research should be valued higher than doing research that gets utilized because the important research might get utilized and then have a far greater payoff. We therefore change the numbers to show that being in Cell A is worth more than being in Cell D, and that importance does dominate utilization. In light of that reasoning, one might also say importance dominates adoption as well. In other words, unused research could be viewed narrowly as being of no value, regardless whether (1) the recommendations get adopted, (2) the research is valid, or (3) the subject matter is important. On the other hand, one could emphasize that unused research could have been used or could even still be used. It is thus worth doing for its expected value, which is the value that it would have if it were used, discounted by the probability of its being used as of the present time or as of when the research was being done. One could also emphasize that unused research has value in itself to policy researchers as a satisfying activity, at least when the research is validly done on an important subject.[11]

Combining Concepts

Table 6 shows there are 16 possible situations which combine the presence or absence of validity, importance, adoption, and utilization. A plus sign shows the characteristic is present. A minus sign shows the characteristic is absent. A question mark shows that it does not make any difference whether the characteristic is present or absent for the purpose of calculating the total value of the situation. In light of the previous discussion, we can rank-order the policy research characteristics

Table 6. Combining Validity, Importance, Adoption and Utilization

Situation	4 Validity	3 Importance	2 Adoption	1 Utilization	Total Value
1	+	+	+	+	10
2	+	+	+	−	9
3	+	+	−	+	8
4	+	+	−	−	7
5	+	−	+	+	7
6	+	−	+	−	6
7	+	−	−	+	5
8	+	−	−	−	4
9 to 16	−	?	?	?	0

+ = Present
− = Absent
? = Could be present or absent

as being validity, importance, adoption, and utilization in terms of their relative value. We can thus give them rank scores of 4, 3, 2, and 1 respectively.

Situation 1 has the highest total value since all four characteristics are present. The total value is shown as being a 10 by summing the four rank scores. Situation 2 has the next to highest total value since it is only missing utilization. As discussed previously, it is possible for one's recommendations to be adopted, even though one's study is uncited and unknown. Situation 3 is the opposite in the sense that there is utilization, but not adoption. It has a total value of 8 points by summing the rank scores of the characteristics that are present. Likewise, one can proceed through the first eight situations. They all have validity. They are arranged in descending order of their total values.

Situations 9 through 16 lack validity. Validity can be considered a constraint in that it must be met for the research study to have any value from the perspective of a professional policy evaluator. Validity is not a variable that can be traded for combinations of other variables, or for higher degrees of importance, adoption, and/or utilization. Thus, situations 9 through 16 all have a total value of zero, regardless how well they score on importance, adoption, or utilization. This brings out the importance of doing valid research as an ethical obligation in policy evaluation. One should also seek to do *important* research whose recommendations are *adopted* and *utilized*, but those are variables in an objective function to be achieved, rather than constraints to which the objective function is subject.

Perhaps one can define a good policy evaluation as one that has validity plus importance, regardless whether it is referred to or its recommendations are adopted. One could also include within a definition of a good policy evaluation a criterion that relates to whether one agrees with what the policy research recommends. That, however, is getting away from criteria that relate to methodology (as validity does) or substance (as importance does). It involves getting into the direction of the recommendations, which is within the criteria of normative philosophy and being a good citizen, but outside the criteria of technical policy evaluation. Policy evaluators can concern themselves with such questions in their roles as political activists, but those roles should be kept separate from the role of objective policy evaluator. One's policy recommendations will have more credibility if the policy research of which they are a part is done from an objective perspective, rather than an advocacy perspective. An objective perspective seeks to determine the policy or combination that is best for achieving a given set of goals in light of the relations between the policies and the goals. An advocacy perspective seeks to justify why a policy or combination should be adopted and avoids providing support for any other policy. It is like the difference between a judge (trying to determine the law and the facts) and a lawyer (trying to argue as to how the law and the facts should be interpreted).

In defining good policy evaluation, one should add as a criterion the concept of originality to the concepts of validity, social/theoretical importance, and utilization/adoption. Originality can be measured in degrees since all research differs to some extent from previous research unless an exact plagiarism is involved. Even highly original research builds on and synthesizes prior research. Feasibility is an additional criterion for judging proposed policy research, as contrasted to completed policy research. Feasibility is concerned with how easily the research can be implemented given the limited time, expertise, interests, funds, and other resources of the researcher.

CONCLUSIONS

Conceptualizing the field of policy analysis or policy evaluation emphasizes the key elements of goals, policies, relations between the policies and goals, and drawing a conclusion as to which policy or combination of policies is best. That basic four-part framework can be crossed with four categories that relate to the source of those elements. Those sources include authority, statistical observation, deduction, and sensitivity analysis. Rationality in this context means using procedures for deriving goals, policies, relations, and conclusions in a way that will maximize benefits minus costs if one has adequate information and average luck.

Such procedures are possible in spite of the subjectivity of goals, missing information, the multiplicity of goals, and the alleged complexity of rational policy evaluation. There have been many recent improvements in dealing with these key elements of goals, policies, relations, and conclusions in policy evaluation.

Conceptualizing a specific policy analysis project emphasizes the nature of the conclusion-drawing and what is done with the conclusions. Conclusion-drawing may involve deciding on an optimum choice with mutually exclusive alternatives or allowing combinations, with or without probabilistic risks. It may also involve finding an optimum level where doing too much or too little is undesirable, or finding an optimum mix of scarce resources across activities or places. The conclusions may have potential usefulness mainly for making, influencing, or predicting decisions. They may have actual usefulness in the sense of being referred to by others. The ideas recommended may or may not be adopted. More important than actual utilization or adoption is internal consistency or logical validity, and external consistency or empirical validity. Also important are conclusions that have societal importance in terms of benefits minus costs, or theoretical importance in terms of explanatory power. Other desirable characteristics of policy analysis projects include originality and feasibility. It is hoped that this analysis of basic concepts in public policy analysis will add to the conceptual framework that is being built by many people in this relatively new, useful, and important field of study.

NOTES AND REFERENCES

1.   For further details on defining policy analysis, see Garry Brewer and Peter deLeon, *The Foundations of Policy Analysis* (Homewood, IL: Dorsey, 1983); Yehezkel Dror, *Public Policy-making Reexamined* (New Brunswick, NJ: Transaction Books, 1983); Phillip Gregg (ed.), *Problems of Theory in Policy Analysis* (Lexington, MA: Lexington-Heath, 1976); Harold Lasswell, *A Pre-View of Policy Sciences* (New York: Elsevier, 1971); and S. Nagel (ed.), *Encyclopedia of Policy Studies* (New York: Marcel Dekker, 1983), iii–xxii and 3–10.

2.   For further details on sources of the elements in policy analysis, see Dickinson McGaw and George Satson, *Political Social Inquiry* (New York: Wiley, 1976) (general); E. E. Schattschneider, et al., *A Guide to the Study of Public Affairs* (New York: Dryden, 1952) (authority); David Hoaglin, et al., *Data for Decisions: Information Strategies for Policymakers* (Cambridge, MA: Abt, 1982) (statistical analysis); Martin Greenberger, et al., *Models in the Policy Process* (New York: Russell Sage, 1976) (deduction); and Carl Moore, *Profitable Applications of the Break-Even System* (Englewood Cliffs, NJ: Prentice-Hall, 1971) (sensitivity analysis).

3.   On rationality, see Edward Friedland, *Introduction to Concepts of Rationality in Political Science* (Morristown, NJ: General Learning Press, 1974) and Herbert Simon, *Reason in Human Affairs* (Palo Alto, CA: Stanford, 1983).

4.   On objections to the feasibility of systematic policy analysis see "The Pros and Cons of Systems Analysis in Policy Studies," in S. Nagel (ed.), *Basic Literature in Policy Studies: A*

Comprehensive Bibliography (Greenwich, CT: JAI Press, 1984), 33–36. A leading work on the pro side is Daniel Lerner and Harold Lasswell (eds.), *Policy Sciences* (Palo Alto, CA: Stanford, 1951). A leading work on the con side is Ida Hoos, *Systems Analysis in Public Policy: A Critique* (Berkeley, CA: University of California Press, 1972). On possible ways of overcoming each of the four separate objections, see chapters 13 through 16 of S. Nagel, *Public Policy: Goals, Means, and Methods* (New York: St. Martin's, 1984).

5.   For further details on trends in policy analysis see Giandomenico Majone, "Applied Systems Analysis: A Genetic Approach," in Edward Quade and Hugh Miser (eds.), *Handbook of Systems Analysis* (New York: Elsevier, 1984); and S. Nagel, *Contemporary Public Policy Analysis* (Tuscaloosa, AL: University of Alabama Press, 1984), 12–37.

6.   For further details on the five basic methodologies, see Edith Stokey and Richard Zeckhauser, *A Primer for Policy Analysis* (New York: Norton, 1978); Michael White, et al., *Managing Public Systems: Analytic Techniques for Public Administration* (N. Scituate, MA: Duxbury, 1980); and S. Nagel, *Policy Evaluation: Making Optimum Decisions* (New York: Praeger, 1982).

7.   For further discussion and examples of the usefulness of policy evaluation models, see Sheen Kassouf, *Normative Decision Making* (Englewood Cliffs, NJ: Prentice-Hall, 1970) (making decisions); Gary Becker and William Landes (eds.), *Essays in the Economics of Crime and Punishment* (New York: Columbia University Press, 1974) (influencing decisions); Martin Greenberger, et al., *Models in the Policy Process* (New York: Russell Sage, 1976) (predicting decisions); and S. Nagel and M. Neef, *Decision Theory and the Legal Process* (Lexington, MA: Lexington-Heath, 1979) (general).

8.   On utilization of policy analysis research, see Albert Cherns, *Using the Social Science and Social Problem Solving* (London: Routledge and Kegan Paul, 1979); Irving Horowitz and James Katz, *Social Science and Public Policy in the United States* (New York: Praeger, 1975), Charles Lindblom and David Cohen, *Usable Knowledge: Social Science and Social Problem Solving* (New Haven, CT: Yale, 1979); and Carol Weiss (ed.), *Using Social Research in Public Policy Making* (Lexington, MA: Lexington-Heath, 1977).

9.   On the adoption of proposed public policies, see James Anderson, *Public Policy-Making* (New York: Holt, Rinehart and Winston, 1979); Robert Eyestone, *From Social Issues to Public Policy* (New York: Wiley, 1978); Charles Jones, *An Introduction to the Study of Public Policy* (N. Scituate, MA: Duxbury, 1977); Charles Lindblom, *The Policy-Making Process* (New Haven, CT: Yale, 1980); and Judith May and Aaron Wildavsky (eds.), *The Policy Cycle* (Beverly Hills, CA: Sage, 1978).

10.   On validity in policy evaluation methods, see Michael Carley, *Rational Techniques in Policy Analysis* (London: Heinemann, 1980); William Dunn, *Public Policy Analysis* (Englewood Cliffs, NJ: Prentice-Hall, 1981); Duncan McRae and James Wilde, *Policy Analysis for Public Decisions* (N. Scituate, MA: Duxbury, 1979); Edward Quade, *Analysis for Public Decisions* (Amsterdam: North Holland, 1982); Edith Stokey and Richard Zeckhauser, *A Primer for Policy Analysis* (New York: Norton, 1978); and S. Nagel, *Public Policy: Goals, Means, and Methods* (New York: St. Martins, 1983).

11.   On the concept of importance or value in policy analysis research, see William Dunn (ed.), *Values, Ethics, and the Practice of Policy Analysis* (Lexington, MA: Lexington-Heath, 1983); Joel Fleishman and Bruce Payne, *Ethical Dilemmas and the Education of Policy-Makers* (Hastings-on-Hudson, NY: Hastings Center, 1981); Fred Frohock, *Public Policy: Scope and Logic* (Englewood Cliffs, NJ: Prentice-Hall, 1979); Wayne Leys, *Ethics for Policy Decisions: The Art of Asking Deliberative Questions* (Englewood Cliffs, NJ: Prentice-Hall, 1952); and Duncan McRae, *The Social Function of Social Science* (New Haven, CT: Yale, 1976).

PART III

METHODS

INTO THE SNAKEPIT:
VALUE-WEIGHTING SCHEMES
IN POLICY ANALYSIS

Michael J. Carley

ABSTRACT

Value weighting schemes are often used as a means of systematically attaching social values to quantitative data in policy analysis. There are different schools of thought on the benefit of such schemes, however, with some analysts embracing them wholeheartedly, and others arguing they are best ignored. This article explores some of the contentious issues in value-weighting by the revealed and expressed preferences of politicians, experts, and the public, especially with regard to distributional equity.

INTRODUCTION

Following the usual quantification of data in the research phase of a policy analysis comes the choice of whether to aggregate (or sum) the resultant data into simpler composite indicators or to leave it in an unaggregated form. The aggregation usually requires that unlike measures be transformed into a common scale so they can be added together, for

Policy Analysis: Perspectives, Concepts, and Methods, pages 269–279.
Copyright © 1986 by JAI Press, Inc.
All rights of reproduction in any form reserved.
ISBN: 0–89232–371–X

example, in studies of housing quality which sum measures of dilapidation and overcrowding into a common indicator. This is sometimes followed by the development of a value-weighting scheme which attempts to express the differential contribution of each piece of data to some specific decision criteria or to the general quality of life of various groups in society. There is considerable divergency, however, among policy analysts as to the relative advantages and disadvantages of aggregation and value-weighting.

Some analysts are generally opposed to aggregation and their main argument is that it hides or loses information important to the decision process and may serve to obscure the strengths and weaknesses of various policy alternatives (Bisset, 1978). Further, they argue that value-weighting all too often does not reflect the values of those persons who are most affected by the decisions. Knox (1978), for example, warns of the pitfalls of "cultural imperialism" where the value-weighting represents an operational definition of some welfare concept reflecting the researcher's values rather than the values of those whose welfare is under consideration. Although this is a danger in most social science research, it becomes a critical issue where a policy analysis may lead to changes in resource allocation. This school of analysts tends to argue that value-weighting is best done, *post* analysis, by the politicians who, when presented with data important to a decision, make mental trade-offs among alternatives which reflect some sum of the value judgements of their constituents.

Other policy analysts propose that aggregation without value-weighting avoids problems, that is simply adding up the quantified measures converted to some common scale (money, utils, units etc.) without regard to value judgements. In fact this simply transfers the value-weighting to the choice of indicators and so the choice becomes all important. Also such a scheme presupposes a model of social behavior which says its components are additive. That might be the case in the housing quality example above, but not the case for example, for measures of health status and social mobility which if combined might give a meaningless indicator. Nor would it necessarily be the case for many combinations of social effects and so, in a number of cases, some form of value-weighting must accompany the aggregation. Those who support value-weighting argue, on the other hand, that a disaggregated analysis usually results in "information overload" in the form of a welter of statistics and mountains of indigestible documentation. Further, since value-weighting is at least implicit in every policy analysis, they argue there is positive value in making the process explicit and thus exposing it to scrutiny and debate (Einhorn and McCoach, 1977). The key question in developing any such value-weighting scheme is, of course, "whose values?" Three answers are generally put forward: the politicians', the experts', or the public's.

POLITICIANS' PREFERENCES

Value-weighting based on politicians' preferences takes two forms. The first is to study past government decisions and, if consistent, to use the implicit revealed preferences in those decisions to impute value-weights. This has recently been done, for example, in a study of the closure of branch railroad lines by British Rail (Brent, 1979). The revealed preference approach argues that the appropriate source of the expression of such value-weights is within the political system and that such studies avoid all the problems associated with trying to get politicians to express preferences directly. It is seen as a useful means for the politician to come to grips with the weightings implicit in past decisions, to use them in all or part if thought satisfactory, or to change them in duration or magnitude in the future if they were wrong. The proponents of the revealed preference approach are quite ready to point out its main limitations: that it is a sufficient, but not necessary, explanation of past behavior in that it assumes rationality and full information for decision makers—a situation which patently does not exist. This causes policy models based on revealed preferences to diverge from reality. However all models diverge from reality and the approach gives a valid, but partial, perspective on policy problems, especially if similar situations are to occur in the future and the preferences revealed demonstrate a consistent pattern in decision making. British Rail, for example, may intend more branch line closures in the 1980s, and this study may well help reveal underlying and more specific criteria for decisions than is normally available for public consumption.

A second way of dealing with the politicians' preferences is, of course, to ask them, and then to operate on the assumption that their preferences reflect some democratic mix of their constituents' values. For example, one recent proposal suggested that various combinations of program outputs could be ranked by asking politicians to put their selected units of output in rank order (Schmid, 1975). The methodology of "asking" is much the same for politicians as it is for experts and involves either more or less rigorous straightforward interviews or the establishment of some panel of value-judgers. For example, one proposal for assessing environmental impact suggested the formation of a weighting panel which would include representatives of government, industry, public interest groups, community organizations, and other parties potentially affected by the outcome of the assessment (Sondheim, 1978).

Sometimes value-weights are developed by using the Delphi technique, which is basically iterative polling of politicians or experts, with feedback. This involves a group of anonymous persons who are interviewed in two or more rounds, and in each round are presented with the cumulative results of the previous round and asked if they would alter their projections accordingly. Anonymity is used to avoid psychological and personality problems of group interaction which may hinder face-to-face dynamics, for example, domination of a value-weighting scheme by a strong personality or a leading reputation. As the rounds progress the panel's membership, which may number seven to 100 or more, are expected to consider the degree their weights differ from group consensus and to revise the estimates they choose. In this way, a consensus of opinion arises.

Studies of the usefulness and validity of Delphi-generated weights are conflicting. Some suggest that Delphi does produce reasonable weightings which stand up to *de post facto* analysis, and that different panels produce similar results (Ament, 1970; Linstone and Turoff, 1975). Others decry Delphi's lack of a theoretical base or criticize it on political grounds. Bisset (1978:53), for example, says, "that averaging the implicit weightings of a group of experts is not satisfactory unless it can be demonstrated that such value judgements meet with popular approval." Sackman (1976), in a study for the Rand Corporation where Delphi was first developed, finds that Delphi is not empirically linked to objective and independently verifiable external validation criteria. He suggests Delphi be replaced by rigorous questionnaire techniques. Probably the biggest limitation to Delphi is the fact that the consensus of opinion is reached not by a comparison of arguments of substance but due to whatever personality factors cause one sort of individual to hold his ground and another to compromise (Fowles, 1976). Both Delphi and rigorously designed questionnaires, however, probably do offer another valid, if partial, approach to structuring value-weighting schemes, as long as their underlying assumptions and methodological limitations are made explicit.

EXPERT OPINION

Although asking politicians to value-weight indicators seems reasonable as they do so implicitly in any event, reliance on so-called "expert" opinion is easily and probably fashionably dismissed as undemocratic. Nevertheless there are issues in which value weightings based on estimation by professionals, administrators, and others with experience in a given area, are useful. These issues are of fairly specific scale and involve those policy problems in which value judgements, attitudes, and social relations play a minimal role. For example, the detailed and fairly routine planning problems pursuant to more general policies, like minimum standards for public provision of correctional facilities or physical infrastructure in a new town design, can often be weighted by professional opinion without any great danger to democratic principle. This is not true of more strategic level policy problems where value judgements constitute one of the main criteria for choice. For example, a decision about whether to build a resource-based new town or expand an existing town is hardly a technical decision. Expert opinion is also not very useful whenever there is likely to be a strong divergence of opinion over a social issue. Research in the United Kingdom, for example, shows that criteria used by "experts" to delineate areas for special housing programs in urban areas were arbitrary and inadequate from the residents' point of view. The question of what constitutes housing dilapidation is obviously contentious, especially in the face of the threat of wholesale "urban renewal" (Dennis, 1978).

PUBLIC PREFERENCES

Tribe (1976) takes the view that the *process* of policy analysis is at least as important as the result itself. In other words, not only must justice be done, it must be seen to be done. Many times useful value-weights come from politicians and experts. There are many cases when this is insufficient however, and the preferences of the public, or some segment of it, must be surveyed as part of the analysis. In recent years there has been a growing trend towards developing public participation in governmental decision making, and one only has to look at the interest in road-building schemes, or applications for new power stations, dams, coal mines or other environmental changes, to see this demonstrated. Such value-weighting based on the surveyed preferences of some sample of the public finds favor with numerous authors in a variety of disciplines concerned with policy analysis (see, e.g., Einhorn and McCoach, 1977; Sondheim, 1978). Dissenting voices tend to be those who are critical of any weighting scheme and who feel that complete disaggregation is the only honest approach to data presentation. However, even highly disaggregated survey data may be of considerable value to policy makers, and such surveys can provide a reasonable base of empirical data with which to begin testing the presupposed value-weighting model.

Survey approaches to value-weighting often form part of a public participation exercise which includes publicizing and interaction among analysts, administrators and the public. The information collected as a result of a public participation exercise can be used to value-weight in two ways. First, some analysts argue that such data, sometimes used in conjunction with expert opinion, can directly structure an explicit mathematical weighting scheme which in turn is applied to objective data (Gordon and Needercorn, 1978). Although such an approach runs the risk of making unsupportable causal assumptions and assuming a monolithic public instead of one made up of diverse and competing groups, it cannot be dismissed out of hand. For although it is no doubt wise to be wary of those who would quantify the unquantifiable, it is unwise to avoid quantifying the quantifiable. Rank ordering is certainly possible and, as in the technique of planning balance sheet analysis (Lichfield, Kettle and Whitbread, 1975), weights can be associated with different sectors of the public. This is best done in the framework of a sensitivity analysis which establishes upper and lower boundaries for the value weights and then demonstrates the "robustness" of different policy options to changes in the weighting scheme. If small changes in value-weights result in an altered ranking of options then it is wise to be very cautious in the application of the weighting scheme.

Another approach to using survey data is to provide it as a complement to the objective data in the analysis and allow the two kinds of information to be synthesized by the decision maker. This indirect approach avoids many theoretical problems but does carry with it the danger that the decision maker will ignore the information or do the synthesis badly. That, however, is the stuff of political debate, and if this seems the best approach, the policy analyst can only exhort that all the relevant opinions be considered.

In either case measuring public preferences may prove difficult, but the importance of doing so cannot be underrated and the methodology is steadily improving. The simple surveys of straightforward questions, which suffer from problems such as respondents' strategic behavior, are now mostly superseded by survey formats using the Likert scale of measuring respondents' satisfactions-dissatisfactions on a five or seven point continuum. This gives a relative intensity of preferences if not interval scales. Other techniques are being developed which may yield interval data, distinguish between personal judgements and judgements about a wider community, and force the respondent to simultaneously consider costs and benefits at the same time—a problem for simpler surveys. Techniques such as "budget pies" for assessing citizen preferences in U.S. urban expenditure, or the use of priority evaluation games in the U.K. for evaluating preferences in environmental and transport planning may well be expanded to other policy fields (Clark, 1974; Hoinville and Prescott-Clark, 1972). These techniques give each respondent a limited amount of "resources" which can be "spent" on a variety of alternative service mixes. A priority evaluation scheme was recently used by London Transport as part of its planning for the rejuvenation of subway stations (Woudhuyson and Law, 1979).

Where active public participation is not feasible, subjective social indicator data may provide important policy information. This may serve to alert policy makers to attitudinal changes which presage actual social change (for example, dissatisfaction with public transport provision leading to increased auto usage) and to make civil servants more accountable by citizen evaluation of services. Although citizen perceptions of poor services may not correspond with the actual service level, such information may serve as a useful "litmus" or warning sign of something amiss between citizen and government. And a well-designed survey of subjective indicators can reveal the diversity of opinion about a policy issue, rather than simply the opinion of the articulate in society.

Where public participation may be useful for value-weighting, it must be actively promoted by those administrators and policy analysts who hope to realize its value, and such promotion includes providing reasonable access to information at a *useful* time in the policy process. The value of public participation is that it provides information essential for the clarification of most policy problems, and increases the incentives for the public to cooperate with, and appreciate, the policy process. The quality of the information collected, and the level of appreciation of the policy process by citizens, will be proportional to the amount of publicizing and interaction which occur. That is, participation is based on sharing information, which in turn really means sharing power. Unfortunately some governmental bodies may well resist public participation for this reason. The links between publicizing and education, and the quality of information collection, are nevertheless quite clear (Vauzelles-Barbier, 1978).

VALUE-WEIGHTING AND DISTRIBUTIONAL EQUITY

One of the most contentious issues in policy analysis may be the role of distributional equity—whether "who gets what?" should structure the value-weighting scheme and thus explicitly influence the analysts' recommendations as to which policy option is preferable. The issue, like many, first arose in relation to the use of cost-benefit analysis (CBA) and the arguments in that field are generally mirrored in the other areas of policy analysis.

The mainstream of CBA analysts generally fall into three schools on the issue. The first argues that CBA should remain silent with regard to the distribution of wealth in society, as it is only competent to consider questions of efficiency and overall additions to or subtractions from social welfare. The argument is not that questions of distributional equity are unimportant, but that equity is best reached through other types of government action like taxes and subsidies, and need not be considered in assessing new programs. All distributional value-weighting should therefore be done *post* analysis by politicians. And since value-weighting requires interpersonal comparisons of utility which can only be highly inaccurate, to engage in such an activity is to confuse clients of policy advice or to lend spurious scientific authority to personal prejudices. Other perceived dangers of explicit value-weighting are: (1) the risk that numerical value-weights are determined by non-representative bodies, for example, bureaucrats masquerading as responsible policy makers, and (2) that such value-weights can and would vary not only from region to region but from time to time according to changing power structure and political fashion (Mishan, 1974). Given this line of argument CBA would avoid value-weighting and have nothing to say on programs, like social security, specifically designed to redistribute income or wealth. It would also ignore the redistributive aspects of other programs like special education for deprived students or new highway construction.

An increasing number of analysts, however, now argue that redistributive effects are an important policy consideration. Little and Mirrlees (1974), for example, say:

> The argument that the project evaluator, if he be a civil servant, should take the existing distribution of income or wealth as ideal (implying that he need not 'weight' the consumption of different income groups differently), on the grounds that the government has the power to make it what it likes through other measures, principally taxation, does not hold water.

Analysts of this school recognize that the weighting of costs and benefits according to some judgement about justice or equity is implicit or explicit in any policy analysis. In this case the economist does not promote any particular income distribution weighting scheme but should certainly consider the implications of any number of schemes put forward by politicians. Meade (1955), for example, has argued that the economist's job is to advise various political factions about the implications for economic welfare of their particular set of distribution weights. These weights cannot be objectively tested but "they are not altogether natural. Indeed they are part of the normal stock in trade of politics." In this view the policy analyst has an important, neutral, technical role in advising on the distributional and efficiency implications of policy options.

Some analysts of this school seek to supplement CBA insofar as it does not sufficiently explore the distributional issues. Within this group are the practitioners of techniques like the planning balance sheet, which seeks to expand CBA to include sector by sector distributional effects; distributional weighting schemes which are inferred from political behavior or reflect a decision-maker's judgement; and social impact assessments which examine projected impacts on various groups in the community, often by means of surveys. Other techniques (e.g., environmental impact assessments), it should be cautioned, may reject a CBA framework for other reasons (e.g., failure to consider externalities) but may themselves be criticized for ignoring questions of distributional equity.

Finally, a last small school take an overtly value-laden stance to distributional equity. Among these are analysts who accept the existing distribution of income and the concept that the market alone can determine value through prices. Others reject this possibility in its entirety, in that their value judgements on distributional equity are quite different—for example, those who have a Marxist perspective on economics (Edwards, 1977). Also in this school are those analysts who argue for a particular distributional arrangement. Their recommendations are often based on research organized to substantiate their particular point.

Of these schools of analysis this author accords with the second but recognizes that attempts to value-weight by distributional equity criteria, however laudatory, do face problems. First, any redistribution may involve administrative and informational costs which have to be considered in the policy analysis. Second, identifying exactly who benefits and who bears the costs can be difficult, especially for the latter. And it is quite possible for any one person to benefit and bear costs from the same project, for example, a person who flies often and lives near a noisy airport. Third, interpersonal comparisons are fraught with difficulty— a new highway can be a benefit to a commuter but a cost to his home-working next door neighbor. Fourth, what economists term the marginal level of utility may vary according to income level, i.e., a dollar to a poor man is worth more than a dollar to a rich man. Fifth, substantial externalities may make it difficult to identify distributional effects. Finally, any incorporation of distributional weights by analysts might be viewed as an attempt to usurp decision makers' power.

CONCLUSION

In conclusion, it can be suggested that equity considerations—who gets the benefits and pays the costs—are vitally important in most policy issues today, and it is no longer sufficient to merely calculate the aggregate costs and benefits of a policy's impacts. A considerable amount of work on the methodology of value-weighting according to distributional impacts remains to be done, however. At present, equity is probably best considered without recourse to a single highly quantified weighting scheme which may mask the essentially value-judgmental nature of income-redistribution. This is not to imply, however, that redistributive effects are better ignored. On the contrary, their importance suggests the policy analyst has a valuable role to play in providing information on the distributional aspects of projects, and the application of a variety of distributional weights in a sensitivity analysis may help demonstrate to decision makers the impacts of various options.

REFERENCES

Ament, R.H. (1970) "Comparison of Delphi forecasting studies in 1964 and 1967." Futures 2:15–23.

Bisset, R. (1978) "Quantification, decision-making and environmental impact assessment in the United Kingdom." Journal of Environmental Management 7:43–58.

Brent, R.J. (1979) "Imputing weights behind past railway closure decisions within a cost-benefit framework." Applied Economics 11:157–170.

Clark, T.N. (1974) "Can you cut a budget pie?" Policy and Politics 3:3–31.

Dennis, N. (1978) "Housing policy areas: criteria and indicators in principle and practice." Institute of British Geographers New Series 3:2–22.

Edwards, M. (1977) "The ideological function of cost-benefit analysis in planning." Town Planning Discussion Paper No. 23, University College, London.

Einhorn, H.J. and W. McCoach (1977) "A simple multiattribute utility procedure for evaluation." Behavioral Science 22:270–282.

Fowles, J. (1976) "An overview of social forecasting procedures." Journal of the American Institute of Planners 42:253–263.

Gordon, P. and J.H. Needercorn (1978) "A procedure for fully evaluating the anticipated impacts of selected public system innovations on various environments using citizen-generated information inputs." Socio-Economic Planning Sciences 12:77–83.

Hoinville, G. and P. Prescott-Clark (1972) Traffic Disturbance and Amenity Values. London: SCPR.

Knox, P.L. (1978) "Territorial social indicators and area profiles." Town Planning Review 49:75–83.

Lichfield, N., P. Kettle and M. Whitbread (1975) Evaluation in the Planning Process. Oxford: Pergamon Press.

Linstone, H.A. and M. Turoff, eds. (1975) The Delphi Method—Techniques and Applications. Reading, MA: Addison-Wesley Publishing.

Little, I.M.O. and J.A. Mirrlees (1974) Project Appraisal for Developing Countries. London: Heinemann Educational Books.

Meade, J.E. (1955) Trade and Welfare. London: Oxford University Press.

Mishan, E.J. (1974) "Flexibility and consistency in project evaluation." Economica 41:81–96.

Sackman, H. (1976) "A skeptic at the oracle." Futures 8:444–446.

Schmid, A.A. (1975) "Systematic choice among multiple outputs of public projects without prices." Social Indicators Research 2:275–286.

Sondheim, M. (1978) "A comprehensive methodology for assessing environmental impact." Journal of Environmental Management 7:27–42.

Tribe, L. (1976) "Ways not to think about plastic trees." In L. Tribe, L.S. Schelling and J. Voss (eds.), When Values Conflict—Essays on Environmental Analysis, Discourse, and Decision. Cambridge, MA: Ballinger.

Vauzelles-Barbier, D. (1978) "Public participation in the rehabilitation of urban centres." International Social Science Journal 30:336–359.

Woudhuyson, J. and H. Law (1979) "Underground transport: how to do it right." Design (371):42–47.

EFFICIENCY, MULTIPLE CLAIMS, AND MORAL VALUES

Stephen H. Linder

ABSTRACT

Most of the restrictions imposed by evaluation techniques such as cost-benefit analysis on the types of information that may be used in making decisions are too severe and, in many instances, highly questionable. The information exclusions are particularly oppressive with regard to soft values and moral claims. This paper considers a multiple-value approach as a strategy for incorporating both values and claims, while aiding the decision maker in appraising the requisite trade-offs.

INTRODUCTION

The shortcomings of relying primarily on the efficiency aspects of alternatives in decisions over large-scale public projects and applications of technology have become increasingly obvious as the social dissatisfaction with these decisions cumulates. As in the case of power generation and development projects, intangible values associated with aesthetic

Policy Analysis: Perspectives, Concepts, and Methods, pages 281–299.
Copyright © 1986 by JAI Press, Inc.
All rights of reproduction in any form reserved.
ISBN: 0–89232–371–X

properties or, more generally, non-consequentialist moral claims have been excluded from decision formulation primarily as the result of the analytic methodology employed. Such claims must then be made outside of the context of the original process undermining both its integrity and effectiveness, while imposing additional costs on society. In many instances, groups whose values were ignored in the initial project decision have been successful in pressing both for judicial relief and for statutory requirements to ensure greater value representation. And yet, the primacy afforded efficiency values remains largely unchanged. In part, this can be attributed to the institutional status of cost-benefit analysis relative to other methods of evaluation, as well as to the ineffectiveness of existing procedural mechanisms for incorporating the public's values into the decision process.

The purpose of this chapter is to examine an alternative class of evaluation methods that are premised upon *multiple* values. Of particular interest is the theory underlying these methods—the requisite assumptions about values and the structured representations derived from them. Further, since several multiple value methods can also accommodate the values of different individuals, attention will be given to the problem of resolving value conflicts and establishing consensus. Following the next section which establishes the ground work for what follows, multiple value approaches will be contrasted with cost-benefit analysis, focusing attention on the issues of valuation and criteria. Several multiple value approaches will then be examined in the order dictated by the complexity of their assumptions. And finally, these methods will be evaluated relative to other procedural and interpersonal strategies for integrating contending values. However, because of space limitations, assessment techniques for eliciting, estimating, or scaling values will be omitted.

BACKGROUND

Hard vs. Soft Values

One of the more insightful maxims of contemporary policy analysis holds that "hard values tend to drive out soft ones." In this context, the "hard values" are those which are tangible and whose realization can be measured with some precision; by and large, they tend to be economic or technological and thus translatable into physical units. "Soft values," on the other hand, are predominantly intangible and non-instrumental. Consequently, they are generally expressed in qualitative terms, rendering them incommensurable with other values. When contrasted with hard values in the course of analyzing project impacts, the soft values appear idiosyncratic and less credible, especially when their articulation is left to concerned citizens often at a disadvantage in terms of information or expertise. Moreover, in most confrontations with soft value advocates, proponents of hard values can legitimate their claims with tangible evidence, converting any value disputes into technical issues to be settled on technical grounds. As a practical matter, soft values are seldom excluded entirely from analyses, they are simply dwarfed by hard ones.

The source of this hard-value bias lies not so much with the individual analysts or evaluators, who exercise their craft in good faith, but rather with the particular evaluative theory they employ. Clearly, it is the theory that determines both the relevancy of values and their appropriate representation. Typically, there are several ways of juxtaposing soft with hard values in project evaluation, each of which serves to reinforce the conclusiveness of the latter. First, soft values impacted by a project may receive separate treatment—to be appended to the results of hard-value analysis as *pro memoria* items. This is a useful practice for demonstrating that any procedural requirements for considering community values have been met. But, for the most part, these results serve only as a caveat to the eventual consumers of the evaluation.

Second, when accompanied by sufficient political might, soft values may operate as constraints in an evaluation, defining the boundaries of feasibility. In this context, their function is essentially a negative one: while limiting the range of certain hard-value parameters and effectively precluding specific outcomes, soft-value constraints have little influence over what values should be included. Accordingly, project alternatives are still evaluated relative to their performance on hard-value criteria; in effect, it is the hard values rather than the soft ones that remain to be maximized once feasibility has been defined.

And third, soft values can be incorporated directly into the hard-value analysis. Of course, in order to satisfy the commensurability requirements of conventional methods, soft values must be replaced with hard-value surrogates. In cost-benefit analysis, for example, this replacement effectively undermines the status of soft values, since any surrogate will invariably be instrumental in nature and must be expressed in monetary units. Consequently, in expanding the hard-value analysis by a dimension or two to accommodate surrogate variables, no changes need be made in the existing decision criteria. The efficiency criterion can be applied with equal fervor both to hard values and to surrogates for the soft values selected for inclusion.

Several obstacles to a balanced analysis of hard and soft values emerge from these three strategies for integrating soft values into project evaluations. On the one hand, there is the problem of valuation: how can the full range of project impacts be translated into value terms? Or, more specifically, how can we appraise the relative performance of alternatives with respect to intangible values? Closely related to this valuation problem is the issue of criteria. The selection of decision criteria effectively determines which values are decisive and which are not and, under certain conditions, what kinds of trade-offs will be made among the incorporated values.

Although these two issues can be separated for analytic purposes, they are generally interdependent; that is, once an assumption is made about the applicable criteria, the valuation of project components is relatively constrained. In terms of evaluation theory, the opposite is true as well. For example, the degree of commensurability among the hard and soft values of project impacts will affect the relationship among relevant criteria. To eliminate the hard-value bias, then, it is necessary not only to change the principles of valuation to accommodate difficulties with soft values, but also to expand the set of decision criteria in order to structure balanced, value trade-offs.

The Efficiency Criterion

At a more fundamental level, any criterion employed in public decision making rests upon the presumption of an ethical consensus regarding its use and implications. The efficiency criterion, which evaluates projects based on their net money-valued benefits, not only presumes that the appropriate costs and benefits have been tabulated, but also that the reallocation of resources instituted by a particular project will be socially desirable. Judgements of relative inefficiency are generally grounded in the notion of pareto improvement, linking social desirability to an aggregate assessment of individual gains and losses. Clearly, there are many instances when society finds it desirable to reject a pareto efficient arrangement of resources and to subordinate the calculation of individual gains to ethical considerations. Desirability, then, may be categorical, the product of a threshold test for violations of rights, rather than simply a tally of money-valued consequences. On the other hand, desirability may be determined by a political mechanism which responds primarily to votes. In either case, the efficiency criterion is effectively divorced from its linkage to social desirability, undermining its justification and prescriptive validity.

As pointed out by Mishan (1980), one of the principal contributors to the literature of cost-benefit analysis, in a pluralist society there is seldom an ethical consensus sufficient to justify the primacy of economic efficiency as an allocative norm independent of the political process. Without such a consensus, efficiency loses its normative power for discriminating "good" projects from "bad" ones, or the socially desirable from the undesirable. Accordingly, the criterion's purported objectivity, derived from avoiding reliance on either political expressions of values or any one individual's subjective judgements, is eroded as well. Unless the basic premises underlying efficiency have wider acceptance than do most other moral or subjective criteria, it is inappropriate to subsume all other objectives under an efficiency umbrella or to treat a potential pareto improvement as the conclusive criterion. Thus, the evaluation of projects relative to their net money-valued benefits, while providing a useful appraisal of economic consequences, typically ignores a variety of moral claims that, although components of social desirability, are systematically excluded from efficiency-based analyses.

This is not to say that cost-benefit methodology precludes the *ex post* consideration of non-efficiency claims—issues of equity and distributional impacts generally supplement most analyses—rather that the propositions underlying this methodology are themselves moral claims deserving scrutiny on equal footing with equity and other issues. The problem, of course, is that the method of analysis is not versatile enough to provide equal footing for competing claims, largely as a consequence of the constraints on admissible information imposed by its underlying propositions. It makes sense then for the analyst to argue for a division of labor, delegating non-efficiency issues to political authorities, as this bolsters his method's prescriptive validity while insulating its implicit moral claims from challenge. Proponents of such a division posit cost-benefit analysis as necessary but not sufficient for justifying public decisions; sufficiency, on the other hand, is taken as essentially a political ingredient representing residual claims. Consequently, while effective in articulating tradeoffs among money-valued components, cost-benefit analysis leaves unstructured the central tradeoff between these necessary and sufficient conditions, perhaps the most difficult one faced by the decision maker.

The Problem of Valuation

With efficiency as the criterion, projects are evaluated on the basis of the money values of their costs and benefits. Presumably, these values reflect the relative preferences of individuals over project consequences; or more specifically, the effective demand expressed by individuals as a willingness to pay certain amounts for project impacts. Under fixed conditions, prices in a competitive market represent the marginal value which individuals place on the goods and services produced or on the opportunities foregone by a particular project decision. As a practical matter, however, prices are at best an approximation of the project's value to individuals: on the one hand, effective demand for project benefits is shaped by both ability to pay and advertising, while on the other, market imperfections due to lack of resource mobility or of competitiveness tend to move prices away from marginal value. More importantly, prices reflect the current value of goods and services available in the market, as opposed to the future value of outputs which would be generated by a project decision (Steiner, 1974). But perhaps the most serious drawback to using prices as a measure of project value is that they ignore a variety of project impacts.

A great deal of attention in public sector economics has been devoted to the technical imperfections in the market which distort prices and lead to inefficient allocations. The presence of external effects is of special interest in that it represents a source of market failure, at times provoking government intervention, as well as an absence of markets for the indirect or intangible impacts of certain decisions. For an appropriate application of the efficiency criterion, all of these impacts must be evaluated as project costs and benefits by simulating market outcomes to estimate the assignment of prices that would have resulted in a perfectly competitive market (Dorfman, 1965; Margolis, 1970). Accordingly, these imputed prices will reflect what individuals are willing to pay for the project's unmarketed impacts and thereby provide an indication of relative value.

However, even though the theory for adjusting distorted prices or imputing nonexistent ones is well developed, the question remains as to whether a market valuation is the most appropriate way of representing the overall value of a project decision. Not only might efficiency be too restrictive a criterion, as has already been pointed out, but the preference revealed by individuals in the market might be too narrow a basis for project appraisal. Clearly, the nonmarketable attributes of projects, encompassing soft values, require alternative criteria that address the problem of commensurability; likewise, the exclusive reliance on a preference-regarding theory of relative desirability should be reexamined.

Before considering the issue of multiple criteria and the inclusion of soft values, the problem of value specification must be addressed. For once we reject the use of pricing mechanisms, we are left with individual preferences as the basis for valuation. Although the choices of individuals serve as a pillar of welfare economic theory, there is a reluctance among economists to consider preferences apart from those revealed in the market, since this would admit non-efficiency criteria and require some interpersonal comparisons of value (Boadway, 1979). Conversely, moral philosophers, typically distrustful of preference-regarding methods of assessment, reject market-revealed preference as egoistic, and thusly an improper basis for social valuation. But rather than considering the pluralism of *nonmarket* preference, some proceed a step further and drive a wedge between values and preferences in general; while the former are seen as community-oriented and encompassing a range of moral qualities, the latter are thought to express self-interested motives free of moral content. This dichotomy effectively undermines the moral validity of any project appraisal that is based upon subjective preferences, regardless of how these preferences are established.

From the non-utilitarian's perspective, preferences over project characteristics are not merely irrelevant to gauging the worth of decision alternatives, they are insidious, often leading to actions that are morally unacceptable. Nevertheless, in the current climate of analytical policy-making, separating moral claims from individual preference relegates them to a subordinate role in project decisions, functioning, at best, as constraints on the alternatives under consideration. Moreover, once the dimensionality of the alternatives is expanded to include non-efficiency objectives, there is no reason to presume that all preference-regarding appraisals will discriminate against values.

On the contrary, preference itself is simply a generic term describing an ordering relation which can be defined in a number of ways, and if the alternatives evoke multiple value considerations then preferences will reflect the requisite value judgements. Thus, the value insensitivity characterizing many analytic methods is not so much a limitation peculiar to subjective preference as it is the product of an artificial restriction on the dimensionality of project alternatives.

Although removing restrictions on criteria and on the representation of project attributes can expand the scope of admissible values, such values tend to be defined in consequentialist terms. These include, for example, environmental values associated with the aesthetic qualities of wilderness or with ecological balance, as well as social values relating to community cohesion or ethos. They are intangible values potentially impacted by project decisions and, in this context, are cast as indirect consequences which either enhance or diminish the overall desirability of project alternatives. In an expanded analysis, each value would be treated simply as an additional goal, perhaps expressive of a particular interest, to be weighed with others in reaching a decision. The most desirable alternative, then, would represent an implicit balance of the contending values, which emphasized some at the expense of others and maximized one particular composite of the objectives.

However, the problem with imposing a consequentialist framework on moral claims is that it fails to accommodate deontic considerations, such as individual rights and obligations, which are thought to preempt all other claims. Rather than having a decisive influence on the worth of a particular alternative, the values described above serve as measuring rods for appraising the relative performance of alternatives; accordingly, worth is expressed as a weighted sum of the component performances. Clearly, there are bases for establishing the moral worth of alternatives that appeal, not to their valued performance, but to moral rules and principles (Fried, 1978). These rules and principles can be used to discriminate among contending values, establishing their rightness or wrongness over and above their contribution to a project's desirability.

An individual right is one type of moral claim founded on principle that acts as a trump over appeals to the beneficial consequences of a particular action in justifying a policy decision. As Dworkin (1978) points out, the practical force of individual rights resides in the claim that some decision disadvantaging a particular individual is wrong even though it makes the community as a whole better off by satisfying the value priorities of most individuals. But he is careful to set the threshold for the emergence of rights at the level of the most persuasive appeals to collective welfare; by definition, then, rights are decisive in any contest with collective goals. Hence, any compromises among competing rights will exclude consideration of community costs and benefits, although the welfare of the individuals whose rights are at stake may be taken into account. Extending this view further, the common notion of rights as constraints on project alternatives is misguided since a balancing of rights generally occurs on a level separate from the balancing of values and, in effect, constitutes an additional set of criteria.

Again the framework of analysis can be expanded further incorporating rights as components of, rather than as constraints upon, policy decisions. This time the offending restriction is the limited form of the underlying decision model. Recall that cost-benefit analysis, although preference-regarding, restricted consideration to market-revealed preferences and thus to market-relevant criteria. When we added new criteria, the scope of admissible preference was enlarged as well. Nonetheless, the resulting multiple-value framework adhered to the basic "adding and averaging" form common to utilitarian models, including cost-benefit analysis.

There are two distinguishing features of this form: first, all alternatives are ultimately described in terms of single values indicating their overall worth; and second, the component values of attribute performance (or costs and benefits) are compensatory in the sense that a low value on one attribute can be compensated for by a high value on some other attribute. In order for these features to apply, the component values of each alternative must be commensurable: for cost-benefit analysis commensurability is based on a weighted dollar valuation, and for multiple-value analyses, a weighted preference valuation. However, once we incorporate rights into the analysis commensurability is no longer at issue, since the very nature of rights precludes any compensatory treatment. That is to say, there are no trade-offs to be made among individual rights. And although rights may be used to establish the appropriate weighting in multiple-value analysis (more of this later), incorporating them into an analytic framework requires a change to a non-compensatory form.

But if we accept Dworkin's notion that the accommodation of rights operates on a level above the accommodation of goals, there is no need to sacrifice the advantages offered by the compensatory treatment of goals: we can simply arrange the analytic framework into a natural hierarchy which establishes a fixed sequence of decision considerations. In this way, each alternative is appraised explicitly in terms of the relevant rights of individuals, as well as the multiple dimensions of its consequences. More of this general approach appears in the second part of this paper. The basic premise is that most restrictions imposed by conventional policy analysis on the types of information that may be used in making decisions are too severe and, in many instances, highly questionable. Although seemingly mild, many of these information exclusions have severe consequences, notably for moral claims.

Structuring Trade-offs

The argument is frequently made that any effort to expand cost-benefit analysis beyond its efficiency values to incorporate other claims undermines the validity and rigor of the method. As we have seen, the use of this method as a second-best means for accommodating soft values typically either side-steps the central trade-off problem or recasts it in efficiency terms. Either way, soft values become a supplement to, rather than an integral part of, the formulation process. Consider an organizational context wherein the decision maker is left with a ranking of alternative states of affairs according to tangible net benefits and a diffuse set of intangible moral claims. Under the pressure of decision, there is a tendency to avoid value conflicts by appealing to apparently objective, benefit calculations together with some disclaimer about contending claims. Here, the hard-value bias is more a matter of cognitive limitations than of moral insensitivity. The question is, how can we structure complex trade-offs in a way that will reduce cognitive demands while appraising a variety of moral claims?

It should be clear at the outset that any attempt to structure complex, multiple-value problems, including cost-benefit analysis, rests on a set of assumptions making implicit moral claims. Moreover, the complexity of assumption is often inversely related to the cognitive simplicity of the resulting decision problem. Thus, the desirable approach should be transparent in its moral claims, and at least sufficiently versatile to embody the claims of those responsible for the eventual decision. Substantively, the approach should structure the trade-offs between hard and soft values, as well as those within each category, to avoid a hard-value bias while at the same time reducing the cognitive demands on the decision maker. And finally, the approach should be inclusive of, rather than neutral to, a variety of moral claims. Inclusiveness is at the root of the hard-value bias problem, since the range of values at issue not only shapes the decision problem but also reflects the implicit weighting of values embodied in the evaluation process.

If we assume that all value conflicts are confined to the *context* of the evaluation, then the analysis itself, as well as its results, will appear to be value-free and objective. Presumably, any judgement exercised in the course of analysis will involve only matters of technical expertise. Alternatively, the analysis may be seen not so much value-free as value-inclusive, in effect, subsuming all lesser values under widely agreed-upon principles for enhancing the general welfare. Conversely, the locus of value conflict may encompass the evaluation of alternatives. In this instance, value disagreements are represented in the analysis proper, shifting concern from the projects under evaluation to the values they serve. In effect, the analytic method is used to develop a systematic analogue for the political process: not only are a variety of contending values taken into account, they are made explicit in order to facilitate trade-offs. And while some technical expertise is sometimes called for in devising the representation and accomplishing specific valuations, the actual trade-offs that lead to a final ordering among project alternatives are generally the responsibility of community officials.

Thus, when value conflict is seen as peripheral to the analysis, there is little rationale for incorporating dissenting values on a competitive footing. However, once disputes over values are acknowledged as a central feature of the analytic process, emphasis is placed on making disagreements or value differences explicit and resolving them. In short, the contrast in assumptions about the locus of value conflict introduces a basic distinction between those evaluation methods that incorporate a wide variety of values and decision criteria and those that adhere to a single criterion and invariably discriminate in favor of certain values.

In the next section attention is turned exclusively to multiple-value frameworks designed to resolve value conflict in a variety of ways. Despite their apparent diversity, all are intended to impart a simplifying structure upon highly complex, and often contentious, decision problems. And contrary to the appearance of having an intelligence of their own—some inherent capacity to generate a "best" alternative, automatically—they are wholly dependent upon the subjective input of participants in the decision process. In a sense, these frameworks are devices for reducing the cognitive demands on decision makers, by providing them systematic assistance in processing information.

The primary difficulty for most decision makers lies, not in having vague or ill-defined value priorities, but in applying these to an ambiguous decision situation. Here ambiguity is an obstacle to the decision maker's attempt to have his values accurately reflected in any alternative that might be selected; frequently, the actual values implicit in a given alternative go unrecognized or are misperceived. Accordingly, all of these methods rely to some extent on a decomposition of the decision problem into several constituent elements, wherein each element can more easily be appraised and then aggregated with other elements to characterize decision alternatives. None of the methods under consideration are neutral with respect to either the elements at issue or their aggregation. Consequently, the selection of an appropriate method, or modification of an inappropriate one, will be determined largely by the salient features of the decision situation—the number of decision participants, their assumptions, values and level of agreement, as well as their institutional context.

AIDING DECISIONS OVER MULTIPLE VALUES

One of the central difficulties associated with the recognition of multiple values arises in determining how competing values should be reconciled. For once multiple values have been defined in a decision situation, it becomes apparent that, except in the trivial case of pure dominance, no one alternative will be "best" on all values. Each is likely to produce a mixed profile of relative worth, with high appraisals on some values and low appraisals on others. In this context, "values" can be taken to represent any evaluative dimension of the decomposed decision problem, including "objectives," "attributes," and individuals' assessments. Any decision over these alternatives necessarily implies that certain values are more highly regarded than the rest. Making these judgements explicit requires that each value be "traded-off" against its complement; that is, values are compared and assigned some relative worth or weightings that influence the overall worth of each alternative. The nature of this influence, of course, depends upon what sort of aggregation takes place.

This issue of trade-offs, or the relative weighting of competing values, is rather complex; not surprisingly, it has discouraged the recognition of multiple values in many instances. Perhaps the most common approach is a solution by assumption, where one value is assigned a preeminent position, a priori: this is the case with the pareto principle in welfare economics and the Rawlsian maximin principle. More generally, any noncompensatory decision model escapes the necessity of trade-offs, and therein lies its advantage. Unfortunately, in many instances, the non-compensatory model will fail to converge on a single alternative, and the decision maker will be forced to employ a supplementary rule.

There are several aspects of the trade-off problem that deserve attention, since how this problem is handled serves as a defining characteristic of multiple-value frameworks. Establishing the relative worth of values involves two interrelated tasks: first, the values must be rendered commensurate; and second, priorities must be assigned. References to trade-offs sometimes refer only to one or the other. For example, in micro-economic theory, the marginal rate of substitution between commodities refers only to commensurability, while the relative weight assigned to GRE scores by admissions committees reflects priority only. The effect of formally assigning a number to represent relative worth is to stretch or shrink each of the dimensions of value in order to exaggerate or minimize the differences among the alternatives along these dimensions. In other words, on an "important" value the alternatives would differ widely, increasing the relative contribution of this value to the decision maker's choice, and possibly making it decisive.

However, before trade-offs can be executed, it must be determined whether the trade-offs will involve the set of values without reference to any alternatives, or relative to the range provided by the alternatives. Assuming a common scale of subjective worth—this shifts the focus from the situation to the decision maker—the former approach assigns priority exclusively; as a result, a poor alternative on an important value may be equivalent to a highly-regarded alternative on an unimportant value. Clearly, the range of the alternatives should affect how values are appraised, but commensurability concerns may interfere with the assignment of priority. Thus, a narrow range of alternatives' performance may be weighted heavily simply to compensate for its relative disadvantage in influencing overall worth. It must also be decided whether the trade-offs remain constant over the entire range of the alternatives' worth; if not, then different weight must be assigned for each level of worth along a given pair of values.

Returning to the context of decisions over public projects, two classes of value conflict emerge. The first involves conflict over the judgements of decision participants, and the second focuses on conflicting values of interests with a stake in the decision outcome. In both instances, reconciling value conflict requires some sort of *interpersonal* comparison. Much of the trepidation surrounding the comparisons can be traced back to early defenses of the pareto principle. The effect of the recommended restrictions on interpersonal comparisons was to make it very difficult to accommodate any non-efficiency values such as equity (Sen, 1979a). Interpersonal comparisons, as Sen (1979b) suggests can be accomplished in several ways, each treating the problem of comparison in a different light.

In one instance, comparison can be largely an introspective exercise, with the decision maker attempting to empathize with the value perspectives of those involved in the decision. Hence, there is no real need to induce the participants to fashion commensurable representations of their values, since these will be the product of the decision maker's intuition. Although not without its problems, this approach has been influential in the social choice theories of Harsanyi and Rawls, among others.

Alternatively, interpersonal comparisons may depend upon finding a widely acceptable criterion that can be applied through simple observation; the problem of comparison, then, is a matter of locating the right piece of information. This is a common approach in social policy which relies upon institutional criteria, like entitlements and relative income comparisons, in order to weight individual claims and interests.

And finally, comparisons may focus on the difficulty of reconciling divergent judgements about an appropriate course of action. Each of the participants in this circumstance is likely to be influenced by interpersonal comparisons of his or her own; unless, of course, an artificial barrier isolates their judgements in every case but one—singling out a decision maker. The resolution rests with establishing a satisfactory consensus, rather than imposing one through the assignment of weightings, since the subject of the comparison is a judgement about what should be done and not a set of explicit individual values or interests.

Consider the kinds of trade-offs required in the first two types of comparisons, from the perspective of selecting a useful framework for simplifying the decision task. In general, there is a single decision maker with responsibility for trading off the values of some individuals against the values of others. To keep the problem manageable, the values selected for inclusion represent the interests of impacted groups of individuals who share similar values, rather than the values of every impacted individual. But, with a single dominant decision maker, the values of impacted groups do not necessarily exhaust the values in contention, nor is the only criterion to maximize the satisfaction of group values. Removing the restriction permits the inclusion of information which is not based exclusively on interests or preferences. Such information enables the decision maker to discriminate among group values normatively, encouraging some values and discouraging others through the weighting of their contribution to overall social desirability. Thus, by admitting non-preference information, the scope of interpersonal comparisons is expanded beyond the difficult assessments of relative satisfaction or welfare to encompass moral distinctions among different kinds of values and claims based on rights.

There is a tendency in public debate to characterize conflicts over public projects in terms of global confrontations between development and conservationist forces. Typically, the central feature of this confrontation is the perceived need for a "trade-off" between the interests of the contending groups. However, by this construction, trading off one interest against the other generally implies a hard-value rate of exchange: most resolutions express the relative level of soft-value achievement in terms of hard-value sacrifice. Hence, the notion of a confrontation among competing interests presents the decision maker with a bargaining problem that closely parallels problems in market allocation. Clearly, the most appealing justification is one based upon a solution mechanism that mimics the market—cost-benefit analysis. Alternatively, once the dimensionality of the decision problem is expanded to include both preference and non-preference elements, trade-offs focus upon interpersonal comparisons. And the decision maker structures his or her discretion in terms of moral and institutional principles, as well as the impacted interests.

In addition to conflicting values, the decision problem may involve conflicts over individual judgements. The relevant comparison, then, is among recommendations for choices, each of which may incorporate trade-offs among contending interests and, at the same time, anticipate the judgements of other participants. This replaces the single, dominant decision maker with a set of them, facing the necessity of reaching a consensus. Without a dominant decision maker, participants must first come to an agreement on the values selected for inclusion before any consensus over an appropriate course of action can be worked out. Of course, there must also be agreement on the appropriate rules for resolving both of these issues.

Social choice theorists have devoted considerable effort to the problem of arriving at collective decisions. However, these efforts generally impose restrictions upon individual preferences and then examine both the implications of these restrictions and the consequences of certain aggregation rules. In effect, our two problems of value inclusion and selection of a decision rule are solved by assumption, and any information which is not drawn from a restricted range of preference is considered irrelevant to social choice. With a number of decision participants, the advantages of a solution-by-assumption approach in any form are sacrificed for a process of resolving differences through interaction.

Intervention Techniques

Frameworks for aiding decision making involving many participants can be thought of as intervention techniques for overcoming the decision constraints peculiar to small group situations. There are a number of interpersonal difficulties that inhibit the formation of consensus in small groups. These include, for example, participation biases and pressures toward conformity, concentrations of power, and the restraint of cognitive ability by dominant personality characteristics (Eils and John, 1980). The decision techniques for dealing with interpersonal problems are usually directed toward enhancing the interaction among group members by structuring their communication in certain ways. An alternative intervention strategy subordinates a concern for group dynamics to the selection of an effective procedural technique for making value differences explicit. Although some procedural strategies advance selected rules for aggregating values, their primary function is to aid decision participants in uncovering and focusing upon their value conflicts.

Strategies for structuring communication among participants range from simple verbal guidelines for avoiding interpersonal biases to multistage methods that build consensus upon feedback between individual and group assessments. While Eils and John (1980) point to successes in the use of verbal techniques, success is usually defined in behavioral terms. On the other hand, the multi-stage methods purposely restrict communication to avoid interpersonal biases, but impose a regimen of successive adjustments to minimize the disparity between the individual's own judgements and the "group" judgement which is an aggregation of individual assessments. The Delphi method and its offspring are representative of this approach. Rather than appraising value trade-offs, each decision maker is induced to bring his values closer to the aggregate profile, compromising for the sake of conformity.

The assumption behind procedural interventions is that the most serious obstacle to any resolution of the participatory decision problem is the existence of cognitive differences over the values in contention. While some individuals perceive the decision problem in terms of certain values, other individuals may base their position and their definition of the problem on an entirely different set of values, leaving no common ground for disagreement. The difficulties posed by differences in perception and understanding are especially evident when the decision problem is cast in terms of project alternatives. Not only is the complexity of the evaluation compounded, but the conflict among values remains implicit and often irresolvable to the point where debate is redirected toward instrumental issues expressed in hard-value language. To counter this, a procedural strategy begins with a decomposition of alternatives into their constituent value elements. The motivation is twofold: first, to make the values in contention explicit, highlighting the bases of disagreement; and second, to reduce the burden and potential errors in evaluation by considering the contending values individually rather than all at once.

Two specific strategies will be examined in the next section; they are both based upon a simple rating approach to subjective assessment, and have proven to be quite robust in comparisons with far more complex methods based on utility theory. Furthermore, these methods will accommodate value conflicts involving judgements, as well as interests, and when taken together can incorporate moral claims along with impacted values.

Matrix and Weighting Methods

The matrix method simply provides a structured format for displaying values, both as a check on inclusiveness and to facilitate comparative assessments. Nevertheless, this device embodies several assumptions that lend importance to its usefulness. In its most basic form, the matrix is made up of rows signifying project alternatives, and columns containing component values. The entries in each cell of the matrix represent subjective assessments of the worth or performance of a particular alternative on a given value. However, the implicit decision rule is noncompensatory: no aggregation across values occurs. The appraisal of alternatives, then, is made up of intra-value assessments along each of the specified dimensions. As a result, there is no need to establish either commensurability or priority among the values. Although this precludes the appraisal of trade-offs, it has the advantage of accommodating moral claims which come to play a central role in trade-offs and interpersonal comparisons at a later stage.

Thus, the matrix method is useful for articulating and appraising moral claims that are inherently noncompensatory. The results of this analysis then can serve as inputs to the weighting method dealing directly with the assessment of trade-offs and the aggregation of values into a metric of overall worth. There are two separate rules for appraising alternatives relative to their implicit moral claims. One is the familiar threshold rule, where certain minimal qualities must obtain for any alternative to remain under consideration. Of course, the thresholds can also be defined in terms of maximal qualities which cannot be exceeded. If we describe rights as barriers against a certain scope of activities, the threshold rule could be applied through a matrix analysis, leaving the entire process open to review or replication.

A second rule is sequential elimination. By this rule, each of the values is applied to the full set of alternatives in some ordered sequence; the values may be considered individually or in subsets, depending upon the context. At the first stage of the sequence, for example, all of the alternatives that did not satisfy a particular moral claim might be eliminated, and so on for each successive claim, until only those alternatives satisfying the decisive claims would be subject to the analysis of trade-offs. One advantage of this rule is that it selects for consideration only those moral claims that discriminate among alternatives. But more importantly, the notion of an ordered sequence to the evaluation accommodates any hierarchy of claims that might result from the balancing of conflicting moral principles.

The weighting method is the product of work by decision theorists in the area of multiattribute utility measurement (Miller, 1960; Edwards, 1977; Einhorn and McCoach, 1977), focusing upon the problem of making individuals' values explicit. In its several versions, the primary emphasis of this method is on value trade-offs. As with the decomposition of alternatives into values, trade-offs are dealt with in two parts. Once the relative dimensions are identified, commensurability in the sense of subjective worth must be established among them. At that point, relative priority is assigned in the form of dimensional weightings. Finally, the overall desirability of the alternatives can be determined by applying the weights to each dimension of worth and aggregating them according to a suitable rule.

In the case of trade-offs among interests, the single dominant decision maker is asked to invent measures, based upon his or her values and judgement, that reflect the worth of alternatives. This approach places the individual decision maker rather than any single criterion at the center of the evaluation process. And yet, the discretion present in this situation is highly structured, and any values employed in the assessment are made explicit. To accommodate trade-offs among judgements, each of the participants can play the role of the unitary decision maker, in turn imposing his or her own assessments of worth and priority. In this way, not only are values spelled out, but the extent of value disagreement is clarified. Presumably, once cognitive differences over the relevant values are settled, disagreements will hinge on matters of degree or relative priority. However, in removing the ambiguity over values by fixing attention on basic disagreements, the conflict over priorities is, as Edwards points out, frequently reduced as well.

The weighting method can accommodate both hard and soft values, but avoids a hard-value bias by placing any hard-value measures onto the same subjective scale as soft values. In practice, the decision maker must specify the location of a given alternative along each dimension of value. A scoring function is developed for each dimension and a subjective worth is assigned to the alternative depending on its level of performance on that dimension. In some instances, specialists may be required to specify the performance of each alternative on the dimensions under consideration. With the alternatives expressed in terms of worth on each dimension, the decision maker must then evaluate the relative importance of the dimensions.

There are several ways of assigning weights to reflect relative importance, but as noted above, the assignment is likely to be sensitive to the shape of the scoring function and to the range of the alternatives' scores. However, in the case of weighting the relative priority of individuals' values, these interpersonal comparisons can be facilitated by employing normative criteria that discriminate among values. This is the second point at which moral claims are brought to bear on the assessment of alternatives. Following the matrix analysis, concern for rights and obligations may form the basis for trade-offs among individual interests as a part of the weighting procedure. Since there are few restrictions on the use of non-preference information, using the matrix and weighting methods in tandem ensures a balanced consideration of soft values and an appraisal of moral claims, while reducing the cognitive demands of trade-offs.

REFERENCES

Boadway, R.W. (1979) Public Sector Economics. Cambridge, MA: Winthrop.

Dorfman, R., ed. (1965) Measuring Benefits of Government Investments. Washington, D.C.: Brookings Institution.

Dworkin, R. (1978) Taking Rights Seriously. Cambridge, MA: Harvard University Press.

Edwards, W. (1977) "Use of multiattribute utility measurement for social decision." In D. Bell, et al. (eds.), Conflicting Objectives in Decisions. New York: Wiley.

Eils, L.C. and R.S. John (1980) "A criterion validation of multiattribute utility analysis and of group communication strategy." Organizational Behavior and Human Performance 25:268–282.

Einhorn, H. and W. McCoach (1977) "A simple multiattribute utility procedure for evaluation." Behavioral Science 22:270–282.

Fried, C. (1978) Right and Wrong. Cambridge, MA: Harvard University Press.

Margolis, J. (1970) "Shadow prices for incorrect or nonexistent market values." In R. Haveman and J. Margolis (eds.), Public Expenditures and Policy Analysis. Chicago: Markham.

Miller, J. (1960) Professional Decision Making. New York: Praeger.

Mishan, E.J. (1980) "How valid are economic evaluations of allocative changes?" Journal of Economic Issues 14 (March):143–161.

Sen, A. (1979a) "Personal utilities and public judgements." Economic Journal 89 (September):537–558.

————(1979b) "Strategies and revelation." In J.J. Laffont (ed.), *Aggregation and Revelation of Preferences*. Amsterdam: North Holland.
Steiner, P. (1974) "Public expenditure budgeting." In A.S. Blinder, et al. (eds.), *The Economics of Public Finance*. Washington, D.C.: Brookings Institution.

ETHICS, RHETORIC, AND THE EVALUATION OF PUBLIC POLICY CONSEQUENCES

George J. Graham, Jr.

ABSTRACT

This paper advances the argument that rhetoric addressed to, and stimulating the development of, a public is the key to proper evaluation of public policy consequences. Current American interest group politics is posited as the barrier to effective political discourse, but the context of the shift in our governmental system from assuming non-zero sum political rewards (as a result of presumed growth) to negative sum games (generated by the recognition of economic limits) makes the possibility of discovering or creating a public by means of rhetorical argument (including increased utilization of ethics argument). Aristotle's discussion of rhetoric and Stephen Toulmin's discussion of ethical argument are introduced as the proper means with which to approach John Dewey's problem of the public and James Madison's conception of responsible leadership. An active public is presented as the necessary balance against special interests in a democratic system. The appeal to visions of moral purpose that is central in rhetorical and ethical discourse is seen as essential in maintaining legitimacy for American political institutions.

Policy Analysis: Perspectives, Concepts, and Methods, pages 301–314.
ISBN: 0–89232–371–X

"Do cats eat bats? Do cats eat bats? " and sometimes "Do bats eat cats?" for, you
see, as she couldn't answer either question, it didn't much matter which way she
put it.

Lewis Carroll[1]

One of the intriguing aspects of political argument is that one need not
be sure of answers before asking questions, so long as questions are
seriously asked and answers seriously attended to before coming to a
decision. It seems that now, by design or by accident, public policy in
the United States is decided in terms of unquestioned answers; that is,
assumptions about the public, about group interests, and about reelection
demands replace for the politician the constructive guidance of public
policy discourse. To be sure, there are many cases whose political resolution can be explained with all-too-much precision in terms of why
certain answers are not questioned because of the objectives of powerful
interests, but not all policy blunders are intentional. The struggle toward
a new public philosophy requires that somehow one must develop a
capacity to generate a fix on the public, to provide a mechanism or
institutional framework within which one can consider generating serious inquiry into the common ends that bind the collectivity. Current
American institutions make difficult serious application of rhetorical
inquiry into the best settlement of a policy issue because, structurally,
the very mechanisms originally designed to make discourse, deliberation,
and decision a common public effort have in recent decades become
transformed by social and economic shifts into institutions which give
presumption and control to the very interests they were designed to
limit. The presumptive power of identifying which values and arguments
will guide the answers to public questions, and the consequential framework for winning a debate and controlling the application of outcomes,
have been given over to the very interests which were to be constrained
by the checks of the American system. Were it possible to view politics
as a non-zero sum game as it at least appears to be in times of strong
growth in the economy, the current governmental practices might easily
be seen as justified. But politics has become a negative sum game, at
least under the current long-view projections of resources, so that issues,
represented by Proposition 13 and inflation, force a public reassessment
of where the current system is moving. Politics, which is necessary only
if there are limited resources, must come to grips with public policy
choices, and the appropriate mechanism for evaluation of concrete
choices.

It was not always necessary to justify such a negative approach to the problem because politics is our allocation of scarce resources, but recently the American economic system has evolved in a particular way that has permitted interests to presume our continued growth under the limited economic perspective of a Keynesian equilibrium. Unfortunately for the model, fortunately soon enough for us we hope, the combination of oil prices and the strain of providing insurance for failing industries, large and small, makes clear that an economic process so attractive on paper can fail in practice. Answers, such as those concerning current models of inflation, do not seem to work; the questions leading to the answers are themselves not yet clear. How can one explain in economic terms the stability of certain forms of inflation that survive traditional techniques for control? Even economic advisers have fallen from the high art of economic theories to the lowly science of psychology in attempting to isolate the reasons for current economic behavior. If rational economic man fails to follow our prescriptions, how surprised can we be if rational political man, too, fails to follow expectations?

The truth of the matter rests in the ancient observation that, in ethical and social matters, we cannot gain more precision than the subject matter permits. In approaching the issue of how to evaluate public policy consequences, we are at a loss in articulating any method or procedure for determining whether the policy's consequences are what they ought to be, given the objectives of policy, because the purposes of a policy are so seldom established by government. Programs, rather than policies, are legislated and continued without the benefits of clear-cut isolation of their creators' intended consequences (Moynihan, 1970: 90–100). And under these conditions one must fail in pursuing ethical and substantive evaluation. The problem of developing some means to improve our capacity to evaluate public policies stimulates this attempt to devise an application of rhetoric—in the positive, classical sense—for grappling with the American policy process. This application, however, can be suggestive only once we clarify the depth of our problem.

I

However, this bottle was *not* marked "poison," so Alice ventured to taste it, and finding it very nice (it had, in fact, a sort of mixed flavour of a cherry-tart, custard, pine-apple, roast turkey, taffy, and hot buttered toast), she very soon finished it off.

Lewis Carroll

The transformation of the American conception of government is difficult to date, but the enormous rise of its new functions usually is associated with the New Deal. One can follow Peter Drucker's (1978: ch.10) conception of "The Sickness of Government" or Theodore J. Lowi's (1979: ch. 10) idea of "The State of Permanent Receivership" in identifying the protective and omnipresent growth of the functions of government. Rising concern for these unsatisfiable promises no longer solely is a concern for the traditional exponent of limited government, but has been recognized as a problem across current American ideological perspectives. American political leaders, who for a few decades promised to achieve a consensus by simultaneously satisfying a diversity of wants, are now forced to reassess policies and programs as we discover that the bottle from which we drink is being "finished off." This reassessment can be a positive event if our grounds for these new difficult choices reach to isolating the purposes that are to be followed; that is, constructive results can occur if we finally recognize that we must choose between cherry-tart and hot buttered toast. Unfortunate consequences might result, however, if one merely assesses who votes for tart or toast, or who wants to cut all portions without considering nutritional values. Scarcity can provide the grounds for an active political discourse into our purposes, objectives, and goals if we seriously confront questions such as energy and inflation not as crises to be given a solution, but as continuing uncertainties that force serious choices upon society.

Along with the warnings of the difficulties attending continuation of too much government comes a shared wisdom of our recognizing the need to limit individual demands on and expectations of government. The essential problem of attempting to apply this shared wisdom is that the corrective must be achieved *within* the very environment that generated the difficulties: Alice found the taste "very fine." This makes ready prescriptions unready. Civic commitment to a public interest is gained, not essayed. Ethical and political prescriptions, no matter how elegant, must be accepted. If too much government promises both heavy indebtedness and reelection, it is difficult to see why a politician would be concerned with Drucker's (1978:234) "reprivitization" or Lowi's (1979:298–313) "juridical democracy." Even if one accepts the prospect of limiting government, one must also be convinced that everyone's interests, not just others' interests, necessarily will be limited. This critical step toward admitting that elected officials need to go beyond their careful allocations to organized constituents in responding to the limited capacities of governments must be achieved in the public arena if a shift of public expectations is to be achieved. More important, the public must recognize that it must limit its own demands if it hopes to maintain its interests over a long period of time. A public must limit itself in its perception of the public interest.

But few of us dare employ the symbol 'public' in a conceptual fashion.

References to the 'public interest,' in the political arena, usually are translated as a mere assertion by an interest that its ends ought to be shared. References to the 'public interest' in the academy are usually followed by a skeptical, and almost cynical, reference to 'public*s*,' portraying a sensitivity to the coalitional politics we observe. Nonetheless, interest in public policy and the pragmatics of current American pressures make clear that if there is no such thing as "the public," then somehow, it must be created. Without a public, political discourse in terms of shared interests, goals, and objectives is without meaning. Settlement of issues over scarce resources will not be politically decided, but decided instead by coercion by the most powerful interests on their own terms. If a public does not exist, then the determination of how scarce resources will be distributed will be remanded to those interests that are the most powerful. This means that creation of a public will be even more difficult.

The dynamic for creation of a public is available in a serious application of rhetorical skills; that is, individuals can be molded into a public by appeals to shared interests, goals, and objectives. In employing rhetorical tools, one may appeal to recognized interests, goals, and objectives that are held by an audience or, when necessary, create them. To borrow from John Dewey:

> The essential need, in other words, is the improvement of the methods and conditions of debate, discussion, and persuasion. That is *the* problem of the public.... It is not necessary that the many should have the knowledge and skill to carry on the needed investigations; what is required is that they have the ability to judge of the bearing of knowledge supplied by others upon common concerns (1954:208–209).

This admittedly prescriptive assertion by Dewey provides the framework for attacking the problem of a public. No public capable of evaluating public goals means simply that there is no constraint on private interest in setting governmental goals. Ethical argument as applied to public policy, as we shall see, depends upon a public audience for its testing— at least in a democratic setting.

II

> "What is a Caucus-race?" said Alice.... "why," said the Dodo, "the best way to explain it is to do it"... "The race is over!" and they all crowded round it, panting, and asking, "But who has won?"... at last the Dodo said "Everybody has won, and *all* must have prizes."

> "I wish I hadn't cried so much!" said Alice, as she swam about, trying to find her

way. "I shall be punished for it now, I suppose, by being drowned in my own tears. That *will* be a queer thing, to be sure! However, everything is queer today."

Lewis Carroll

Movement toward the domination of American politics by minority political factions is a recent phenomenon not because interests have never in the past been able to dictate public policy, but rather because the success of factions (often through Senate control or through Supreme Court decisions limiting government actions) never required positive government action in all segments of economic and political life. The rise of the politics of direct accountability along with the diminution of the belief in a representative's responsibility, has led to more responsiveness on particular demands by interests and less rewards for restructuring and limiting demands. Low rates of participation and the advantages of incumbency seduce a representative into paying his interest accounts and avoiding potentially controversial issues. The now old story is the growth of governmental programs in both numbers and size as responses to organized interests. Even "public interest" organizations become constituents with accounts. Everybody wins. All receive prizes. There never was an adequate theory explaining how the model could continue, but the effort to invent one has been displaced by the concrete limits of inflation and taxation, a combination that attracts even the politician's attention.

If one could transform the human wants that led to governmental programs into a new spiritual awareness, as E.F. Schumacher prescribes,[2] then one could move from our sea of tears over having lost our material excess by wanting too much, to a spiritual excess by learning to want less. Unfortunately tears are shed unevenly in a society—those with the least material success have the most, relatively, to lose. A budget cut that affects all portions equally is but a regressive policy solution whose effects are likely to be felt most by the least well off. Unless interest group liberalism is fully displaced with serious public deliberation, the potential public benefits of its crisis will not be realized. The losses may generate self-pity over losses rather than constructive efforts to emerge from the privitization of social existence.

III

It was high time to go, for the pool [of tears] was getting quite crowded with the birds and animals that had fallen into it; there was a Duck and a Dodo, a Lory and an Eaglet, and several other curious creatures. Alice led the way, and the whole party swam to shore.

Lewis Carroll

The proper contrast with interest group liberalism is deliberation. Original conceptions of representation in the American system, as articulated by James Madison in *Federalist #63*, provide the specification of responsibility by leaders under pressures of untempered interests:

> As the cool and deliberate sense of the community ought, in all government, and actually will, in all free government, ultimately prevail over the view of its rulers; so there are particular moments in public affairs when the people, stimulated by some irregular passion, or some illicit advantage, or misled by the artful misrepresentations of interested men, may call for the measures which they themselves will afterwards be the most ready to lament and condemn. In these critical moments, how salutary will be the interference of some temperate and respectable body of citizens, in order to check the misguided career, and to suspend the blow mediated by the people against themselves, until reason, justice, and truth can regain their authority over the public mind.

The roles of political leaders and institutions, here of the Senate, include raising the recognition of limits in terms of common public concerns to weigh against private wants. But the very language employed by Madison is seemingly archaic: "sense of community," "temperate," "justice," "truth," and "public mind" are not only abstract, but alien to us in our political discourse. Abstract rights and individual entitlements, the language of special interest requests to government, are not balanced against shared conceptions of community, justice, and temperance. If deliberation is the proper contrast with interest group liberalism, common conceptions of purpose and meaning must be developed in order to balance the universal claims to entitlement.

Deliberation, or political discussion in general, is possible only where there are *or can be* found common values, shared assumptions, and common interests—the very foundation for a notion of public. To move privatized interest claims on government to political deliberation on proper actions of government, someone must appeal to or, in some cases, develop common grounds for discourse. Once these grounds are attended to by articulate leaders, it is possible to imagine public policy evaluation based upon ethical concerns and serious pursuit of the best policy though deliberative rhetoric. But someone must first lead toward this shore.

There is no novelty in recognizing that some political figures pursue their own interests. The American system was designed to limit such leaders. The novelty today (though not for Aristotle or John Stuart Mill) is recognition of the fact that the *same* tools for political control in a democratic society can be used for good and for selfish ends. That is, politics depends upon persuasion to explicit actions which can be in the

common interest or be merely selfishly inspired. We now employ "rhetoric" often as a negative label—"He gives us nothing but 'rhetoric'!"—
yet rhetoric is a neutral faculty, defined by Aristotle as the "faculty of
discovering in the particular case what are the available means of persuasion" (1960:7). Like its sister-faculty, dialectic, rhetoric is based on
understanding the rules of argument with enthymemes in rhetoric par-
alleling syllogisms in dialectic. The important points are that (1) the
reasoning process is separable from purposes because, like logic, rhetoric
concerns the structure of available arguments, and that (2) success in
argument (i.e. persuasion) depends upon knowing *all* available means
of persuasion. Thus, techniques employed by the opposition can be
neutralized in order to focus attention on proper arguments. If there
are public ends that are superior to selfish interests, the public can be
brought to the proper persuasion. Indeed, like the later promise seen
in competitive free speech by John Stuart Mill, Aristotle argues:

> But the art of Rhetoric has its value. It is valuable, first, because truth and justice
> are by nature more powerful than their opposites, so that, when decisions are not
> made as they should be, the speakers with right on their side have only themselves
> to thank for the outcome. Their neglect of the art needs correction.... it is char-
> acteristic of Rhetoric and Dialectic alone that, abstractly considered, they may in-
> differently prove opposite statements. Still, their basis, in the facts, is not a matter
> of indifference, for, speaking broadly, what is true and preferable is by nature
> always easier to prove, and more convincing (1960:5–6).

Aristotle presupposes that the truth will out, a proposition concerning
values that is subject to intellectual doubt. Fortunately within democratic
societies one can accept this presupposition until counterarguments are
provided: all things equal, the public will accept the best arguments.
These arguments, often mixing persuasion and science according to
Aristotle, are affected by lesser dimensions of persuasion—ethos of the
speaker, for example—but these can be neutralized or made to have
negative consequences. Public arguments will appeal to shared beliefs
in the effort to persuade the public. Deliberative arguments permit insights into the best resolution of issues because *all* routes of persuasion
are explored. These applications of rhetoric, though we may doubt certainty of the truth always being persuasive, will make considerations
deliberative in the sense of James Madison and Edmund Burke and will
raise the probability of achieving the best policy choices in the sense of
the public's own shared values.

Application of rhetorical search for the best public policy requires two
things: (a) a public, and (b) leaders who appeal to the public. The former
is often *created* by the latter in order to create a larger political arena
when one is losing in a smaller one. As E. E. Schattschneider (1960)

likens expansion of the political conflict to enlisting the masses on a playground to your defense in a losing individual battle, politicians can learn that only an expanded conflict that activates a larger public can balance special interest demands without leading to an electoral defeat. This is the dynamic that rhetoric generates, for it can be used by others to replace politicians who ignore the values that could mold a public. It is this potential activation of the "input" side of the public policy process through rhetoric that can make deliberation *essential* in governmental institutions. And it is only through deliberation that decision makers can begin to consider what are the desired and undesired consequences of particular public policies in terms of the public interest.

Since rhetoric is neutral, truth will depend upon the substance of issues to which it is applied. Therefore, rhetoric will employ the findings of the sciences, which for Aristotle included politics and ethics. Serious pursuit of arguments with the public in mind open the politician to ethical arguments as well as to the best possible collection of empirical studies in the area of a policy issue. Especially in consideration of a potentially unpopular decision, an official will wish to know how to persuade constituents that the decision was what they should want. This desire for an expanded consideration of ethical and factual consequences can even be based on the least ethical of reasons—merely a selfish desire to be reelected—with a positive consequence—improving political deliberations in order to achieve reelection. The explanation of interest group liberalism's success in terms of the easiest route to reelection can in fact be altered if reelection becomes dependent upon persuading the public that certain long-term policy consequences are in the public's interest. The key is to transform the evaluation of public policy consequences into serious concern for achieving "public acceptability" as the best means for assuring reelection.[3]

It is ethical argument that permits development of an attentive public willing to see policy issues as "something more" than governmental response to constituent special interests. The mode of ethical argument as here introduced is not that of traditional ethical approaches—though they can be used or translated into the mode under consideration. The mode of ethical argument of importance here is ethical reasoning that can guide moral judgments. Arguments of this sort are ethics-in-use, ethics as they occur in human settings, rather than the theoretical ethics of the academy. It is a meaning based on the assumption of a community for the purposes of discussion of what ought to be done, and presumes a mutual search for correct action. As Stephen Toulmin (1960:136) defines the " 'function' of ethics," it is "to correlate our feelings and behavior in such a way as to make everyone's aims and desires as far as possible compatible." The method of realizing the end of ethical reasoning is, of course, argument. Ethical arguments of all modes can be employed in the process, but the end of the process—even if an argument is academically brilliant—is dependent on persuasiveness. For Toulmin, there is a difference between scientific and moral judgments in that science is "concerned to alter expectations" while moral judgments attempt "to alter feelings and behavior."[4] What alters feelings or behavior are appeals to overlooked consequences or values relevant to our choice, appeals leading to evaluation of purposes, shared values, and consequences of our judgment. In sum, ethical arguments provide good reasons for choice beyond unreflective selfish response. It is in strengthening and developing the community norms and mutual trust that ethical arguments contribute to the creation of a public.

This public provides the counterbalance for special interests as either a protection for or as an ominous threat to elected representatives. Decisions must be clear, however, if arguments are to be convincing. Positive and negative consequences, uncovered and projected by deliberative considerations of facts and values as best can be developed, are the grounds for persuasion and public evaluation. Ethical discourse and considerations can be advanced by rhetoric. But without this public as counterbalance, the public will not (indeed, cannot) be the audience for political discourse. Clarity of policy position, a requirement for meaningful public discourse, is the enemy of interest group liberalism. If policy decisions provided rules and projected consequences clear enough for public comprehension, the problems of bureaucracy and, indeed, of evaluation would be simplified. One would have moved to a public evaluation of the action of leaders who are entitled to make their best cases for their decisions.

The model appears utopian in the context of the pluralist-interest group politics of old, but the new recognition of limits on government holds promise for the realization *if* adequate rhetorical methods are pursued. Remembering that the nonrational modes of persuasion can be neutralized by one who understands, say, the impact of fifteen second television commercials or the potential of media events, the level of political discourse can be raised as a public becomes defined. The very instrumentalities that plague traditional images of rhetoric as practiced currently in public settings facilitate the development of grounds for public challenges to interests. Investigative reporting, distasteful as it sometimes is, sets the ground for shared understandings once the facts uncovered are called forth by argument. Political discourse is rhetorical, but in the best sense. It draws upon science, ethics, and sentiments through rationally based arguments. These arguments inevitably combine factual and evaluative dimensions, sometimes in parasitic, sometimes symbiotic relations. This treatment of policy evaluation in the promulgation stage, played before an attentive public, forces one to link consequences to expectations, the only meaningful democratic ground for evaluation. To be sure the leader, in Madison's sense discussed above, must be able to persuade the public that his actions avoid consequences "they themselves will afterwards be most ready to lament and condemn." But that is what leadership is meant to be.

American institutions seem to work against this simple model because the election terms are short, making it possible that lamenting and condemnation of an aspiration may occur after election day, and the public is, at best, distrustful and disinterested except in terms of consequences. There are proposals, some simple, that would tune legislative functions for the public, but each change demands prior public attention. Unless the public recognizes its shared interest in preserving legislative authority in the Congress, powers will be delegated. Unless the public recognizes its shared interest in lowering its expectations of the government—and especially of presidential leadership—then we shall continue to have a decline in respect for these very institutions. Someone, within or without the government, must begin the move toward lessening the demands on institutions—whether under reprivitization, spiritual, or juridical arguments depends on the persuasive potential of the arguments—if the construction of a public is to occur. Once an active public is created, the pressures for adjusting institutions will become at once both more probable and less necessary. The public will become the judge of acceptable public policy consequences.

IV

There was no label this time with the words "DRINK ME," but nevertheless she uncorked it and put it to her lips. "I know *something* interesting is sure to happen," she said to herself, "whenever I eat or drink something; so I'll just see what this bottle does."

Lewis Carroll

Rhetoric and ethical discourse share a procedural neutrality in that the outcome of the reasoning is open-ended. The conclusions of political debate depend on who the participants are, and what audience is relevant. The outcome of the discourse will be different if it is played out before constituent interests than it would be before the public. The expansion of discourse to the public is proper under democratic presuppositions, but frightens some as much as it will surprise others who presume the public will share their way of seeing policy issues. When considering everyday actions, the individual members of the public seem selfish, prejudiced, and biased. To be sure, we can ourselves verify these individual attributes. We may have good reason to hesitate taking a draught from this bottle.

There are also good reasons to dare an experiment with the public's involvement in government. Just as there was an American dilemma resulting from abstract commitment to equality and hesitancy to accept its consequences, laws can be forged from the higher commitments of a public.[5] Martin Luther King persuaded America by means of arguments and actions that led the public to see segregation as he did, through the vision of moral purpose. The capacity for these appeals to mold a public indicates possibilities of achieving correlations of "our feelings and behavior in such a way as to make everyone's aims and desires as far as possible compatible." This dichotomy of America is not peculiar; it is built into the character of balancing moral and personal existence. The American dilemma provides a tension that yields an openness to a "morality of distant contemplation" with which to balance a "morality of immediate confrontation," to borrow the terms of Charles S. Hyneman (1964:272). The prospect for moral discourse in achieving policy settlements is enhanced by introducing appeals to the public.

In conclusion, it is important to note that the reintroduction of the public into American politics has significance for surviving as an open polity. If politically acceptable settlements cannot be achieved, then the scarcity and limitations will require an alternative model for allocating resources. Current visions of state organizations with which to contrast a pluralistic, open society based on public legitimation scarcely prove consistent with democratic values. The prescribed activation of the public can be justified on the basis of legitimacy needs, as the only viable means for long-term increases in legitimating our institutions. The move toward public involvement in public policy evaluation through ethical and rhetorical explorations of consequences is also a move away from the systematic distortion of interest group liberalism's definition—or lack thereof—of the public interest.[6] Permit me to end with a quote from Jurgen Habermas's assessment of legitimacy, which uses terms more technical than but nonetheless congruent with our prescriptions:

> By *legitimacy* I understand the worthiness of a political order to be recognized. The *claim to legitimacy* is related to the social integrative preservation of a normatively determined social identity. *Legitimations* serve to make good this claim, that is, to show how and why existing (or recommended) institutions are fit to employ political power in such a way that the values constitutive for the identity of the society will be realized. Whether legitimations are convincing, whether they are believed, depends naturally on empirical motives, but these motives are not formed independently of the (formal analyzable) justificatory force of the legitimations themselves. We can also say that they are not independent of the legitimation potential, of the

grounds or reasons, that can be mobilized. What are accepted as reasons and have the power to produce consensus, and thereby to shape motives, depends on the *level of justification* required in a given situation (1979:182–183).

* * * * *

There was nothing else to do, so Alice began talking again.

Lewis Carroll

ACKNOWLEDGMENTS

This paper is based on *Humanizing Public Policy*, a book-length essay dealing with relating contributions from the humanities to public policy analysis. The larger project was commenced while a Fellow of the National Humanities Institute— New Haven, 1976–1977, and continued under support from the National Endowment for the Humanities Education Division (EN-20798-74-372 and EN-31833-78-896, respectively). Current work is supported as a Senior Research Fellow of the Vanderbilt Institute for Public Policy Analysis. Special thanks go to Scarlett G. Graham for her criticisms and suggestions. Portions of the arguments herein parallel more extensive treatment in two articles: Graham (1981a) and (1981b).

NOTES

1. The quotes, *passim*, are, of course, from his *Alice's Adventures in Wonderland*.
2. Even though Schumacher's later work provides a mixture of metaphysics and theology in support of spiritual over Cartesian perspectives that is highly attractive to those seeking individual guidance (1977), the work generating political discourse no doubt will remain his *Small Is Beautiful: Economics as if People Mattered* (1973).
3. "Public acceptability" is explicated in Graham and Graham (1976). On exploring the research capacity for measuring "public acceptability," in addition to the works cited in Graham and Graham, see Cook (1979).
4. Toulmin (1960:129). For a useful summary of Toulmin, see Fischer (1980:91–98). Fischer's own arguments, especially on vindication, should be studied in conjunction with Toulmin (1960 and 1958). Several additional recent efforts to articulate formal models and/or categories for analysis of political rhetoric are discussed in Graham (1980).
5. The concept is borrowed from Myrdal (1964).
6. These arguments do not presume a simple "public interest" against "private interests" dichotomy; the public must incorporate the private interests through deliberative settlement. The policy outcomes of deliberation are forced beyond simple *political* acceptability—the outcome of special interest deliberation—to *public* acceptability (see Graham and Graham, 1976).

REFERENCES

Aristotle (1960) The Rhetoric of Aristotle (trans. Lane Cooper). Englewood Cliffs, NJ: Prentice-Hall.

Cook, F.L. (1979) Who Should Be Helped? Public Support for Public Services. Beverly Hills, CA: Sage Publications.

Dewey, J. (1954) The Public and Its Problems. Chicago: Swallow.

Drucker, P. (1978) The Age of Discontinuity: Guidelines to Our Changing Society. New York: Harper Colophon Books.

Fischer, F. (1980) Politics, Values, and Public Policy. Boulder, CO: Westview Press.

Graham, G.J., Jr. (1981a) "Ethics and public policy: a course designed to integrate policy contributions from the humanities." News for Teachers of Political Science (Summer):1, 5–6.

——(1981b) "The role of the humanities in public policy evaluation." Soundings LXIV 2:150–169.

——(1980) "Values and rhetoric in politics and political studies." Paper delivered at the Philosophy of Science Association Meetings, Toronto.

—— and S.G. Graham (1976) "Evaluating drift in policy systems." Ch. 8 in P.M. Gregg (ed.), Problems of Theory in Policy Analysis. Lexington, MA: Lexington Books.

Gregg, P.M., ed. (1976) Problems of Theory in Policy Analysis. Lexington, MA: Lexington Books.

Habermas, J. (1979) Communication and the Evolution of Society (trans. Thomas McCarthy). Boston: Beacon Press.

Hyneman, C.S. (1964) The Supreme Court on Trial. New York: Atherton.

Lowi, T.J. (1979) The End of Liberalism: The Second Republic of the United States, 2nd ed. New York: W.W. Norton.

Moynihan, D.P. (1970) "Policy v. program in the 1970s." The Public Interest 20(Summer):90–100.

Myrdal, G. (1964) The American Dilemma, 2 vol. New York: McGraw-Hill.

Schattschneider, E.E. (1960) The Semi-Sovereign People: A Realist's View of Democracy in America. New York: Holt, Rinehart and Winston.

Schumacher, E.F. (1977) A Guide for the Perplexed. New York: Harper and Row.

——(1973) Small Is Beautiful: Economics as if People Mattered. New York: Harper and Row.

Toulmin, S.E. (1958) The Uses of Argument. Cambridge: Cambridge University Press.

——(1960) An Examination of the Place of Reason in Ethics. Cambridge: Cambridge University Press.

PRACTICAL DISCOURSE IN POLICY ARGUMENTATION

Frank Fischer

ABSTRACT

The search for a normative methodology for policy evaluation raises fundamental epistemological questions about the relationship between facts and values, particularly the question of how to integrate them methodologically. Missing are methodological rules for mediating between empirical and normative perspectives. It is suggested here that a framework for such a method can be developed from the informal logic of practical reason. Such an approach facilitates the development of a logic of questions designed for probing policy judgments. Integrating value questions and empirical data, these questions are presented as a rational-analytic guide for policy inferences. As a theoretical framework, the approach is offered to promote epistemological discussion in the political and policy sciences.

FACTS AND VALUES

Few subjects have been discussed more extensively than the relation of facts to values in the social sciences (Riley, 1974). Most of the polemic

Policy Analysis: Perspectives, Concepts, and Methods, pages 315–332.

has centered around social science's reluctance to loosen its grip on the fact-value dichotomy derived from positivism and its variants (Bernstein, 1976). Even though prolonged debate about the fact-value dichotomy in philosophy and social science remains inconclusive, most mainstream social scientists have been unwilling to entertain nonpositivistic alternatives. Generally they continue to adhere to the positivistic principle of value neutrality and its methodological prescription, the strict separation of facts and values. In recent years, however, it has become increasingly evident that the costs of this adherence are quite significant, at least when measured in terms of relevant contributions to contemporary social problems. This has led a growing number of theorists, including policy-oriented social scientists, to suggest that the fact-value problem raises basic questions about the nature and purposes of social science, particularly about its relation to social and political action. Martin Rein (1976:249), for one, argues that the question of methodological integration of facts and values is one of the major barriers to a social science that can contribute to policy questions.

Under the methodological prescription of the fact-value dichotomy, only empirical judgments can be subjected to rational assessment. Value choices are understood to be emotive judgments or responses—matters of personal conviction, taste or faith—that are beyond the reach of rational methods. Social scientists are free to adopt value-oriented positions as public citizens but to do so in the conduct of research is to risk the introduction of bias and misjudgment.

For mainstream social science, value neutrality is traced to the writings of Max Weber (1949). Weber founded his position on a distinction between formal and substantive rationality. Formal rationality is the procedural rationality of the scientific method. The task of social science is to investigate those aspects of the social world that lend themselves to formal procedures, such as the analysis of particular means to specific ends. Substantive rationality, in contrast, is identified with propositions about the nature of reality and statements of value, which form the basis for selecting the specific ends to pursue. As such, values (or normative statements based on values) are concerned with the question of "what is to be done," rather than the empirically-based questions of either "what is the case," or "what is the best (or most efficient) means" to pursue that which is to be done. Value judgments, as statements about what we should do, are beyond the reach of rational methods and must be relegated to the province of philosophy and metaphysics. In a social or policy science founded upon these epistemological distinctions, the only admissible normative statements are those based on formal rationality.

These methodological principles establish the framework of a policy science that emphasizes empirically-oriented technical criticisms of means designed to efficiently achieve goals or ends taken as given. The policy scientist functions as a social engineer whose task is to calculate the costs and benefits of alternative means for achieving goals hammered out by (or justified through) legitimate political processes. From this perspective, many policy scientists view the value-laden political dimensions of policy as irrational interruptions that impede the methodological requirements of efficient decision-making (Wildavsky, 1966).

The limitations of a policy science dominated by efficiency came to the fore dramatically in the late 1960s and early 1970s. In response to the domestic crises of the period, the Federal government and some states initiated a number of reform measures that emphasized policy evaluation. Spurred by the Federal adoption of program budgeting and a vast amount of Great Society legislation carrying policy analysis requirements, policy evaluation developed into a small industry. However, early enthusiasm about the utilization of policy evaluation findings gave way to skepticism in a relatively short period of time. As one analyst summed it up, everyone is in principle for policy evaluation but few have much hope that its conclusions will be utilized in real-world policy-making processes. Significantly, a growing number of writers attribute the failures that policy evaluation has encountered to its narrow instrumental focus. Most of our social crises involve more that matters of inefficient programs. First and foremost, they involve basic value conflicts. In this respect, it can be argued that policy science aims at the relatively less important aspects of our social problems and has, in turn, developed no method for assessing the more fundamental normative questions that underlie them.

POLICY METHODOLOGY

Such questions have renewed methodological discussion in the political and policy sciences. Policy theorists such as Rein (1976) and Dror (1967) have begun to point to the necessity of studying the normative political dimensions of policy evaluation and decision-making. Beyond the emphasis on efficiency, these theorists recognize the need to include the political assessment of policy goals. For the policy analyst, this poses the problem of how to evaluate the normative acceptability of proposed policies to various relevant political participants—decision-makers, interest groups, administrators, and so on—whose consents are required for policies to be translated into political action. According to Meltsner (1972:859), focus on this political dimension of policy "will be the lever by which the analyst achieves some measure of usefulness and success."

From a scientific perspective, the logic of the task is clear. The analyst must empirically sort out the political norms and values that bear on a particular policy problem and relate them to a causal model of the social processes that underlie the policy issue. The policy scientist can turn here to techniques such as value mapping (Rein, 1976:43). The task is first to determine the logical compatibility of a desired goal with other accepted goals in the larger normative framework or ideology, and then to integrate the goal into the policy model as a causal variable related to specific empirical conditions and consequences. A methodology of normative or political acceptability is translated here into a scheme for modeling and prediction. The ideal, according to Meltsner, is an analytic integration of normative categories and empirical data into the structure of a mathematical policy model. Similarly, Dror (1969) and Majone (1975) state that political feasibility should be expressed as a "probability distribution" of each policy alternative. Work by Hammond and Adelman (1978) and Rae and Taylor (1970) provide important illustrations of efforts in this direction. Conceived within the framework of a stochastic model, the influences of normative political knowledge will depend on the ability to quantify political factors.

These writers generally recognize the major operational dilemmas posed by the scientific ideal. Given both the state-of-the-art of quantification and the enormous complexity of the linkages between values expressed in the phenomenological world of policy-making and their statistical designations in an abstract causal policy model, a rigorous scientific approach is far removed from the realm of real-world decision-making techniques, particularly in the case of the normatively complex problems that press for policy solutions. The explanatory power of the available scientific policy models falls short of the level needed to provide the foundation for the design and development of effective intervention strategies (Arrow, 1967; Scott and Shore, 1979). Such models can retrospectively isolate variables that assist in explanation, but are far too imprecise to generate usable predictions. While such decision models have *heuristic* value in a range of social problems, generally they can provide *solutions* only in well-defined technically-oriented problems that lend themselves to quantification and calculation. In social policy, answers can be calculated only under restricted circumstances—such as uncomplicated, simple situations with quick and easy information, or perhaps where calculations are based on preemptory values (Frohock, 1979:60). The more sophisticated and compelling the mathematical formulation, as Dahl (1975:130) puts it, the more it tends to apply to less controversial technical problems.

Perhaps even more problematic than these empirical limitations of the modeling process is the overly simplistic conception of values and normative relationships that underlie the scientific conception of value mapping (Rein, 1976; Brown, 1976). The policy analyst's normative assignment in this approach is limited to tracing out the relationship of an established goal to a fixed or static web of values that surrounds a social problem. Beyond this task, little further reflection about values is required. Examination of the actual policy research process, however, shows the approach to be a misleading simplification, if not a fundamental epistemological error. Value positions in policy research seldom prove to be static conceptions that remain fixed and unchanging. Instead, they tend to shift iteratively as the analyst moves through the phases of data collection, analysis and interpretation. New data or knowledge frequently have a direct impact on the content and desirability of normative policy goals. Normative analysis, therefore, must in actual practice be an ongoing process that continues to occur throughout the phases of empirical policy research. This suggests that value perspectives are as much a function of processes internal to policy inquiry as they are fixed and unchangeable entities to be measured and mapped into the policy model.

The policy analyst has a dilemma here. The methodological tools for both the empirical and normative dimensions of the policy mapping process are underdeveloped. Causal models can locate variables that assist in explaining social observations but their margins of error are too wide to provide a firm basis for policy decision-making. At the same time, the methods of normative analysis rest upon simplistic assumptions about the role of values in the social process. In view of these limitations, writers such as Dror (1968) and Meltsner (1972) maintain that the policy sciences must develop less rigorous, but more practical, approaches to normative policy analysis such as scenario writing and the Delphi method, techniques based on the use of trained insight, imagination and conjecture. In this respect, Meltsner maintains that scientific methodology should be supplemented with training in the art of "political judgment."

The urgency and complexity of the problem has led to renewed epistemological exploration within the policy sciences. Mitroff and Pondy (1975), for example, maintain that new methodological directions "can only be gotten outside of the usual models of thinking by going to fields of inquiry, like the philosophy of science, which traditionally have been conceived to be far removed from the concerns of . . . policy analysis." Similarly, others argue that policy scientists must begin to explore policy evaluation as an alternative mode of inquiry with its own logic, rules and procedures (Anderson, 1978; Lindblom and Cohen, 1979).

A FORENSIC APPROACH

One of the most interesting directions to emerge from such explorations is that of a "forensic" social science. Writers such as Churchman (1971),

Brown (1976), and MacRae (1971) suggest that normative analysis can be facilitated by an organized dialogue between normative and empirical perspectives. In such a scheme, policy analysts and political decision-makers both take on the assignment of preparing briefs for or against particular policy positions. Each party confronts the other with a counterproposal based on alternative sets of facts (or varying perceptions of the facts) organized around the competing world-views that underlie their respective arguments. The grounds for accepting or rejecting a normative proposal must be the same grounds for accepting or rejecting a counterproposal; and they must be subjected to corresponding types of data, judged or tested by the same rigorous empirical methods. What is lost in logical and theoretical elegance is compensated for through relevance and practicality. Rather than seek to "prove" policy decisions in the traditional scientific sense of the term, analysts and decision-makers base their judgments on the most persuasive arguments, employing both empirical methods and the discursive logic of normative discourse.

This approach is an important step toward the development of a dynamic methodology designed to facilitate a dialectical interplay between empirical and normative processes in policy evaluation. But like any step forward, it only brings the methodologist to the next set of hurdles. The logical question that arises is this: If both analysts and policymakers must employ the same grounds or criteria in their respective arguments, what are these criteria? What are the rules governing the integration of empirical and normative judgments? Here the technique encounters the fundamental fact-value problem, particularly the question of normative criteria. There is little question about criteria governing empirical discourse, but the question as to whether there are criteria or grounds for mediating normative discourse is methodologically problematic. The introduction of normative debate brings the value dimensions of policy into sharper focus, but this is not to be confused with methodology per se. Given the long history of arguments in philosophy and the social sciences about value judgments, it is reasonable to surmise that the methodological success of the forensic model ultimately rests on the elaboration of rules that govern the exchange between empirical and normative perspectives.

The question, then, is how to develop a practical framework capable of incorporating the full range of empirical and normative judgments. An important clue can be gleaned from the work of ordinary-language philosophers engaged in the explication of the logic and purposes of practical discourse. The problem posed by the forensic approach is quite similar to the one that concerns ordinary-language philosophers such as Toulmin (1950), Baier (1958), Taylor (1961), and Perry (1976). The similarity of concerns, in fact, is significant enough to suggest the study of practical reason as a potential avenue of methodological exploration for policy theorists (Fischer, 1980).

THE LOGIC OF PRACTICAL DISCOURSE

In recent decades, as Dallmayr (1976) explains, "philosophical trends in a variety of contexts have pointed toward a revival of normative arguments even in the absence of cognitive premises; by means of a careful and critical scrutiny of normative statements, philosophers of different persuasions have progressively uncovered the distinctive and autonomous status of moral and normative discourse vis-à-vis empirical propositions." Stimulated by linguistic philosophy—especially the ordinary-language approach—a number of political theorists have begun to seek knowledge about values through the metaethical analysis of the structure of normative arguments in politics.

The primary purpose of metaethics is to explicate the distinctive logic of practical discourse to determine how people make reasoned judgments—i.e., how they choose and systematically employ rules and standards as criteria to arrive at conclusions. The basic aim is to come to a clear understanding of what it means to be rational in the process of dealing with values and norms, particularly in relation to empirical statements (Taylor, 1961). Where conceptual linguistic analysis focuses on the definitions and meanings of concepts employed in practical discourse, metaethics examines the nature of the judgments in which normative concepts are used; it inquires about the logic of practical discourse that governs reasoning about values; and it asks whether value judgments can be justified, proven, or shown to be valid.

An outgrowth of the later work of Wittgenstein, the ordinary-language approach to practical deliberation represents a loosely connected set of orientations characterized as much by ambiguity as by unity and agreement (Wellman, 1961). On the most general level, however, these orientations share a common response to positivism and the fact-value dichotomy. Fundamentally, the study of practical reason represents an effort to circumvent the methodological pitfalls of the fact-value separation, without necessarily resolving the underlying epistemological problems that it poses. Instead of emphasizing the failure of attempts to validate fundamental ideals, ordinary-language writers focus on the rational elements that make normative practical discourse possible in everyday life. Accepting the fact that values may in the final analysis rest on irrational components, they reject the positivistic conclusion that all normative discourse must be relegated to an epistemological limbo. They point to a number of dimensions of practical discourse that militate against such a conclusion. For example, in everyday life, actors are seldom faced with the lofty intellectual task of establishing the validity of fundamental values. Also, they have succeeded, at least to a degree, in explicating the outlines of an "informal logic" that governs practical deliberation. Such theorists argue that positivists, in their overemphasis on the irrationality of fundamental values, overlook the normative inferential methods that mediate the wide range of normative discussion about practical world affairs carried on within a framework of fundamental values. As most of the deliberation about practical affairs is conducted within a general social consensus about ideal values, it is possible from this view to argue that positivistic philosophers, and mainstream social scientists, have thrown the proverbial baby out with the bathwater.

The analysis of practical reason begins with the recognition that normative and scientific discourse are two distinct types of reason, each with its own logic and purpose. Writers such as Toulmin (1958) argue that the fundamental distinction between the two rests on purpose or function: the function of scientific judgment is to alter expectations about what will happen, while that of normative judgment is to alter attitudes, behavior and decisions about what should happen. Scientific judgments are based on the formal logic of the hypothetico-deductive model of causal demonstration. In contrast, normative judgments follow an informal logic that can be better understood in terms of something akin to a "jurisprudential analogy." Drawing attention to the similarities between normative arguments and those used by lawyers in a courtroom, Toulmin demonstrates that a good lawyer does not simply present the facts of the case but rather marshals them to stress those aspects of the situation that favor his or her clients. The lawyer selects language and structures arguments designed to persuade or convince a jury to decide in favor of the client. Similarly, moral and political judgments are statements in support of decisions that can be forceably or poorly defended. They are neither factual nor emotive statements, but rather "like records of practical decisions or positions taken which can be defended or supported much like a lawyer defends his client" (MacDonald, 1953:52). They are rationally constructed but not proven inductively or deductively like a scientific proposition. In this respect, one does not refer to J. S. Mill's "proof" of liberty but rather to his persuasive defense of it (MacDonald, 1953).

For present purposes, the contribution of a normative logic rests on its ability to provide the logical structure of the rational evaluative argument. The task is to present standards for decision-making that can serve as guides to be used as pointers or direction-finders, turning attention to facts, values and norms that might not otherwise be seen (Hambrick, 1974; Brock, et al., 1973; Dunn, 1981). They should, as Leys put it, "help voters, administrators, judges and anyone who participates in the determination of policy by providing a 'rational-analytic' for reviewers, investigators, auditors, surveyors, and consultants who are asked to pass judgment upon what others have done." Organized as a framework of questions, it can "improve and systematize practical judgments by finding out whether the right questions are being asked" (Leys, 1952:11).

The development of such a framework of questions has clear implications for policy-making. As a normative foundation, it could serve as a metanormative guide for probing the acceptability of policy judgments. Ideally, such a logical structure would integrate the full range of empirical and normative questions that arise in policy deliberations. It would provide each participant in a policy debate with a common framework for laying out his or her arguments. All parties would be subject to the same methodological questions and rules of judgment. Where agreement or consensus proves beyond reach, it should be possible to specify the exact points of tension and disagreement and suggest the kinds of evidence, if any, that might resolve these tensions.

As a preliminary step toward the development of an informal logic of policy questions, it is possible here to suggest twelve points or loci around which discussion and debate might take place. Cutting across both empirical and normative domains of policy inquiry, they are based on Taylor's study of the logic of evaluation and an examination of specific policy arguments (Fischer, 1980).

Following Toulmin's lead, Taylor (1961) has laid out an informal logic of evaluative discourse. A full evaluation, in Taylor's scheme, has to answer to questions that arise in four distinct but interrelated levels of evaluation. Ranging from the most concrete empirical questions up to abstract normative questions concerning the 'way of life,' each of the four levels has its own specific logic and purpose in evaluative inquiry. Specified as verification, validation, vindication and rational choice, the first two constitute first-order discourse concerned with reasoning within a specific value system; the second two constitute second-order discourse addressed to fundamental questions about the value system itself. Each of the two levels involves an interplay between empirical and normative questions. Although Taylor's explication of these four phases of evaluation largely speaks to the abstract epistemological concerns of philosophers, it also provides a basis for the development of specific evaluative questions applicable to policy decision-making. The translation from epistemology to practical questions adapted to policy evaluation has been the primary focus of the work presented here. As such, it is offered only as a suggestive beginning, designed to promote further exploration in this direction.

Evaluative inquiry can be initiated by a problem emerging in any of the four levels of discourse, requiring the participants to proceed to higher or lower levels of inquiry, depending upon the specific nature of the problem. However, for purposes of systematic presentation, it is helpful to present them in a formal order, ranging from the lowest concrete level up to the highest abstract questions. The phase or level of verification, then, is the starting point.

Verification is the simplest of the levels to describe. It is addressed to the basic empirical questions which have monopolized the attention of social and policy scientists. At this level, the evaluator will seek answers to problems revolving around the four following questions: Is the program objective derived from the policy goal(s)? Does the program empirically fulfill its stated objectives? Does the program fulfill the objective(s) more efficiently then alternative means available? Does empirical analysis uncover secondary system effects resulting from the program that offset other important objectives?

These are familiar questions in the empirical methodology of the policy evaluation. For purposes of brief illustration, consider the case of the Head Start compensatory education program. After determining whether Head Start policy goals have been properly translated into an empirically measurable program, analysts must question whether the program in fact efficiently achieves its stated objectives. They have to ask whether it accomplishes its objectives better than alternative programs, without offsetting other relevant objectives pertinent to compensatory educational policies as a whole. As in the case of the public debate about the Head Start findings of the Westinghouse Learning Corporation, much of the deliberation at this level focuses on the concerns of empirical methodology: Was the control group adequate? Was sufficient attention paid to program variations? Was the sample random? And so on (Williams and Evans, 1972).

Criticisms directed at the technocratic conception of policy evaluation largely derive from its failure to extend inquiry beyond the verification of program objectives. After technical verification, the logic of evaluation leads to questions of validation, concerned with whether the particular goals from which the policy objectives are drawn are the relevant goals in the specific situation. In this phase, the evaluator must turn from the methodological principles of empirical verification to the logical rules of first-order normative discourse. As a process of reasoning that takes place *within* an adopted value system, the focus of discussion here centers around the following questions: Is the policy goal(s) relevant? Can it be justified or grounded by an appeal to a higher principle(s) or established causal knowledge? Are there circumstances in the situation which require that an exception be made to the policy goal? Are two or more goals equally relevant to the situation? Does the decision-maker's value system place higher precedence on one of the conflicting criteria? Or does it make contradictory prescriptions in this situation?

The validation of a policy goal shifts the focus from program objectives to the relevance of the more general goals from which the objectives are derived. The general relevance of a policy goal can be justified by an appeal to two interrelated modes of reasoning. A goal can be justified by pointing to its logical link to a higher level of normative principle (e.g., the goal of efficiency can be derived from the principles of economic development); or it can be justified by an appeal to data about specific causal consequences that have previously resulted from adhering to the goal. In philosophy, this latter appeal is known as "rule-utilitarianism." Beyond this first step, the evaluator must examine the relevance of the goal to the specific circumstances to which it is applied; and, if relevant, determine whether it conflicts with other goals relevant to the same situation.

To pursue the Head Start illustration further, assume that policy evaluators fail to statistically verify an improvement in the reading scores of Head Start children, leading some to argue for the elimination of the program. Against this judgment, minority leaders might raise questions about the validity of reading scores as a criterion in this situation. Are they a valid criterion for judging the overall success of a program based on policies designed to improve the life opportunities of socially deprived ghetto children? What about providing "socially relevant experiences"? Wouldn't this objective have at least equal bearing on the determination of success or failure of Head Start programs? For those holding equality to be the highest human value, socially relevant experiences would most likely take precedent over academic merit measured as reading scores.

At this point, evaluative discourse shifts fundamentally from first to second-order discourse. The vindication of a political choice between reading scores and socially relevant experiences requires the evaluator to step outside of the value systems from which these preferences are drawn and to examine their implications for the larger social system as a whole. Deliberation here revolves around these two basic questions: Do the practical consequences resulting from a commitment to the decision-maker's basic value system facilitate the realization of the ideals of the accepted social order? Do other value systems, which reflect interests and needs in the social system as a whole, judge the consequences (as benefits and costs) to be distributed equitably?

The questions of vindication are essentially second-order empirical questions concerned with the functional consequences of individual and group values for the social system as a whole. In this respect, they reflect the types of concerns advanced by philosophers and social theorists of the systems persuasion (Sutherland, 1973). As such, vindication is the second-order counterpart of verification in first-order discourse. Although the empirical complexity of the questions raised in vindication is frequently a major obstacle, it is nonetheless possible to locate the concerns of this level of evaluation in policy debates. In the issues surrounding Head Start, probably the most salient example has been the controversy about the "culture of poverty." Debate here revolves around the question of whether ghetto children are socialized into value systems that lack instrumentality for the American 'way of life,' and if so, what to do about it. Empirical evidence demonstrating the presence and consequences of a culture of poverty can be offered as support for arguing the primacy of socially relevant experiences. The character of the solution, however, will depend on the relationship of the empirical findings to the accepted standards of social equity.

The second question of vindication is concerned with whether the system consequences satisfy the accepted standards of social equity held by competing interest groups or social classes that benefit from or pay for the outcomes. Disparities between these standards and the empirical results trigger political debate about the social system itself, which ultimately leads to the philosophical concerns of the fourth level of evaluation, rational choice.

At the level of rational political choice, the central problem is the construction of an ideal model. The political philosopher's task is to construct an ideal model of the "rational" way of life by identifying values (such as equity, freedom or community) to be adopted as the ultimate goals of all subsequent political undertakings. While policy science by virtue of its function is not concerned with this level of evaluation (Meehan, 1975), it is essential that policy evaluators recognize the systematic links between the normative questions that arise in policy debates and higher levels of evaluation, including political philosophy. Even though policy scientists are not directly concerned with the construction of alternative social systems, they are consumers of the ideological framework of the society within which they are working. Utilization of the full range of normative questions provides the analyst with a framework for exploring the value conflicts and contradictions operating within the system. In analytical terms, the clarification of the relationship between fundamental normative assumptions and empirical data must be an essential component of political feasibility studies in policy evaluation. In the broader context of political theory, explication of these relationships would contribute significantly to the elimination of the ideological shroud that hovers over the technocratic approach to policy analysis (Habermas, 1970; Kramer, 1975).

Summarized in Table 1, these questions are designed to serve as a

Table 1. A Logic of Policy Questions

Program Objectives:	Is the program objective(s) logically derived from the relevant policy goals?
Empirical Consequences:	Does the program empirically fulfill its stated objective(s)?
Alternative Means:	Does the program fulfill the objective(s) more efficiently than alternative means available?
Unanticipated Effects:	Does empirical analysis uncover secondary system effects resulting from the program that offset other important objectives?
Relevance:	Is the policy goal(s) relevant? Can it be justified or grounded by an appeal to a higher principle(s) or established causal knowledge?
Situational Context:	Are there circumstances in the situation which require that an exception be made to the policy goal?
Multiple Goals:	Are two or more goals equally relevant to the situation?
Precedence:	Does the decision-maker's value system place higher precedence on one of the conflicting criteria? Or does it make contradictory prescriptions in this situation?
System Consequence:	Do the practical consequences resulting from a commitment to the decision-maker's basic value system facilitate the realization of the ideals of the accepted social order?
Social Equity:	Do other value systems, which reflect interests and needs in the social system as a whole, judge the consequences (as benefits and costs) to be distributed equitably?
Ideological Conflicts:	Do the fundamental ideals that organize the accepted social order provide a basis for an equitable resolution of conflicting judgments?
Alternative Social Order:	If the social order is unable to resolve value system conflicts, do other social orders equitably prescribe for the relevant interests the needs that the conflicts reflect?

rational-analytic guide for policy deliberation. Rather than as a normative calculus, they are presented as a framework of component parts of a policy judgment that requires investigation. Instead of supplying information per se, they point to unperceived angles and forgotten dimensions that must be explored, as well as the kinds of empirical and normative data pertinent to the deliberative processes in general. The task of the evaluator is to tease out the answers to these questions and formally organize them in such a way that the strengths and weaknesses, inconsistencies and contradictions of a policy decision are revealed.

While such a logic of evaluation has prescriptive implications for evaluating the outcomes of policy deliberation, it is essential that it be recognized as an ideal structure. To properly introduce an ideal logic of discourse, an evaluator must be prepared to anticipate the inherent conflicts that it will generate in the modern bureaucratic decision-making process, where patterns of communication are sharply limited by hierarchical authority and the chain of command. In actuality, it is intentionally designed to exploit the tensions between the real and the ideal, between bureaucratic domination and legitimate human discourse. Dialectically, the explication of such tensions can serve as a critical force facilitating policy change. In this regard, an ideal logic may better serve those who suffer the consequences of public policies than the officials responsible for them. Like policy analysis in general, an ideal logic of evaluation must be approached as a tool for bureaucratic reform (Daneke, 1977).

In addition to the clarification of empirical and normative relations in policy argumentation, viewed as organizational reform, this alternative approach also facilitates the exploration of important epistemological questions emerging in the philosophy of the social sciences that bear on the policy sciences. Given the interplay between empirical research (facts) and ideology (values), it is clear that the construction of policy arguments necessarily remains as much an art as a science. Accordingly, policy scientists must begin to confront the less scientific, more interpretive dimensions of policy evaluation and the methodological problems they imply. As Mitroff and Pondy (1975) maintain, this requires methodological exploration of more recent developments in the philosophy of the social sciences. Careful reading of this literature, in fact, suggests that some of the main "technical" problems that plague policy research are less matters of research design and data collection than problems with normative epistemological assumptions. As a suggestive beginning, the advantage of the methodological framework presented here is its compatibility with such investigation, particularly investigation of problems concerning the integration of empirical and normative judgments, and the relation of causal explanation to interpretation. To the extent that the development and logical analysis of policy proposals is a deliberative exercise employing conjecture and speculation, analogy and metaphor, and extrapolation from empirically established causal propositions, policy methodology must be attuned to questions concerning the relation of cause to understanding, insight and discovery to demonstration and proof. As a logical structure, the methodological framework can help to facilitate the exploration of these linkages.

Drawing on the epistemological literature, especially the contributions of phenomenological sociologists and political philosophers, the policy methodologist must confront the fact that, unlike the scientifically de-rived policy proposal (based on a closed, generalized model), a politically-based policy proposal must be open and contextual. Where scientific judgment can be based on a computational algorithm, the validity of a normative policy argument is in the final analysis determined by the communicative power or persuasive force it has for its audience. Such judgments are not true or false in the scientific sense of the term; rather they portray policies as better or worse, powerful or weak, or persuasive and unconvincing for members of the policy audience. The test criteria for the proposal is the breadth of its appeal, its ability to synthesize conflicting arguments, the number of people willing to accept it, and so on. It is difficult to state precise rules about how to do this. As one leading writer put it, "policy analysis with its emphasis on originality, imagination and foresight cannot be simply described" (Wildavsky, 1969:190). However, from the analytical insights offered by ordinary-language philosophers, it is clear that the logic of the process is not beyond rational inquiry.

The existing policy literature provides some important clues as to how or where to begin such studies. Barry and Rae (1975), for example, suggest that those interested in evaluation should place greater emphasis on the study of "political-rhetoric"—the way in which arguments are marshaled in politics to reconcile people pursuing different goals and objectives. House (1980) and Anderson (1979) similarly call for the study of the "metapolitical" languages of policy evaluation; and Johnson (1975) alludes to instructive parallels that can be drawn between literary criti-cism and public policy evaluation as policy criticism. Outside of main-stream social science, the study of the rules and principles of criticism are widely endorsed as a serious, systematic endeavor. It may well be here, through further exploration of policy languages and modes of argumentation, that normative political theorists can make one of their most important contributions to public policy studies (Graham, 1977).

If it is true that the ability of the social sciences to contribute to policy questions rests upon their ability to relate empirical and normative judg-ments, policy methodologists must begin to translate the import of these epistemological discussions into their own language and concerns. In contrast to the sophisticated nature of the challenge, claims about the present discussion must remain modest. The purpose has only been to point to these methodological issues and offer some suggestive direc-tions. It is hoped that the discussion will encourage others interested in policy evaluation to join in. Both policy analysts and political theorists have important roles to play here. Analysts in particular can examine policy arguments to determine the types of questions and responses that actually arise in such deliberations, while political theorists should focus on adapting the methods of normative inquiry to practical empirical problems. The central task at this stage is to nurture a dialogue about the normative methodological dimensions of policy evaluation. Toward this end, policy analysts and political theorists must join together in a common effort.

REFERENCES

Anderson, C.W. (1979) "The place of principles in policy analysis." American Political Science Review 73:711–723.

———(1978) "The logic of public problems: evaluation in comparative policy research." In D.E. Ashford (ed.), Comparing Public Policies. Beverly Hills, CA: Sage Publications.

Arrow, K.J. (1967) "Public and private values." In S. Hook (ed.), Human Values and Economic Policy. New York: New York University Press.

Baier, K. (1958) The Moral Point of View. Ithaca, NY: Cornell University Press.

Barry, B. and D.W. Rae (1975) "Political evaluation." In N. Polsby and F.D. Greenstein (eds.), The Handbook of Political Science. Reading, MA: Addison-Wesley.

Bernstein, R.J. (1976) The Restructuring of Social and Political Theory. New York: Harcourt, Brace, Jovanovich.

Brock, B. et al. (1973) Public Policy Decision-Making: Systems Analysis and Comparative Advantages Debate. New York: Harper and Row.

Brown, P.G. (1976) "Ethics and policy research." Policy Analysis 2:259–274.

Churchman, C.W. (1971) The Design of Inquiring Systems. New York: Basic Books.

———and A.H. Schainblatt (1969) "PPB: how can it be implemented?" Public Administration Review 29:178–189.

Dahl, R.A. (1975) Modern Political Analysis. Englewood Cliffs, NJ: Prentice-Hall.

Dallmayr, F.R. (1976) "Beyond dogma and despair: toward a critical theory of politics." American Political Science Review 52:64–79.

Daneke, G. (1977) "Policy analysis as bureaucratic reform." Southern Review of Public Administration 1:109–128.

Dror, Y. (1969) "The prediction of political feasibility." Futures 1:282–288.

——— (1968)Public Policymaking Reexamined. San Francisco: Chandler.

——— (1967) "Policy analysts: a new profession in government service." Public Administration Review 27:200–208.

Dunn, W.N. (1981) Public Policy Analysis. Englewood Cliffs, NJ: Prentice-Hall.

———and B. Fozouni (1976) Toward a Critical Administrative Theory. Beverly Hills, CA: Sage Publications.

Fischer, F. (1980) Politics, Values, and Public Policy: The Problem of Methodology. Boulder, CO: Westview Press.

Frohock, F.M. (1979) Public Policy: Scope and Logic. Englewood Cliffs, NJ: Prentice-Hall.

Graham, G.J. (1977) "Rhetorical analysis and political evaluation: knowledge, beliefs, and discourse in normative judgment." Prepared for delivery at the Annual Meeting of the American Political Science Association, Washington, D.C.

Habermas, J. (1970) Toward a Rational Society. Boston: Beacon Press.

Hambrick, R. (1974) "A guide for the analysis of policy arguments." Policy Sciences 5:469–478.

Hammond, K.R. and L. Adelman (1978) "Science, values and human judgment." In K.R. Hammond (ed.), Judgment and Decision in Public Policy Formation. Boulder, CO: Westview Press.

House, E.R. (1980) Evaluating with Validity. Beverly Hills, CA: Sage Publications.

Johnson, R.W. (1975) "Research objectives for policy analysis." In K.M. Dolbeare (ed.), Public Policy Evaluation. Beverly Hills, CA: Sage Publications.

Kramer, F. (1975) "Policy analysis as ideology." Public Administration Review 36: 509–517.

Leys, W.A.R. (1952) Ethics for Policy Decisions. Englewood Cliffs, NJ: Prentice-Hall.

Lindblom, C.E. and D.K. Cohen (1979) Usable Knowledge: Social Science and Social Problem Solving. New Haven, CT: Yale University Press.

MacDonald, M. (1953) "Natural rights." In P. Laslett (ed.), Philosophy, Politics and Society. Oxford: Oxford University Press.

MacRae, D. (1976) The Social Function of Social Science. New Haven, CT: Yale University Press.

———(1971) "Scientific communication, ethical argument, and public policy." American Political Science Review 56:38–50.

Majone, G. (1975) "On the notion of political feasibility." European Journal of Political Research 3:259–274.

Meehan, E.J. (1975) "Science, values, and policies." American Behavioral Scientist 17:53–100.

Meltsner, A. (1972) "Political feasibility and policy analysis." Public Administration Review 32:859–867.

Mitroff, I. and L. Pondy (1975) "On the organization of inquiry: a comparison of some radically different approaches to policy analysis." Public Administration Review 24:471–479.

Perry, T.D. (1976) Moral Reasoning and Truth. Oxford: Clarendon.

Rae, D.W. and M. Taylor (1971) "Decision rules and policy outcomes." British Journal of Political Science 1:71–90.

Rein, M. (1976) Social Science and Public Policy. New York: Penguin.

Riley, G., ed. (1974) Values, Objectivity, and the Social Sciences. Reading, MA: Addison-Wesley.

Rivlin, A. (1973) "Forensic social science." Perspectives on Inequality. Cambridge: Educational Reprint Series, No. 8.

Scott, R.A. and A.R. Shore (1979) Why Sociology Does Not Apply: A Study of the Use of Sociology in Public Policy. New York: Elsevier.

Sutherland, J.W. (1973) A General Systems Philosophy for the Social and Behavioral Sciences. New York: George Braziller.

Taylor, P.W. (1961) Normative Discourse. Englewood Cliffs, NJ: Prentice-Hall.

Toulmin, S. (1958) The Uses of Argument. Cambridge: Cambridge University Press.

———(1950) An Examination of the Place of Reason in Ethics. Cambridge: Cambridge University Press.

Weber, M. (1949) "The meaning of ethical neutrality." In E. Shils and H.A. Finch (trans. and eds.), The Methodology of the Social Sciences. New York: Free Press.

Wellman, C. (1961) The Language of Ethics. Cambridge, MA: Harvard University Press.

Wildavsky, A. (1969) "Rescuing policy analysis from PPBS." Public Administration Review 29:189–202.

——(1966) "The political economy of efficiency: cost-benefit analysis, systems analysis, and program budgeting." Public Administration Review 26:292–310.

Williams, W. and J.W. Evans (1972) "The politics of evaluation: the case of Head Start." In P. Rossi and W. Williams (eds.), Evaluating Social Programs. New York: Free Press.

THE ANALYTIC HIERARCHY PROCESS AND POLICY ARGUMENTATION

Kevin P. Kearns

ABSTRACT

The Analytic Hierarchy Process (Saaty, 1980) was incorporated as one component of an 18-month research project designed to assess alternative technical assistance resources for fostering intermunicipal cooperation in Allegheny County, Pennsylvania. Diverse local government stakeholders participated in the AHP workshop including representatives of state, county, municipal governments, civic agency administrators, and business executives. This paper summarizes the results of the workshop and comments on the strengths and weaknesses technique. The paper concludes that the AHP would be strengthened through the incorporation of an explicit "value-critical" perspective that systematically surfaces assumptions underlying contending policy arguments.

INTRODUCTION

This chapter describes a research endeavor which explored a promising yet highly controversial strategy for enhancing the efficiency and effec-

Policy Analysis: Perspectives, Concepts, and Methods, pages 333–354.
Copyright © 1986 by JAI Press, Inc.
All rights of reproduction in any form reserved.
ISBN: 0–89232–371–X

tiveness of municipal services. The strategy, known as voluntary inter-governmental cooperation, requires a formal agreement between two or more autonomous jurisdictions for the joint delivery of a service. Examples of such arrangements include joint provision of police or fire services, joint purchasing of supplies or equipment, joint tax collection, or even "circuit-riding" management personnel who attend to the affairs of several autonomous jurisdictions. The critical attribute of these interjurisdictional agreements is that they are voluntary; that is they develop in a "bottom-up" manner from the mutual needs and initiatives of the communities involved rather than being imposed in a "top-down" fashion by a higher level of government such as the county or the state.

Despite several apparent advantages of the cooperative approach to municipal service delivery, it has received mixed reviews from public officials and policy analysts. Some have hailed it as a promising long term solution to the urban fiscal crisis and a viable alternative to the consolidation or structural reorganization of local governments (Honadle, 1981b). Others claim that intergovernmental cooperation has thus far failed to yield benefits proportionate to the substantial investments required to initiate, negotiate, and sustain multijurisdictional ventures (Ostrom, et al., 1973).

These divergent perceptions suggest that strategies for promoting intergovernmental cooperation on a regional basis will succeed to the extent that they seek to resolve stakeholder conflicts regarding the perceived efficacy of this management innovation. Thus the design of such strategies is an inherently ill-structured problem (Mitroff and Sagasti, 1973; Ackoff, 1974) the resolution of which requires the application of new problem structuring and problem solving techniques which build upon rather than ignore conflicting perceptions, beliefs, and motives held by multiple policy stakeholders. This chapter describes how the Analytic Hierarchy Process (Saaty, 1980) contributed to the resolution of this ill-structured problem. While the discussion is limited substantively to intergovernmental cooperation and geographically to the Pittsburgh metropolitan area, the conceptual and methodological approach outlined below is generalizable to many other contexts.

The first section of the chapter outlines the background and rationale for intergovernmental cooperation and identifies factors which have inhibited its widespread utilization. The second section describes an 18-month research project which sought to identify strategies for promoting intergovernmental cooperation among communities in the Pittsburgh area. Special attention is devoted to the application of the Analytic Hierarchy Process (Saaty, 1980), a new and highly promising technique for structuring and resolving ill-structured systemic problems. The last section of the chapter discusses the strengths and weaknesses of the Analytic Hierarchy Process.

INTERGOVERNMENTAL COOPERATION IN PERSPECTIVE

Despite a massive investment of federal resources over the past two decades, there has been little meaningful progress toward the resolution of the myriad problems facing municipal governments. Indeed the cancerous spread of fiscal and social distress appears to be gaining momentum. Today the manifestations of urban problems no longer are confined to the jurisdictional boundaries of large metropolitan centers. Many suburban and quasi-rural communities are plagued by the same challenges of fiscal distress, population decline, and decaying capital infrastructure as their larger urban counterparts. Satellite communities in the industrial Northeast and Midwest have been especially hard hit by shifts in domestic and international economies. For example, more than three-quarters of the 129 suburban jurisdictions surrounding Pittsburgh recorded population losses during the 1970s. With steel production down by more than 70 percent since 1978, the regional unemployment rate is well above the national average. Essential components of the capital infrastructure—such as roads, bridges, and sewer lines—are in dire need of repair and replacement, and basic public services such as police protection have been curtailed or eliminated. In some suburban jurisdictions municipal employees have worked temporarily without pay, while in others they have been laid off in an effort to bridge the widening gap between revenues and expenditures.

While these problems are especially acute in the older, industrialized suburbs in the Northeast and Midwest, small municipalities in all parts of the country are feeling the fiscal squeeze. In 1983 the Department of Housing and Urban Development classified more than 50 percent of all small cities in the United States as "distressed," according to criteria such as population lag/decline, job lag/decline, and age of housing stock.

Some observers have concluded that suburban municipalities should be absorbed within larger units of government such as the metropolitan center or the county. Structural reorganization strategies such as city-county mergers and metropolitan consolidation have promised to produce economies of scale and eliminate regional fiscal disparities, thereby improving the overall quality of public services. While there is some evidence suggesting that various forms of metropolitan consolidation have contributed to efficiency and effectiveness, these structural solutions have faced strong opposition from suburban municipal officials who correctly perceive them as posing a threat to their political autonomy and administrative authority. Citizens have mounted opposition to these plans based on their belief that a metropolitan government would place even greater distance between themselves and an already bewildering local bureaucracy. In Allegheny County, for example, there have been half a dozen attempts since the 1920s to restructure the system of municipal service delivery (Gow, 1952). All such efforts have been vigorously opposed and effectively stymied by officials and residents of suburban jurisdictions.

Voluntary intergovernmental cooperation is a multijurisdictional approach which appears to offer many of the benefits of structural reorganization strategies but few of the political and social costs, since it requires no tampering with the jurisdictional boundaries or functional responsibilities of autonomous government units (Zimmerman, 1974; Honadle, 1981a, 1981b). Among the benefits attributed to the cooperative approach are the following:

- It can reduce the costs of services through economies of scale;
- It can improve the quality of services through the pooling of financial resources and technical expertise;
- It can facilitate the delivery of new services such as emergency medical services which are not feasible for small autonomous jurisdictions.

While some communities in the Pittsburgh area have successfully implemented cooperative arrangements with neighboring communities, others have either not explored the cooperative approach or have failed in their efforts to initiate and sustain joint undertakings. Moreover, some community officials have publicly criticized the cooperative approach, claiming that it is little more than a political "smokescreen" designed to mask a trend toward metropolitanism. A consensus of this topic is conspicuously absent.

Method

The Intergovernmental Cooperation Project, an 18-month research endeavor sponsored by the corporate community of Pittsburgh, sought to map the divergent perceptions of intermunicipal cooperation and to design a strategy for promoting the establishment and maintenance of cooperative arrangements among the 129 suburban communities in the

Pittsburgh area. Several interrelated research problems were addressed:

- To what extent is the cooperative approach to municipal service delivery used by localities in Allegheny County?
- Has the cooperative approach produced tangible or intangible benefits?
- Do public officials and citizens perceive potential for new cooperative arrangements?
- Do municipal officials need assistance in the design and implementation of cooperative arrangements?
- Are existing technical assistance resources sufficient to meet municipal needs?

These questions were addressed through three interrelated data gathering activities: surveys of citizens, surveys of public officials, and interviews with technical assistance providers. The fourth component of the research design was a stakeholder workshop structured around the Analytic Hierarchy Process (Saaty, 1980). The AHP workshop facilitated discussions of survey findings and assisted in the formulation of program goals, the selection of performance criteria, and the comparative assessment of policy alternatives.

In seeking to maximize stakeholder involvement in the research undertaking, thereby capturing the range of divergent perspectives on intermunicipal cooperation, the investigators convened a project advisory committee. The committee was composed of diverse stakeholders including municipal, county, and state government officials as well as representatives of technical assistance agencies and local universities. Chief executive officers of leading corporations in the Pittsburgh area, as well as representatives of privately funded civic agencies, such as the Chamber of Commerce, also served on the committee. The group was conceived of as a working body, not merely a means to legitimate the project recommendations. Thus the committee members were intimately involved in all phases of the research undertaking from the design of survey instruments through the drafting of interim and final project reports. The following section highlights the findings of the three data gathering efforts.

The Surveys

The survey of citizens, conducted via a telephone interview with 258 randomly selected County residents, demonstrated that citizens support the idea of cooperative service delivery. Moreover, citizens displayed a high level of awareness regarding salient issues in the design and implementation of cooperative arrangements. The vast majority of respondents were able to provide reasoned, cogent justifications for their preferences even though they were not prompted with a list of possible responses. Those who favored cooperative service delivery generally cited the potential for cost savings, while those who were less supportive expressed the fear that their communities would lose control over municipal services.

The survey of public officials was conducted via a self-administered questionnaire sent to 761 municipal officials including council members, appointed city managers, police chiefs, fire chiefs, and public works supervisors. The survey results indicated that cooperative arrangements are prevalent in routine services such as purchasing and police dispatching, yet they are rare in technically complex or politically sensitive municipal functions such as cash management, risk management, police patrolling, and municipal tax collection. The larger and more affluent communities are more likely to be involved in a cooperative arrangement ($p < .05$), a finding that may be attributable to the level of training and professional experience of management personnel. The most important policy-relevant finding concerned the expressed needs of municipal officials for various types of technical assistance in the design and implementation of cooperative arrangements, including general information on cooperative arrangements undertaken by others, feasibility studies, and assistance in the implementation of cooperative ventures with demonstrated records of success. Municipal officials indicated that they prefer to receive assistance from voluntary associations of governments such as municipal leagues and councils of governments whose staff members are most intimately involved in the day-to-day operations of municipal management. A discouraging finding from the perspective of a university-based policy analyst is that universities were identified as the least preferred source of technical assistance, due to a perceived lack of practical understanding of municipal problems by faculty and students.

Finally, interviews in nearly two dozen technical assistance agencies indicated that their activities were not directed at the high priority needs identified by municipal officials. None of the agencies, for example, served as a general clearinghouse for information on cooperative arrangements, and none facilitated peer exchanges among local public officials. Few agencies provided follow-up assistance in the implementation of technically complex or politically sensitive arrangements. Also the interviews revealed a high degree of overlap and duplication of assistance efforts.

On the basis of these and other secondary data-gathering activities, the project advisory committee reached the following conclusions:

- Voluntary intergovernmental cooperation has produced tangible and intangible benefits for municipalities;
- There is substantial unrealized potential for cooperation in technically complex and politically sensitive public services;
- Municipal officials need various types of technical assistance to initiate and sustain cooperative arrangements;
- A single organization should be responsible for promoting intergovernmental cooperation by coordinating the activities of existing technical assistance agencies and directing resources toward the high priority needs expressed by municipal officials.

Thus the survey findings provided some parameters for this ill-structured problem, yet many questions remained unanswered. For example, there was no way to objectively assess the relative importance of the political, economic, and administrative factors that would determine the success of the coordinating agency. Also there was no way to objectively evaluate the strengths and weaknesses of alternative models of a coordinating agency. Finally, as in most group decision-making settings, there was an undercurrent of conflict within the project advisory committee concerning the goals to be pursued by the coordinating agency. Several members had been affiliated with prior unsuccessful efforts to reform the system of municipal service delivery and were cognizant of the political sensitivity of this undertaking. They appeared to favor a narrowly defined and conservative mandate for the coordinating agency while other committee members espoused more dramatic actions. Thus despite progress in the clarification of some issues, the advisory committee still faced a textbook example of an ill-structured problem, a situation characterized by uncertainty and conflict concerning the precise nature of the problem itself and faith in the viability of alternative solutions.

THE AHP WORKSHOP

To resolve these issues, the investigators explored a variety of techniques for structuring and resolving problems in group settings including policy delphi (Turoff, 1970), strategic assumption surfacing and testing (Mitroff and Emshoff, 1979), multi-attribute utility analysis (Gardiner and Edwards, 1975), and social judgment analysis

(Mumpower, et al., 1979). The Analytic Hierarchy Process (Saaty, 1980) ultimately was selected.

The Analytic Hierarchy Process (AHP) is a systematic procedure for representing the elements of any policy problem hierarchically. The hierarchic representation accounts for the interdependence of actors, objectives, and policy alternatives, and guides decision-makers in breaking down the problem through a series of pairwise comparisons which express judgments or perceptions concerning the relative strength, intensity of impact, or desirability of the elements in a hierarchy. Developed by Thomas L. Saaty, the AHP has been applied to many problems including transportation design (Saaty, 1977a), forecasting (Saaty and Rogers, 1976), energy management (Saaty and Mariano, 1979) and general policy planning (Saaty and Kearns, 1985). A complete elaboration on the theory and practice of the AHP is provided elsewhere (Saaty, 1980). This discussion will, therefore, be limited to an abbreviated illustration of the technique and a description of its use in the Intergovernmental Cooperation Project.

The first step in the AHP is the construction of a hierarchic representation of a decision problem. While the hierarchic structure will vary depending on the type of problem, the top level usually reflects the overall goal or objective of the exercise. Intermediate levels are composed of environmental factors or performance criteria which affect the attainment of goals. Actors who affect the attainment of goals may also be included in the intermediate level. The lowest level is generally a list of policy alternatives. The hierarchic structure of the problem in the present study is illustrated in Figure 1.

The overall objective of the exercise, i.e., the top level of the hierarchy, was the selection of an agency to promote intergovernmental cooperation by coordinating the delivery of technical assistance to municipalities. In the course of structuring the hierarchy, the project advisory committee identified four goals of equal importance to be pursued by the coordinating agency:

- Identify opportunities for new cooperative arrangements and rank these opportunities according to their need for assistance.
- Develop integrated assistance strategies in response to the expressed needs of municipal officials.
- Create the capacity for continuous monitoring and evaluation of assistance strategies.
- Disseminate information on intergovernmental cooperation and provide assistance in the transfer of proven technologies between municipalities.

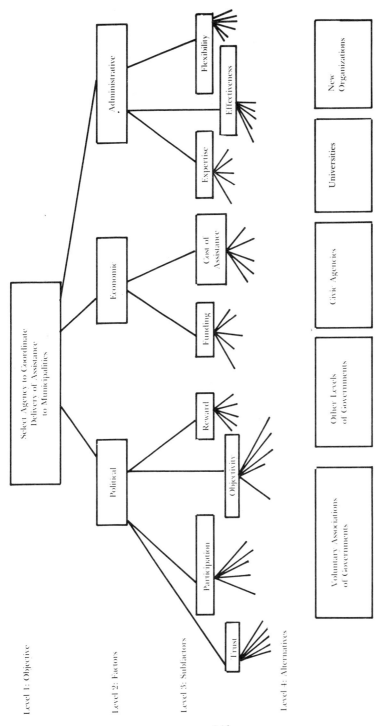

Level 1: Objective

Level 2: Factors

Level 3: Subfactors

Level 4: Alternatives

Select Agency to Coordinate Delivery of Assistance to Municipalities

Political

Economic

Administrative

Trust

Participation

Objectivity

Reward

Funding

Cost of Assistance

Expertise

Effectiveness

Flexibility

Voluntary Associations of Governments

Other Levels of Governments

Civic Agencies

Universities

New Organizations

Figure 1. Hierarchic Portrayal of the Decision Problem.

341

The second and third levels of the hierarchy in Figure 1 refer to factors and subfactors respectively. The members of the advisory committee agreed that the following sets of factors, drawn largely from results of the surveys discussed earlier, would exert substantial influence on the success or failure of the coordinating agency:

Political Factors

- *Trust*: the agency should be trusted by municipal officials.
- *Participation*: municipal officials should have direct access to the organization and should be formally involved in its decision making processes.
- *Objectivity*: the organization should be free of partisan political influence.
- *Reward*: the organization should offer prestige and other non-financial incentives to municipalities.

Economic Factors

- *Funding*: the coordinating agency should have an adequate and stable source of funding.
- *Cost of Assistance*: the agency should provide low cost assistance to municipalities.

Administrative Factors

- *Expertise*: the agency should be staffed by persons who are experienced in municipal government.
- *Effectiveness*: the agency should have a documented record of effectiveness or be able to demonstrate how it proposes to effectively address municipal needs.
- *Flexibility*: the agency should be responsive to expressed needs and have the ability to modify its activities as needs change.

Finally, the bottom level of the hierarchy includes several alternative types of assistance agencies which could serve as the coordinating vehicle:

- *Voluntary Associations of Governments*: Municipal leagues and councils of governments.
- *Other Levels of Government*: County and State agencies.
- *Civic Agencies*: Non-profit research and technical assistance agencies.
- *Universities*: Faculty and students of graduate programs in public affairs and management.

- *New Organization*: Hybrid or replica of programs in place in other regions.

The AHP demands that the hierarchic representation of a problem be devised by the participants in the decision process. This requires considerable dialogue to ensure that the definition of the problem reflects the range of perceptions and preferences of those who affect and are affected by the outcome. When constructing the hierarchy, errors of *commission* are insignificant since participants will have the opportunity to express the strength or intensity of their preferences for criteria and alternative solutions. Errors of *omission*, on the other hand, can jeopardize the integrity of the results. Thus the hierarchic representation of a problem should be based on prior research (if possible) and extensive dialogue among policy stakeholders. Participants in AHP workshops frequently note that hierarchical problem structuring is an intuitively appealing process. Hierarchic structures capture the systemic complexity of messy problems while simultaneously placing manageable boundaries on that complexity so that decision makers can focus on goals, performance criteria, and alternative solutions.

Having constructed a hierarchic representation of a problem, the next step in the AHP is the establishment of priorities among relevant factors in the second level with respect to their impact on the overall objective. This is accomplished through pairwise comparisons of factors using a scale of relative importance (see Saaty, 1977b). Table 1 outlines the scale of relative importance. The use of this scale will be described shortly.

First a matrix is arranged to facilitate the ranking of factors in the second level with respect to their relative impact on the overall objective. Similar matrices must be constructed for pairwise comparisons of subfactors in the third level with respect to the factors in the second level and so on through the bottom level of the hierarchy. The matrix is set up by listing the elements to be compared down the left and across the top margins. The matrix for the second level of this hierarchy is illustrated in Figure 2.

Note the matrix in Figure 2 has numbers in its nine cells. These numbers, derived from the scale of relative importance, reflect the judgments of the advisory committee regarding the relative impact each of the three factors will have on the success of a coordinating agency. The following question was asked of the group: "With respect to the success of a coordinating agency in meeting its four goals, what is the importance of political factors relative to economic and administrative factors?" Similarly, in the third level (see Figure 4), the group was asked: "With respect to political factors, what is the importance of trust relative to participation, objectivity, and reward?" The same line of questioning continued

Table 1.   Scale of Relative Importance

Intensity of Relative Importance	Definition	Explanation
1	Equal importance	Two activities contribute equally to the objective.
3	Moderate importance of one over another	Experience and judgment slightly favor one activity over another.
5	Essential or strong importance	Experience and judgment strongly favor one activity over another.
7	Demonstrated importance	An activity is strongly favored and its dominance is demonstrated in practice.
9	Absolute importance	The evidence favoring one activity over another is of the highest possible order of affirmation.
2,4,6,8	Intermediate values between the two adjacent judgments	When compromise is needed.
Reciprocals of above non-zero numbers	If an activity has one of the above numbers (e.g., 3) compared with a second activity, then the second activity has the reciprocal value (i.e., 1/3) when compared to the first.	

Source: Saaty (1980).

through the economic and administrative factors, concluding with comparisons of alternatives in the fourth level with respect to the subfactors in the third level.

The convention is to compare the importance of elements on the left

Select Coordinating Agency	Political Factors	Economics Factors	Administrative Factors
Political Factors	1	3	4
Economic Factors	1/3	1	3
Administrative Factors	1/4	1/3	1

Figure 2.   Matrix for Comparing the Relative Impact of Factors with Respect to the Overall Objective.

Select Coordinating Agency	Political	Economic	Administrative	Local Priorities
Political	1	3	4	.61
Economic	1/3	1	3	.27
Administrative	1/4	1/3	1	.12

Figure 3. Level Two with Respect to Level One.

margin of the matrix with those across the top. Thus, if an element on the left is perceived to be more important than an element on the top, a positive integer from 2 to 9, drawn from the scale of relative importance, is inserted in the cell. If it is judged to be less important, the reciprocal value of the integer will be entered. The relative importance of any element compared with itself is 1. Therefore, the diagonal vector of the matrix in Figure 2 contains only the integer 1.

Finally, reciprocal values are automatically entered for reverse comparisons. Since political factors were judged by the committee to be "moderately more important" than economic factors (3 in cell a_{12} of Figure 2), economic factors must be "moderately less important" (1/3 in cell a_{21}) than political factors. This procedure ensures that reverse com-

Political	Trust	Participation	Objectivity	Rewards	Local Priorities
Trust	1	3	2	2	.39
Participation	1/3	1	3	1	.25
Objectivity	1/2	1/3	1	1/3	.11
Rewards	1/2	1	3	1	.25

Economic	Funding	Cost of Assistance		
Funding	1	1/7		.125
Cost of Assistance	7	1		.875

Administrative	Expertise	Effectiveness	Flexibility	
Expertise	1	1	1	.33
Effectiveness	1	1	1	.33
Flexibility	1	1	1	.33

Figure 4. Level Three with respect to Level Two.

parisons are consistent. The AHP allows for a margin of inconsistency in nonreverse judgments. Nine pairwise comparison matrices were needed to elicit all of the relevant judgments from advisory committee members. Figures 3 and 4 illustrate the matrices for the first three levels of the hierarchy.

Note that these matrices have percentages listed down the right-hand margin. These percentages, obtained by solving the matrices of pairwise comparisons, are local priorities which express the relative importance of the factors and subfactors when compared with each other. The percentages are obtained by computing a set of eigenvectors for each matrix and then normalizing the result to obtain the vectors of local priorities.

Computing eigenvectors is not difficult but it can be time consuming. An approximation of the eigenvector is the geometric mean, obtained by multiplying the judgments in each row and taking their nth root where n is the number of judgments. The resulting column of numbers is then normalized to obtain the vector of local priorities. Thus, for the matrix of Figure 2 we have:

	Pol.	Econ.	Admin.	Approximate Eigenvector		Local Priorities
Pol.	1	3	4	$\sqrt[3]{1 \times 3 \times 4}$	$= 2.29$	$2.29/3.72 = .61$
Econ.	1/3	1	3	$\sqrt[3]{1/3 \times 1 \times 3}$	$= 0.9$	$0.99/3.72 = .27$
Admin.	1/4	1/3	1	$\sqrt[3]{1/4 \times 1/3 \times 1}$	$= 0.44$	$0.44/3.72 = .12$
					3.72	

The local priorities clearly indicate that advisory committee members perceived political factors to be more important than economic or administrative factors in determining the success of a coordinating agency.

Next, "global" priorities are derived by multiplying the local priorities of subfactors in the third level of the hierarchy by the priorities of their corresponding factors in the level above. Table 2 illustrates how global priorities are calculated.

With the aid of an on-site computer terminal, the advisory committee received immediate feedback of the local and global priorities generated from their judgments. On the basis of this feedback, committee members agreed to simplify their subsequent analysis by eliminating two subfactors—objectivity and predictability of funding—from further consideration. In addition, the committee members found it difficult to draw operational distinctions between the three administrative subfactors and, therefore, aggregated them into a single factor with a combined global priority of .12. When elements of a hierarchy are eliminated in this

Table 2. Calculation of Global Priorities

	Local Priorities	Global Priorities
Political	.61	
Economic	.27	
Administrative	.12	
Political		
Trust	.39 × .61 =	.283*
Participation	.25 × .61 =	.153*
Objectivity	.11 × .61 =	.067
Reward	.25 × .61 =	.153*
Fiscal		
Funding	.125 × .27 =	.034
Cost of Assistance	.875 × .27 =	.236*
Administrative		
Expertise	.33 × .12 =	.040 ⎤
Effectiveness	.33 × .12 =	.040 ⎬ .12*
Flexibility	.33 × .12 =	.040 ⎦

*Subfactors included in subsequent analyses.

manner, the global priorities of the surviving elements are normalized. Thus, we have:

Subfactors	Normalized Global Priorities
Trust	.264
Participation	.170
Reward	.170
Cost of Assistance	.262
Administrative Factors (combined)	.133

Five additional matrices were required to compare the relative efficacy of alternative types of assistance agencies with respect to the surviving factors identified above. These matrices, which are not illustrated here, were filled in with the judgments of the advisory committee and solved in accordance with the procedures described above. The questions posed to the advisory committee were of the following kind: "With respect to the subfactor trust, what is the desirability of voluntary associations of government as a coordinating agency relative to the remaining alternatives?" Once again, committee members used the scale of relative importance (Table 1) to fill in the cells of the matrix.

Finally, the global priorities of the alternative assistance agencies are obtained by constructing a matrix of their local priorities with respect to each subfactor in the level above. Each column of local priority vectors is multiplied by the global priority of the corresponding subfactor in the third level. The rows are then added across to obtain the global priority for each alternative. Thus, in Table 3 the global priority for Voluntary Associations of Governments is (.264 × .54) + (.170 × .62) + ... + (.133 × .50) = .555.

Table 3 illustrates that voluntary associations of governments emerged as the preferred vehicle (55.5 percent) for coordinating the delivery of assistance to municipalities due, in large part, to their apparent political palatability.

It is important to note that the local and global priorities produced by the AHP are ratio level values. Thus from a resource allocation perspective, the global priorities of Table 3 would suggest that 55.5 percent of available resources be devoted to developing the technology transfer capabilities of voluntary associations of governments, 19.5 percent to other levels of governments, and so on (Saaty and Kearns, 1985).

Discussion

The AHP is one of the most innovative and significant developments in the methodology of the applied policy sciences. It has provided a rigorous yet generic methodological foundation for general systems theory which thus far has proven to be conceptually elegant yet operationally sparse (Saaty and Kearns, 1985). Also it has managed to achieve a balance between "politics" or inductive problem solving on the one hand and "analysis" or deductive problem solving on the other. These two modes of policy analysis had been perceived by Lindblom (1980), Lindblom and Cohen (1979), and Wildavsky (1979), among others, to be hopelessly incongruous. Finally, the use of the AHP in the present study was instrumental in overcoming barriers which, on occasion, had stood in the way of earnest and meaningful dialogue among policy stakeholders. Some of these barriers might be attributable to divergent professional experiences while others apparently were based upon deeply rooted philosophical differences. These differences threatened to jeopardize the project prior to the AHP workshop. Following the workshop the recommendations were clarified and implemented.

With those strengths of the AHP in mind, a precaution should be offered to those considering its use. Many policy analysts have suggested that truly relevant policy debates revolve not around the conflicting

Table 3. Global Priorities of Alternative Coordinating Agencies

	Subfactors					
Agencies	Trust (.264)	Participation (.170)	Reward (.170)	Cost (.262)	Admin. (.133)	Global Priorities
Voluntary Assoc. of Gov'ts.	.54	.62	.53	.57	.50	.555
Other Levels of Gov't.	.15	.10	.25	.23	.25	.195
Civic Agencies	.22	.18	.14	.11	.14	.160
Universities	.05	.06	.05	.05	.03	.053
New Organization	.04	.04	.03	.04	.06	.037

policy *preferences* of multiple actors and stakeholders. Rather, such debates are most valuable when they address the implicit, and often conflicting, *assumptions* upon which policy preferences are based (e.g., Mitroff and Sagasti, 1973; Rein, 1976; MacRae, 1976; Mitroff and Emshoff, 1979; Fischer, 1980; Dunn, 1982). While underlying values and assumptions may be uncovered as a natural consequence of debates concerning the hierarchic structure of a problem and the subsequent pairwise comparisons, the AHP does not systematically *elicit* these assumptions. The AHP lacks an explicit assumption surfacing and challenging component and, therefore, is not a value-critical technique. As a consequence, when judgments of relative importance diverge, the AHP offers no method of resolution other than to forge a pseudo-consensus by taking the geometric mean of the various judgments. Also, the absence of a value-critical perspective allows workshop participants who are unusually charismatic or forceful to impose their unchallenged judgments on the group as a whole. This phenomenon, known as the Asch Effect, prompted the developers of the Delphi technique to require that judgments be made anonymously without face-to-face dialogue, a strategy that carries with it substantial costs.

Finally, the failure to continuously surface and critique the assumptions underlying policy preferences can cause the discussion in an AHP workshop to gradually deteriorate as participants become complacent and their collective "learning curve" prematurely peaks and becomes flat. This deterioration can actually be charted using a schema developed by Stephen Toulmin (1958) for mapping the structure of complex "arguments" (see Dunn, 1982). The Toulmin framework allows one to qualitatively assess the complexity of policy arguments, thereby drawing preliminary conclusions on the extent to which intra-group dialectics yield alternative and, perhaps, more viable policy claims.

Figure 5 is a Toulmin-type map of a debate which actually transpired during the early stages of the AHP workshop. The debate focused on the first pairwise comparisons made by the advisory committee concerning the importance of political factors relative to economic and administrative concerns in determining the success of a coordinating agency.

Note that the Claim, proposed during the AHP workshop by a member of the advisory committee, was supported by an explicitly stated warrant and backing. A second committee member, however, posed unique counter-assumptions by first, noting the importance of longitudinal concerns in assessing the relative importance of political factors, and second, by reversing the order of the prerequisites. Substantial discussion ensued on this matter which resulted in a modification of initial judgments concerning the relative importance of political factors. Thus, in the early stages of the AHP workshop, the argument structures were reasonably

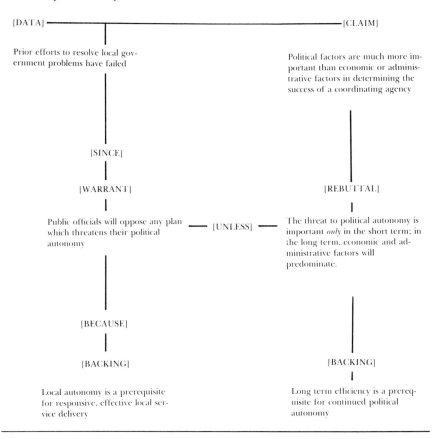

[DATA] ——————————————————————————— [CLAIM]

Prior efforts to resolve local government problems have failed

Political factors are much more important than economic or administrative factors in determining the
success of a coordinating agency

[SINCE]

[WARRANT]   [REBUTTAL]

Public officials will oppose any plan   — [UNLESS] —   The threat to political autonomy is
which threatens their political   important *only* in the short term; in
autonomy   the long term, economic and ad-
                                                         ministrative factors will
                                                         predominate.

[BECAUSE]

[BACKING]   [BACKING]

Local autonomy is a prerequisite   Long term efficiency is a prereq-
for responsive, effective local ser-   uisite for continued political
vice delivery   autonomy

Figure 5. Toulmin Map of a Policy Argument.

complex, yielding innovative and highly useful assumptions and counter-
assumptions.

Without a systematic effort to maintain this deep structure of argument, however, the dialogue gradually deteriorated as the workshop
progressed. Toward the end of the exercise, the committee allowed one
member to fill in an entire matrix with his own judgments, none of which
were supported by even cursory references to available data. The claim
illustrated in Figure 6, proposed very late in the AHP workshop, was
actually in direct contradiction with data made available by the surveys.
Nevertheless, the claim was allowed to stand unchallenged. This illustrates that the dialogue and debate in an AHP workshop can deteriorate
into little more than the unchallenged positing of arbitrary opinions.

The gradual deterioration of value-critical debates could be attribut-

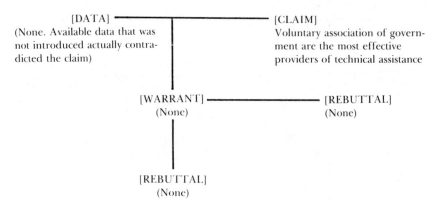

Figure 6. Disintegration of Value-Critical Debates.

able to a sense of mutual trust and confidence among workshop participants which gains momentum as the AHP progresses. Alternatively, the
deterioration may be due to fatigue which begins to take its toll on the
physical energy and mental acuity of workshop participants. Finally, it
may be that, after receiving the computer assisted feedback of their early
judgments, workshop participants become intuitively, and perhaps sub-
consciously, aware of the conclusions which the AHP will eventually elicit.
There may be a general feeling that the important decisions have already
been made in the upper levels of the hierarchy and all that remains is
to "grind out" an increasingly obvious solution.

These explanations, however, do not address the initial proposition
that policy debates are more relevant and productive when they display
a value-critical dimension and the AHP lacks a systematic procedure for
raising the level of dialogue beyond simple policy preferences. Aug-
menting the AHP with additional techniques such as Strategic Assumption Surfacing and Testing (Mitroff and Emshoff, 1979) complicate the
technique. It appears, instead, that the responsibility for maintaining a
meaningful level of dialogue in an AHP workshop falls squarely on the
shoulders of the discussion leader. By simply prodding participants to
justify their judgments and continuously encouraging others to explore
alternative propositions, the discussion leader can prevent the AHP from
becoming merely a device for legitimating the predetermined preferences of one or a few influential participants.

CONCLUSION

The interdependent, holistic, and subjective dimensions of ill-structured problems demand that attention be given to the preferences, values, beliefs, and assumptions of multiple policy stake-holders. Raiffa (1968) poignantly observed that the analysts' primary concern when faced with an ill-structured problem is not arriving at the wrong solution, but rather asking the wrong questions and subsequently solving the wrong problem. Yet what policy analytic methods will ensure the "right" questions are asked and the "right" problem formulated and solved? What technique will adequately account for the subjectivity embedded in stakeholder's values and assumptions without becoming mired in psychoanalysis? Finally, what technique can draw pragmatic applications from the theory and philosophy of dialectical inquiry in a manner that is non-threatening and intuitively appealing to participants?

This chapter has suggested that the AHP in concert with other modes of inquiry is capable of fulfilling these criteria and therefore is a highly appropriate technique for formulating and resolving ill-structured policy problems. The shortcomings of the AHP in comparison with other value-critical techniques can, in the wrong hands, lead to spurious conclusions and highly tenuous recommendations. The inherent strengths of the AHP, on the other hand, are its simplicity, its adaptability to policy problems in many different contexts, and its capacity to characterize the systemic relations among elements of a problem.

REFERENCES

Ackoff, R. (1974) Redesigning the Future. New York: John Wiley.

Dunn, W.N. (1982) "Reforms as arguments." In E. House (ed.), Evaluation Studies Review Annual. Beverly Hills, CA: Sage Publications.

Fischer, F. (1980) Politics, Values, and Public Policy: The Problem of Methodology. Boulder, CO: Westview.

Gardiner, P. and W. Edwards (1975) "Public value: multiattribute utility measurement for social decision making." In S. Schwartz and M. Kaplan (eds.), Human Judgment and Decision Processes. New York: Academic Press.

Gow, J.S. (1952) "Metropolitics in Pittsburgh." Unpublished Ph.D. dissertation, University of Pittsburgh.

Honadle, B.W. (1981a) "Providing community services: the cooperative factor." National Civic Review (July):353–355.

———(1981b) "Voluntary interlocal cooperation: a big idea for small towns." Municipal Management (January):152–155.

Lindblom, C. (1980) The Policy-Making Process, 2nd ed. Englewood Cliffs, NJ: Prentice-Hall.

Lindblom, C. and D. Cohen (1979) Usable Knowledge. New Haven, CT: Yale University Press.

MacRae, D., Jr. (1976) The Social Function of Social Science. New Haven, CT: Yale University Press.

Mitroff, I. and J. Emshoff (1979) "On strategic assumption-making: a dialectical approach to policy and planning." Academy of Management Review (January):1–11.

Mitroff, I. and F. Sagasti (1973) "Epistemology as general systems theory: an approach to the design of complex decision-making experiments." Philosophy of the Social Sciences 3:117–134.

Mumpower, J., V. Vreis and K. Hammond (1979) "Scientific information, social values, and policy formation." IEEE Transactions on Systems, Man and Cybernetics SMC-9(9):464–478.

Ostrom, E., R. Parks and G. Whitaker (1973) "Do we really want to consolidate urban police forces?" Public Administrative Review (Sept/Oct):423–432.

Raiffa, H. (1968) Decision Analysis Introductory Lectures on Choices Under Uncertainty. Reading, MA: Addison-Wesley.

Rein, M. (1976) Social Science and Public Policy. New York: Penguin.

Saaty, T.L. (1977a) "Scenarios and priorities in transportation planning: application to the Sudan." Transportation Research 11(5):343–350.

———(1977b) "A scaling method for priorities in hierarchical structures." Journal of Math Psychology 15(3):234–281.

———(1980) The Analytic Hierarchy Process. New York: McGraw-Hill.

Saaty, T.L. and K.P. Kearns (1985) Analytic Planning: The Anatomy of Systems. London: Pergamon Press.

Saaty, T.L. and R. Mariano (1979) "Rationing energy to industries: priorities and input-output dependence." Energy Systems and Policy (January):85–111.

Saaty, T.L. and P. Rogers (1976) "Higher education in the United States (1985–2000): scenario construction using a hierarchical framework with Eigenvector weighting." Socio-Economic Planning Sciences 10:251–263.

Toulmin, S. (1958) The Uses of Argument. Cambridge: Cambridge University Press.

Turoff, M. (1970) "The design of a policy Delphi." Technological Forecasting and Social Change 2(2):149–171.

Wildavsky, A. (1979) Speaking Truth to Power: The Art and Craft of Policy Analysis. Boston: Little Brown.

Zimmerman, J. (1974) "Intergovernmental service agreements and transfer of functions." Pp. 29–50 in Substate Regionalism and the Federal System, vol. III: The Challenge of Local Government Reorganization. Washington, D.C.: ACIR.

THE POLICY GRID:
A COGNITIVE METHODOLOGY FOR
ASSESSING POLICY DYNAMICS

William N. Dunn, Anthony G. Cahill,
Mary J. Dukes, and Ari Ginsberg

ABSTRACT

This chapter accepts Heclo's challenge to develop a methodology for investigating the cumulative movement and reinterpretation of policy through "systems of interpretation" by which policy stakeholders attach meaning to events. The chapter outlines the contours of a cognitive model of policy dynamics; describes a set of procedures (the policy grid) which yields measures of the structure and content of systems of interpretation; illustrates the application of the policy grid in a pilot study of criminal justice information policies; and discusses the reliability and validity of policy grid data and their implications for the study of policy dynamics.

INTRODUCTION

The policy sciences are frequently crippled by their inability to penetrate the systems of interpretation (Heclo, 1976) by which individual and collective meanings are attached to policy choices. While it has become commonplace to acknowledge that policy-relevant information does not exist independently of a person's conceptual representations (models) of reality (Allison, 1971; Scarpino, Dunn, and Mitroff, 1983:335), stu-

Policy Analysis: Perspectives, Concepts, and Methods, pages 355–375.
ISBN: 0–89232–371–X

dents of policymaking have not learned to investigate systematically the origins, development, and consequences of what have been called reference frames (Rein and Schon, 1977; Holzner and Marx, 1979; Weiss and Bucuvalas, 1980), generative metaphors (Schon, 1979), theories-in-use (Argyris and Schon, 1975; Schon, 1983), and schemas (Taylor and Crocker, 1980; Kahneman, Slovic, and Tversky, 1982).

The challenge, therefore, is to develop a systematic methodology which enables us to discern changes in these systems of interpretation. In Heclo's words, we need a methodology for investigating:

> the cumulative movement and reinterpretation of policy, one applicable both to the stream of observable events and to the equally powerful stream of development in ideas, basic paradigms, dominant metaphors, standard operating procedures, or whatever we choose to call the systems of interpretation by which we attach meaning to events (Heclo, 1976:253–54).

This chapter accepts Heclo's challenge by applying a methodology designed to deal simultaneously with the dynamics of observable events and the systems of interpretation by which events are given meaning in particular policy contexts. This chapter (1) outlines the main contours of a cognitive model of policy dynamics; (2) describes the policy grid, a set of procedures which yields empirical measures of the structure and content of systems of interpretation; (3) illustrates the application of the policy grid in a pilot study of frames of reference towards criminal justice information policies in a large urban municipality; and (4) discusses the reliability and validity of policy grid data and their implications for the study of policy dynamics.

A COGNITIVE MODEL OF POLICY DYNAMICS

Policy dynamics are a consequence of changes in the ways that policy stakeholders attach meanings to policy goals, options, and consequences. Policy stakeholders, including policy analysts within and outside formal policy arenas, act in accordance with their own abstract understandings of the policies which affect them. Yet, "policy" has multiple meanings to different stakeholders; it is not a self-defining phenomenon. As Jones (1977:5) warns, "there is no unambiguous datum constituting policy and waiting to be discovered in the world."

The cumulative movement and reinterpretation of policy are based in part on changes in the "cognitive infrastructure" of the policy-making process. This cognitive infrastructure is composed of organized systems of constructs used to interpret and anticipate events (Wacker, 1981). Characteristics of this infrastructure have been described in terms of schematic information processing (Taylor and Crocker, 1980), problem structuring (Dunn, 1981; Mitroff and Mason, 1981), problem setting (Rein and Schon, 1977), organizational learning (Argyris and Schon, 1977), and government learning (Etheredge, 1979).

The model of cognitive infrastructure described below is based on the psychology of personal constructs (Kelly, 1955; Bannister and Mair, 1968; Bannister, 1970; Slater, 1977). The central element of this cognitive model is that of the reference frame, or what Kelly (1955) called "construction system." A reference frame (Holzner and Marx, 1979) is an experientially acquired system of constructs which contains sets of criteria, standards of assessment, and decision rules which facilitate and restrict interpretations of policy.

In the course of experience policy stakeholders develop, maintain, and alter their frames of reference towards policies. Frames of reference and their basic units, constructs, may vary on a number of dimensions. They may vary in structure—one stakeholder's frame of reference may be relatively undifferentiated and simple, while another's may be highly differentiated and complex, as illustrated by typical differences in frames of reference of the ordinary citizen and the scientific expert. Reference frames also vary in content. The content of an ordinary citizen's constructs may be "ideological," while those of the scientific expert may be "technical," even though both observe the same policy events. Thus, policy stakeholders differ not only because there are differences in the events they observe, but also because they use different systems of constructs to interpret these events (Kelly, 1955; compare Allison, 1971).

A cognitive model of policy dynamics may proceed from several sensitizing propositions (Dunn, 1985) which have been adapted from Kelly (1955) to fit the domain of policy studies.

- *Individuality.* Policy stakeholders differ from one another in their interpretation of events, not only because there are differences in the events that they seek to anticipate, but also because they have different approaches to the interpretation of the same events.
- *Organization.* Policy stakeholders evolve for their convenience in interpreting events a frame of reference constituted by organized relationships among constructs. Stakeholders differ not only in their interpretations of events, but also because they organize such interpretations in different ways. This organizational principle is what makes them *systems* of interpretation.
- *Range.* Policy stakeholders employ constructs that are convenient for the interpretation of a finite range of events. Some events lie within the range of convenience of a construct, while others lie beyond it and may not be interpreted.

- *Experience.* Frames of reference change as policy stakeholders successively experience and (re)interpret events. Constructs and the organized reference frames of which they are parts represent working hypotheses that are revised in the course of experience.
- *Modulation.* Changes in frames of reference are limited by the permeability of constructs relevant to a particular domain. The more permeable a stakeholder's superordinate (governing) constructs, the more likely that subordinate constructs will be changed.
- *Fragmentation.* Policy stakeholders may successively employ subsystems of constructs that are inconsistent. Subsystems of constructs are inconsistent only when they are directly compared; inconsistencies disappear when a subsystem is viewed in terms of its links to a superordinate system.
- *Communality.* Policy stakeholders' cognitive processes are similar to the extent that they share a common frame of reference. We should expect similarities in cognitive processes among stakeholders with similar frames of reference, even when they experience different events, rather than expect similarities in cognitive processes among stakeholders who experience the same events.
- *Sociality.* Policy stakeholders play a role in common social processes to the extent that they understand each others' frame of reference. To understand the frames of reference of others does not require a common frame of reference, but a frame of reference that incorporates the constructs of others within its range of convenience.
- *Rationality.* Policy stakeholders are rational to the extent that they successfully interpret events. Rationality is a property of persons; it is not a property of events.
- *Capacity.* The success of policy stakeholders in interpreting events is a function of their capacity to extend and order constructs within their frame of reference. Rationality, then, is a function of cognitive capacity.

The concept of frame of reference provides a unifying principle for the study of policy dynamics. The policy grid provides researchers with means to investigate empirically the underlying structure and content of the systems of interpretation.

PROPERTIES AND INDICES OF THE POLICY GRID

The policy grid operationalizes the concept of frame of reference. Procedures for obtaining and analyzing data on the structure and content of individual and group reference frames are an extension of Kelly's Role Construct Repertory Test (Rep-Test), which has been used in numerous domains including: psychotherapy (see Bannister and Mair, 1968; Fransella and Bannister, 1977; Slater, 1977); marketing (e.g., Sampson, 1972); computer system usage (e.g., Stabell, 1978); organization design (e.g., Wacker, 1981); and job training (Dunn, Kearns, and Cahill, 1984).

The policy grid is both a process and product. As a process, the policy grid is a semi-structured interview procedure in which respondents classify and evaluate policy elements (goals, options, events) according to their own personal constructs. The policy grid is also a product of these procedures. As a product, the policy grid is a matrix of *mxn* elements and constructs. This matrix provides a geometric, quantitative, and qualitative representation of a person's frame of reference towards policy. There are four basic steps in administering the policy grid (Wacker, 1981; Dunn, Kearns, and Cahill, 1984):

1. *Element Selection.* Policy elements—which may be sets of goals, options, or events—constitute the objects, cues, or standard stimuli to which stakeholders are asked to respond. Elements may be selected by respondents or supplied by researchers. Elements are presented in the form of cards with brief descriptions of the element or labeled pictures. Elements are selected with reference to the domain under consideration. For example, in counseling psychiatric patients, elements may be the names of the patient's family, friends, or significant others. In marketing studies, elements may be brands of soap, cars or other objects of interest. In the application of the policy grid described in the following section, the elements were six policy options. In every case, elements are chosen so as to diverge from one another, thus maximizing the likelihood that a full range of underlying constructs will be elicited.

2. *Element Comparison.* Elements are randomly divided into sets of three (triads). The respondent is asked to name a way in which two of these elements are similar and different from the third. What the respondent names is a construct. A second set of three triads is then presented to the respondent, who supplies another construct. Additional triads are presented until the respondent is unable to supply new (i.e., non-duplicative) constructs. At this point the respondents are assumed to have exhausted the *n* constructs which define the boundaries of their frame of reference toward a given set of policies.

3. *Element Evaluation.* In the course of supplying constructs, each respondent is asked to evaluate the extent to which each element may be characterized by each construct. The evaluation of policy options, goals, or events may follow one or more of three procedures: classification, ranking, and rating. If elements are *classified*, the respondent will

be asked to state whether a construct applies or does not apply to elements in the set. If elements are *ranked*, the respondent will be asked to state the order in which elements are characterized by a construct. Elements may also be *rated* on a scale (e.g., 1 = strongly present, 2 = present, . . . , 5 = absent).

4. *Grid Analysis*. Classifications, rankings, or ratings form a grid (matrix) of *mxn* elements and constructs. Each element is a column in the grid, while each construct is a row. In each cell of the grid numerical values are entered to express the extent to which each element shares characteristics implied by each construct. Grid data may be analyzed to create a geometric, quantitative, and qualitative representation of a person's frame of reference. The analysis of grid data yields measures of the structure (e.g., complexity) and content (e.g., "ideological") of reference frames.

Numerical Properties of the Policy Grid

Each policy grid is a unique set of subjective coordinates which represents a stakeholder's frame of reference towards policy. If elements are fixed (e.g., $m = 10$) then all column vectors for all respondents have the same number of dimensions and are conformable. Yet the number of constructs varies among persons. Some respondents have few constructs while others have many. For this reason, the row vectors of two or more grids have different dimensions which are not conformable. The typical policy grid is asymmetrical.

Since few grids yield symmetrical matrices ($m = n$ is a rare condition), statistical procedures which assume conformable dimensions (e.g., factor analysis) are inapplicable. This stricture applies only to the parallel analysis of data which have been pooled or aggregated across individual grids; it does not apply to the serial analysis of individual grids (see Wacker, 1981). Individual grids may be analyzed with a variety of statistical techniques, including principal components analysis, factor analysis, and multidimensional scaling (Slater, 1977; Kruskal and Wish, 1978).

Indices of Grid Structure and Content

Indices of grid structure and content have been reviewed by Fransella and Bannister (1977), Slater (1977), and Stabell (1978). The main purpose of these indices, when used with a policy grid, is to uncover and quantify differences in the structure and content of reference frames. Structural differences are of three major kinds:

- *Differentiation.* Differentiation refers to the number of constructs used to compare and contrast elements. A highly differentiated reference frame has many constructs, while one with low differentiation has few constructs. The degree of differentiation alone does not provide an adequate representation of structural differences, since two or more persons with the same number of constructs may use these constructs in a more or less consistent way. For example, a thought-disordered schizophrenic and a police officer may each use twelve different constructs to compare and contrast criminal justice policies. But the consistency of the police officer's constructs, measured by correlations among scores for all pairs of constructs, will be much greater than that of the schizophrenic. A schizophrenic's grid is likely to resemble a table of random numbers (see Fransella and Bannister, 1977).
- *Complexity.* Complexity refers to the degree to which each construct performs a different function from every other construct. A schizophrenic's policy grid is likely to be maximally complex, with each construct in the grid performing a different function. This maximal complexity would be indicated by weak correlations among scores for all pairs of constructs. By contrast, a minimally complex reference frame is one where each construct performs the same function as all other constructs. This would be indicated by perfect correlations (i.e., unity) among scores for all pairs of constructs in the policy grid.
- *Integration.* Integration refers to the degree of connectedness of each construct. A maximally integrated reference frame, as indicated by perfect correlations among all pairs of constructs, will be minimally complex, since each construct performs the same function as every other construct. A minimally integrated reference frame, as indicated by weak or zero correlations among all pairs of constructs—for example, as in a random grid—will also be highly complex. Thus, complexity and integrations are negatively related in the limit.

The content of a policy grid is what gives specific meanings to differences in reference frames. Differences in content are of three major kinds:

- *Policy Preference.* Policy preference refers to the perceived desirability of each policy element (e.g., policy option) in relation to every other element. An element which is more preferred is one which has a higher average score than another element, as measured by column means in the policy grid.

- *Policy Distance.*   Policy distance refers to differences in the meaning of policy elements (e.g., policy options) to respondents. Elements which are close together in meaning will have low interelement distance (D) values, while those which are far apart will have high interelement D values.

- *Construct Centrality.*   Construct centrality refers to the importance of a construct in relation to other constructs. Constructs with high centrality are those which are more closely related to every other construct, as measured by average correlations between each construct and all other constructs. Constructs with more or less centrality are labelled by using the natural language of respondents, for example "just," "sensible," "political," or "crooked." This permits naturalistic (qualitative) generalizations about the core meanings which underlie policy preferences.

These indices of structure and content may be calculated for individuals as well as groups. The next section demonstrates how these indices were calculated for a sample of stakeholders who affect and are affected by criminal justice information policies in a large urban municipality.

USING THE POLICY GRID IN APPLIED RESEARCH

A prototype version of the policy grid was used as part of a larger study conducted in 1982. The larger study was designed to investigate attitudes towards criminal justice information policies in a large urban municipality. In the first stage of the study a 123-item questionnaire was administered to a sample of 61 stakeholders, including line and supervisory police officers, assistant district attorneys, criminal justice researchers, and citizens. Respondents were asked to assess the utility of information about six police functions: crime prevention, crime detection and apprehension, social order, traffic control, emergency services, and community relations. Each police function was described in a brief statement which stated the purpose(s) of the function and provided examples of the kinds of information typically available to determine whether the function is being successfully performed by police. For example, information about crime prevention was described as follows:

> A key function of the police is to minimize the occurrence of personal and property crimes. Typical measures associated with this function are: the total number of

personal crimes (homicide, rape, etc.) and property crimes (burglary, larceny, vehicle theft, etc.).

After reading each of the six statements, respondents were asked to indicate on a 5-point Likert scale the extent to which information about the performance of that function satisfied various criteria of utility. For example, respondents were asked the extent to which information about the police crime prevention function "gives practical information on how well policies or programs are operating." Respondents were also asked to rank in order of priority the extent to which information about each function was useful to them. Questionnaire data were reduced to four factors through principal components analysis and compared by role (police, district attorneys, researchers, citizens). With the exception of the police emergency services function, there were no statistically significant differences ($p = .05$) in the perceived utility of information about the performance of the six police functions.

＇In the second phase of the study a policy grid was administered to a convenience sample of 17 of the original respondents. The brief descriptions of information about the six police functions were placed on cards and used as elements in grid interviews. Each of the elements (e.g., police crime prevention) represents a distinct criminal justice informational policy. Randomly ordered sets of three elements were presented on cards to each respondent, who was asked to name a way in which two elements were similar and different from the third. Using this procedure with the 17 respondents, interviewers generated a total of 73 constructs of which 23 were unique, that is, not duplicated among respondents.

Calculating Frame Scores

Data obtained from grid interviews may be analyzed in various ways. The analysis presented below is based on data obtained from eight criminal justice practitioners (assistant district attorneys and police officers) and nine non-CJS stakeholders (citizens and criminal justice researchers). The size of this sample does not permit statistical inferences, for example, those based on the interpretation of Chi-square or F values. As such, it is not possible to infer characteristics of the reference frames of stakeholders in the larger population. What follows, therefore, is an illustration of how data obtained with the policy grid may be analyzed and interpreted.

The results of two grid interviews are presented in Table 1. These two policy grids depict the rankings of the six informational policies on the constructs generated by each respondent. Note that respondent 01 has five constructs, while respondent 02 has four. The three structural indices described in the preceding section (differentiation, complexity, integration) may be calculated from data in these two grids.

Differentiation.   Differentiation refers to the number of constructs used to compare and contrast policies. The index of frame differentiation (FD) is given by the equation:

$$FD = \sum_{i=1}^{k} k$$

where k is the number of elements.

Using the data for the two respondents given above,

$$FD_{(01)} = \sum_{i=1}^{k} k = 5$$

$$FD_{(02)} = \sum_{i=1}^{k} k = 4$$

Complexity.   Complexity refers to the degree to which each construct performs a unique function in a stakeholder's overall reference frame. Maximal complexity is indicated by large absolute differences in cell values for all pairs of constructs, while minimal complexity is indicated by small absolute differences. The index of frame complexity, adapted from Bieri and Tripodi (1964), is given by the equation:

$$FC = \frac{1}{m} \frac{2}{k(k-1)} \sum_{j=1}^{m} \sum_{i=1}^{k-1} \sum_{k=i+1}^{k} f(a_{ji} - a_{jk})$$

where a_{ij}.is the rank of the ith element on the jth construct;
$(a_{ji} - a_{jk})$ is the absolute difference in the ranks of two constructs on the
    ith element;
k is the number of constructs; and
m is the number of elements.

This index, standardized for both the number of elements and con-

Table 1. Ranking of Elements on Constructs for Two Respondents

Respondent O1

Construct			Element			
	1	2	3	4	5	6
C1	6	5	4	2	1	3
C2	2	1	4	6	5	3
C3	6	1	2	4	5	3
C4	1	6	2	4	5	3
C5	6	1	2	5	4	3

Respondent O2

Construct			Element			
	1	2	3	4	5	6
C1	1	2	3	4	5	6
C2	1	2	3	4	5	6
C3	2	1	5	4	3	6
C4	2	1	3	5	4	6

Note: The values in each matrix represent the ranking of each element on each construct.

structs, yields the following complexity scores for respondents 01 and 02:

$$FC_{(01)} = \frac{1}{m} \times \frac{2}{k(k-1)} \sum_{j=1}^{m} \sum_{i=1}^{k-1} \sum_{k=i+1}^{k} f(a_{ji} - a_{jk})$$

$$= \frac{1}{6} \times \frac{2}{5(5-1)} \times 105$$

$$.167 \times .1 \times 105 = 1.75$$

$$FC_{(02)} = \frac{1}{6} \times \frac{2}{4(4-1)} \times 24 =$$

$$.167 \times .167 \times 24 = .67$$

Integration.   Integration refers to the degree of connectedness of each construct. A reference frame which is maximally integrated is indicated by perfect correlations among all pairs of constructs. A maximally integrated reference frame is minimally complex, since each construct performs the same function as all other constructs. The index of frame integration is given by the equation:

$$FI = \frac{1}{k^2} \sum_{j=1}^{k-1} \sum_{j=j+1}^{k} r_{ij}^2$$

where k^2 is the number of constructs squared; and
r_{ij}^2 is the coefficient of determiniation for the ith element on the jth pair
of constructs.

The values of r are derived from an interconstruct correlation matrix calculated for all constructs taken two at a time. Integration scores for respondents are 01 and 02 are:

$$FI_{(01)} = \frac{1}{k^2} \sum_{j=1}^{k-1} \sum_{i=j+1}^{k} r_{ij}^2$$

$$= \frac{1}{5^2} \times 5.27 = .04 \times 5.27 = .21$$

$$FI_{(02)} = \frac{1}{4^2} \times 8.706 = .0625 \times 8.71 = .54$$

Three indices of grid content described in the preceding section may also be calculated from data in Table 1. These indices of content are: policy preference, policy distance, and construct centrality.

Policy Preference.   Policy preference refers to the perceived desirability

Table 2.   Policy Preference Scores for Two Respondents

Respondent 01	*Respondent 02*
PP = 1/5 × 21 = 4.2	PP = 1/4 × 6 = 1.6
PP = 1/5 × 14 = 2.8	PP = 1/4 × 6 = 1.6
PP = 1/5 × 14 = 2.8	PP = 1/4 × 14 = 3.5
PP = 1/5 × 21 = 4.2	PP = 1/4 × 21 = 5.25
PP = 1/5 × 20 = 4.0	PP = 1/4 × 17 = 4.25
PP = 1/5 × 15 = 3.0	PP = 1/4 × 24 = 6.0

Note: Lower scores signify more preferred.

of each policy option among stakeholders. Policy preference is defined as:

$$PP = \frac{1}{k} \sum_{i=1}^{k-1} \sum_{i=j+1}^{k} a_{ji}$$

where a_{ji} is the rank of the jth element on the ith construct; and k is the number of constructs.

The policy preference scores for each of the two respondents are provided in Table 2.

When policy preference scores are used to rank the six policies, the most preferred informational policy is crime prevention. Thirty-five percent preferred this informational policy, while the informational policy designated as community service was not preferred by any of the 17 respondents. The emergency service informational policy was preferred by only one percent of the respondents.

Policy Distance.   Policy distance refers to differences in the semantic meaning of informational policies to respondents. Policies which are perceived as being close together in meaning will have low interelement distance (D) values, while those which are far apart will have high interelement (D) values (see Osgood, Suci, and Tannenbaum, 1957).

Policy Distance is defined as:

$$PD = \sum_{i=1}^{k} d_{ij}^2$$

where d_{ij}^2 is the squared distance between the rank value of the jth construct on the ith occupation.

Calculating policy distance scores for each respondent results in an inter-policy distance matrix. The matrices for respondents 01 and 02 are presented in Table 3.

Table 3.   Inter-Policy Distance Scores for Two Respondents

	Respondent 01				
	1	*2*	*3*	*4*	*5*	*6*
1	—	8.77	6.4	6.78	7.42	5.66
2		—	5.29	7.94	7.62	5.0
3			—	5.0	5.66	2.23
4				—	2.24	4.0
5					—	4.12
6						—

	Respondent 02				
	1	*2*	*3*	*4*	*5*	*6*
1	—	3.0	4.47	6.0	8.37	8.66
2		—	3.87	5.92	7.14	8.72
3			—	4.47	4.47	7.94
4				—	4.90	7.68
5					—	7.55
6						—

For respondent 01, the policies perceived as most distant (D = 8.77) are crime prevention (element 1) and crime detection (element 2) while those perceived as least distant (D = 2.24) are traffic control (element 5) and emergency services (element 4). Respondent 02, on the other hand, perceives crime detection (element 2) and community services (element 6) as most distant (D = 8.72), while crime prevention (element 1) and crime detection (element 2) are least distant (D = 3.0).

Construct Centrality.   This refers to the importance of a construct in relation to all other constructs. Constructs with high centrality are those which are more closely associated with every other construct, as measured by average correlations between each construct and all other constructs. Constructs with more or less centrality are labeled by using the natural language of respondents, thus permitting naturalistic (qualitative) generalizations about the central meanings which underlie policy preferences. Construct centrality is defined as:

$$CC = \frac{1}{k} \sum_{i=1}^{k} r_{ij}^2$$

where k is the number of contstructs; and
r_{ij}^2 is the coefficient of determination for the jth pair of constructs on the ith element.

Construct centrality scores for respondent 01 are given in Table 4. For respondent 01 the central underlying construct (CC = .665) described

Table 4. Construct Centrality Scores for Respondent 01

Construct	Centrality Score
(1) Day-to-day, mundane activities (traffic control) *vs.* hard-core crime (felonies, etc.).	.292
(2) High-prioritiy duties *vs.* low priority duties.	.421
(3) Definite call for help where response is known *vs.* routine or ambiguous activities.	.665
(4) Police behavior differs in dealing with "ordinary citizens" (traffic) and "hard core" criminals.	.645
(5) Police role as arbitrator (service needs) *vs.* apprehender of those who have broken the law.	.630

by the respondent was a "definite call for help where activities and responses are known," *vs.* "routine or ambiguous activities." For this same respondent (see Table 3) the most preferred policy options are social order (PP = 2.8) and crime detection (PP = 2.8). In performing both functions police must deal with situations calling for a definitive and planned (known) response, as distinguished from situations where ambiguous or routine activities are appropriate. Accordingly, the policy preference and construct centrality scores of respondent 01 are consistent.

Analyzing Collective Grids

Several methods are available to analyze the structure and content of collective grids, including analysis of variance, R- and Q-type factor analysis, and distance-cluster analysis. Among these methods, distance-cluster analysis is particularly appropriate for representing the structure of collective meanings among groups of stakeholders whose shared frames of reference constitute a "system of interpretation" (Heclo, 1976). Here, policy distance scores may be correlated across respondents. The matrix of correlation coefficients may then be input into a factor analysis routine which yields clusters of persons defined in terms of the best linear combination of distance scores for all pairs of policies. A factor (cluster) is defined as:

$$F = \sum_{i=1}^{p=C} w X$$

where w is an estimated factor weight for the ith pair of elements; X is the distance correlation for the ith pair of elements; and C is the combination of all elements taken two at a time.

The output of distance cluster analysis is a set of K clusters that represent membership groups with shared meanings towards a set of policies.

Strictly speaking, data gathered in this study are not appropriate for distance-cluster analysis. Nevertheless, the type of results that may be derived from distance-cluster analysis is illustrated below in Figure 1. Here, policy distance scores for each respondent were first multiplied by the reciprocal of the number of constructs held by each individual, thus eliminating differences due to the number of constructs. These transformed policy distance (D) scores were then placed on a coordinate system composed of X and Y axes which show the intersection of distance scores for pairs of policies (Figure 1). The X axis displays the distances (D scores) for the two policies: social order and community services. On the basis of aggregate analysis this pair of policies proved to be the most distant. The Y axis shows D scores for another pair of policies: traffic control and emergency services. These were the least distant policies in the sample as a whole. As can be seen from the graph, the eight criminal justice professionals (represented by Os) show a narrower range of D scores, while the nine citizens and university researchers show a wider range of D scores (represented by ☆s).

RELIABILITY AND VALIDITY OF THE POLICY GRID

Attempts to assess the reliability and validity of the policy grid are and should be directly dependent on the theory from which grid methodology is derived. That theory, labeled "constructivist alternativism" by Kelly (1955), makes several key assumptions which dictate special forms of reliability and validity analysis.

Theoretical Assumptions of the Policy Grid

The first key assumption is that all persons are hypothetico-deductive reasoners ("scientists") whose constructs *change*. Constructs are working hypotheses about future states of the world, predictions which are validated or invalidated through experience. In this sense "man is a form of motion" (Kelly, 1955), a dynamic information processor whose systems of interpretation are continuously changing.

A second key assumption is methodological. The policy grid and other procedures which enable subjects to project *their own* systems of interpretation on external objects, events, or persons are more objective than procedures (e.g., standardized questionnaires) which do not. The policy grid is more objective because it yields constructs which are meaningful

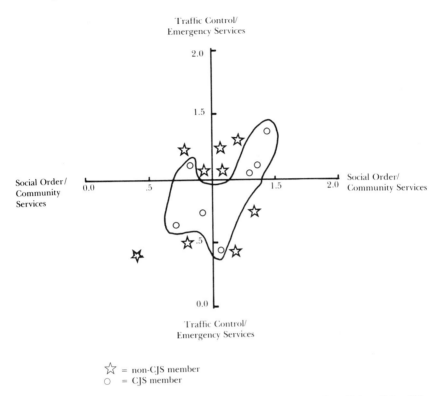

Figure 1.   Graph of Distance Scores for Two Pairs of Policies (N = 17).

and important to stakeholders, as distinguished from those which are meaningful and important to researchers. Accordingly, the policy grid is consistent with principles of "representative design" (Brunswick, 1956) according to which cognitive elements should be representative of the universe of meanings habitually attached by persons to particular contexts (Bannister and Mair, 1968:98–99).

A third key assumption is that relations between constructs constitute *organized* systems of interpretation. The structure of a reference frame is no less important than its semantic content. Two or more reference frames may be semantically equivalent, in the sense that they are composed of constructs with the same or similar meanings, but have different structures. The structure of reference frames enables and constrains processes of policy interpretation. Hence, we may investigate the differentiation, complexity, and integration of reference frames, as well as the particular constructs that permit us to label individual and collective choices as "ideological," "pragmatic," "technical," "political," and so on.

These three assumptions—dynamism, objectivity, and structuralism—dictate particular forms of reliability and validity analysis (Bannister and Mair, 1968; Slater, 1977). For example, if reliability is defined as *stability* and measured by test-retest coefficients, what appears to be an unreliable policy grid in fact may be one that has captured a reference frame that is receptive to change. Similarly, if reliability is defined as *consistency* and measured by an internal consistency reliability coefficient (e.g., alpha), what may appear to be an unreliable policy grid may in fact represent low frame integration.

The interpretation of several standard validation procedures is also affected by these theoretical assumptions (Dunn, Kearns, and Cahill, 1984). Face validity, given the assumption about the objectivity of projective techniques, cannot be determined by researchers alone. Subjects themselves establish the face validity of their constructs (although the validity of structural constructs such as differentiation, complexity and integration must be established by researchers). Construct validation procedures, including the assessment of convergent and discriminant validity, are applicable if multiple measures of the same construct are used, and if constructs which are predicted to converge and diverge are reflected in the strength and sign of correlation coefficients. Finally, the content validity of the policy grid may be determined by constructing a cumulative frequency distribution which displays the number of new constructs generated by a sample of respondents.

To determine whether the policy grid adequately samples constructs actually used by stakeholders in the criminal justice system, a cumulative frequency distribution was constructed by arranging (left to right) persons with the highest to lowest number of new constructs. By graphing the number of new constructs elicited from each respondent, the cumulative frequency curve will display a point at which the set of constructs has approximated the "universe of meaning" surrounding a particular set of policies. Typically, the majority of all constructs will be generated by a relatively small number of respondents (15–25) within a population.

In this pilot study the content validity of the policy grid was reasonably well established. The seventeen respondents generated a total of twenty-three unique constructs, which are displayed in Figure 2 as a cumulative frequency distribution. The universe of meaning, represented by the 23 unique constructs, was approximated after the tenth interview.

CONCLUSION

The results presented above are illustrative of the considerable potential of the policy grid in eliciting the diverse systems of interpretation surrounding public policy. While this pilot study was cross-sectional, and

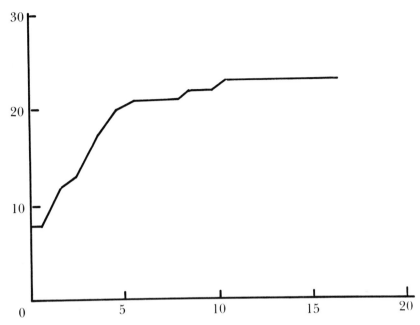

Figure 2. Cumulative Frequency distribution of New Constructs
(N = 17).

thus does not permit generalizations about the dynamics of policy change, it nevertheless provides a basis for designing and conducting real-time studies which employ the policy grid to obtain and analyze data on the frames of reference of policy stakeholders. The policy grid not only enables us to investigate the systems of interpretation by which individual and collective meanings are attached to observable events; it also promises to enlarge present capacities to understand their cumulative movement and reinterpretation.

REFERENCES

Allison, G.T. (1971) Essence of Decision: Explaining the Cuban Missile Crisis. Boston: Little, Brown.

Argyris, C. and D.A. Schon (1975) Theory in Practice: Increasing Professional Effectiveness. San Francisco: Jossey-Bass.

———(1977) Theory in Practice. New York: Jossey-Bass.

Bannister, D., ed. (1970) Perspectives in Personal Construct Theory. New York: Academic Press.

————and J.M.M. Mair (1968) The Evaluation of Personal Constructs. New York: Academic Press.

Brunswick E. (1956) Perceptions and the Representative Design of Psychological Experiments. Berkeley, CA: University of California Press.

Dunn, W.N. (1981) Public Policy Analysis: An Introduction. Englewood Cliffs, NJ: Prentice-Hall.

————(1985) "Usable knowledge: a metatheory of policy research in the social sciences." In W. Bennis, K. Benne and R. Chin (eds.), The Planning of Change: Readings in the Applied Social Sciences, 4th ed. New York: Holt, Rinehart and Winston.

————, K.P. Kearns and A.G. Cahill (1984) "Application of the policy grid to work-related frames of reference." University Program for the Study of Knowledge Use, University of Pittsburgh, PA.

Etheredge, L.S. (1979) "Government learning: an overview." Center for International Studies, Massachusetts Institute of Technology, Cambridge, MA.

Fransella, F. and D. Bannister (1977) A Manual for Repertory Grid Technique. London: Academic Press.

Heclo, H.H. (1976) "Policy dynamics." Pp. 236–266 in R. Rose (ed.), The Dynamics of Public Policy: A Comparative Analysis. Beverly Hills, CA: Sage Publications.

Holzner, B. and J. Marx (1979) Knowledge Application: The Knowledge System in Society. Boston: Allyn and Bacon.

Jones, C.O. (1977) An Introduction to the Study of Public Policy, 2nd ed. North Scituate, MA: Duxbury Press.

Kahneman, D., P. Slovic and A. Tversky, eds. (1982) Judgment Under Certainty. Cambridge: Cambridge University Press.

Kelly, G.A. (1955) The Psychology of Personal Constructs, vol. 1 and 2. New York: W.W. Norton.

Kruskal, J.B. and M. Wish (1978) Multidimensional Scaling. Beverly Hills, CA: Sage Publications.

Mitroff, I.I. and R.O. Mason (1981) Challenging Strategic Planning Assumptions. New York: Wiley.

Osgood, C., G. Suci and P. Tannenbaum (1957) The Measurement of Meaning. Urbana, IL: University of Illinois Press.

Rein, M. and D.A. Schon (1977) "Problem setting in policy research." Pp. 235–251 in C.H. Weiss (ed.), Using Social Research in Public Policy Making. Lexington, MA: D.C. Heath.

Sampson, P. (1972) "Can consumers create new products?" Journal of the Market Research Society 12:40–51.

Scarpino, G.M., W.N. Dunn and I.I. Mitroff (1983) "The role of conceptual models in knowledge acquisition for policymaking." In Knowledge: Creation, Diffusion, Utilization. Beverly Hills, CA: Sage Publications.

Schon, D.A. (1979) "Generative metaphor: a perspective on problem setting in social policy." In A. Ortony (ed.), Metaphor in Thought. Cambridge: Cambridge University Press.

————(1983) The Reflective Practitioner: How Professionals Think in Action. New York: Basic Books.

Slater, P. (1977) Dimensions of Interpersonal Space. London: Wiley.

Stabell, C.B. (1978) "Integrative complexity of information environment perception and information use: an empirical investigation." Organizational Behavior and Human Performance 22:116–142.

Taylor, S.E. and J. Crocker (1980) "Schematic bases of social information processing." Pp. 89–134 in E. Higgins, C. Herman and M. Zanna (eds.), Social Cognition. Hillsdale, NJ: Erlbaum.

Tripodi, T. and J. Bieri (1964) "Information transmission in clinical judgments as a function of stimulus dimensionability and cognitive complexity." Journal of Personality 32:119–137.

Wacker, G. (1981) "Toward a cognitive methodology of organizational assessment." Journal of Applied Behavioral Science 17(1):114–129.

Weiss, C. and M. Bucuvalas (1980) "Truth tests and utility tests: decision makers' frame of reference for social science." The American Sociological Review 45(2):302–312.

BIOGRAPHICAL SKETCHES
OF CONTRIBUTORS

Guy B. Adams is a member of the faculty at the Evergreen State College, where he directs the Graduate Program in Public Administration. His research interests include new approaches to theory development in public administration and interdisciplinary innovations in teaching methods. He is editor of *Dialogue*, a critical review of contributions to administrative theory.

Robert W. Backoff is Associate Professor, School of Public Administration and Department of Political Science, the Ohio State University. His research interests focus on the comparative study of strategic management in state agencies in the United States, the development of new approaches to formulating public policy in structuring policy issues, and the study of dialogue processes in strategic decision making. His most recent publications include "The Incentive Relation in Implementation" with Barry M. Mitnick, in *Public Policy Implementation* (George C. Edwards, III, ed., 1984), and "Mutual Understanding and Its Role in Formulation During Planning" with Paul C. Nutt, in *Technological Forecasting and Social Change* (1986).

Anthony G. Cahill is the Assistant Director of the Program for the Study of Knowledge Use of the University of Pittsburgh. His primary research and teaching interests lie in the transfer of university-based scientific and technical knowledge to public policymakers, information systems design, and applied policy analysis. His most recent publication is "The Role of Information in Emergency Management" with Louise K. Comfort, in *Managing Disasters* (Duke University Press, forthcoming). He is the Managing Editor of *Knowledge: Creation, Diffusion, Utilization*, and has served as a consultant to numerous government agencies.

Michael J. Carley is a Research Fellow of the Policy Studies Institute in London. He is the author of *Social Measurement and Social Indicators* (Allen and Unwin), *Rational Techniques in Policy Analysis* (Heinemann), and *Social Impact Assessment and Monitoring* (Westview). For the past three years, on leave from the Institute, he has served as a consultant to, among others, the Canadian federal and territorial governments, UNICEF, and the National Centre for Human Resources in Brazil. His current focus is on the socioeconomic impacts of industrial change.

Erve Chambers is Professor and Chairperson, Department of Anthropology, University of Maryland. His research interests include applications of anthropological theory and methods to contemporary social problems. He is editor of *Practicing Anthropology*.

Fred R. Dallmayr is Dee Professor of Government at Notre Dame University. His research interests include applications of critical theory and critical phenomenology to problems of the social sciences. Among his recent books is *Polis and Praxis: Exercises in Contemporary Political Theory* (MIT Press, 1984).

Mary J. Dukes is currently a Market Research Analyst for Mobay Chemical Corporation. Her primary specialties include management science, operations research, and computer applications of ill-structured policy problems.

William N. Dunn is Professor in the Graduate School of Public and International Affairs, University of Pittsburgh, where he directs the Program for the Study of Knowledge Use, a research center devoted to empirical, theoretical, and methodological investigations of the impact of the social sciences and professions on public problem solving. As the editor of *Knowledge: Creation, Diffusion, Utilization*, his main interests include the development of an interdisciplinary social science of knowledge applications. His recent books include *Public Policy Analysis* (Prentice-Hall) and *Values, Ethics and the Practice of Policy Analysis* (D.C. Heath).

Frank Fischer is Associate Professor in the Department of Political Science, Rutgers University. His research interests include the application of theories of practical reason to ethical problems facing policymakers and practitioners. He is author of *Politics, Values, and Public Policy: The Problem of Methodology* (Westview Press).

Baruch Fischhoff is Research Associate at Decision Research in Eugene, Oregon, and a major contributor to innovations in contemporary decision theory, including fields of technology assessment, risk assessment, and the study of errors, biases, and heuristics in human judgment. His recent publications include *Acceptable Risk* (Cambridge University Press, 1981), "Setting Standards" (*Management Science*, 1984), "Managing Risk Perceptions" (*Issues in Science and Technology*), "Defining Risk" (*Policy Sciences*) and "Informal Use of Formal Models" (*Academy of Management Review*).

G. David Garson is Assistant Dean for Planning Management in the School of Humanities and Social Sciences at North Carolina State University. He is the author of various works on public administration, research methods, and computing. He has authored numerous books, including *Handbook of Political Science Methods* (Allyn and Bacon), and is editor of the *Social Science Micro-computer Journal*.

Ari Ginsberg is Assistant Professor of Management in the Graduate School of Business Administration, New York University. He received his Ph.D. in Strategic Planning and Policy from the Graduate School of Business at the University of Pittsburgh. He has published articles on organizational strategy, strategic change, cognitive perspectives of policy formulation, and corporate entrepreneurship. His current research interests include cognitive approaches to the study of strategy formulation, strategic adaptation and changing competitive environments, and corporate entrepreneurship.

George J. Graham, Jr. is Professor of Political Science at Vanderbilt University and Senior Research Associate of the Policy Institute. His primary interests include rhetoric, ethics, and science in public policy evaluations. He has published *Founding Principles in American Government: 200 Years of Democracy on Trial* (co-edited with Scarlett G. Graham) and *Methodological Foundations for Political Analysis*. He is co-editor of *Post-Behavioral Era* (with George W. Carey).

Kevin P. Kearns is Assistant Director of executive programs at the School of Urban and Public Affairs at Carnegie-Mellon University. His research

interests focus on municipal management and the diffusion of technological innovations in the public sector. He has consulted extensively
with municipal officials on a wide range of topics including risk management, intergovernmental relations, and computer applications. Recent publications include *Analytical Planning: The Organization of Systems*,
with Thomas Saaty (Pergamon Press, 1985).

William Leiss is Professor in the Department of Communications, Simon
Fraser University. He has also taught environmental studies and
social theory at York University and the University of Toronto. Among
his interests are the relation between science and public policy and the
analysis of advertising imagery. He is the author of *The Domination of
Nature*, *The Limits to Satisfaction* and *Social Communication in Advertising*,
and has edited *Ecology vs. Politics in Canada*.

Stephen H. Linder is Research Associate Professor of Health Policy at
the Center for Health and Manpower Policy Studies, School of Public
Health, The University of Texas Health Science Center at Houston. He
is currently interested in the design of public policy, and public health
policy at the state level. His publications include "From Social Theory
to Policy Design" (with B. Guy Peters) in the *Journal of Public Policy*.

Duncan MacRae, Jr. is William Rank Kenan, Jr. Professor of Political
Science and Sociology at the University of North Carolina at Chapel Hill.
His research interests include the application of ethical theories to policy
analysis and the utilization of policy indicators to inform public debate.
His most recent books include *The Social Function of Social Science* (Yale
University Press) and *Policy Indicators: Links Between Social Science and
Public Debate* (University of North Carolina Press).

Barry M. Mitnick is Associate Professor in the Graduate School of Business at the University of Pittsburgh. His research interests include the
theory of agency, incentive systems in organizations, and theories and
design of strategic behavior under regulation. He is the author of *The
Political Economy of Regulation: Creating, Designing and Removing Regulatory
Forms*.

Alex C. Michalos is Professor of Philosophy at the University of Guelph
where he has taught philosophy and social science since 1966. He is the
author of numerous books, including the five-volume *North American
Social Report* which won the Secretary of State's award for excellence in
interdisciplinary research in 1984. He is the Editor and founder of two
journals: *Social Indicators Research* and *The Journal of Business Ethics*. He

is Past President of the Society for Philosophy and Technology and is on the editorial board of several journals.

Stuart S. Nagel is a Professor of Political Science at the University of Illinois. He is the secretary-treasurer and publications coordinator of the Policy Studies Organization. He is the author of such recent books as *Public Policy: Goals, Means, and Methods* (St. Martin's, 1984) and *Microcomputers, Evaluation Research, and Policy Analysis* (Sage Publications, 1986). He is also the editor of the *Encyclopedia of Policy Studies* (Marcel Dekker, 1983).

Frederic G. Reamer is Associate Professor at the School of Social Work, Rhode Island College. His primary interests include professional ethics, criminal and juvenile justice, and mental health. His most recent authorships include *Ethical Dilemmas in Social Service* (Columbia University Press), *Rehabilitating Juvenile Justice* with Charles H. Shireman (to be published by Columbia University Press, 1986), and a monograph published by the Hastings Center, *The Teaching of Social Work Ethics*, with Marcia Abramson.

Herbert G. Reid is Professor of Political Science at the University of Kentucky. His interests focus on Appalachian politics, American political thought and culture, and problems of ideology and change in advanced capitalist societies. He has published recent articles in the *Appalachian Journal* and the *Canadian Journal of Political and Social Theory*, among others.

AUTHOR INDEX

SUBJECT INDEX